Neural Network Learning: Theoretical Foundations

This book describes recent theoretical advances in the study of artificial neural networks. It explores probabilistic models of supervised learning problems, and addresses the key statistical and computational questions. Research on pattern classification with binary-output networks is surveyed, including a discussion of the relevance of the Vapnik-Chervonenkis dimension. Estimates of this dimension are calculated for several neural network models. A model of classification by real-output networks is developed, and the usefulness of classification with a large margin is demonstrated. The authors explain the role of scale-sensitive versions of the Vapnik-Chervonenkis dimension in large margin classification, and in real estimation. They also discuss the computational complexity of neural network learning, describing a variety of hardness results, and outlining two efficient constructive learning algorithms. The book is self-contained and is intended to be accessible to researchers and graduate students in computer science, engineering, and mathematics.

Martin Anthony is Reader in Mathematics and Executive Director of the Centre for Discrete and Applicable Mathematics at the London School of Economics and Political Science.

Peter Bartlett is a Senior Fellow st the Research School of Information Sciences and Engineering at the Australian National University.

T0296947

Neural Network Learning:
Theoretical Foundations

Martin Anthony and Peter L. Bartlett

CAMBRIDGE
UNIVERSITY PRESS

CAMBRIDGE UNIVERSITY PRESS
Cambridge, New York, Melbourne, Madrid, Cape Town, Singapore, São Paulo, Delhi

Cambridge University Press
The Edinburgh Building, Cambridge CB2 8RU, UK

Published in the United States of America by Cambridge University Press, New York

www.cambridge.org
Information on this title: www.cambridge.org/9780521118620

First published 1999
Reprinted 2001, 2002
This digitally printed version 2009

A catalogue record for this publication is available from the British Library

Library of Congress Cataloguing in Publication data
Anthony, Martin.
Learning in neural networks : theoretical foundations /
Martin Anthony and Peter L. Bartlett.
p. cm.
Includes bibliographical references.
ISBN 0 521 57353 X (hardcover)
1. Neural networks (Computer science). I. Bartlett, Peter L.,
1966– . II. Title.
QA76.87.A58 1999
006.3′2–dc21 98–53260 CIP

ISBN 978-0-521-57353-5 hardback
ISBN 978-0-521-11862-0 paperback

To Colleen, Selena and James.

Contents

vii

Preface

Results from computational learning theory are important in many aspects of machine learning practice. Understanding the behaviour of systems that learn to solve information processing problems (like pattern recognition and prediction) is crucial for the design of effective systems. In recent years, ideas and techniques in computational learning theory have matured to the point where theoretical advances are now contributing to machine learning applications, both through increased understanding and through the development of new practical algorithms.

In this book, we concentrate on statistical and computational questions associated with the use of rich function classes, such as artificial neural networks, for pattern recognition and prediction problems. These issues are of fundamental importance in machine learning, and we have seen several significant advances in this area in the last decade. The book focuses on three specific models of learning, although the techniques, results, and intuitions we obtain from studying these formal models carry over to many other situations.

The book is aimed at researchers and graduate students in computer science, engineering, and mathematics. The reader is assumed to have some familiarity with analysis, probability, calculus, and linear algebra, to the level of an early undergraduate course. We remind the reader of most definitions, so it should suffice just to have met the concepts before.

Most chapters have a 'Remarks' section near the end, containing material that is somewhat tangential to the main flow of the text. All chapters finish with a 'Bibliographical Notes' section giving pointers to the literature, both for the material in the chapter and related results. However these sections are not exhaustive.

It is a pleasure to thank many colleagues and friends for their contributions to this book. Thanks, in particular, to Phil Long for carefully and thoroughly reading the book, and making many helpful suggestions, and to Ron Meir for making many thoughtful comments on large sections of the book. Jon Baxter considerably improved the results in Chapter 5, and made several useful suggestions that improved the presentation of topics in Chapter 7. Gábor Lugosi suggested significant improvements to the results in Chapter 4. Thanks also to James Ashton, Shai Ben-David, Graham Brightwell, Mostefa Golea, Ying Guo, Ralf Herbrich, Wee Sun Lee, Frederic Maire, Shie Mannor, Llew Mason, Michael Schmitt and Ben Veal for comments, corrections, and suggestions. It is also a pleasure to thank the many collaborators and colleagues who have influenced the way we think about the topics covered in this book: Andrew Barron, Jon Baxter, Shai Ben-David, Norman Biggs, Soura Dasgupta, Tom Downs, Paul Fischer, Marcus Frean, Yoav Freund, Mostefa Golea, Dave Helmbold, Klaus Höffgen, Adam Kowalczyk, Sanjeev Kulkarni, Wee Sun Lee, Tamás Linder, Phil Long, David Lovell, Gábor Lugosi, Wolfgang Maass, Llew Mason, Ron Meir, Eli Posner, Rob Schapire, Bernhard Schölkopf, John Shawe-Taylor, Alex Smola, and Bob Williamson. We also thank Roger Astley of Cambridge University Press for his support and for his efficient handling of this project.

Parts of the book were written while Martin Anthony was visiting the Australian National University, supported by the Royal Society and the Australian Telecommunications and Electronics Research Board, and while Peter Bartlett was visiting the London School of Economics. Martin Anthony's research has also been supported by the European Union (through the 'Neurocolt' and 'Neurocolt 2' ESPRIT projects) and the Engineering and Physical Sciences Research Council. Peter Bartlett's research has been supported by the Australian Research Council and the Department of Industry, Science and Tourism. We are grateful to these funding bodies and to our respective institutions for providing the opportunities for us to work on this book.

We thank our families, particularly Colleen and Selena, for their help, encouragement and tolerance over the years.

Martin Anthony and Peter Bartlett
London and Canberra
March 1999.

1
Introduction

1.1 Supervised Learning

This book is about the use of artificial neural networks for supervised learning problems. Many such problems occur in practical applications of artificial neural networks. For example, a neural network might be used as a component of a face recognition system for a security application. After seeing a number of images of legitimate users' faces, the network needs to determine accurately whether a new image corresponds to the face of a legitimate user or an imposter. In other applications, such as the prediction of future price of shares on the stock exchange, we may require a neural network to model the relationship between a pattern and a real-valued quantity.

In general, in a supervised learning problem, the learning system must predict the *labels* of patterns, where the label might be a class label or a real number. During *training*, it receives some partial information about the true relationship between patterns and their labels in the form of a number of correctly labelled patterns. For example, in the face recognition application, the learning system receives a number of images, each labelled as either a legitimate user or an imposter. Learning to accurately label patterns from training data in this way has two major advantages over designing a hard-wired system to solve the same problem: it can save an enormous amount of design effort, and it can be used for problems that cannot easily be specified precisely in advance, perhaps because the environment is changing.

In designing a learning system for a supervised learning problem, there are three key questions that must be considered. The first of these concerns *approximation*, or representational, properties: we can associate with a learning system the class of mappings between patterns and labels

1

that it can produce, but is this class sufficiently powerful to approximate accurately enough the true relationship between the patterns and their labels? The second key issue is a statistical one concerning *estimation*: since we do not know the true relationship between patterns and their labels, and instead receive only a finite amount of data about this relationship, how much data suffices to model the relationship with the desired accuracy? The third key question is concerned with the computational efficiency of learning algorithms: how can we *efficiently* make use of the training data to choose an accurate model of the relationship?

In this book, we concentrate mainly on the estimation question, although we also investigate the issues of computation and, to a lesser extent, approximation. Many of the results are applicable to a large family of function classes, but we focus on artificial neural networks.

1.2 Artificial Neural Networks

Artificial neural networks have become popular over the last ten years for diverse applications from financial prediction to machine vision. Although these networks were originally proposed as simplified models of biological neural networks, we are concerned here with their application to supervised learning problems. Consequently, we omit the word 'artificial,' and we consider a neural network as nothing more than a certain type of nonlinear function. In this section we introduce two of the neural network classes that are discussed later in the book and use them to illustrate the key issues of approximation, estimation, and computation described above.

The simple perceptron

First we consider the *simple (real-input) perceptron*, which computes a function from $\mathbb{R}^n$ to $\{0,1\}$. Networks such as this, whose output is either 0 or 1, are potentially suitable for pattern classification problems in which we wish to divide the patterns into two classes, labelled '0' and '1'. A simple perceptron computes a function f of the form

$$f(x) = \operatorname{sgn}(w \cdot x - \theta),$$

for input vector $x \in \mathbb{R}^n$, where $w = (w_1, \ldots, w_n) \in \mathbb{R}^n$ and $\theta \in \mathbb{R}$ are adjustable parameters, or *weights* (the particular weight θ being known

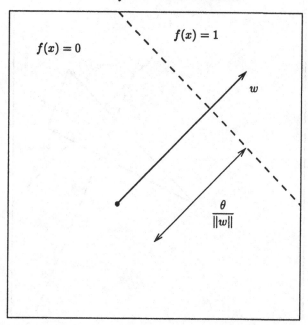

Fig. 1.1. The decision boundary in $\mathbb{R}^2$ computed by a simple perceptron with parameters w, θ.

as the *threshold*). Here, $w \cdot x$ denotes the inner product $\sum_{i=1}^{n} w_i x_i$, and

$$\operatorname{sgn}(\alpha) = \begin{cases} 1 & \text{if } \alpha \geq 0 \\ 0 & \text{otherwise.} \end{cases}$$

Clearly, the decision boundary of this function (that is, the boundary between the set of points classified as 0 and those classified as 1) is the affine subspace of $\mathbb{R}^n$ defined by the equation $w \cdot x - \theta = 0$. Figure 1.1 shows an example of such a decision boundary. Notice that the vector w determines the orientation of the boundary, and the ratio $\theta / \|w\|$ determines its distance from the origin (where $\|w\| = \left(\sum_{i=1}^{n} w_i^2\right)^{1/2}$).

Suppose we wish to use a simple perceptron for a pattern classification problem, and that we are given a collection of labelled data ((x, y) pairs) that we want to use to find good values of the parameters w and θ. The *perceptron algorithm* is a suitable method. This algorithm starts with arbitrary values of the parameters, and cycles through the training data, updating the parameters whenever the perceptron misclassifies an example. If the current function f misclassifies the pair (x, y) (with

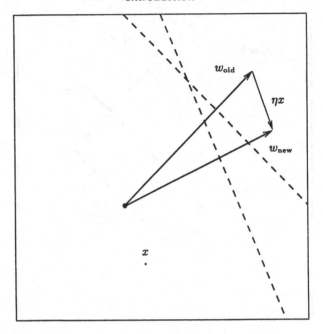

Fig. 1.2. The perceptron algorithm updates the parameters to move the decision boundary towards a misclassified example.

$x \in \mathbb{R}^n$ and $y \in \{0,1\}$), the algorithm adds $\eta(y - f(x))x$ to w and $\eta(f(x) - y)$ to θ, where η is a (prescribed) fixed positive constant. This update has the effect of moving the decision boundary closer to the misclassified point x (see Figure 1.2).

As we shall see in Chapter 24, after a finite number of iterations this algorithm finds values of the parameters that correctly classify all of the training examples, provided such parameters exist.

It is instructive to consider the key issues of approximation, estimation, and computation for the simple perceptron. Although we shall not study its approximation capabilities in this book, we mention that the representational capabilities of the simple perceptron are rather limited. This is demonstrated, for instance, by the fact that for binary input variables ($x \in \{0,1\}^n$), the class of functions computed by the perceptron forms a tiny fraction of the total number of boolean functions. Results in the first two parts of this book provide answers to the estimation question for classes of functions such as simple perceptrons. It might not suffice simply to find parameter values that give correct classifications for all of the training examples, since we would also like the perceptron to perform well on subsequent (as yet unseen) data. We are led to the problem of *generalization*, in which we ask how the performance on the training data relates to subsequent performance. In the next chapter, we describe some assumptions about the process generating the training data (and subsequent patterns), which will allow us to pose such questions more precisely. In the last part of the book, we study the computation question for a number of neural network function classes. Whenever it is possible, the perceptron algorithm is guaranteed to find, in a finite number of iterations, parameters that correctly classify all of the training examples. However, it is desirable that the number of iterations required does not grow too rapidly as a function of the problem complexity (measured by the input dimension and the training set size). Additionally, if there are no parameter values that classify all of the training set correctly, we should like a learning algorithm to find a function that minimizes the number of mistakes made on the training data. In general the perceptron algorithm will not converge to such a function. Indeed, as we shall see, it is known that no algorithm can efficiently solve this problem (given standard complexity theoretic assumptions).

The two-layer real-output sigmoid network

As a second example, we now consider the *two-layer real-output sigmoid network*. This network computes a function f from $\mathbb{R}^n$ to $\mathbb{R}$ of the form

$$f(x) = \sum_{i=1}^{k} w_i \sigma \left(v_i \cdot x + v_{i,0} \right) + w_0,$$

where $x \in \mathbb{R}^n$ is the input vector, $w_i \in \mathbb{R}$ $(i = 0, \ldots, k)$ are the output weights, $v_i \in \mathbb{R}^n$ and $v_{i,0}$ $(i = 0, \ldots, k)$ are the input weights, and $\sigma : \mathbb{R} \to \mathbb{R}$, the *activation function*, is the *standard sigmoid function*, given by

$$\sigma(\alpha) = \frac{1}{1 + e^{-\alpha}}. \tag{1.1}$$

This function is illustrated in Figure 1.3. Each of the functions

$$x \mapsto \sigma \left(v_i \cdot x + v_{i,0} \right)$$

can be thought of as a smoothed version of the function computed by a simple perceptron. Thus, the two-layer sigmoid network computes an affine combination of these 'squashed' affine functions. It should be

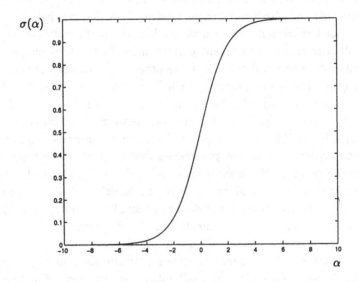

Fig. 1.3. The graph of the function $\sigma(\cdot)$ defined in Equation (1.1).

noted that the output of this network is a real number, and is not simply either 0 or 1 as for the simple perceptron. To use a network of this kind for a supervised learning problem, a learning algorithm would receive a set of labelled examples $((x,y)$ pairs, with $x \in \mathbb{R}^n$ and $y \in \mathbb{R})$ and attempt to find parameters that minimize some measure of the error of the network output over the training data. One popular technique is to start with small initial values for the parameters and use a 'gradient descent' procedure to adjust the parameters in such a way as to locally minimize the sum over the training examples (x_i, y_i) of the squared errors $(f(x_i) - y_i)^2$. In general, however, this approach leads only to a local minimum of the squared error.

We can consider the key issues of approximation, estimation, and computation for this network also. The approximation question has a more positive answer in this case. It is known that two-layer sigmoid networks are 'universal approximators', in the sense that, given any continuous function f defined on some compact subset S of $\mathbb{R}^n$, and any desired accuracy ϵ, there is a two-layer sigmoid network computing a function that is within ϵ of f at each point of S. Of course, even though such a network exists, a limited amount of training data might not provide enough information to specify it accurately. How much data *will* suffice depends on the complexity of the function f (or more precisely on the complexity—number of computation units and size of parameters—of a network that accurately approximates f). Results in Part 3 address these questions, and Part 4 considers the computational complexity of finding a suitable network.

General neural networks

Quite generally, a neural network N may be regarded as a machine capable of taking on a number of 'states', each of which represents a function computable by the machine. These functions map from an input space X (the set of all possible patterns) to an output space Y. For neural networks, inputs are typically encoded as vectors of real numbers (so $X \subseteq \mathbb{R}^n$ for some n), and these real numbers often lie in a bounded range. In Part 1, we consider binary output networks for classification problems, so, there, we have $Y = \{0, 1\}$. In Parts 2 and 3 we consider networks with real outputs.

Formalizing mathematically, we may regard a neural network as being characterized by a set Ω of states, a set X of inputs, a set Y of outputs, and a parameterized function $F : \Omega \times X \to Y$. For any $\omega \in \Omega$, the function *represented by state ω* is $h_\omega : X \to Y$ given by

$$h_\omega(x) = F(\omega, x).$$

The function F describes the functionality of the network: when the network is in state ω it computes the function h_ω. The set of functions *computable by N* is $\{h_\omega : \omega \in \Omega\}$, and this is denoted by H_N. As a concrete example of this, consider the simple perceptron. Here, a typical state is $\omega = (w_1, w_2, \ldots, w_n, \theta)$, and the function it represents is

$$
\begin{aligned}
h_\omega(x) &= F(\omega, x) \\
&= F\left((w_1, w_2, \ldots, w_n, \theta), (x_1, x_2, \ldots, x_n)\right) \\
&= \operatorname{sgn}\left(\sum_{j=1}^{n} w_j x_j - \theta\right).
\end{aligned}
$$

1.3 Outline of the Book

The first three parts of the book define three supervised learning problems and study how the accuracy of a model depends on the amount of training data and the model complexity. Results are generally of the form

$$\text{error} \leq (\text{estimate of error}) + (\text{complexity penalty}),$$

where the complexity penalty increases with some measure of the complexity of the class of models used by the learning system, and decreases as the amount of data increases. How 'complexity' is defined here depends both on the definition of error and on how the error is estimated. The three different learning problems are distinguished by the types of labels that must be predicted and by how the network outputs are interpreted.

In Part 1, we study the *binary classification problem*, in which we want to predict a binary-valued quantity using a class of binary-valued functions. The correct measure of complexity in this context is a combinatorial quantity known as the *Vapnik-Chervonenkis dimension*. Estimates of this dimension for simple perceptrons and networks of perceptrons have been known for some time. Part 1 reviews these results, and presents some more recent results, including estimates for the more commonly used sigmoid networks. In all cases, the complexity of a neural network is closely related to its size, as measured by the number of parameters in the network.

In Part 2, we study the *real classification problem*, in which we again want to predict a binary-valued quantity, but by using a class of real-valued functions. Learning algorithms that can be used for classes of real-valued functions are quite different from those used for binary-valued classes, and this leads to some anomalies between experimental experience and the VC theory described in Part 1. Part 2 presents some recent advances in the area of *large margin classifiers*, which are classifiers based on real-valued functions whose output is interpreted as a measure of the confidence in a classification. In this case, the correct measure of complexity is a scale-sensitive version of the VC-dimension known as the *fat-shattering dimension*. We shall see that this analysis can lead to more precise estimates of the misclassification probability (that is, better answers to the estimation question), and that the size of a neural network is not always the most appropriate measure of its complexity, particularly if the parameters are constrained to be small.

In Part 3, we study the *real prediction problem*. Here, the problem is to predict a real-valued quantity (using a class of real-valued functions). Once again, the fat-shattering dimension emerges as the correct measure of complexity. This part also features some recent results on the use of convex function classes for real prediction problems. For instance, these results suggest that for a simple function class, using the convex hull of the class (that is, forming a two-layer neural network of functions from the class, with a constraint on the output weights) has considerable benefits and little cost, in terms of the rate at which the error decreases.

Part 4 concerns the *algorithmics* of supervised learning, considering the computational limitations on learning with neural networks and investigating the performance of particular learning algorithms (the perceptron algorithm and two constructive algorithms for two-layer networks).

1.4 Bibliographical Notes

There are many good introductory books on the topic of artificial neural networks; see, for example, (Hertz, Krogh and Palmer, 1991; Haykin, 1994; Bishop, 1995; Ripley, 1996; Anderson and Rosenfeld, 1988). There are also a number of books on the estimation questions associated with general learning systems, and many of these include a chapter on neural networks. See, for example, the books by Anthony and Biggs (1992), Kearns and Vazirani (1995), Natarajan (1991a), Vidyasagar (1997), and Vapnik (1982; 1995).

The notion of segmenting the analysis of learning systems into the key questions of approximation, estimation and computation is popular in learning theory research (see, for instance, (Barron, 1994)).

The simple perceptron and perceptron learning algorithm were first discussed by Rosenblatt (1958). The notion of adjusting the strengths of connections in biological neurons on the basis of correlations between inputs and outputs was earlier articulated by Hebb (1949) who, in trying to explain how a network of living brain cells could adapt to different stimuli, suggested that connections that were used frequently would gradually become stronger, while those that were not used would fade away. A classic work concerning the power (and limitations) of simple perceptrons is the book by Minsky and Papert (1969). Around the time of the publication of this book, interest in artificial neural networks waned, but was restored in the early 1980's, as computational resources became more abundant (and with the popularization of the observation that gradient computations in a multi-layer sigmoid network could share intermediate calculations). See, for example, (Rumelhart, Hinton and Williams, 1986a; Rumelhart, Hinton and Williams, 1986b). Since this time, there have been many international conferences concentrating on neural networks research.

The 'universal approximation' property of neural networks has been proved under many different conditions and in many different ways; see (Cybenko, 1989; Hornik, Stinchcombe and White, 1990; Leshno, Lin, Pinkus and Schocken, 1993; Mhaskar, 1993).

Part one

Pattern Classification with Binary-Output Neural Networks

2
The Pattern Classification Problem

2.1 The Learning Problem
Introduction
In this section we describe the basic model of learning we use in this part of the book. This model is applicable to neural networks with one output unit that computes either the value 0 or 1; that is, it concerns the types of neural network used for *binary classification* problems. Later in the book we develop more general models of learning applicable to many other types of neural network, such as those with a real-valued output.

The definition of learning we use is formally described using the language of probability theory. For the moment, however, we move towards the definition in a fairly non-technical manner, providing some informal motivation for the technical definitions that will follow.

In very general terms, in a supervised learning environment, neural network 'learning' is the adjustment of the network's state in response to data generated by the environment. We assume this data is generated by some random mechanism, which is, for many applications, reasonable. The method by which the state of the network is adjusted in response to the data constitutes a *learning algorithm*. That is, a learning algorithm describes how to change the state in response to training data. We assume that the 'learner'† knows little about the process generating the data. This is a reasonable assumption for many applications of neural networks: if it is known that the data is generated according to a particular type of statistical process, then in practice it might be better to take advantage of this information by using a more restricted class of functions rather than a neural network.

† The 'learner' in this context is simply the learning algorithm.

Towards a formal framework

In our learning framework, the learner receives a sequence of training data, consisting of ordered pairs of the form (x, y), where x is an input to the neural network ($x \in X$) and y is an output ($y \in Y$). We call such pairs *labelled examples*. In this part of the book, and in Part 2, we consider classification problems, in which $Y = \{0, 1\}$. It is helpful to think of the label y as the 'correct output' of the network on input x (although this interpretation is not entirely valid, as we shall see below). We assume that each such pair is chosen, independently of the others, according to a fixed probability distribution on the set $Z = X \times Y$. This probability distribution reflects the relative frequency of different patterns in the environment of the learner, and the probability that the patterns will be labelled in a particular way. Note that we do *not* necessarily regard there to be some 'correct' classification function $t :$ $X \to \{0, 1\}$: for a given $x \in X$, both $(x, 0)$ and $(x, 1)$ may have a positive probability of being presented to the learner, so neither 0 nor 1 is the 'correct' label. Even when there is some correct classification function $f :$ $X \to \{0, 1\}$ (that is, f is such that the probability of the set $\{(x, f(x)) : x \in X\}$ is one), we do not assume that the neural network is capable of computing the function f. This is a very general model of training data generation and it can model, among other things, a classification problem in which some inputs are ambiguous, or in which there is some 'noise' corrupting the patterns or labels. The aim of successful learning is that, after training on a large enough sequence of labelled examples, the neural network computes a function that matches, almost as closely as it can, the process generating the data; that is, we hope that the classification of subsequent examples is close to the best performance that the network can possibly manage.

It is clear that we have to make the above notions mathematically precise. We first discuss the formal expression of the statement that the training data is randomly generated. We assume that there is some probability distribution P defined on Z. The probability distribution P is fixed for a given learning problem, but it is *unknown*. The information presented to the neural network during training consists only of a sequence of *labelled examples*, each of the form (x, y). Formally, for some positive integer m, the network is given during training a *training sample*

$$z = ((x_1, y_1), (x_2, y_2), \ldots, (x_m, y_m)) = (z_1, z_2, \ldots, z_m) \in Z^m.$$

The labelled examples $z_i = (x_i, y_i)$ are drawn independently, according to the probability distribution P. In other words, a random training sample of length m is an element of Z^m distributed according to the product probability distribution P^m.

We now turn our attention to measuring how well a given function computed by the network 'approximates' the process generating the data. Let us denote the set of all functions the network can compute by H rather than H_N (to keep the notation simple, but also because the model of learning to be defined can apply to learning systems other than neural networks). Given a function $h \in H$, the *error of h with respect to P* (called simply the *error* of h when P is clear) is defined as follows:†

$$\mathrm{er}_P(h) = P\left\{(x, y) \in Z : h(x) \neq y\right\}.$$

This is the probability, for (x, y) drawn randomly according to P, that h is 'wrong' in the sense that $h(x) \neq y$. The error of h is a measure of how accurately h approximates the relationship between patterns and labels generated by P. A related quantity is the *sample error* of h on the sample z (sometimes called the *observed error*), defined to be

$$\hat{\mathrm{er}}_z(h) = \frac{1}{m} \left|\{i : 1 \leq i \leq m \text{ and } h(x_i) \neq y_i\}\right|,$$

the proportion of labelled examples (x_i, y_i) in the training sample z on which h is 'wrong'. The sample error is a useful quantity, since it can easily be determined from the training data and it provides a simple estimate of the true error $\mathrm{er}_P(h)$.

It is to be hoped that, after training, the error of the function computed by the network is close to the minimum value it can be. In other words, if h is the function computed by the network after training (that is, h is the *hypothesis* returned by the learning algorithm), then we should like to have $\mathrm{er}_P(h)$ close to the quantity

$$\mathrm{opt}_P(H) = \inf_{g \in H} \mathrm{er}_P(g).$$

This quantity can be thought of as the *approximation error* of the class H, since it describes how accurately the best function in H can approximate the relationship between x and y that is determined by the probability distribution P. (Note that we take an infimum rather than simply a minimum here because the set of values that er_P ranges over

---

† The functions in H have to be measurable, and they also have to satisfy some additional, fairly weak, measurability conditions for the subsequent quantities to be well-defined. These conditions are satisfied by all function classes discussed in this book.

may be infinite.) More precisely, a positive real number ϵ is prescribed in advance, and the aim is to produce $h \in H$ such that

$$\mathrm{er}_P(h) < \mathrm{opt}_P(H) + \epsilon.$$

We say that such an h is ϵ-*good (for P)*. The number ϵ (which we may take to belong to the interval $(0,1)$ of positive numbers less than 1), is known as the *accuracy parameter*. Given the probabilistic manner in which the training sample is generated, it is possible that a large 'unrepresentative' training sample will be presented that will mislead a learning algorithm. It cannot, therefore, be guaranteed that the hypothesis will always be ϵ-good. Nevertheless, we can at least hope to ensure that it will be ϵ-good *with high probability*—specifically, with probability at least $1 - \delta$, where δ, again prescribed in advance, is a *confidence parameter*. (Again, we may assume that $\delta \in (0,1)$.)

Formal definition of learning

We are now in a position to say what we mean by a *learning algorithm*.

Informally, a learning algorithm takes random training samples and acts on these to produce a hypothesis $h \in H$ that, provided the sample is large enough, is, with probability at least $1 - \delta$, ϵ-good for P. Furthermore, it can do this for each choice of ϵ and δ and regardless of the distribution P. We have the following formal definition.

Definition 2.1 *Suppose that H is a class of functions that map from a set X to $\{0,1\}$. A learning algorithm L for H is a function*

$$L : \bigcup_{m=1}^{\infty} Z^m \to H$$

from the set of all training samples to H, with the following property:

- *given any $\epsilon \in (0,1)$,*
- *given any $\delta \in (0,1)$,*

there is an integer $m_0(\epsilon,\delta)$ such that if $m \geq m_0(\epsilon,\delta)$ then,

- *for any probability distribution P on $Z = X \times \{0,1\}$,*

if z is a training sample of length m, drawn randomly according to the product probability distribution P^m, then, with probability at least $1 - \delta$, the hypothesis $L(z)$ output by L is such that

$$\mathrm{er}_P(L(z)) < \mathrm{opt}_P(H) + \epsilon.$$

More compactly, for $m \geq m_0(\epsilon, \delta)$,

$$P^m \left\{ \text{er}_P(L(z)) < \text{opt}_P(H) + \epsilon \right\} \geq 1 - \delta.$$

We say that H is learnable if there is a learning algorithm for H.

Equivalently, a function L is a learning algorithm if there is a function $\epsilon_0(m, \delta)$ such that, for all m, δ, and P, with probability at least $1 - \delta$ over $z \in Z^m$ chosen according to P^m,

$$\text{er}_P(L(z)) < \text{opt}_P(H) + \epsilon_0(m, \delta),$$

and for all $\delta \in (0, 1)$, $\epsilon_0(m, \delta)$ approaches zero as m tends to infinity. We refer to $\epsilon_0(m, \delta)$ as an *estimation error bound* for the algorithm L. In analysing learning algorithms, we often present results either in the form of sample complexity bounds (by providing a suitable $m_0(\epsilon, \delta)$) or estimation error bounds. It is usually straightforward to transform between the two.

For a neural network N, we sometimes refer to a learning algorithm for H_N more simply as a learning algorithm for N.

There are some aspects of Definition 2.1 that are worth stressing. Note that the learning algorithm L must 'succeed' for all choices of the accuracy and confidence parameters ϵ and δ. Naturally, the quantity $m_0(\epsilon, \delta)$, known as a *sufficient sample size for (ϵ, δ)-learning H by L*, is allowed to vary with ϵ and δ. This is to be expected since decreasing the value of either ϵ or δ makes the learning problem more difficult (and hence we should be prepared to use a larger sample). Note, however, that $m_0(\epsilon, \delta)$ depends in no way on P; that is, a sufficient sample size can be given that will work for any fixed distribution P. This is desirable because P is unknown; it is not given as an input to the learning problem in the way that ϵ and δ are. We could have defined the learning problem so that the sample size is allowed to vary with the distribution. However, if the sample complexity depends on the probability distribution, we would need to have some information about the distribution in order to get sample size bounds. Many simple pattern classification techniques (such as certain nearest neighbour algorithms and kernel methods) are known to give predictions that are asymptotically optimal, in the sense that for any probability distribution, the error approaches that of the best deterministic classifier (the 'Bayes optimal'), as the amount of training data increases. On the other hand, the rate at which the error converges can be made arbitrarily slow by suitable choice of the probability distribution. This is one of the main motivations for considering classes like neural networks. We shall see that, because these classes are not too complex, we can prove estimation error convergence rates that apply to every probability distribution.

Learnability may appear difficult to achieve, particularly in view of the 'distribution-independence' (that is, the need for a sufficient sample size that is independent of P). However, we show in this chapter that if the class H consists of a finite number of functions then H is learnable, and in subsequent chapters we establish the learnability of many other classes.

It is of central importance to determine whether a given set H of functions is learnable and, if so, to design a learning algorithm for H. One measure of the efficiency of a learning algorithm is the minimum sample size $m_0(\epsilon, \delta)$ sufficient for learning to the levels of accuracy and confidence prescribed by ϵ and δ. We define the *sample complexity* function $m_L(\epsilon, \delta)$ of L as the smallest integer that can be taken to be $m_0(\epsilon, \delta)$ in Definition 2.1; that is,

$$m_L(\epsilon, \delta) \;=\; \min\{m : m \text{ is a sufficient sample size}$$
$$\text{for } (\epsilon, \delta)\text{-learning } H \text{ by } L\}.$$

Similarly, we define the *estimation error* $\epsilon_L(m, \delta)$ of L to be the smallest possible estimation error bound. It is also useful to define the *inherent sample complexity* $m_H(\epsilon, \delta)$ *of the learning problem for H*:

$$m_H(\epsilon, \delta) = \min_L m_L(\epsilon, \delta),$$

where the minimum is taken over all learning algorithms for H. The inherent sample complexity $m_H(\epsilon, \delta)$ provides an absolute lower bound on the size of sample needed to (ϵ, δ)-learn H, no matter what learning algorithm is being used. The inherent estimation error $\epsilon_H(m, \delta)$ may be defined similarly.

Notice that these definitions allow us to separate the problems of approximation and estimation introduced in Chapter 1. The approximation error is measured by $\mathrm{opt}_P(H)$, and a quantitative answer to the estimation question is provided by $\epsilon_H(m, \delta)$ (and $m_H(\epsilon, \delta)$).

Although we have used the term 'algorithm', we have not been at all specific about the computational or algorithmic aspects of learning. Later in the book, we investigate the important issue of the *computational complexity* of learning. For the moment, we simply regard a learning algorithm as a function and concentrate on quantifying the *sample complexity* of learning.

2.2 Learning Finite Function Classes

In this section we show that there are particularly simple learning algorithms for finite classes of functions. These algorithms use the sample error as an estimate for the true error and choose as output hypothesis a function in the class with minimal sample error. This works since the sample errors converge in a certain manner to the true errors, as the sample length is increased.

For many neural networks N, the class H_N of functions computable by the network is finite. For example, any neural network with a binary output defined on a finite input set (such as a neural network accepting only binary-valued inputs) will compute a finite number of functions. Furthermore, neural networks defined on real inputs but having weights that can take only a finite number of values also have finite H_N.

A 'uniform convergence' result, and learning using sample error

The aim of learning is to produce a function h in H that has near-minimal error $\mathrm{er}_P(h)$. Given that the true errors of the functions in H are unknown, it seems natural to use the sample errors as estimates. We might believe that if a function has small sample error then it has small true error. In this vein, suppose that an algorithm L chooses $L(z)$ having minimal sample error on z; that is,

$$\hat{\mathrm{er}}_z(L(z)) = \min_{h \in H} \hat{\mathrm{er}}_z(h).$$

In the remainder of this section we show that such an L is a learning algorithm whenever H is finite.

The following result will be useful. It shows that, given any $h \in H$ and given a large enough random sample, the sample error of h is close to the true error of h. This is unsurprising, as it is just a 'Law of Large Numbers' result from probability theory, telling us how rapidly the tails of a binomial distribution approach zero. (If we toss a coin a number of times, this theorem describes the rate at which the relative frequency of heads approaches the probability of a head. In this analogy, the probability of a head is $\mathrm{er}_P(h)$, and the relative frequency of heads is $\hat{\mathrm{er}}_z(h)$.)

Theorem 2.2 *Suppose that h is a function from a set X to $\{0,1\}$. Then*

$$P^m \left\{ |\hat{\mathrm{er}}_z(h) - \mathrm{er}_P(h)| \geq \epsilon \right\} \leq 2\exp(-2\epsilon^2 m),$$

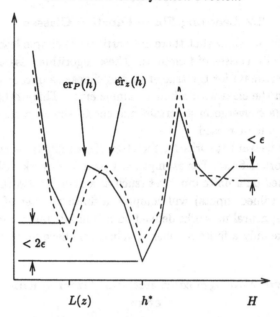

Fig. 2.1. If every h in function class H has $\mathrm{er}_P(h)$ close to $\hat{\mathrm{er}}_z(h)$, minimizing $\hat{\mathrm{er}}_z(h)$ will approximately minimize $\mathrm{er}_P(h)$.

for any probability distribution P, any ϵ, and any positive integer m.

Proof The theorem is a restatement of Hoeffding's inequality (Inequality (1.16) in Appendix 1). To see this, let $X_1, X_2, \ldots, X_m$ be a sequence of m $\{0, 1\}$-valued random variables, where X_i is 1 on $z_i = (x_i, y_i) \in Z$ if and only if $h(x_i) \neq y_i$. Then the sample error of h on z is $(1/m)(X_1 + X_2 + \cdots + X_m)$, and the expectation of each X_i equals $P\{h(x) \neq y\}$, which is $\mathrm{er}_P(h)$. □

We wish to show that any algorithm L that minimizes sample error on z is a learning algorithm when H is finite. Theorem 2.2 shows that for any particular $h \in H$, the sample error and error of h are close with high probability. But this is not quite sufficient to ensure that L learns. Rather, since L examines the sample error of *every* $h \in H$ and chooses the one that gives minimal sample error, we would like the sample error of *every* $h \in H$ to be close to its true error. Figure 2.1 illustrates why, if this is so, then minimizing $\hat{\mathrm{er}}_z(h)$ will approximately minimize $\mathrm{er}_P(h)$. The following result is of the required type.

Theorem 2.3 *Suppose that H is a finite set of functions from a set X to $\{0,1\}$. Then*

$$P^m \left\{ \max_{h \in H} |\hat{\mathrm{er}}_z(h) - \mathrm{er}_P(h)| \geq \epsilon \right\} \leq 2|H| \exp(-2\epsilon^2 m),$$

for any probability distribution P, any ϵ, and any positive integer m.

Proof We use Theorem 2.2, as follows.

$$
\begin{aligned}
&P^m \left\{ \max_{h \in H} |\hat{\mathrm{er}}_z(h) - \mathrm{er}_P(h)| \geq \epsilon \right\} \\
&\quad = \; P^m \left(\bigcup_{h \in H} \{z \in Z^m : |\hat{\mathrm{er}}_z(h) - \mathrm{er}_P(h)| \geq \epsilon \} \right) \\
&\quad \leq \; \sum_{h \in H} P^m \{|\hat{\mathrm{er}}_z(h) - \mathrm{er}_P(h)| \geq \epsilon \} \\
&\quad \leq \; |H| \left(2 \exp(-2\epsilon^2 m) \right),
\end{aligned}
$$

as required. (The first inequality—that the probability of a union of events is no more than the sum of their probabilities—is known as the *union bound*.) $\square$

Theorem 2.3 is an example of a *uniform convergence* result; it shows that the sample errors converge (in probability) to the true errors, *uniformly over H*, as m tends to infinity. We apply this theorem to obtain our first learnability result.

Theorem 2.4 *Suppose that H is a finite set of functions from a set X to $\{0,1\}$. Let $L : \bigcup_{m=1}^{\infty} Z^m \to H$ be such that for any m and any $z \in Z^m$,*

$$\hat{\mathrm{er}}_z(L(z)) = \min_{h \in H} \hat{\mathrm{er}}_z(h).$$

Then L is a learning algorithm for H, with estimation error

$$\epsilon_L(m, \delta) \leq \left(\frac{2}{m} \ln \left(\frac{2|H|}{\delta} \right) \right)^{1/2},$$

and sample complexity

$$m_L(\epsilon, \delta) \leq \frac{2}{\epsilon^2} \ln \left(\frac{2|H|}{\delta} \right).$$

Proof We must show that $\mathrm{er}_P(L(z))$ is not much bigger than $\mathrm{opt}_P(H) =$

$\inf_{h \in H} \mathrm{er}_P(h)$. Since H is finite, this infimum is attained; that is, there is $h^* \in H$ such that $\mathrm{er}_P(h^*) = \mathrm{opt}_P(H)$. Theorem 2.3 states that

$$P^m \left\{ \max_{h \in H} |\hat{\mathrm{er}}_z(h) - \mathrm{er}_P(h)| \geq \epsilon \right\} \leq 2|H| \exp\left(-2\epsilon^2 m\right),$$

and this is no more than δ if

$$\epsilon \geq \left(\frac{1}{2m} \ln\left(\frac{2|H|}{\delta} \right) \right)^{1/2}.$$

In this case, with probability at least $1 - \delta$, for *every* $h \in H$,

$$\mathrm{er}_P(h) - \epsilon < \hat{\mathrm{er}}_z(h) < \mathrm{er}_P(h) + \epsilon,$$

and so,

$$
\begin{aligned}
\mathrm{er}_P(L(z)) &\leq \hat{\mathrm{er}}_z(L(z)) + \epsilon \\
&= \min_{h \in H} \hat{\mathrm{er}}_z(h) + \epsilon \\
&\leq \hat{\mathrm{er}}_z(h^*) + \epsilon \\
&< (\mathrm{er}_P(h^*) + \epsilon) + \epsilon \\
&= \mathrm{opt}_P(H) + 2\epsilon.
\end{aligned}
$$

Hence, with probability at least $1 - \delta$, L returns a function h with

$$\mathrm{er}_P(h) \leq \mathrm{opt}_P(H) + \left(\frac{2}{m} \ln\left(\frac{2|H|}{\delta} \right) \right)^{1/2}.$$

Solving for m gives the sample complexity bound. $\square$

2.3 Applications to Perceptrons

We have already mentioned that for many neural networks N the class H_N of computable functions is finite. We now give two specific examples, both of which are types of *perceptron*. The perceptron was introduced in Section 1.2. Recall that, for an input $x \in \mathbb{R}^n$, the parameterized function describing the mapping computed by a perceptron is

$$
\begin{aligned}
F(\omega, x) &= F\left((w_1, w_2, \ldots, w_n, \theta), (x_1, x_2, \ldots, x_n)\right) \\
&= \mathrm{sgn}\left(\sum_{j=1}^{n} w_j x_j - \theta \right).
\end{aligned}
$$

In order to ensure that the function class is finite, we now consider perceptrons in which there are restrictions on the allowable values of the weights and threshold. First, we consider what we call the *binary-weight perceptron*, where each non-threshold weight can be only 0 or 1, and the threshold θ can only be an integer in the range 0 to n (where n, as usual, is the number of inputs). Since there are 2 choices for each of the n non-threshold weights and $n + 1$ choices for the threshold, the total number of states is $(n + 1)2^n$. Hence, for this network N, $|H_N| \leq (n + 1)2^n$, using the fact that the number of functions computable by a neural network is bounded by the number of states. Secondly, we consider the *k-bit perceptron*, in which the states are those for which the weights and threshold are expressible in binary as integers of length k (where one of the bits encodes the sign of the weight or threshold). There are 2^k possibilities for each weight and threshold and so, for this network N', $|H_{N'}| \leq (2^k)^{n+1} = 2^{k(n+1)}$.

We may apply Theorem 2.4 directly. (We state only sample complexity bounds in the following result, but estimation error bounds follow immmediately.)

Theorem 2.5 *Let N be the binary-weight perceptron on n inputs, and let $Z = \mathbb{R}^n \times \{0,1\}$. Suppose that $L : \bigcup_{m=1}^{\infty} Z^m \to H_N$ is such that for any m and any $z \in Z^m$,*

$$\hat{\mathrm{er}}_z(L(z)) = \min_{h \in H_N} \hat{\mathrm{er}}_z(h).$$

Then L is a learning algorithm for H_N and its sample complexity satisfies the inequality

$$m_L(\epsilon, \delta) \leq m_0(\epsilon, \delta) = \frac{2}{\epsilon^2}\left(n\ln 2 + \ln(n+1) + \ln\left(\frac{2}{\delta}\right) \right),$$

for all $\epsilon, \delta \in (0,1)$. The same statement holds for the k-bit perceptron N', with $m_0(\epsilon, \delta)$ replaced by

$$m_0'(\epsilon, \delta) = \frac{2}{\epsilon^2}\left(k(n+1)\ln 2 + \ln\left(\frac{2}{\delta}\right) \right).$$

2.4 Restricted Model

Definitions

As we emphasized, in the model of learning we have considered, it is not assumed that there is a 'target function' computable by the network. But if this *is* the case, one can obtain learnability results with smaller sufficient sample sizes.

To describe this *restricted model* of learning, let H be a set of $\{0,1\}$-valued functions on a set X and, rather than having an arbitrary distribution P on $Z = X \times \{0,1\}$, let us imagine that we have some *target function* t, belonging to H, and a probability distribution μ on the set X of inputs. We define the *error* of $h \in H$ with respect to t and μ to be

$$\text{er}_\mu(h, t) = \mu\{x \in X : h(x) \neq t(x)\}.$$

In this context, the training samples (rather than being arbitrary members of Z) are of the form

$$((x_1, t(x_1)), (x_2, t(x_2)), \ldots, (x_m, t(x_m))),$$

which we call the *training sample corresponding to x and t*. A learning algorithm maps from such samples to H and satisfies the following: given any $\epsilon, \delta \in (0,1)$, there is $m_0(\epsilon, \delta)$ such that for $m \geq m_0(\epsilon, \delta)$, for any $t \in H$ and any probability distribution μ on X, with μ^m-probability at least $1 - \delta$, a random $x \in X^m$ is such that if

$$z = ((x_1, t(x_1)), (x_2, t(x_2)), \ldots, (x_m, t(x_m)))$$

is the corresponding training sample, then $\text{er}_\mu(L(z))$, the error of the output hypothesis, is less than ϵ. (In this case, since $t \in H$, we can aim for arbitrarily small error, since the optimal error is 0.)

The restricted model may be regarded as a straightforward special case of the model of learning described in this chapter. For, given any $t \in H$ and a distribution μ on X, there is a corresponding distribution P on Z, in the sense that for any measurable subset A of X,

$$P\{(x, t(x)) : x \in A\} = \mu(A),$$
$$P\{(x, y) : x \in A, \ y \neq t(x)\} = 0,$$

and, furthermore, $\text{er}_P(h) = \text{er}_\mu(h, t)$. Thus the restricted learning problem corresponds to considering only a subset of all possible distributions P on Z.

Consistent learning algorithms

Given any training sample z corresponding to a function $t \in H$, there is always at least one function in H that matches t on the sample, in the sense that its values on the x_i agree with the labels $t(x_i)$. (Indeed, the target function t itself obviously has this property, and there may be other such functions.) It turns out that any L returning a function

$h \in H$ that matches the sample is a learning algorithm for a finite class H. (Such a learning algorithm is said to be *consistent*.)

Theorem 2.6 *Suppose that H is a finite set of functions from a set X to $\{0,1\}$. Let L be such that for any m and for any $t \in H$, if $x \in X^m$ and z is the training sample corresponding to x and t, then the hypothesis $h = L(z)$ satisfies $h(x_i) = t(x_i)$ for $i = 1, 2, \ldots, m$. Then L is a learning algorithm for H in the restricted model, with sample complexity*

$$m_L(\epsilon, \delta) \le m_0(\epsilon, \delta) = \frac{1}{\epsilon} \ln \left(\frac{|H|}{\delta} \right).$$

Proof Let $t \in H$ and suppose $h \in H$ is such that

$$\mathrm{er}_\mu(h,t) = \mu\{x \in X : h(x) \ne t(x)\} \ge \epsilon.$$

Then the probability (with respect to the product distribution μ^m) that h agrees with t on a random sample of length m is clearly at most $(1 - \epsilon)^m$. This is at most $\exp(-\epsilon m)$, using a standard approximation. Thus, since there are certainly at most $|H|$ such functions h, the probability that *some* function in H has error at least ϵ *and* matches t on a randomly chosen training sample of length m is at most $|H| \exp(-\epsilon m)$. For any fixed positive δ, this probability is less than δ provided

$$m \ge m_0(\delta, \epsilon) = \frac{1}{\epsilon} \ln \left(\frac{|H|}{\delta} \right),$$

as required. $\qquad\square$

The main difference between this sample complexity bound and that given in Theorem 2.4 is the presence of $1/\epsilon$ rather than the larger $1/\epsilon^2$. We shall see this difference arise in a number of contexts. The intuitive explanation of this improvement is that less data is needed to form an accurate estimate of a random quantity if its variance is smaller.

2.5 Remarks

Learning with respect to a touchstone class

It is often useful to weaken the requirement of a learning algorithm by asking only that (with high probability)

$$\mathrm{er}_P(L(z)) < \mathrm{opt}_P(T) + \epsilon = \inf_{t \in T} \mathrm{er}_P(t) + \epsilon$$

where T, called the *touchstone class*, is a subset of H. We call this *learning with respect to a touchstone class*. What we require in this modified framework is that L outputs a function whose error is close to the smallest error achievable by a function in the class T (and not necessarily to the smallest error of a function in the full class H). For example, in learning with a multi-layer neural network, we might be satisfied if, after training, the network computes a function that is almost as good as any function a simple perceptron could compute. The model of learning we have considered may be viewed as the case in which $T = H$. Sometimes it is computationally easier to learn with respect to a touchstone class when T is a strict subset of H.

Bounding the expected value of error

In our definition of learning, we demand that if $m \geq m_0(\epsilon, \delta)$, then with probability at least $1 - \delta$, $\mathrm{er}_P(L(z)) < \mathrm{opt}_P(H) + \epsilon$. An alternative approach would be to require a bound on the expected value of the random variable $\mathrm{er}_P(L(z))$. Explicitly, we could ask that, given $\alpha \in (0, 1)$, there is $m'_0(\alpha)$ such that

$$\mathbf{E}\left(\mathrm{er}_P(L(z))\right) < \mathrm{opt}_P(H) + \alpha$$

for $m \geq m'_0(\alpha)$, where $\mathbf{E}$ denotes the expectation over Z^m with respect to P^m. This model and the one of this chapter are easily seen to be related. By Markov's inequality (see Appendix 1),

$$\mathbf{E}\left(\mathrm{er}_P(L(z))\right) < \mathrm{opt}_P(H) + \epsilon\delta$$
$$\iff \quad \mathbf{E}\left(\mathrm{er}_P(L(z)) - \mathrm{opt}_P(H)\right) < \epsilon\delta$$
$$\implies \quad P^m\left\{\mathrm{er}_P(L(z)) - \mathrm{opt}_P(H) \geq \epsilon\right\} < \frac{\epsilon\delta}{\epsilon} = \delta.$$

Therefore, learnability in the alternative model implies learnability in our model, and we may take $m_0(\epsilon, \delta) = m'_0(\epsilon\delta)$. Conversely, suppose

$$P^m\left\{\mathrm{er}_P(L(z)) - \mathrm{opt}_P(H) \geq \frac{\alpha}{2}\right\} < \frac{\alpha}{2}.$$

Then, since $\mathrm{er}_P(L(z)) - \mathrm{opt}_P(H) \leq 1$ for all z, we have

$$\mathbf{E}\left(\mathrm{er}_P(L(z)) - \mathrm{opt}_P(H)\right) \leq \frac{\alpha}{2} P^m\left\{\mathrm{er}_P(L(z)) - \mathrm{opt}_P(H) < \frac{\alpha}{2}\right\} +$$
$$P^m\left\{\mathrm{er}_P(L(z)) - \mathrm{opt}_P(H) \geq \frac{\alpha}{2}\right\}$$
$$< \quad \alpha.$$

It follows that learnability in the sense of this chapter implies learnability in the alternative model, and we may take $m_0'(\alpha) = m_0(\alpha/2, \alpha/2)$.

2.6 Bibliographical Notes

For an introduction to measure theory and probability, see, for example, (Billingsley, 1986; Feller, 1971).

The problem of supervised learning for pattern classification is an old one, and there are many books discussing it. See, for instance, the books of Duda and Hart (1973), and Devroye, Györfi and Lugosi (1996). The probablistic models of learning discussed in this chapter derive from a model due to Valiant (1984b). (Valiant, however, emphasizes the computational complexity of learning, something we do not address until later in this book.) In fact, the 'Probably Approximately Correct' (PAC) model as originally developed is precisely our restricted model of learning; our main model of learning is a form of 'agnostic PAC learning', studied by Haussler (1992), Kearns, Schapire and Sellie (1994), Maass (1995), and others.

The existence of universal asymptotically optimal pattern classification schemes was first shown by Stone (1977). Devroye (1982) showed that the rate at which the error of such schemes converges to the Bayes optimal can be arbitrarily slow.

The fact that finite hypothesis spaces are learnable in the restricted model was shown by Valiant (1984b). Blumer, Ehrenfeucht, Haussler and Warmuth (1989) highlighted the important role of consistent learning algorithms in learning, building on work of Vapnik and Chervonenkis (1971).

The notion of a touchstone class has been studied by Kearns et al. (1994). Later in the book, we shall see an example of a neural network class that can be learnt efficiently using a larger class of functions.

The learning model that focuses on the expected value of error has been investigated by Haussler, Littlestone and Warmuth (1994); see also (Devroye and Lugosi, 1995). The relationship between this model, the restricted model, and many other learning models is studied in (Haussler, Kearns, Littlestone and Warmuth, 1991).

There has been a great deal of work on learning models that relax Valiant's PAC model (the restricted model). For instance, these models allow noisy labels (Angluin and Laird, 1988; Kearns and Li, 1993; Sloan, 1995; Cesa-Bianchi, Fischer, Shamir and Simon, 1997), relax the assumptions of the independence of training examples (Aldous and Vazirani, 1990; Bartlett, Fischer and Höffgen, 1994), relax the assumption that the distribution generating training examples is fixed (Bartlett, 1992; Bartlett, Ben-David and Kulkarni, 1996; Barve and Long, 1997; Freund and Mansour, 1997), relax the assumption that the relationship between the examples and their labels is fixed (Kuh, Petsche and Rivest, 1991; Blum and Chalasani, 1992; Helmbold and Long, 1994), relax the requirement that the sample size bounds apply to all distributions (Benedek and Itai, 1991) and functions (Benedek and Itai, 1988), and restrict consideration to some restricted set of probability distributions (Li and Vitányi, 1991; Li and Vitányi, 1993). In other models, the training examples are not randomly chosen; they may be chosen by the learner, and labelled by an oracle (Angluin, 1988; Angluin, 1992), or they may be chosen by a helpful teacher (Shinohara and Miyano, 1991; Goldman and Kearns, 1991; Jackson and Tomkins, 1992; Anthony, Brightwell and Shawe-Taylor, 1995).

3

The Growth Function and VC-dimension

3.1 Introduction

The previous chapter gave a formal definition of the learning problem, and showed that it can be solved if the class H_N of functions is finite. However, many interesting function classes are not finite. For example, the number of functions computed by the perceptron with real-valued weights and inputs is infinite. Many other neural networks can also be represented as a parameterized function class with an infinite parameter set. We shall see that learning is possible for many (but not all) function classes like this, provided the function class is not too complex. In this chapter, we examine two measures of the complexity of a function class, the growth function and the VC-dimension, and we show that these are intimately related. In the next two chapters, we shall see that the growth function and VC-dimension of a function class determine the inherent sample complexity of the learning problem.

3.2 The Growth Function

Consider a finite subset S of the input space X. For a function class H, the restriction of H to the set S (that is, the set of restrictions to S of all functions in H) is denoted by $H_{|S}$. If $H_{|S}$ is the set of all functions from S to $\{0, 1\}$, then clearly, H is as powerful as it can be in classifying the points in S. We can view the cardinality of $H_{|S}$ (and in particular how it compares with $2^{|S|}$) as a measure of the classification complexity of H with respect to the set S.

The growth function of H, $\Pi_H : \mathbb{N} \to \mathbb{N}$, is defined as

$$\Pi_H(m) = \max \left\{ \left| H_{|S} \right| : S \subseteq X \text{ and } |S| = m \right\}.$$

Notice that $\Pi_H(m) \le 2^m$ for all m. If H is finite, then clearly $\Pi_H(m) \le$

$|H|$ for all m, and $\Pi_H(m) = |H|$ for sufficiently large m, so the growth function can be considered to be a refinement of the notion of cardinality that is applicable to infinite sets of functions.

As an example, we shall calculate the growth function for the perceptron. By a *dichotomy* (by H) of a finite subset S of the input space, we mean one of the $\Pi_H(S)$ ways in which the set S can be classified by functions in H into positive and negative examples; that is, a dichotomy is one of the functions $f : S \to \{0, 1\}$ in $H_{|_S}$. To count the number of dichotomies of a subset of the input space, it is convenient to consider the parameter space. If we divide the parameter space into a number of regions, so that in each region all parameters correspond to the same dichotomy of the set, we can then count these regions to obtain an upper bound on the number of dichotomies. We shall see in later chapters that this approach is also useful for more complex function classes.

Theorem 3.1 *Let N be the real-weight simple perceptron with $n \in \mathbb{N}$ real inputs and H the set of functions it computes. Then*

$$\Pi_H(m) = 2\sum_{k=0}^{n}\binom{m-1}{k}.$$

Here,

$$\binom{a}{b} = \frac{a(a-1)\cdots(a-b+1)}{b!}$$

for any $a \geq 0$ and $b > 0$. By convention, we define $\binom{a}{0} = 1$ for any $a \geq 0$. Notice that $\binom{a}{b} = 0$ for $b > a$, and it is easy to see that $\sum_{k=0}^{n}\binom{m}{k} = 2^m$ for $n \geq m$.

The proof of Theorem 3.1 involves three steps. We first show that the number of dichotomies of a set of m points is the same as the number of cells in a certain partition of the parameter space (defined by the points). Then we count the number of these cells when the points are in general position. (A set of points in $\mathbb{R}^n$ is in general position if no subset of $k+1$ points lies on a $(k-1)$-plane, for $k = 1, \ldots, n$.) Finally, we show that we can always assume that the points lie in general position, in the sense that if they are not, then this can only decrease the number of dichotomies.

The set of parameters for a real-weight simple perceptron with n inputs is $\mathbb{R}^n \times \mathbb{R}$, which we identify with $\mathbb{R}^{n+1}$. For a subset $S \subseteq \mathbb{R}^{n+1}$ of this space, we let $\mathrm{CC}(S)$ denote the number of connected components of S. (A connected component of S is a maximal nonempty subset $A \subseteq S$

such that any two points of A are connected by a continuous curve lying in A.)

Lemma 3.2 *For a set $S = \{x_1, \ldots, x_m\} \subseteq \mathbb{R}^n$, let $P_1, P_2, \ldots, P_m$ be the hyperplanes given by*

$$P_i = \left\{ (w, \theta) \in \mathbb{R}^{n+1} : w^T x_i - \theta = 0 \right\}.$$

Then

$$\left| H_{|s} \right| = \mathrm{CC} \left(\mathbb{R}^{n+1} - \bigcup_{i=1}^{m} P_i \right).$$

Proof Clearly, $\left| H_{|s} \right|$ is the number of nonempty subsets of parameter space $\mathbb{R}^{n+1}$ of the form

$$\left\{ (w, \theta) \in \mathbb{R}^{n+1} : \mathrm{sgn}(w^T x_i - \theta) = b_i \quad \text{for } i = 1, \ldots, m \right\}, \quad (3.1)$$

where $(b_1, b_2, \ldots, b_m)$ runs through all 2^m $\{0,1\}$-vectors. Let $C = \mathbb{R}^{n+1} - \bigcup_{i=1}^{m} P_i$. In every connected component of C, the sign of $w^T x_i - \theta$ is fixed, for $i = 1, \ldots, m$. Hence each distinct connected component of C is contained in a distinct set of the form (3.1), and so

$$\left| H_{|s} \right| \geq \mathrm{CC}(C).$$

To prove the reverse inequality, we show that every set of the form (3.1) intersects exactly one connected component of C. First, if a set (3.1) contains (w, θ) for which $w^T x_i - \theta \neq 0$ for all i, then it intersects exactly one connected component of C, as desired. But every set of the form (3.1) contains such a point. To see this, suppose (w, θ) satisfies $\mathrm{sgn}(w^T x_i - \theta) = b_i$ for $i = 1, \ldots, m$. Define

$$\delta = \min \left\{ \left| w^T x_i - \theta \right| : w^T x_i - \theta \neq 0 \right\}.$$

Then $(w, \theta - \delta/2)$ also satisfies $\mathrm{sgn}(w^T x_i - \theta) = b_i$ for all i, but in addition $w^T x_i - \theta \neq 0$ for all i. It follows that

$$\left| H_{|s} \right| \leq \mathrm{CC}(C).$$

$\square$

Figure 3.1 shows an example of an arrangement of three hyperplanes in $\mathbb{R}^2$, defined by three points in $\mathbb{R}$. It turns out that the number of cells does not depend on the choice of the planes P_i when the points in S are in general position, as the following lemma shows. Before stating

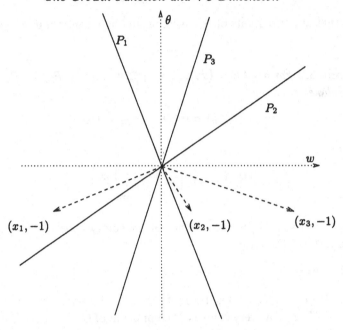

Fig. 3.1. The planes P_1, P_2, and P_3 (defined by points $x_1, x_2, x_3 \in \mathbb{R}$) divide $\mathbb{R}^2$ into six cells.

this lemma, we note that the planes in Lemma 3.2 may be expressed in the form

$$P_i = \left\{ v \in \mathbb{R}^{n+1} : v^T z_i = 0 \right\},$$

for $i = 1, \ldots, m$, where $z_i^T = (x_i^T, -1)$. When the x_i are in general position, every subset of up to $n+1$ points in $\{z_1, z_2, \ldots, z_m\}$ is linearly independent. To apply the lemma, we shall set $d = n + 1$.

Lemma 3.3 *For $m, d \in \mathbb{N}$, suppose $T = \{z_1, \ldots, z_m\} \subseteq \mathbb{R}^d$ has every subset of no more than d points linearly independent. Let $P_i = \{v \in \mathbb{R}^d : v^T z_i = 0\}$ for $i = 1, \ldots, m$, and define*

$$C(T) = \mathrm{CC} \left(\mathbb{R}^d - \bigcup_{i=1}^{m} P_i \right).$$

Then $C(T)$ depends only on m and d, so we can write $C(T) = C(m, d)$,

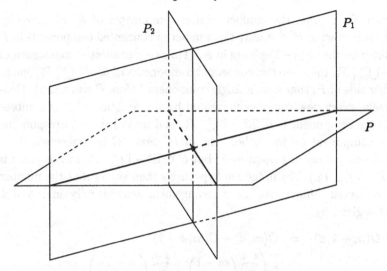

Fig. 3.2. Planes P_1, P_2, and P in $\mathbb{R}^3$. The intersections of P_1 and P_2 with P are shown as bold lines.

and for all $m, d \geq 1$, we have

$$C(m, d) = 2 \sum_{k=0}^{d-1} \binom{m-1}{k}. \tag{3.2}$$

Proof First notice that linear independence of every subset of up to d points of T is equivalent to the condition that the intersection of any $1 \leq k \leq d$ linear subspaces P_i is a $(d-k)$-dimensional linear subspace (a '$(d-k)$-plane'). With this condition, it is clear that $C(1, d) = 2$ for $d \geq 1$, and $C(m, 1) = 2$ for $m \geq 1$, so (3.2) holds in these cases. (Recall that $\binom{m-1}{0} = 1$ for any positive m.)

We shall prove the lemma by induction. Assume that the claim is true for all $T \subseteq \mathbb{R}^j$ with $|T| \leq m$ and $j \leq d$. Then suppose that we have m planes $P_1, \ldots, P_m$ satisfying the independence condition, and that we introduce another plane P so that the linear independence condition for the corresponding $m + 1$ points is satisfied. (See Figure 3.2.)

Consider the m intersections of the new plane P with each of the previous planes. By the linear independence condition, each intersection is a $(d-2)$-plane in the $(d-1)$-plane P, and all of these $(d-2)$-planes satisfy the independence condition in P (that is, the intersection of any $1 \leq k \leq d-1$ of them is a $(d-1-k)$-plane). Clearly, having intersected $P_1, \ldots, P_m$, the number of new components of $\mathbb{R}^d$ obtained by then introducing P is exactly the number of connected components in P defined by the m $(d-2)$-planes in P. (For every connected component of $P - \bigcup_{i=1}^m P_i$, there are two connected components of $\mathbb{R}^d - \bigcup_{i=1}^m P_i$, one to either side of P, that were a single component before P was added. Conversely, every new component created by the addition of P is a subset of some component C of $\mathbb{R}^d - \bigcup_{i=1}^m P_i$, and must have a corresponding new component on the 'other side' of P. Since C is connected, there must be a connecting point in P, but $C \subset \mathbb{R}^d - \bigcup_{i=1}^m P_i$, so this point is in $P - \bigcup_{i=1}^m P_i$.) The inductive hypothesis then shows that the number of connected components in our arrangement depends only on m and d, and is given by

$$
\begin{aligned}
C(m+1, d) &= C(m, d) + C(m, d-1) \\
&= 2 \left(\sum_{k=0}^{d-1} \binom{m-1}{k} + \sum_{k=0}^{d-2} \binom{m-1}{k} \right) \\
&= 2 \left(\binom{m-1}{0} + \sum_{k=1}^{d-1} \left(\binom{m-1}{k} + \binom{m-1}{k-1} \right) \right) \\
&= 2 \left(\binom{m}{0} + \sum_{k=1}^{d-1} \binom{m}{k} \right).
\end{aligned}
$$

It follows that (3.2) is true for all $m, d \geq 1$. $\qquad\square$

Proof (**of Theorem 3.1**) Let $S = \{x_1, x_2, \ldots, x_m\}$ be an arbitrary subset of $X = \mathbb{R}^n$. Applying Lemmas 3.2, 3.3, and the observations before Lemma 3.3, we see that if S is in general position then

$$
|H_{|S}| = C(m, n+1) = 2 \sum_{k=0}^n \binom{m-1}{k}.
$$

If S is not in general position, then suppose that $H_{|S} = \{f_1, \ldots, f_K\}$, and that, for $i = 1, 2, \ldots, m$, (w_j, θ_j) corresponds to the function f_j as follows:

$$
f_j(x_i) = \begin{cases} 1 & \text{if } w_j^T x_i - \theta_j \geq 0 \\ 0 & \text{otherwise.} \end{cases}
$$

Then let

$$
\delta_j = \min\{|w_j^T x_i - \theta_j| : 1 \leq i \leq m, \ w_j^T x_i - \theta_j \neq 0\},
$$

and $\delta = \min_j \delta_j$. Now if we replace each θ_j by $\theta' = \theta_j - \delta/2$, we obtain a set of parameters (w_j, θ'_j) corresponding to the functions in $H_{|S}$, with the additional 'separation' property that $|w_j^T x_i - \theta'_j| \geq \delta/2 > 0$ for all i and j.

Clearly, it is possible to perturb the points in S so that for any set $\tilde{S}$ within some sufficiently small ball,

$$\left|H_{|S}\right| \leq \left|H_{|\tilde{S}}\right|. \tag{3.3}$$

(If we define $W = \max_j \|w_j\|$, then any point in S can be moved any distance less than $\delta/(2W)$ without altering the classifications of the point by the functions f_j.) Now, general position is a generic property of a set of points in $\mathbb{R}^n$, in the sense that the set of m-tuples of points in $\mathbb{R}^n$ that are not in general position has Lebesgue measure zero† when regarded as a subset of $\mathbb{R}^{mn}$. As a result, within the ball of perturbed sets $\tilde{S}$ satisfying (3.3), we can always find some set in general position, so that

$$\left|H_{|\tilde{S}}\right| = C(m, n+1),$$

which, together with (3.3), shows that the number of dichotomies is maximal for points in general position. $\square$

3.3 The Vapnik-Chervonenkis Dimension

For a function class H and a set S of m points in the input space X, if H can compute all dichotomies of S (in our notation, if $\left|H_{|S}\right| = 2^m$), we say that H *shatters* S. The Vapnik-Chervonenkis dimension (or VC-dimension) of H is the size of the largest shattered subset of X (or infinity, if the maximum does not exist). Equivalently, the VC-dimension of H is the largest value of m for which the growth function $\Pi_H(m)$ equals 2^m. We shall see that the behaviour of the growth function is strongly constrained by the value of the VC-dimension, so the VC-dimension can be viewed as a 'single-integer summary' of the behaviour of the growth function.

---

† If S is not in general position, some subset of S of size $k+1$ lies on a $(k-1)$-plane, for some $1 \leq k \leq n$. This means that the determinant of some $(k+1) \times (k+1)$ matrix constructed from an axis-orthogonal projection of the elements of this subset is zero. However, there is a finite number of these matrices, and their determinants are analytic (polynomial) functions of the m points. Clearly, each of these functions is not identically zero, so the set of points that are not in general position has Lebesgue measure no more than the sum of the measures of the zero sets of these analytic functions, which is zero.

For the perceptron, we have

$$\Pi_H(m) = 2\sum_{k=0}^{n} \binom{m-1}{k}$$

$$= \begin{cases} 2^m & \text{if } n \geq m-1 \\ 2^m - 2\sum_{k=n+1}^{m-1} \binom{m-1}{k} & \text{otherwise,} \end{cases}$$

and this is less than 2^m exactly when $m \geq n+2$, so $\mathrm{VCdim}(H) = n+1$.

As an illustration of the notion of VC-dimension, the proof of the following theorem gives an alternative derivation of the VC-dimension of the perceptron.

Theorem 3.4 *Let N be the real-weight simple perceptron with $n \in \mathbb{N}$ real inputs. Then a set $S = \{x_1, \ldots, x_m\} \subseteq \mathbb{R}^n$ is shattered by H if and only if S is affinely independent; that is, if and only if the set $\{(x_1^T, -1), \ldots, (x_m^T, -1)\}$ is linearly independent in $\mathbb{R}^{n+1}$. It follows that $\mathrm{VCdim}(H) = n+1$.*

Proof We first show that if S is shattered by H then it must be affinely independent. Suppose, to the contrary, that S is shattered by H, but is affinely dependent. Then for any $b \in \{0,1\}^m$ there is a weight vector w in $\mathbb{R}^n$, threshold θ in $\mathbb{R}$, and vector $v \in \mathbb{R}^m$ such that

$$\begin{pmatrix} x_1^T & -1 \\ x_2^T & -1 \\ & \vdots \\ x_m^T & -1 \end{pmatrix} \begin{pmatrix} w \\ \theta \end{pmatrix} = v,$$

with $v_i \geq 0$ if and only if $b_i = 1$. Let $\{(w_1, \theta_1), \ldots, (w_{2^m}, \theta_{2^m})\}$ be a representative set of weights satisfying these constraints for binary vectors $b_1, b_2, \ldots, b_{2^m}$, the 2^m possible values of b. Then there are vectors $v_1, \ldots, v_{2^m}$ (whose components have the appropriate signs, determined by the b_i) such that

$$\begin{pmatrix} x_1^T & -1 \\ x_2^T & -1 \\ & \vdots \\ x_m^T & -1 \end{pmatrix} \begin{pmatrix} w_1 & w_2 & \cdots & w_{2^m} \\ \theta_1 & \theta_2 & & \theta_{2^m} \end{pmatrix} = (v_1 \cdots v_{2^m}).$$

But since we have assumed that S is affinely dependent, without loss of generality we can write

$$\left(x_m^T - 1\right) = \sum_{i=1}^{m-1} \alpha_i \left(x_i^T - 1\right)$$

for some $\alpha_1 \dots, \alpha_{m-1}$. It follows that all column vectors v_i have $v_{mi} = \sum_{j=1}^{m-1} \alpha_j v_{ji}$. If we choose i such that $\alpha_j v_{ji} \geq 0$ for all $1 \leq j \leq m - 1$, then, necessarily, $v_{mi} \geq 0$, which contradicts our assumption that the v_i together take on all 2^m sign patterns. It follows that VCdim$(H) \leq n + 1$.

For the second part of the proof, suppose that S is affinely independent. Then the matrix

$$\begin{pmatrix} x_1^T & -1 \\ x_2^T & -1 \\ \vdots & \\ x_m^T & -1 \end{pmatrix}$$

has row-rank m. So for any vector $v \in \mathbb{R}^m$ there is a solution (w, θ) to the equation

$$\begin{pmatrix} x_1^T & -1 \\ x_2^T & -1 \\ \vdots & \\ x_m^T & -1 \end{pmatrix} \begin{pmatrix} w \\ \theta \end{pmatrix} = v,$$

from which it immediately follows that S can be shattered. Clearly, VCdim$(H) \geq n + 1$. □

This result can be generalized to any function class H whose members are thresholded, shifted versions of elements of a vector space of real functions; that is, to a class of the form $H = \{\text{sgn}(f + g) : f \in F\}$, where g is some fixed real function and F satisfies the linearity condition: for all $f_1, f_2 \in F$ and $\alpha_1, \alpha_2 \in \mathbb{R}$, the function $\alpha_1 f_1 + \alpha_2 f_2$ also belongs to F. Recall that the linear dimension dim(F) of a vector space F is the size of a basis, that is, of a linearly independent subset $\{f_1, \dots, f_d\} \subseteq F$ for which $\left\{\sum_{i=1}^{d} \alpha_i f_i : \alpha_i \in \mathbb{R}\right\} = F$.

Theorem 3.5 *Suppose F is a vector space of real-valued functions, g is a real-valued function, and $H = \{\text{sgn}(f + g) : f \in F\}$. Then* VCdim$(H) = $ dim(F).

Proof The proof is similar to that of Theorem 3.4. Let $\{f_1, \dots, f_d\}$ be a basis for F. Then, if $\{x_1, x_2, \dots, x_m\}$ is shattered by H, there are vectors $v_1, v_2, \ldots, v_{2^m}$ taking (as in the previous proof) all possible sign patterns, and corresponding $w_1, w_2, \ldots, w_{2^m} \in \mathbb{R}^d$ such that

$$
M(w_1 \cdots w_{2^m}) = (v_1 \cdots v_{2^m}) - \begin{pmatrix} g(x_1) & g(x_1) & \cdots & g(x_1) \\ g(x_2) & g(x_2) & \cdots & g(x_2) \\ \vdots & \vdots & & \vdots \\ g(x_m) & g(x_m) & \cdots & g(x_m) \end{pmatrix},
$$

(3.4)

where

$$
M = \begin{pmatrix} f_1(x_1) & f_2(x_1) & \cdots & f_d(x_1) \\ f_1(x_2) & f_2(x_2) & \cdots & f_d(x_2) \\ \vdots & \vdots & & \vdots \\ f_1(x_m) & f_2(x_m) & \cdots & f_d(x_m) \end{pmatrix}.
$$

(The proof for the simple perceptron effectively uses the basis functions $f_i : x \mapsto x_i$ for $i = 1, \ldots, n$ and $f_{n+1} : x \mapsto -1$, it has $g : x \mapsto 0$, and it denotes the last entry of w_j by θ_j.)

If $m > d$ then the matrix M on the left of Equation (3.4) is not of row-rank m, so as in the proof of Theorem 3.4, we may assume that its last row can be written as a linear combination of the other rows. With v_{ji} and α_i defined as in the previous proof, we then have

$$
v_{mi} = \sum_{j=1}^{m-1} \alpha_j v_{ji} + g(x_m) - \sum_{j=1}^{m-1} \alpha_j g(x_j).
$$

If $g(x_m) - \sum_j \alpha_j g(x_j) \geq 0$, choose i such that $\alpha_j v_{ji} \geq 0$ for all $1 \leq j \leq m - 1$, and we see that $v_{mi} \geq 0$. Otherwise, choose i such that $\alpha_j v_{ji} \leq 0$ for all j, and we see that $v_{mi} < 0$. In either case, the v_i do not take all 2^m sign patterns, and so VCdim$(H) \leq d$.

Conversely, since $\{f_1, f_2, \ldots, f_d\}$ is a basis of F, there is a d-set $\{x_1, x_2, \ldots, x_d\}$ such that the linear system of equations (3.4) is full-rank. To see why, suppose that for any d-set $\{x_1, \ldots, x_d\}$, the rows of the matrix M form a linearly dependent set. Then the vector space V spanned by all vectors of the form $(f_1(x), f_2(x), \ldots, f_d(x))$ as x ranges through all of the domain of F, has linear dimension at most $d - 1$, since it has no basis of length d. But this would mean that $f_1, \ldots, f_d$ were linearly dependent, which is not the case. It now follows, as in the proof of Theorem 3.4, that VCdim$(H) \geq d$.   □

As mentioned above, we shall see that the growth function determines the inherent sample complexity of the learning problem. The following useful result shows that the behaviour of the growth function is strongly constrained by the VC-dimension.

Theorem 3.6 *For a function class H with* VCdim$(H) = d$,

$$\Pi_H(m) \leq \sum_{i=0}^{d} \binom{m}{i}, \qquad (3.5)$$

for all positive integers m.

Proof For $m \leq d$, inequality (3.5) is trivially true since in that case the sum is 2^m. Assume, then, that $m > d$ and fix a set $S = \{x_1, \ldots, x_m\} \subseteq X$. We will make use of the natural correspondence between $\{0, 1\}$-valued functions on a set and subsets of that set by defining the set system (or family of sets)

$$\mathcal{F} = \{\{x_i \in S : f(x_i) = 1\} : f \in H\}.$$

The proof proceeds by creating a transformed version $\mathcal{F}^*$ of $\mathcal{F}$ that is an *ideal* and has the same cardinality as $\mathcal{F}$. (A set $\mathcal{F}^*$ of subsets is an ideal if each set in $\mathcal{F}^*$ has all of its subsets also in $\mathcal{F}^*$.) We then prove that

$$|\mathcal{F}| = |\mathcal{F}^*| \leq \sum_{i=0}^{d} \binom{m}{i},$$

which will yield the result, since S was chosen arbitrarily.

For an element x of S, let T_x denote the operator that, acting on a set system, removes the element x from all sets in the system, unless that would give a set that is already in the system:

$$T_x(\mathcal{F}) = \{A - \{x\} : A \in \mathcal{F}\} \cup \{A \in \mathcal{F} : A - \{x\} \in \mathcal{F}\}.$$

Consider now $\mathcal{F}^* = T_{x_1}(T_{x_2}(\cdots T_{x_m}(\mathcal{F}) \cdots))$. Clearly, $|\mathcal{F}^*| = |\mathcal{F}|$. Furthermore, for all x in S, $T_x(\mathcal{F}^*) = \mathcal{F}^*$, so F^* is an ideal.

To prove the bound on the cardinality of $\mathcal{F}^*$, it will be useful to define the notion of shattering for a family of subsets, in the same way as for a family of $\{0, 1\}$-valued functions. For $R \subseteq S$, we say that $\mathcal{F}$ shatters R if $\mathcal{F} \cap R = \{A \cap R : A \in \mathcal{F}\}$ is the set of all subsets of R.

Suppose we can show that any subset shattered by $\mathcal{F}^*$ is also shattered by $\mathcal{F}$. This would imply that $\mathcal{F}^*$ can only shatter sets of cardinality at most d. Since $\mathcal{F}^*$ is an ideal, this would mean that the largest set in $\mathcal{F}^*$

has cardinality no more than d. It would then follow that

$$|\mathcal{F}^*| \le \sum_{i=0}^{d} \binom{m}{i},$$

(since this expression is the number of subsets of S containing no more than d elements), and hence that $|\mathcal{F}|$ is bounded as required.

It suffices therefore to show that, whenever $\mathcal{F}^*$ shatters a set, so does $\mathcal{F}$. For x in S, and $R \subseteq S$, suppose, then, that $T_x(\mathcal{F})$ shatters R. If x is not in R, then, trivially, $\mathcal{F}$ shatters R. If x is in R, then for all $A \subseteq R$ with x not in A, since $T_x(\mathcal{F})$ shatters R we have $A \in T_x(\mathcal{F}) \cap R$ and $A \cup \{x\} \in T_x(\mathcal{F}) \cap R$. By the definition of the operator T_x, this implies $A \in \mathcal{F} \cap R$ and $A \cup \{x\} \in \mathcal{F} \cap R$. This shows that $\mathcal{F}$ shatters R. The result follows.   □

Theorem 3.6 has the following corollary, which makes it explicit that a function class of finite VC-dimension has polynomially-bounded growth function.

Theorem 3.7 *For $m \ge d \ge 1$,*

$$\sum_{i=0}^{d} \binom{m}{i} < \left(\frac{em}{d}\right)^d. \tag{3.6}$$

Hence, for a function class H with $\mathrm{VCdim}(H) = d$,

$$\Pi_H(m) \begin{cases} = 2^m & \text{if } m \le d \\ < \left(\frac{em}{d}\right)^d & \text{if } m > d, \end{cases} \tag{3.7}$$

and, for $m \ge 1$, $\Pi_H(m) \le m^d + 1$.

Proof For $0 \le i \le d$ and $m \ge d$, $(m/d)^d (d/m)^i \ge 1$. Hence,

$$\sum_{i=0}^{d} \binom{m}{i} \le (m/d)^d \sum_{i=0}^{d} \binom{m}{i} (d/m)^i \le (m/d)^d (1 + d/m)^m < (me/d)^d,$$

where the second inequality follows from the Binomial Theorem (Equation (1.6) in Appendix 1), and the last inequality follows from Euler's Inequality (Inequality (1.4) in Appendix 1).

The bound $\Pi_H(m) \le m^d + 1$ follows from Theorem 3.6.   □

This result, together with the definition of the VC-dimension, immediately gives the following corollary, which shows that the log of the growth function is within a log factor of the VC-dimension.

Corollary 3.8 *For a function class* H *with* $\text{VCdim}(H) = d$, *if* $m \geq d$ *then*

$$d \leq \log_2 \Pi_H(m) \leq d\log_2(em/d).$$

3.4 Bibliographical Notes

The notion of VC-dimension was introduced by Vapnik and Chervonenkis (1971). It has subsequently been investigated by many authors. See, for example, (Bollobás, 1986, Chapter 17), in which it is referred to as the *trace number* of a set system. Wenocur and Dudley (1981) named $\text{VCdim}(H) + 1$ the *VC-number* of the class H. It seems that it was first called the VC-dimension by Haussler and Welzl (1987). A number of other notions of shattering and dimension have been studied (see, for example, (Cover, 1965; Sontag, 1992; Kowalczyk, 1997; Sontag, 1997)), but we shall see that the VC-dimension is the crucial quantity for the learning problem that we study here. The VC-dimension has found application in other areas of mathematics and computer science, including logic (Shelah, 1972) and computational geometry (Haussler and Welzl, 1987; Matousek, 1995).

The inductive argument to count the number of cells in a hyperplane arrangement was apparently first discovered by Schläfli in the last century (see (Schläfli, 1950)). A number of authors have presented this argument; see (Cover, 1965; Makhoul, El-Jaroudi and Schwartz, 1991).

The linear algebraic proof of the VC-dimension of a thresholded vector space of real functions (Theorem 3.5 and its corollary, Theorem 3.4) are due to Dudley (1978) (see also (Wenocur and Dudley, 1981)).

The question of the possible rates of growth of $\Pi_H(m)$ was posed by Erdös in 1970, and the answer (Theorem 3.6) was independently discovered by a number of authors (Sauer, 1972; Shelah, 1972; Vapnik and Chervonenkis, 1971); see (Assouad, 1983). This theorem is widely known as *Sauer's Lemma*. The proof presented here was first presented by Steele (1978); see also (Frankl, 1983; Alon, 1983; Bollobás, 1986). The theorem can also be proved using an inductive argument that is very similar to the argument used to prove the bound on the growth function of the real-weight simple perceptron (Theorem 3.1). In addition, we shall encounter a linear algebraic proof in Chapter 12.

The proof of Theorem 3.7 is due to Chari, Rohatgi and Srinivasan (1994).

4

General Upper Bounds on Sample Complexity

4.1 Learning by Minimizing Sample Error

In Chapter 2, we showed that if a set H of functions is finite then it is learnable, by a particularly simple type of learning algorithm. Specifically, if, given a training sample z, L returns a hypothesis $L(z)$ such that $L(z)$ has minimal sample error on z, then L is a learning algorithm for H. Generally, for any set H of $\{0,1\}$-valued functions (that need not be finite), we define a *sample error minimization algorithm*† *for H—* or *SEM algorithm*—to be any function $L : \bigcup_{m=1}^{\infty} Z^m \to H$ with the property that for any m and any $z \in Z^m$,

$$\mathrm{\hat{e}r}_z(L(z)) = \min_{h \in H} \mathrm{\hat{e}r}_z(h).$$

Thus, a SEM algorithm will produce a hypothesis that, among all hypotheses in H, has the fewest disagreements with the labelled examples it has seen. Using this terminology, the learnability result of Chapter 2 (Theorem 2.4) has the following consequence.

Theorem 4.1 *Suppose that H is a finite set of $\{0,1\}$-valued functions. Then any SEM algorithm for H is a learning algorithm for H.*

Our main aim in this chapter to show that the conclusion of Theorem 4.1 also holds for many infinite function classes. Explicitly, we shall show that if H has finite Vapnik-Chervonenkis dimension then any SEM algorithm for H is a learning algorithm. Theorem 2.4 provides bounds on the estimation error and sample complexity of SEM algorithms for finite function classes. But as these bounds involve the cardinality of the

---

† We are not yet explicitly concerned with questions of computability or computational complexity; thus, for the moment, we are content to use the term 'algorithm' when speaking simply of a function.

function class, they are clearly inapplicable when H is infinite. We shall see, however, that, for H of finite VC-dimension, the estimation error and sample complexity of any SEM algorithm can be bounded in terms of the VC-dimension of H. (To a first approximation, $\ln |H|$ is replaced by VCdim(H).) Moreover, we shall see that, for some finite classes, the new bounds are better than those given earlier.

The main theorem is the following.

Theorem 4.2 *Suppose that H is a set of functions from a set X to $\{0,1\}$ and that H has finite Vapnik-Chervonenkis dimension$\dagger$ $d \geq 1$. Let L be any sample error minimization algorithm for H. Then L is a learning algorithm for H. In particular, if $m \geq d/2$ then the estimation error of L satisfies*

$$\epsilon_L(m,\delta) \leq \epsilon_0(m,\delta) = \left(\frac{32}{m} \left(d \ln \left(\frac{2em}{d} \right) + \ln \left(\frac{4}{\delta} \right) \right) \right)^{1/2}$$

and its sample complexity satisfies the inequality

$$m_L(\epsilon,\delta) \leq m_0(\epsilon,\delta) = \frac{64}{\epsilon^2} \left(2d \ln \left(\frac{12}{\epsilon} \right) + \ln \left(\frac{4}{\delta} \right) \right).$$

This is a very general result: the bound applies to all function classes H with finite VC-dimension. It may seem surprising that such a simple learning algorithm should suffice. In fact, we shall see in the next chapter that the sample complexity bound applying to the SEM algorithm is tight in the rather strong sense that no learning algorithm can have a significantly smaller sample complexity. (In Part 4, we shall also see that the computational complexity of learning cannot be significantly less than that of minimizing sample error.)

4.2 Uniform Convergence and Learnability

As with the learnability result of Chapter 2, the crucial step towards proving learnability is to obtain a result on the *uniform convergence* of sample errors to true errors. The use of a SEM algorithm for learning is motivated by the assumption that the sample errors are good indicators of the true errors; for, if they are, then choosing a hypothesis with minimal error is clearly a good strategy (as indicated in Chapter 2 by Figure 2.1). The following result shows that, given a large enough

---

$\dagger$ The restriction $d \geq 1$ is just for convenience. In any case, classes of VC-dimension 0 are uninteresting, since they consist only of one function.

random sample, then with high probability, *for every $h \in H$*, the sample error of h and the true error of h are close. It is a counterpart to Theorem 2.2.

Theorem 4.3 *Suppose that H is a set of $\{0,1\}$-valued functions defined on a set X and that P is a probability distribution on $Z = X \times \{0,1\}$. For $0 < \epsilon < 1$ and m a positive integer, we have*

$$P^m \left\{ |\mathrm{er}_P(h) - \hat{\mathrm{er}}_z(h)| \geq \epsilon \text{ for some } h \in H \right\} \leq 4\,\Pi_H(2m) \exp\left(-\frac{\epsilon^2 m}{8}\right).$$

The proof of this uniform convergence result is rather involved and is deferred until the next section. However, notice that if $\Pi_H(2m)$ grows exponentially quickly in m then the bound is trivial (it never drops below 1). On the other hand, if $\Pi_H(2m)$ grows only polynomially quickly in m, the bound goes to zero exponentially fast. So Theorem 4.2 follows fairly directly from this result, as we now show.

Proof **(of Theorem 4.2)** We first show that if

$$|\mathrm{er}_P(h) - \hat{\mathrm{er}}_z(h)| < \epsilon \qquad \text{for all } h \in H, \tag{4.1}$$

then $\mathrm{er}_P(L(z))$ is close to $\mathrm{opt}_P(H)$. We then use Theorem 4.3 to show that the condition on ϵ suffices (and we solve for m).

Suppose that (4.1) holds. Then we have

$$\begin{aligned}
\mathrm{er}_P(L(z)) &\leq \hat{\mathrm{er}}_z(L(z)) + \epsilon \\
&= \min_{h \in H} \hat{\mathrm{er}}_z(h) + \epsilon. \tag{4.2}
\end{aligned}$$

Now, since H might be infinite, we cannot be sure that the infimum $\mathrm{opt}_P(H) = \inf_{h \in H} \mathrm{er}_P(h)$ is attained; we can, however, assert (since the infimum is a *greatest* lower bound) that for any $\alpha > 0$ there is an $h^* \in H$ with $\mathrm{er}_P(h^*) < \mathrm{opt}_P(H) + \alpha$. It follows from (4.1) and (4.2) that

$$\begin{aligned}
\mathrm{er}_P(L(z)) &\leq \hat{\mathrm{er}}_z(h^*) + \epsilon \\
&< \mathrm{er}_P(h^*) + 2\epsilon \\
&< \mathrm{opt}_P(H) + 2\epsilon + \alpha.
\end{aligned}$$

Since this is true for all $\alpha > 0$, we must have

$$\mathrm{er}_P(L(z)) \leq \mathrm{opt}_P(H) + 2\epsilon.$$

Now, Theorem 4.3 shows that (4.1) holds with probability at least $1 - \delta$

provided

$$4\,\Pi_H(2m)\exp(-\epsilon^2 m/8) \le \delta;$$

that is, provided

$$\epsilon^2 \ge \frac{8}{m}\ln\left(4\,\Pi_H(2m)/\delta\right).$$

So, applying Theorem 3.7, we have that, with probability at least $1-\delta$,

$$\mathrm{er}_P(L(z)) < \mathrm{opt}_P(H) + \left(\frac{32}{m}\left(d\ln(2em/d) + \ln(4/\delta)\right)\right)^{1/2}.$$

For the second part of the theorem, we need to show that $m \ge m_0(\epsilon, \delta)$ ensures that $\mathrm{er}_P(L(z)) < \mathrm{opt}_P(H) + \epsilon$. Clearly, by the above, it suffices if

$$m \ge \frac{32}{\epsilon^2}\left(d\ln m + d\ln(2e/d) + \ln(4/\delta)\right).$$

Now, since $\ln x \le \alpha x - \ln\alpha - 1$ for all $\alpha, x > 0$ (Inequality (1.2) in Appendix 1), we have

$$\begin{aligned}
\frac{32d}{\epsilon^2}\ln m &\le \frac{32d}{\epsilon^2}\left(\frac{\epsilon^2}{64d}m + \ln\left(\frac{64d}{\epsilon^2}\right) - 1\right)\\
&= \frac{m}{2} + \frac{32d}{\epsilon^2}\ln\left(\frac{64d}{e\epsilon^2}\right).
\end{aligned}$$

Therefore, it suffices to have

$$m \ge \frac{m}{2} + \frac{32}{\epsilon^2}\left(d\ln(128/\epsilon^2) + \ln(4/\delta)\right),$$

so

$$m \ge \frac{64}{\epsilon^2}\left(2d\ln(12/\epsilon) + \ln(4/\delta)\right)$$

suffices. $\square$

4.3 Proof of Uniform Convergence Result

We now embark on the proof of Theorem 4.3. This is rather long and can, at first sight, seem mysterious. However, we shall try to present it in digestible morsels.

High-level view

First, we give a high-level indication of the basic thinking behind the proof. Our aim is to bound the probability that a given sample z of length m is 'bad', in the sense that there is some function h in H for which $|\mathrm{er}_P(h) - \hat{\mathrm{er}}_z(h)| \geq \epsilon$. We transform this problem into one involving samples $z = rs$ of length $2m$. For such a sample, the sub-sample r comprising the first half of the sample may be thought of as the original randomly drawn sample of length m, while the second half s may be thought of as a 'testing' sample which we use to estimate the true error of a function. This allows us to replace $\mathrm{er}_P(h)$ by a sample-based estimate $\hat{\mathrm{er}}_s(h)$, which is crucial for the rest of the proof. Next we need to bound the probability that some function h has $\hat{\mathrm{er}}_r(h)$ significantly different from $\hat{\mathrm{er}}_s(h)$. Since the labelled examples in the sample are chosen independently at random (according to the distribution P), a given labelled example is just as likely to occur in the first half of a random $2m$-sample as in the second half. Thus, if we randomly swap pairs of examples between the first and second halves of the sample, this will not affect the probability that the two half-samples have different error estimates. We can then bound the probability of a bad sample in terms of probabilities over a set of permutations of the double sample. This allows us to consider the restriction of the function class to a fixed double sample and hence, for classes with finite VC-dimension, it reduces the problem to one involving a finite function class. As in the proof for the finite-case (Theorem 2.2), we can then use the union bound and Hoeffding's inequality.

Symmetrization

As indicated above, the first step of the proof is to bound the desired probability in terms of the probability of an event based on two samples. This technique is known as *symmetrization*. In what follows, we shall often write a vector in Z^{2m} in the form rs, where $r, s \in Z^m$. The symmetrization result is as follows.

Lemma 4.4 *With the notation as above, let*

$$Q = \{z \in Z^m : |\mathrm{er}_P(h) - \hat{\mathrm{er}}_z(h)| \geq \epsilon \text{ for some } h \in H\}$$

and

$$R = \left\{(r, s) \in Z^m \times Z^m : |\hat{\mathrm{er}}_r(h) - \hat{\mathrm{er}}_s(h)| \geq \frac{\epsilon}{2} \text{ for some } h \in H\right\}.$$

Then, for $m \geq 2/\epsilon^2$,

$$P^m(Q) \leq 2\,P^{2m}(R).$$

Proof We prove that $P^{2m}(R) \geq P^m(Q)/2$. By the triangle inequality, if

$$|\mathrm{er}_P(h) - \hat{\mathrm{er}}_r(h)| \geq \epsilon \text{ and } |\mathrm{er}_P(h) - \hat{\mathrm{er}}_s(h)| \leq \epsilon/2,$$

then $|\hat{\mathrm{er}}_r(h) - \hat{\mathrm{er}}_s(h)| \geq \epsilon/2$, so

$$
\begin{aligned}
P^{2m}(R) \geq{} & P^{2m}\left\{\exists h \in H,\ |\mathrm{er}_P(h) - \hat{\mathrm{er}}_r(h)| \geq \epsilon \text{ and}\right. \\
& \left. |\mathrm{er}_P(h) - \hat{\mathrm{er}}_s(h)| \leq \epsilon/2\right\} \\
={} & \int_Q P^m\left\{s : \exists h \in H,\ |\mathrm{er}_P(h) - \hat{\mathrm{er}}_r(h)| \geq \epsilon \text{ and}\right. \\
& \left. |\mathrm{er}_P(h) - \hat{\mathrm{er}}_s(h)| \leq \epsilon/2\right\}\, dP^m(r). \quad (4.3)
\end{aligned}
$$

Now, for $r \in Q$ fix an $h \in H$ with $|\mathrm{er}_P(h) - \hat{\mathrm{er}}_r(h)| \geq \epsilon$. For this h, we shall show that

$$P^m\left\{|\mathrm{er}_P(h) - \hat{\mathrm{er}}_s(h)| \leq \epsilon/2\right\} \geq 1/2. \qquad (4.4)$$

It follows that, for any $r \in Q$ we have

$$P^m\left\{s : \exists h \in H,\ |\mathrm{er}_P(h) - \hat{\mathrm{er}}_r(h)| \geq \epsilon \text{ and } |\mathrm{er}_P(h) - \hat{\mathrm{er}}_s(h)| \leq \epsilon/2\right\}$$
$$\geq 1/2,$$

and combining this result with (4.3) shows that $P^{2m}(R) \geq P^m(Q)/2$.

To complete the proof, we show that (4.4) holds for any $h \in H$. For a fixed h, notice that $m\,\hat{\mathrm{er}}_s(h)$ is a binomial random variable, with expectation $m\,\mathrm{er}_P(h)$ and variance $\mathrm{er}_P(h)(1 - \mathrm{er}_P(h))m$. Chebyshev's inequality (Inequality (1.11) in Appendix 1) bounds the probability that $|\mathrm{er}_P(h) - \hat{\mathrm{er}}_s(h)| > \epsilon/2$ by

$$\frac{\mathrm{er}_P(h)(1 - \mathrm{er}_P(h))m}{(\epsilon m/2)^2},$$

which is less than $1/(\epsilon^2 m)$ (using the fact that $x(1 - x) \leq 1/4$ for x between 0 and 1). This is at most $1/2$ for $m \geq 2/\epsilon^2$, which implies (4.4).
$\square$

Permutations

The next step of the proof is to bound the probability of the set R of Lemma 4.4 in terms of a probability involving a set of permutations on the labels of the double sample, exploiting the fact that a given labelled example is as likely to occur among the first m entries of a random $z \in Z^{2m}$ as it is to occur among the second m entries.

Let Γ_m be the set of all permutations of $\{1, 2, \ldots, 2m\}$ that swap i and $m+i$, for all i in some subset of $\{1, \ldots, m\}$. That is, for all $\sigma \in \Gamma_m$ and $i \in \{1, \ldots, m\}$, either $\sigma(i) = i$, in which case $\sigma(m+i) = m+i$, or $\sigma(i) = m+i$, in which case $\sigma(m+i) = i$. Then we can regard σ as acting on coordinates, so that it swaps some entries z_i in the first half of the sample with the corresponding entries in the second half. For instance, a typical member σ of Γ_3 might give

$$\sigma(z_1, z_2, z_3, z_4, z_5, z_6) = (z_1, z_5, z_6, z_4, z_2, z_3).$$

The following result shows that by randomly choosing a permutation $\sigma \in \Gamma_m$ and calculating the probability that a permuted sample falls in the bad set R, we can eliminate the dependence on the distribution P.

Lemma 4.5 *Let R be any subset of Z^{2m} and P any probability distribution on Z. Then*

$$P^{2m}(R) = \mathbf{E} \Pr(\sigma z \in R) \leq \max_{z \in Z^{2m}} \Pr(\sigma z \in R),$$

where the expectation is over z chosen according to P^{2m}, and the probability is over σ chosen uniformly from Γ_m, the set of swapping permutations on $\{1, \ldots, 2m\}$ described above.

Proof First notice that for any σ in Γ_m,

$$P^{2m}(R) = P^{2m}\{z : \sigma z \in R\},$$

since coordinate permutations preserve the product distribution P^{2m}. Since Γ_m is finite we can interchange summation and integration as follows. (Here, $1_R(z)$ is the indicator function of R, taking value 1 if $z \in R$ and 0 otherwise.)

$$
\begin{aligned}
P^{2m}(R) &= \int_{Z^{2m}} 1_R(z) \, dP^{2m}(z) \\
&= \frac{1}{|\Gamma_m|} \sum_{\sigma \in \Gamma_m} \int_{Z^{2m}} 1_R(\sigma z) \, dP^{2m}(z) \\
&= \int_{Z^{2m}} \left(\frac{1}{|\Gamma_m|} \sum_{\sigma \in \Gamma_m} 1_R(\sigma z) \right) dP^{2m}(z)
\end{aligned}
$$

$$= \int_{Z^{2m}} \Pr\left(\sigma z \in R\right) dP^{2m}(z)$$

$$\leq \max_{z \in Z^{2m}} \Pr\left(\sigma z \in R\right).$$

Notice that the maximum exists, since there is only a finite set of values that the probability under a random permutation can take. $\square$

Reduction to a finite class

In order to bound $P^{2m}(R)$, we see now that it suffices to obtain an upper bound on the maximum over $z \in Z^{2m}$ of the probability $\Pr(\sigma z \in R)$ under random σ.

Lemma 4.6 *For the set $R \subseteq Z^{2m}$ defined in Lemma 4.4, and permutation σ chosen uniformly at random from Γ_m,*

$$\max_{z \in Z^{2m}} \Pr\left(\sigma z \in R\right) \leq 2\,\Pi_H(2m) \exp\left(\frac{-m\epsilon^2}{8}\right).$$

Proof Suppose that $z = (z_1, z_2, \ldots, z_{2m}) \in Z^{2m}$, where the labelled example z_i equals (x_i, y_i), and let $S = \{x_1, x_2, \ldots, x_{2m}\}$. Let $t = |H|_S|$, which is at most $\Pi_H(2m)$. Then there are functions $h_1, h_2, \ldots, h_t \in H$ such that for any $h \in H$, there is some i between 1 and t with $h_i(x_k) = h(x_k)$ for $1 \leq k \leq 2m$.

Recalling that

$$\hat{\mathrm{er}}_z(h) = \frac{1}{m}\left|\{1 \leq i \leq m : h(x_i) \neq y_i\}\right|,$$

we see that $\sigma z \in R$ if and only if some h in H satisfies

$$\left|\frac{1}{m}\left|\{1 \leq i \leq m : h(x_{\sigma(i)}) \neq y_{\sigma(i)}\}\right| - \right.$$
$$\left.\frac{1}{m}\left|\{m+1 \leq i \leq 2m : h(x_{\sigma(i)}) \neq y_{\sigma(i)}\}\right|\right| \geq \frac{\epsilon}{2}.$$

Hence, if we define

$$v_i^j = \begin{cases} 1 & \text{if } h_j(x_i) \neq y_i \\ 0 & \text{otherwise} \end{cases}$$

for $1 \leq i \leq 2m$ and $1 \leq j \leq t$, we have that $\sigma z \in R$ if and only if some j in $\{1, \ldots, t\}$ satisfies

$$\left|\frac{1}{m}\sum_{i=1}^{m} v_{\sigma(i)}^j - \frac{1}{m}\sum_{i=1}^{m} v_{\sigma(m+i)}^j\right| \geq \epsilon/2.$$

Then the union bound for probabilities gives

$$\Pr(\sigma z \in R) \;\leq\; t \max_{1 \leq j \leq t} \Pr\left(\left|\frac{1}{m}\sum_{i=1}^{m}(v_{\sigma(i)}^{j} - v_{\sigma(m+i)}^{j})\right| \geq \epsilon/2\right)$$

$$\leq\; \Pi_H(2m) \max_{1 \leq j \leq t} \Pr\left(\left|\frac{1}{m}\sum_{i=1}^{m}(v_{\sigma(i)}^{j} - v_{\sigma(m+i)}^{j})\right| \geq \epsilon/2\right).$$

Given the distribution of the permutations σ, for each i, $v_{\sigma(i)}^{j} - v_{\sigma(m+i)}^{j}$ equals $\pm|v_i^j - v_{m+i}^j|$, with each of these two possibilities equally likely. Thus,

$$\Pr\left(\left|\frac{1}{m}\sum_{i=1}^{m}(v_{\sigma(i)}^{j} - v_{\sigma(m+i)}^{j})\right| \geq \epsilon/2\right)$$

$$= \Pr\left(\left|\frac{1}{m}\sum_{i=1}^{m}|v_i^j - v_{m+i}^j|\beta_i\right| \geq \epsilon/2\right),$$

where the probability on the right is over the β_i, which are independently and uniformly chosen from $\{-1, 1\}$. Hoeffding's inequality shows that this probability is no more than $2\exp(-m\epsilon^2/8)$, which gives the result. $\qquad\square$

Combining Lemmas 4.4, 4.5, and 4.6 shows that, for $m \geq 2/\epsilon^2$,

$$P^m\{\exists h \in H, \; |\mathrm{er}_P(h) - \hat{\mathrm{er}}_z(h)| \geq \epsilon\}$$

$$\leq\; 2P^{2m}(R) \leq 4\,\Pi_H(2m)\,\exp(-m\epsilon^2/8).$$

The same bound holds for $m < 2/\epsilon^2$ since in that case the right-hand side is greater than one. Theorem 4.3 is now established.

4.4 Application to the Perceptron

Perhaps the primary motivation of the work in this chapter is to obtain for infinite function classes the type of learnability result we earlier obtained for finite classes. For example, although we were able earlier to prove learnability for the (finite) classes of functions computed by the binary-weight perceptron and the k-bit perceptron, we could not obtain any such result for the general perceptron, as this is capable of computing an infinite number of functions on $\mathbb{R}^n$. However, the theory of this chapter applies, since the n-input perceptron has a finite VC-dimension of $n + 1$, as shown in Chapter 3. We immediately have the following result.

Theorem 4.7 *Let N be the perceptron on n inputs, and let $Z = \mathbb{R}^n \times \{0,1\}$. Suppose that $L : \bigcup_{m=1}^{\infty} Z^m \to H_N$ is such that for any m and any $z \in Z^m$,*

$$\hat{\text{er}}_z(L(z)) = \min_{h \in H_N} \hat{\text{er}}_z(h).$$

(That is, L is a SEM algorithm.) Then L is a learning algorithm for H_N, with estimation error

$$\epsilon_L(m,\delta) \leq \left(\frac{32}{m} \left((n+1)\ln(2em/(n+1)) + \ln(4/\delta) \right) \right)^{1/2}$$

for $m \geq (n+1)/2$ and $0 < \delta < 1$. Furthermore, L has sample complexity

$$m_L(\epsilon,\delta) \leq \frac{64}{\epsilon^2}\left(2(n+1)\ln\left(\frac{12}{\epsilon}\right) + \ln\left(\frac{4}{\delta}\right) \right),$$

for all $\epsilon, \delta \in (0,1)$.

It is worth noting how Theorem 4.2 compares with the corresponding result for finite function classes, Theorem 2.4. We start by comparing the two sample complexity results for the case of the k-bit perceptron. As we saw in Chapter 2, Theorem 2.4 gives an upper bound of

$$\frac{2}{\epsilon^2}\left(k(n+1) + \ln\left(\frac{2}{\delta}\right) \right)$$

on the sample complexity of a SEM learning algorithm for the k-bit, n-input perceptron. Since a k-bit perceptron is certainly a perceptron, Theorem 4.7 applies to give a sample complexity bound of

$$\frac{64}{\epsilon^2}\left(2(n+1)\ln\left(\frac{12}{\epsilon}\right) + \ln\left(\frac{4}{\delta}\right) \right)$$

for such an algorithm. For many values of ϵ and δ, this is worse (that is, it is larger), but it should be noted that it has no explicit dependence on k, and so for large enough k, there are ranges of ϵ and δ for which the new bound is better.

A more striking example of the use of the new bound for finite function classes may be given by considering the *boolean perceptron*, the perceptron restricted to binary-valued inputs. Here, the perceptron functions as usual, but the relevant domain is $X = \{0,1\}^n$ rather than $X = \mathbb{R}^n$. It is clear that, since X is finite, so is the set of functions H computed by the boolean perceptron. It can be shown that (if n is large enough), $|H| \geq 2^{(n^2-n)/2}$. It is clear that the VC-dimension of the boolean perceptron is no more than that of the perceptron—namely, $n+1$. (In fact, the VC-dimension is precisely $n+1$.) Suppose that L is a SEM learning algorithm for the boolean perceptron. The results of Chapter 2 yield an upper bound of

$$\frac{2}{\epsilon^2} \ln \left(\frac{2|H|}{\delta} \right)$$

on its sample complexity, which, given that $|H| \geq 2^{(n^2-n)/2}$, is at least

$$\frac{2}{\epsilon^2} \left(\frac{(n^2 - n)}{2} \ln 2 + \ln \left(\frac{2}{\delta} \right) \right).$$

By contrast, the sample complexity bound obtained from Theorem 4.2 is

$$\frac{64}{\epsilon^2} \left(2(n + 1) \ln \left(\frac{12}{\epsilon} \right) + \ln \left(\frac{4}{\delta} \right) \right).$$

This latter bound has worse constants, but note that it depends linearly on n, whereas the first bound is quadratic in n. Thus, in a sense, the bound of this chapter can be markedly better for the boolean perceptron than the simple bound of Chapter 2.

4.5 The Restricted Model

We now briefly consider the restricted model of learning, in which there is a target function in H and a probability distribution μ on the domain X of H. (See Chapter 2.) Here, any algorithm returning a consistent hypothesis is a learning algorithm, a result that follows from the theory of this chapter, since such an algorithm constitutes a SEM algorithm. Moreover, it is possible to obtain a better upper bound on the sample complexity of such learning algorithms than that obtained above for the general learning model. To do so, instead of using a general uniform convergence result, we use the following bound (where the notation is as usual): for any t and any $m \geq 8/\epsilon$ let P_{bad} be the probability

$$\mu^m \left\{ \text{for some } h \in H, \, h(x_i) = t(x_i), \, (1 \leq i \leq m) \text{ and } \text{er}_\mu(h, t) \geq \epsilon \right\}.$$

Then

$$P_{\text{bad}} \leq 2 \, \Pi_H(2m) \, 2^{-\epsilon m/2}.$$

(The proof is similar to that of Theorem 4.3, except that Hoeffding's inequality is replaced by a simple counting argument: the probability of a permutation that gives no mistakes on the first half sample but at least $\epsilon m/2$ on the second half sample is no more than $2^{-\epsilon m/2}$. This replaces the larger factor of $\exp(-\epsilon^2 m/8)$ that arose from Hoeffding's inequality.) This bound can be used to obtain the following result. The proof is similar to that of Theorem 4.2.

Theorem 4.8 *Suppose that H is a set of functions from a set X to $\{0,1\}$ and that H has finite Vapnik-Chervonenkis dimension $d \geq 1$. Let L be a consistent algorithm; that is, for any m and for any $t \in H$, if $x \in X^m$ and z is the training sample corresponding to x and t, then the hypothesis $h = L(z)$ satisfies $h(x_i) = t(x_i)$ for $i = 1, 2, \ldots, m$. Then L is a learning algorithm for H in the restricted model, with sample complexity*

$$m_L(\epsilon, \delta) \leq \frac{4}{\epsilon} \left(d \ln \left(\frac{12}{\epsilon} \right) + \ln \left(\frac{2}{\delta} \right) \right)$$

and with estimation error

$$\epsilon_L(m, \delta) \leq \frac{2}{m} \left(d \ln \left(\frac{2\dot{e}m}{d} \right) + \ln \left(\frac{2}{\delta} \right) \right).$$

The constants in this result can be improved, but that need not concern us here. What is most important in the sample complexity bound is the dependence on ϵ: for the general model, the upper bound we obtained involved a $1/\epsilon^2$ factor, whereas for the restricted model, we can obtain an upper bound involving the much smaller $1/\epsilon$ factor. Equivalently, the error of the hypothesis returned by a SEM algorithm approaches the optimum at rate $(\ln m)/m$ in the restricted model, whereas the corresponding rate in the general model is $\sqrt{(\ln m)/m}$. The intuitive explanation of this improvement is that less data is needed to form an accurate estimate of a random quantity if its variance is lower.

4.6 Remarks
A better uniform convergence result

Theorem 4.3 is not the best uniform convergence result that can be obtained. It is possible to prove the following result, although the proof is a little more involved.

Theorem 4.9 *There are positive constants c_1, c_2, and c_3 such that the following holds. Suppose that H is a set of $\{0,1\}$-valued functions defined on a domain X and that H has finite Vapnik-Chervonenkis dimension d. Let P be a probability distribution on $Z = X \times \{0,1\}$, ϵ any real* *number between 0 and 1, and m any positive integer. Then*

$$P^m \left\{ |\mathrm{er}_P(h) - \hat{\mathrm{er}}_z(h)| \geq \epsilon \text{ for some } h \in H \right\} \leq c_1 c_2^d e^{-c_3 \epsilon^2 m}.$$

This leads to the following learnability result.

Theorem 4.10 *There is a positive constant c such that the following holds. Suppose that H is a set of functions from a set X to $\{0,1\}$ and that H has finite Vapnik-Chervonenkis dimension $d \geq 1$. Let L be any sample error minimization algorithm for H. Then L is a learning algorithm for H and its sample complexity satisfies the inequality*

$$m_L(\epsilon, \delta) \leq m_0'(\epsilon, \delta) = \frac{c}{\epsilon^2} \left(d + \ln \left(\frac{1}{\delta} \right) \right).$$

The sample complexity bound $m_0'(\epsilon, \delta)$ should be compared with the bound $m_0(\epsilon, \delta)$ of Theorem 4.2, which contains an additional $\ln(1/\epsilon)$ term multiplying the VC-dimension.

The proof of Theorem 4.9 is similar to that of Theorem 4.3, except that we use the following improvement of Lemma 4.6. Ignoring constants, the growth function of H in Lemma 4.6 is replaced by an expression of the form $c^{\mathrm{VCdim}(H)}$, and this leads to the improvement in the sample complexity bound by a factor of $\ln m$.

Lemma 4.11 *For the set $R \subseteq Z^{2m}$ defined in Lemma 4.4, and permutation σ chosen uniformly at random from Γ_m, if $m \geq 400(\mathrm{VCdim}(H) + 1)/\epsilon^2$, then*

$$\max_{z \in Z^{2m}} \Pr(\sigma z \in R) \leq 4 \cdot 41^{\mathrm{VCdim}(H)} \exp \left(\frac{-m\epsilon^2}{576} \right).$$

The proof of Lemma 4.11 involves the following result. In this lemma, the VC-dimension of a subset of $\{0,1\}^m$ is defined by interpreting a vector in $\{0,1\}^m$ as a function mapping from $\{1, \ldots, m\}$ to $\{0,1\}$. We omit the proof (see the Bibliographical Notes).

Lemma 4.12 *For any $G \subseteq \{0,1\}^m$, if all distinct $g, g' \in G$ satisfy*

$$\frac{1}{m} |\{i : g_i \neq g_i'\}| > \epsilon,$$

then

$$|G| \leq \left(\frac{41}{\epsilon} \right)^{\mathrm{VCdim}(G)}.$$

This lemma shows that the size of any set of pairwise ϵ-separated points in $\{0,1\}^m$ is bounded by an exponential function of its VC-dimension. In the lemma, the separation of two points is measured using the distance d_1 defined for two vectors g, g' in $\mathbb{R}^m$ as

$$d_1(g, g') = \frac{1}{m} \sum_{i=1}^{m} |g_i - g_i'|.$$

In later chapters, we introduce the notion of a *packing number* (see Section 12.2); we shall see that Lemma 4.12 corresponds to a bound on the d_1 packing number of a class with finite VC-dimension.

The proof of Lemma 4.11 uses a *chaining* argument. The idea is to split each function of interest in the original class $H_{|_{\boldsymbol{z}}}$ into a sum of functions chosen from a sequence of classes of progressively increasing complexity. Then the desired uniform convergence result for the original class is obtained by combining uniform convergence results for all of these classes. The classes are constructed carefully to balance the complexity of the class and the magnitude of functions in the class. For classes that are more complex, although the uniform convergence result must apply to a richer class, that class contains smaller functions, so the variables of interest have smaller variance. This delicate balance leads to a slight improvement over Lemma 4.6, in which we considered the whole class $H_{|_{\boldsymbol{z}}}$ at once by directly applying the union bound and Hoeffding's inequality.

Proof (of Lemma 4.11) Notice that $\max_{z \in Z^{2m}} \Pr(\sigma z \in R)$ is equal to the maximum over $z \in Z^{2m}$ of

$$\Pr\left(\exists h \in H, \left|\sum_{i=1}^{m} \beta_i \left(\ell(h(x_i), y_i) - \ell(h(x_{m+i}), y_{m+i})\right)\right| \geq \frac{\epsilon}{2}\right),$$

where the probability is over β_i chosen uniformly from $\{\pm 1\}$, and the function $\ell(h(x_i), y_i)$ takes value 1 if $h(x_i) \neq y_i$ and 0 otherwise.

Fix $z = ((x_1, y_1), \ldots, (x_{2m}, y_{2m})) \in Z^{2m}$ and define

$$G = \{(\ell(h(x_1), y_1), \ldots, \ell(h(x_{2m}), y_{2m})) : h \in H\}.$$

Let

$$
\begin{aligned}
p &= \Pr\left(\exists h \in H, \left|\sum_{i=1}^{m} \beta_i \left(\ell(h(x_i), y_i) - \ell(h(x_{m+i}), y_{m+i})\right)\right| \geq \frac{\epsilon}{2}\right) \\
&= \Pr\left(\exists g \in G, \left|\sum_{i=1}^{m} \beta_i \left(g_i - g_{m+i}\right)\right| \geq \frac{\epsilon}{2}\right).
\end{aligned}
$$

Let $d = \text{VCdim}(H)$. It is easy to verify that $\text{VCdim}(G) \leq d$.

Let $n = \lfloor \log_2 m \rfloor + 2$†. We define a sequence of sets $G_0, \ldots, G_n$ as follows, so that as i increases it constitutes a progressively better approximation of G. Fix G_0 as a set containing a single (arbitrary) element of G. Then, for each $j = 1, \ldots, n$, first set $G_j = G_{j-1}$, then add to G_j an element $g \in G$ for which $d_1(g, g') > 2^{-j}$ for all $g' \in G_j$. Keep adding these distinct elements until it is no longer possible to do so. Then it is easy to verify that the sets G_j have the following properties, for $j = 1, \ldots, n$.

- $G_{j-1} \subseteq G_j$,
- for all $g \in G$, some $\hat{g}_j \in G_j$ has $d_1(\hat{g}_j, g) \leq 2^{-j}$,
- for all distinct $g, g' \in G_j$, $d_1(g, g') > 2^{-j}$,
- $G_n = G$.

We now define a sequence of sets $V_0, \ldots, V_n$ that contain differences between vectors in the sets G_j. Let $V_0 = G_0$. For $j = 1, \ldots, n$, define

$$V_j = \{g - \hat{g}_{j-1} : g \in G_j\},$$

where for each $g \in G$ and $j = 0, \ldots, n$, $\hat{g}_j$ denotes an element of G_j that has $d_1(\hat{g}_j, g) \leq 2^{-j}$. It is easy to see that these difference sets V_j have the following properties, for $j = 0, \ldots, n$.

- for all $v \in V_j$,

$$\sum_{i=1}^{m} |v_i| \leq 2^{-(j-2)} m,$$

- for all $g \in G_j$, there are vectors $v_0 \in V_0, v_1 \in V_1, \ldots, v_j \in V_j$, such that $g = \sum_{i=0}^{j} v_i$. In particular, for all $g \in G$, there are $v_0 \in V_0, \ldots, v_n \in V_n$ with $g = \sum_{i=0}^{n} v_i$.

Hence,

$$p \leq \Pr\left(\exists v_0 \in V_0, \ldots, v_n \in V_n, \left| \sum_{i=1}^{m} \beta_i \sum_{j=0}^{n} (v_{j,i} - v_{j,m+i}) \right| \geq \frac{\epsilon}{2} \right),$$

where $v_j = (v_{j,1}, \ldots, v_{j,2m})$. By the triangle inequality,

$$p \leq \Pr\left(\exists v_0 \in V_0, \ldots, v_n \in V_n, \sum_{j=0}^{n} \left| \sum_{i=1}^{m} \beta_i (v_{j,i} - v_{j,m+i}) \right| \geq \frac{\epsilon}{2} \right),$$

---

† Recall that the floor function, $\lfloor \cdot \rfloor$, is defined as the largest integer no larger than its real argument, and that the ceiling function, $\lceil \cdot \rceil$, is defined as the smallest integer no smaller than its argument.

and if we choose $\epsilon_0, \ldots, \epsilon_n$ such that

$$\sum_{j=0}^{n} \epsilon_j \le \epsilon/2, \tag{4.5}$$

then

$$p \le \sum_{j=0}^{n} \Pr\left(\exists v \in V_j, \left|\sum_{i=1}^{m} \beta_i(v_i - v_{m+i})\right| \ge \epsilon_j\right).$$

We shall use Hoeffding's inequality (Inequality (1.16) in Appendix 1) to give a bound on each of these probabilities, exploiting the fact that $\sum_{i=1}^{m}(v_i - v_{m+i})^2$ gets progressively smaller as i increases. Indeed, since $\sum_{i=1}^{2m} |v_i| \le 2^{-(j-2)}m$ and $v_i \in \{-1, 0, 1\}^{2m}$, we have

$$
\begin{aligned}
\sum_{i=1}^{m}(v_i - v_{m+i})^2 &= 4\left|\{i : |v_i - v_{m+i}| = 2\}\right| + \left|\{i : |v_i - v_{m+i}| = 1\}\right| \\
&\le 2\sum_{i=1}^{2m} |v_i| \\
&\le m2^{-(j-4)}.
\end{aligned}
$$

Applying Hoeffding's inequality shows that for each j

$$
\Pr\left(\exists v \in V_j, \left|\sum_{i=1}^{2m} \beta_i(v_i - v_{m+i})\right| \ge \epsilon_j\right)
$$
$$
\le 2|V_j| \exp\left(-\epsilon_j^2 m 2^{j-2}\right).
$$

Now $|V_j| \le |G_j|$, points in G_j are 2^{-j}-separated, and $\mathrm{VCdim}(G_j) \le \mathrm{VCdim}(G) \le d$, so Lemma 4.12 implies that

$$|V_j| \le \left(41 \cdot 2^j\right)^d.$$

Hence,

$$p \le 2 \cdot 41^d \sum_{j=0}^{n} \exp\left(jd\ln 2 - \epsilon_j^2 m 2^{j-2}\right).$$

If we choose $\epsilon_j = \epsilon\sqrt{(j+1)2^{-j}}/12$, then it is easy to verify that (4.5) is satisfied. Substituting shows that

$$p \le 2 \cdot 41^d \sum_{j=0}^{n} \exp\left(j\left(d\ln 2 - \frac{\epsilon^2 m}{576}\right) - \frac{\epsilon^2 m}{576}\right)$$

$$\leq \ 2 \cdot 41^d \exp\left(\frac{-\epsilon^2 m}{576}\right) \sum_{j=0}^{\infty} \exp\left(j\left(d\ln 2 - \frac{\epsilon^2 m}{576}\right)\right)$$

$$= \ \frac{2 \cdot 41^d \exp\left(\frac{-\epsilon^2 m}{576}\right)}{1 - 2^d \exp\left(\frac{-\epsilon^2 m}{576}\right)}.$$

For $m \geq 400(d+1)/\epsilon^2$, the denominator is at least $1/2$, which gives the result.   □

4.7 Bibliographical Notes

The results presented in this chapter are to a great extent derived from the work of Vapnik and Chervonenkis (1971) in probability theory (see also the book of Vapnik (1982)). In particular, Theorem 4.3 is from Vapnik and Chervonenkis (1971). Instead of using the 'swapping group' Γ_m, however, their original proof involved the use of the full symmetric group (all permutations of $\{1, 2, \ldots, 2m\}$). It was subsequently noted that the former resulted in easier proofs of this and similar results; see Pollard (1984), for example. (See also (Dudley, 1978).) Our use of Hoeffding's inequality follows Haussler (1992). The use of Inequality (1.2) from Appendix 1 in the proof of Theorem 4.2 follows Anthony, Biggs and Shawe-Taylor (1990). That paper gave sample complexity bounds for the restricted model with improved constants; see also (Lugosi, 1995). In our discussion of sample complexity bounds for the boolean perceptron, we noted that the number of such functions is at least $2^{(n^2-n)/2}$. This is due to Muroga (1965; 1971). Results of Chapter 3 lead to an upper bound $2^{n^2(1+o(1))}$. In fact, a recent paper of Zuev (1989) shows that if $N(n)$ is the number of functions computable by the n-input boolean perceptron, then, as $n \to \infty$, $\log_2 N(n) \sim n^2$. The results on the complexity of learning in the restricted model are from Blumer et al. (1989). Theorem 4.9 is due to Talagrand (1994). (See also (Alexander, 1984).) The proof of Lemma 4.11 is due to Long (1998a). Although this lemma does not have the best constant in the exponent, it has a simple proof. For related chaining arguments, see (Pollard, 1984; Pollard, 1990). Lemma 4.12 is due to Haussler (1995). For large values of the VC-dimension, it improves Theorem 18.4 for the special case of $\{0, 1\}$-valued functions.

5

General Lower Bounds on Sample Complexity

5.1 Introduction

In the previous chapters we showed that a class of functions of finite VC-dimension is learnable by the fairly natural class of SEM algorithms, and we provided bounds on the estimation error and sample complexity of these learning algorithms in terms of the VC-dimension of the class. In this chapter we provide lower bounds on the estimation error and sample complexity of any learning algorithm. These lower bounds are also in terms of the VC-dimension, and are not vastly different from the upper bounds of the previous chapter. We shall see, as a consequence, that the VC-dimension not only characterizes learnability, in the sense that a function class is learnable if and only if it has finite VC-dimension, but it provides precise information about the number of examples required.

5.2 A Lower Bound for Learning

A technical lemma

The first step towards a general lower bound on the sample complexity is the following technical lemma, which will also prove useful in later chapters. It concerns the problem of estimating the parameter describing a Bernoulli random variable.

Lemma 5.1 *Suppose that α is a random variable uniformly distributed on $\{\alpha_-, \alpha_+\}$, where $\alpha_- = 1/2 - \epsilon/2$ and $\alpha_+ = 1/2 + \epsilon/2$, with $0 < \epsilon < 1$. Suppose that $\xi_1, \ldots, \xi_m$ are i.i.d. (independent and identically distributed) $\{0,1\}$-valued random variables with $\Pr(\xi_i = 1) = \alpha$ for all* *i. Let f be a function from $\{0,1\}^m$ to $\{\alpha_-, \alpha_+\}$. Then*

$$\Pr\left(f(\xi_1,\ldots,\xi_m) \neq \alpha\right) > \frac{1}{4}\left(1 - \sqrt{1 - \exp\left(\frac{-2\lceil m/2 \rceil \epsilon^2}{1 - \epsilon^2}\right)}\right). \quad (5.1)$$

Hence, if this probability is no more than δ, where $0 < \delta < 1/4$, then

$$m \geq 2\left\lfloor \frac{1 - \epsilon^2}{2\epsilon^2} \ln\left(\frac{1}{8\delta(1 - 2\delta)}\right)\right\rfloor. \quad (5.2)$$

In this lemma, f can be viewed as a decision rule. That is, based on the observations ξ_i, $f(\xi_1,\ldots,\xi_m)$ represents a guess of whether $\alpha = \alpha_-$ or $\alpha = \alpha_+$. The lemma shows that for every decision rule there is a limitation on its accuracy that depends on the similarity of the two choices (ϵ) and the amount of data (m).

Proof For a random sequence $\xi = (\xi_1,\ldots,\xi_m)$, define $N(\xi) = |\{i : \xi_i = 1\}|$. We first show that the maximum likelihood decision rule, which returns $\alpha = \alpha_-$ if and only if $N(\xi) < m/2$, is optimal, in the sense that for any decision rule f, the probability of guessing α incorrectly satisfies

$$\Pr(f(\xi) \neq \alpha) \geq \frac{1}{2}\Pr\left(N(\xi) \geq m/2 | \alpha = \alpha_-\right) + \frac{1}{2}\Pr\left(N(\xi) < m/2 | \alpha = \alpha_+\right). \quad (5.3)$$

To see this, fix a decision rule f. Clearly,

$$\begin{aligned}
\Pr(f(\xi) \neq \alpha) &= \frac{1}{2}\Pr\left(f(\xi) = \alpha_- | \alpha = \alpha_+\right) + \\
&\quad \frac{1}{2}\Pr\left(f(\xi) = \alpha_+ | \alpha = \alpha_-\right) \\
&= \frac{1}{2}\Pr\left(f(\xi) = \alpha_- \text{ and } N(\xi) \geq m/2 | \alpha = \alpha_+\right) + \\
&\quad \frac{1}{2}\Pr\left(f(\xi) = \alpha_- \text{ and } N(\xi) < m/2 | \alpha = \alpha_+\right) + \\
&\quad \frac{1}{2}\Pr\left(f(\xi) = \alpha_+ \text{ and } N(\xi) \geq m/2 | \alpha = \alpha_-\right) + \\
&\quad \frac{1}{2}\Pr\left(f(\xi) = \alpha_+ \text{ and } N(\xi) < m/2 | \alpha = \alpha_-\right) (5.4)
\end{aligned}$$

But the probability of a particular sequence ξ is equal to

$$\alpha^{N(\xi)}(1 - \alpha)^{m - N(\xi)},$$

so if $N(\xi) \geq m/2$, $\Pr(\xi|\alpha = \alpha_+) \geq \Pr(\xi|\alpha = \alpha_-)$. Hence,

$$\Pr\left(f(\xi) = \alpha_- \text{ and } N(\xi) \geq m/2 | \alpha = \alpha_+\right) \geq$$
$$\Pr\left(f(\xi) = \alpha_- \text{ and } N(\xi) \geq m/2 | \alpha = \alpha_-\right).$$

Similarly,

$$\Pr\left(f(\xi) = \alpha_+ \text{ and } N(\xi) < m/2 | \alpha = \alpha_-\right) \geq$$
$$\Pr\left(f(\xi) = \alpha_+ \text{ and } N(\xi) < m/2 | \alpha = \alpha_+\right).$$

Substituting into (5.4), and using the fact that either $f(\xi) = \alpha_-$ or $f(\xi) = \alpha_+$, gives Inequality (5.3).

Now, we assume that m is even (for, if it is not, we may replace m by $m + 1$, which can only decrease the probability), and discard the second term to show that

$$\Pr(f(\xi) \neq \alpha) \geq \frac{1}{2}\Pr\left(N(\xi) \geq m/2 | \alpha = \alpha_-\right),$$

which is the probability that a binomial $(m, 1/2 - \epsilon/2)$ random variable is at least $m/2$. Slud's Inequality (Inequality (1.22) in Appendix 1) shows that

$$\Pr(f(\xi) \neq \alpha) \geq \frac{1}{2}\Pr\left(Z \geq \frac{m/2 - m(1/2 - \epsilon/2)}{\sqrt{m(1/2 - \epsilon/2)(1/2 + \epsilon/2)}}\right)$$
$$= \frac{1}{2}\Pr\left(Z \geq \sqrt{\frac{m\epsilon^2}{1 - \epsilon^2}}\right),$$

where Z is a normal $(0, 1)$ random variable. Standard tail bounds for the normal distribution (see Inequality (1.23) in Appendix 1) show that

$$\Pr(Z \geq \beta) \geq \frac{1}{2}\left(1 - \sqrt{1 - e^{-\beta^2}}\right)$$

for any $\beta > 0$. Hence,

$$\Pr\left(f(\xi) \neq \alpha\right) > \frac{1}{4}\left(1 - \sqrt{1 - \exp\left(-\frac{m\epsilon^2}{1 - \epsilon^2}\right)}\right).$$

It follows that $\Pr(f(\xi) \neq \alpha) > \delta$ when

$$m < \frac{1 - \epsilon^2}{\epsilon^2}\ln\left(\frac{1}{8\delta(1 - 2\delta)}\right),$$

provided $0 < \delta < 1/4$. Recall that if m was odd, we replaced it with $m + 1$, which gives (5.1) and (5.2). $\qquad\square$

The general lower bound

Using Lemma 5.1, we can now obtain the following general lower bound on the sample complexity of a learning algorithm.

Theorem 5.2 *Suppose that H is a class of $\{0,1\}$-valued functions and that H has Vapnik-Chervonenkis dimension d. For any learning algorithm L for H, the sample complexity $m_L(\epsilon, \delta)$ of L satisfies*

$$m_L(\epsilon, \delta) \geq \frac{d}{320\epsilon^2}$$

for all $0 < \epsilon, \delta < 1/64$. Furthermore, if H contains at least two functions, we have

$$m_L(\epsilon, \delta) \geq 2 \left\lfloor \frac{1 - \epsilon^2}{2\epsilon^2} \ln \left(\frac{1}{8\delta(1 - 2\delta)} \right) \right\rfloor$$

for all $0 < \epsilon < 1$ and $0 < \delta < 1/4$.

Proof At the heart of the proof of these inequalities is a simple application of the *probabilistic method*, a useful technique for proving the existence of objects with certain properties. To apply the method, we assume that the underlying probability distribution P is itself chosen uniformly at random from a specified finite class of distributions. We then show that, for any learning algorithm, the expectation (over this random choice of P) of the probability of failure is at least δ, which implies that for *some* distribution P, the probability of failure is at least δ. Notice that we can prove that, for each algorithm, there is a distribution that leads to failure of the algorithm, even though we do not explicitly construct a distribution that is problematic for that algorithm. The main idea behind showing that the expected probability of failure is at least δ for the first inequality of the theorem is to concentrate the distribution on a shattered set, and then set the conditional probability $\Pr(y = 1 | x)$ near $1/2$ (actually $(1 \pm c\epsilon)/2$, for some constant c) for each point x in the shattered set. To get near-optimal error, the algorithm must estimate these conditional probabilities to accuracy $c\epsilon$ for a significant proportion of the points, but Lemma 5.1 shows that this means that it must see at least of order $1/\epsilon^2$ examples of each point. Having given this overview, we now proceed with the technical details.

Since H has VC-dimension d, there is a set $S = \{x_1, x_2, \ldots, x_d\}$ of d examples that is shattered by H. (We may assume $d \geq 1$; the theorem clearly holds if $d = 0$.) Let $\mathcal{P}$ be the class of all distributions P with the following properties:

- P assigns zero probability to all sets not intersecting $S \times \{0, 1\}$,
- for each $i = 1, 2, \ldots, d$, *either*
  - $P(x_i, 1) = (1 + \alpha)/(2d)$ and $P(x_i, 0) = (1 - \alpha)/(2d)$, *or*
  - $P(x_i, 1) = (1 - \alpha)/(2d)$ and $P(x_i, 0) = (1 + \alpha)/(2d)$,

  where $0 < \alpha < 1$. (The parameter α will be chosen later.)

First, we note that for a given $P \in \mathcal{P}$, the optimal error $\mathrm{opt}_P(H)$ is achieved by any function $h^* \in H$ for which $h^*(x_i) = 1$ if and only if $P(x_i, 1) = (1 + \alpha)/(2d)$. (The class H contains such functions h^* because it shatters S.) The optimal error is given as follows:

$$\mathrm{opt}_P(H) = \mathrm{er}_P(h^*) = P\{h^*(x) \neq y\} = \sum_{i=1}^{d} \frac{1 - \alpha}{2d} = \frac{1}{2} - \frac{\epsilon}{2}.$$

Furthermore, for any $h \in H$ we have

$$
\begin{aligned}
\mathrm{er}_P(h) &= \sum_{i=1}^{d} \left(\frac{1 + \alpha}{2d} 1_{h(x_i) \neq h^*(x_i)}(x_i) + \frac{1 - \alpha}{2d} 1_{h(x_i) = h^*(x_i)}(x_i) \right) \\
&= \mathrm{er}_P(h^*) + \frac{\alpha}{d} \sum_{i=1}^{d} 1_{h(x_i) \neq h^*(x_i)}(x_i).
\end{aligned}
\tag{5.5}
$$

For any sample $z \in Z^m$, let $N(z) = (N_1(z), \ldots, N_d(z))$, where $N_i(z)$ is the number of occurrences of either $(x_i, 0)$ or $(x_i, 1)$ in z. Then for any $h = L(z)$ we have

$$
\begin{aligned}
& \mathbf{E} \left(\frac{1}{d} \sum_{i=1}^{d} 1_{h(x_i) \neq h^*(x_i)}(x_i) \right) \\
&= \frac{1}{d} \sum_{i=1}^{d} \mathbf{E} \left(1_{h(x_i) \neq h^*(x_i)}(x_i) \right) \\
&= \frac{1}{d} \sum_{N} \sum_{i=1}^{d} \mathrm{Pr} \left(h(x_i) \neq h^*(x_i) \mid N(z) = N \right) \mathrm{Pr}(N(z) = N),
\end{aligned}
$$

where $N = (N_1, \ldots, N_d)$ ranges over the set of d-tuples of positive integers with $\sum_{i=1}^{d} N_i = m$. From Lemma 5.1,

$$
\begin{aligned}
& \mathrm{Pr} \left(h(x_i) \neq h^*(x_i) \mid N(z) = N \right) \\
&= \mathrm{Pr} \left(h(x_i) \neq h^*(x_i) \mid N_i(z) = N_i \right)
\end{aligned}
$$

$$> \frac{1}{4}\left(1 - \sqrt{1 - \exp\left(-\frac{(N_i + 1)\epsilon^2}{1 - \epsilon^2}\right)}\right).$$

It is easy to check that this is a convex function of N_i, and so

$$\mathbf{E}\left(\frac{1}{d}\sum_{i=1}^{d} 1_{h(x_i)\neq h^*(x_i)}(x_i)\right)$$

$$> \sum_N \Pr(N(z) = N)\frac{1}{d}\sum_{i=1}^{d}\frac{1}{4}\left(1 - \sqrt{1 - \exp\left(-\frac{(N_i + 1)\epsilon^2}{1 - \epsilon^2}\right)}\right)$$

$$\geq \frac{1}{4}\left(1 - \sqrt{1 - \exp\left(-\frac{(m/d + 1)\epsilon^2}{1 - \epsilon^2}\right)}\right),$$

by Jensen's inequality (see Appendix 1). Let B denote the quantity on the right hand side of the last inequality.

Using the fact that any $[0, 1]$-valued random variable Z satisfies

$$\Pr(Z > \gamma) \geq \frac{\mathbf{E}Z - \gamma}{(1 - \gamma)} > \mathbf{E}Z - \gamma$$

for $0 \leq \gamma < 1$, we have

$$\Pr\left(\frac{1}{d}\sum_{i=1}^{d} 1_{h(x_i)\neq h^*(x_i)}(x_i) > \gamma B\right) > (1 - \gamma)B$$

for any $0 < \gamma < 1$. Hence,

$$\mathbf{E}P^m\left\{\mathrm{er}_P(L(z)) - \mathrm{opt}_P(H) > \gamma B\alpha\right\} > (1 - \gamma)B,$$

where the expectation is over the random choice of the probability distribution P from $\mathcal{P}$. It follows that some P has

$$P^m\left\{\mathrm{er}_P(L(z)) - \mathrm{opt}_P(H) > \gamma B\alpha\right\} > (1 - \gamma)B.$$

Then

$$B \geq \frac{\delta}{1 - \gamma} \tag{5.6}$$

and

$$\epsilon \leq \gamma B\alpha \tag{5.7}$$

together imply

$$P^m\left\{\mathrm{er}_P(L(z)) - \mathrm{opt}_P(H) > \epsilon\right\} > \delta. \tag{5.8}$$

Now, to satisfy (5.6) and (5.7), choose $\gamma = 1 - 8\delta$. Then (5.7) follows from

$$m \leq d \left(\frac{1 - \alpha^2}{\alpha^2} \ln(4/3) - 1 \right).$$

Setting $\alpha = 8\epsilon/(1 - 8\delta)$ implies $\epsilon = \gamma\alpha/8$, which together with (5.6) and the choice of γ implies (5.7), since $B \geq 1/8$ in that case. Hence,

$$m \leq d \left(\frac{(1 - 8\delta)^2 - (8\epsilon)^2}{64\epsilon^2} \ln(4/3) - 1 \right)$$

implies (5.8). Using the fact that $0 < \epsilon, \delta < 1/64$ shows that

$$m \leq \frac{d}{320\epsilon^2}$$

will suffice, which gives the first inequality of the theorem.

The proof of the second inequality is similar but simpler. Since H contains at least two functions, there is a point $x \in X$ such that two functions $h_1, h_2 \in H$ have $h_1(x) \neq h_2(x)$. Consider the distributions P_- and P_+ that are concentrated on the labelled examples $(x, h_1(x))$ and $(x, h_2(x))$, and satisfy $P_\pm(x, h_1(x)) = \alpha_\pm$ and $P_\pm(x, h_2(x)) = 1 - \alpha_\pm$, with $\alpha_\pm = (1 \pm \epsilon)/2$ as in Lemma 5.1. If P is one of these distributions and the learning algorithm chooses the 'wrong' function, then

$$\mathrm{er}_P(L(z)) - \mathrm{opt}_P(H) = (1 + \epsilon)/2 - (1 - \epsilon)/2 = \epsilon.$$

Hence, learning to accuracy ϵ is equivalent to guessing which distribution generated the examples.

Now, if we choose a probability distribution P uniformly at random from the set $\{P_-, P_+\}$, then Lemma 5.1 shows that, for any learner L, the expectation (over the choice of P) of the probability (over $z \in Z^m$) that the learner has $\mathrm{er}_P(L(z)) - \mathrm{opt}_P(H) \geq \epsilon$ is at least δ if

$$m < 2 \left\lfloor \frac{1 - \epsilon^2}{2\epsilon^2} \ln \left(\frac{1}{8\delta(1 - 2\delta)} \right) \right\rfloor$$

provided $0 < \delta < 1/4$. ☐

As an important consequence of this theorem, we see that if a class of functions is learnable then it necessarily has finite VC-dimension.

5.3 The Restricted Model

It is natural to ask whether finite VC-dimension is also necessary for learnability in the restricted model, and if so to seek lower bounds on the sample complexity and estimation error of learning in this model. Theorem 5.2 tells us nothing about the restricted model since the probability distributions used in the proof of that theorem do not correspond to target functions combined with probability distributions on the domain. However, it is still possible to use the probabilistic method to obtain lower bounds in this model.

Theorem 5.3 *Suppose that H is a class of $\{0,1\}$-valued functions and that H has Vapnik-Chervonenkis dimension d. For any learning algorithm L for H in the restricted model, the sample complexity $m_L(\epsilon,\delta)$ of L satisfies*

$$m_L(\epsilon,\delta) \geq \frac{d-1}{32\epsilon}$$

for all $0 < \epsilon < 1/8$ and $0 < \delta < 1/100$. Furthermore, if H contains at least three functions, we have

$$m_L(\epsilon,\delta) > \frac{1}{2\epsilon}\ln\left(\frac{1}{\delta}\right),$$

for $0 < \epsilon < 3/4$ and $0 < \delta < 1$.

Proof Suppose that $S = \{x_0, x_1, \ldots, x_r\}$ is shattered by H, where $r = d-1$. (We assume that $d \geq 2$.) Let P be the probability distribution on the domain X of H such that $P(x) = 0$ if $x \notin S$, $P(x_0) = 1 - 8\epsilon$, and for $i = 1, 2, \ldots, d$, $P(x_i) = 8\epsilon/r$. With probability one, for any m, a P^m-random sample lies in S^m, so henceforth, to make the analysis simpler, we assume without loss of generality that $X = S$ and that H consists precisely of all 2^d functions from S to $\{0,1\}$. For convenience, and to be explicit, if a training sample z corresponds to a sample $x \in X^m$ and a function $t \in H$, we shall denote $L(z)$ by $L(x,t)$.

Let $S' = \{x_1, x_2, \ldots, x_r\}$ and let H' be the set of all 2^r functions $h \in H$ such that $h(x_0) = 0$. We shall make use of the probabilistic method, with target functions t drawn at random according to the uniform distribution U on H'. Let L be any learning algorithm for H. We obtain a lower bound on the sample complexity of L under the assumption that L always returns a function in H'; that is, we assume that whatever sample z is given, $L(z)$ classifies x_0 correctly. (This assumption causes no loss of generality: if the output hypothesis of L does not always belong to H', we can consider the 'better' learning algorithm derived from L whose output hypotheses are forced to classify x_0 correctly. Clearly a lower bound on the sample complexity of this latter algorithm is also a lower bound on the sample complexity of L.) Let m be any fixed positive integer and, for $x \in S^m$, denote by $l(x)$ the number of distinct elements of S' occurring in the sample x. It is clear that for any $x \in S'$, exactly half of the functions h' in H' satisfy $h'(x) = 1$ (and exactly half satisfy $h'(x) = 0$). It follows that for any fixed $x \in S^m$,

$$\mathbf{E}_{t \sim U} \operatorname{er}_P(L(x,t)) = \frac{8\epsilon}{r} \frac{r - l(x)}{2}, \tag{5.9}$$

where $\mathbf{E}_{t \sim U}(.)$ denotes expected value when t is drawn according to U, the uniform distribution on H'. We now focus on a special subset S of S^m, consisting of all x for which $l(x) < r/2$. If $x \in S$ then, by (5.9),

$$\mathbf{E}_{t \sim U} \operatorname{er}_P(L(x,t)) > 2\epsilon. \tag{5.10}$$

Now, let Q denote the restriction of P^m to S, so that for any $A \subseteq S^m$, $Q(A) = P^m(A \cap S)/P^m(S)$. Then

$$\mathbf{E}_{x \sim Q} \mathbf{E}_{t \sim U} \operatorname{er}_P(L(x,t)) > 2\epsilon,$$

since (5.10) holds for every $x \in S$. (Here, $\mathbf{E}_{x \sim Q}(\cdot)$ denotes the expected value when x is drawn according to Q.) By Fubini's theorem, the two expectations operators may be interchanged. In other words,

$$\mathbf{E}_{t \sim U} \mathbf{E}_{x \sim Q} \operatorname{er}_P(L(x,t)) = \mathbf{E}_{x \sim Q} \mathbf{E}_{t \sim U} \operatorname{er}_P(L(x,t)) > 2\epsilon.$$

But this implies that for *some* $t' \in H'$,

$$\mathbf{E}_{x \sim Q} \operatorname{er}_P(L(x,t')) > 2\epsilon.$$

Let p_ϵ be the probability (with respect to Q) that $\operatorname{er}_P(L(x,t')) \geq \epsilon$. Given our assumption that L returns a function in H', the error of $L(x,t')$ with respect to P is never more than 8ϵ (the P-probability of S'). Hence we must have

$$2\epsilon < \mathbf{E}_{x \sim Q} \operatorname{er}_P(L(x,t')) \leq 8\epsilon p_\epsilon + (1 - p_\epsilon)\epsilon,$$

from which we obtain $p_\epsilon > 1/7$. It now follows (from the definition of Q) that

$$
\begin{aligned}
P^m \{\operatorname{er}_P(L(x,t')) \geq \epsilon\} &\geq Q \{\operatorname{er}_P(L(x,t')) \geq \epsilon\} P^m(S) \\
&= p_\epsilon P^m(S) \\
&> \frac{1}{7} P^m(S).
\end{aligned}
$$

Now, $P^m(S)$ is the probability that a P^m-random sample z has no more than $r/2$ distinct entries from S'. But this is at least $1 - \operatorname{GE}(8\epsilon, m, r/2)$

(in the notation of Appendix 1). If $m \leq r/(32\epsilon)$ then, using the Chernoff bound (see Inequality (1.14) in Appendix 1), it can be seen that this probability is at least $7/100$. Therefore, if $m \leq r/(32\epsilon)$ and $\delta \leq 1/100$,

$$P^m \{ \text{er}_P \left(L(x, t') \right) \geq \epsilon \} > \frac{1}{7}\frac{7}{100} = \frac{1}{100} \geq \delta,$$

and the first part of the result follows.

To prove the second part of the theorem, notice that if H contains at least three functions, there are examples a, b and functions $h_1, h_2 \in H$ such that $h_1(a) = h_2(a)$ and $h_1(b) = 1, h_2(b) = 0$. Without loss of generality, we shall assume that $h_1(a) = h_2(a) = 1$. Let P be the probability distribution for which $P(a) = 1 - \epsilon$ and $P(b) = \epsilon$ (and such that P is zero elsewhere on the example set X). The probability that a sample $x \in X^m$ has all its entries equal to a is $(1-\epsilon)^m$. Now, $(1-\epsilon)^m \geq \delta$ if and only if

$$m \leq \frac{1}{-\ln(1-\epsilon)} \ln \left(\frac{1}{\delta} \right).$$

Further, $-\ln(1-\epsilon) \leq 2\epsilon$ for $\epsilon \leq 3/4$. It follows that if m is no more than $(1/(2\epsilon)) \ln(1/\delta)$ then, with probability greater than δ, a sample $x \in X^m$ has all its entries equal to a. Let a^1 denote the training sample $a^1 = ((a, 1), \ldots, (a, 1))$ of length m. Note that a^1 is a training sample corresponding *both* to h_1 and to h_2. Suppose that L is a learning algorithm for H and let L_a denote the output $L(a^1)$ of L on the sample a^1. If $L_a(b) = 1$ then L_a has error at least ϵ (the probability of b) with respect to h_2, while if $L_a(b) = 0$ then it has error at least ϵ with respect to h_1. It follows that if $m \leq (1/(2\epsilon)) \ln(1/\delta)$ then either

$$P^m \{ \text{er}_P \left(L(z, h_1) \right) > \epsilon \} \geq P^m \{a^1\} > \delta$$

or

$$P^m \{ \text{er}_P \left(L(z, h_2) \right) > \epsilon \} \geq P^m \{a^1\} > \delta.$$

We therefore deduce that the learning algorithm 'fails' for some $t \in H$ if m is this small. □

As in the corresponding upper bounds, the key difference to be observed between the sample complexity lower bound for the restricted model and that given in Theorem 5.2 for the general model is that the former is proportional to $1/\epsilon$ rather than $1/\epsilon^2$.

5.4 VC-Dimension Quantifies Sample Complexity and Estimation Error

Combining Theorem 5.2 and Theorem 4.10, we obtain the following result.

Theorem 5.4 *Suppose that H is a set of functions that map from a set X to $\{0,1\}$. Then H is learnable if and only if it has finite Vapnik-Chervonenkis dimension. Furthermore, there are constants $c_1, c_2 > 0$ such that the inherent sample complexity of the learning problem for H satisfies*

$$\frac{c_1}{\epsilon^2}\left(\text{VCdim}(H) + \ln\left(\frac{1}{\delta}\right)\right) \le m_H(\epsilon,\delta) \le \frac{c_2}{\epsilon^2}\left(\text{VCdim}(H) + \ln\left(\frac{1}{\delta}\right)\right).$$

for all $0 < \epsilon < 1/40$ and $0 < \delta < 1/20$.

In particular, since Theorem 4.10 applies to sample error minimization algorithms, if L is a SEM algorithm for H, then its sample complexity satisfies these inequalities, and so its estimation error grows as $\sqrt{(\text{VCdim}(H) + \ln(1/\delta))/m}$.

This result shows that the VC-dimension of a function class determines its statistical properties in a rather strong sense. It also shows that the simple SEM algorithms have a nearly optimal estimation rate. The results presented in this chapter and the previous chapter together imply the following theorem. In this theorem, we use the $\Theta(\cdot)$ notation†, which indicates that the functions are asymptotically within a constant factor of each other.

Theorem 5.5 *For a class H of functions mapping from a set X to $\{0,1\}$, the following statements are equivalent.*

(i) *H is learnable.*

(ii) *The inherent sample complexity of H, $m_H(\epsilon,\delta)$, satisfies*

$$m_H(\epsilon,\delta) = \Theta\left(\frac{1}{\epsilon^2}\ln\left(\frac{1}{\delta}\right)\right).$$

† Recall that, for functions $f, g : \mathbb{N}^k \to \mathbb{N}$, $f = O(g)$ means that there are positive numbers c and $b_1,\ldots,b_k$ such that for any $a_i \ge b_i$ (for $i = 1,\ldots,k$), $f(a_1,\ldots,a_k) \le cg(a_1,\ldots,a_k)$. Similarly, $f = \Omega(g)$ means that there are positive numbers c and $b_1,\ldots,b_k$ such that for any $a_i \ge b_i$ (for $i = 1,\ldots,k$), $f(a_1,\ldots,a_k) \ge cg(a_1,\ldots,a_k)$. Also, $f = \Theta(g)$ means that both $f = O(g)$ and $f = \Omega(g)$. For convenience, we extend this notation in the obvious way to functions that increase as some real argument gets small.

(iii) *The inherent estimation error of H, $\epsilon_H(m, \delta)$, satisfies*

$$\epsilon_H(m, \delta) = \Theta\left(\sqrt{\frac{1}{m} \ln\left(\frac{1}{\delta}\right)}\right).$$

(iv) $\text{VCdim}(H) < \infty$.

(v) *The growth function of H, $\Pi_H(m)$, is bounded by a polynomial in m.*

(vi) H *has the following uniform convergence property: There is a function $\epsilon_0(m, \delta)$ satisfying*

- *for every probability distribution P on $X \times \{0, 1\}$,*

$$P^m\left\{\sup_{h \in H} |\text{er}_P(h) - \hat{\text{er}}_z(h)| > \epsilon_0(m, \delta)\right\} < \delta,$$

- $\epsilon_0(m, \delta) = \Theta\left(\sqrt{(1/m) \ln(1/\delta)}\right).$

This theorem shows that the learning behaviour of a function class H and its uniform convergence properties are strongly constrained by its VC-dimension. Recall that, in order to be able to apply Theorem 4.3 (or its improvement, Theorem 4.9) in the previous chapter, we only need the growth function $\Pi_H(m)$ to grow more slowly with m than $e^{\epsilon^2 m}$. In fact, Theorem 3.7 shows that it either grows as 2^m (if the VC-dimension is infinite) or as m^d (if the VC-dimension is finite). So Theorem 4.3 can only be used to show that estimation error decreases as $1/\sqrt{m}$ (equivalently, that sample complexity grows as $1/\epsilon^2$). Now the lower bounds in this chapter show that this is essentially the only rate possible: while the constants are different for different function classes, if the VC-dimension is finite, we have this rate, and if it is infinite, the class is not learnable.

The same characterization is of course also possible for the restricted model, by making use of Theorems 5.3 and 4.8. The following theorem implies that we can add the property 'H is learnable in the restricted model' to the list of equivalent statements in Theorem 5.5.

Theorem 5.6 *Suppose that H is a set of functions from a set X to $\{0, 1\}$. Then H is learnable in the restricted model if and only if H has finite Vapnik-Chervonenkis dimension. Furthermore, there are constants $c_1, c_2 > 0$ such that the inherent sample complexity of the restricted learning problem for H satisfies*

$$\frac{c_1}{\epsilon}\left(\text{VCdim}(H) + \ln\left(\frac{1}{\delta}\right)\right)$$

$$\leq\ m_L(\epsilon, \delta)$$
$$\leq\ \frac{c_2}{\epsilon}\left(\text{VCdim}(H)\ln\left(\frac{1}{\epsilon}\right) + \ln\left(\frac{1}{\delta}\right)\right).$$

5.5 Remarks

Relative uniform convergence results

The results in this chapter show that the rate of uniform convergence of $\text{er}_P(h)$ to $\hat{\text{er}}_z(h)$ can be no faster than $1/\sqrt{m}$ (if we require an upper bound that is valid for all probability distributions). In fact, the rate of uniform convergence of $\text{er}_P(h)$ to a slightly larger value is considerably faster; the following theorem shows that if the VC-dimension of the class is finite, $\text{er}_P(h)$ decreases to $(1+\alpha)\hat{\text{er}}_z(h)$ at least as quickly as $\ln m/m$, for any fixed $\alpha > 0$.

Theorem 5.7 *Suppose that H is a set of $\{0,1\}$-valued functions defined on a set X and that P is a probability distribution on $Z = X \times \{0,1\}$. For $0 < \epsilon < 1$, $\alpha > 0$, and m a positive integer, we have*

$$P^m\left\{\exists h \in H : \text{er}_P(h) > (1+\alpha)\hat{\text{er}}_z(h) + \beta\right\}$$
$$\leq\ 4\Pi_H(2m)\exp\left(\frac{-\alpha\beta m}{4(\alpha+1)}\right).$$

The theorem follows immediately from the following theorem, on setting ν to $2\beta/\alpha$ and ϵ to $\alpha/(2+\alpha)$.

Theorem 5.8 *For H and P as in Theorem 5.7, and $0 < \epsilon, \nu < 1$,*

$$P^m\left\{\exists h \in H : \frac{\text{er}_P(h) - \hat{\text{er}}_z(h)}{\text{er}_P(h) + \hat{\text{er}}_z(h) + \nu} > \epsilon\right\} \leq 4\Pi_H(2m)\exp\left(\frac{-\nu\epsilon^2 m}{2(1-\epsilon^2)}\right).$$

Proof The theorem follows from the inequality

$$P^m\left\{\exists h \in H : \frac{\text{er}_P(h) - \hat{\text{er}}_z(h)}{\sqrt{\text{er}_P(h)}} > \eta\right\} \leq 4\Pi_H(2m)\exp\left(\frac{-\eta^2 m}{4}\right).$$

$$(5.11)$$

We omit the proof of this inequality, but note that it uses similar ideas to the proof of Theorem 4.3. To see that the inequality implies the theorem, suppose that $\text{er}_P(h) - \hat{\text{er}}_z(h) \leq \eta\sqrt{\text{er}_P(h)}$. Then for any $\alpha > 0$ we have two cases:

(i) If $\text{er}_P(h) < (1 + 1/\alpha)^2\eta^2$, then $\text{er}_P(h) < \hat{\text{er}}_z(h) + \eta^2(1 + 1/\alpha)$.

(ii) If $\mathrm{er}_P(h) \geq (1+1/\alpha)^2\eta^2$, then $\mathrm{er}_P(h) \leq \hat{\mathrm{er}}_z(h) + \alpha/(1+\alpha)\mathrm{er}_P(h)$, and so $\mathrm{er}_P(h) \leq (1+\alpha)\hat{\mathrm{er}}_z(h)$.

In either case, $\mathrm{er}_P(h) \leq (1+\alpha)\hat{\mathrm{er}}_z(h) + \eta^2(1+1/\alpha)$. Hence,

$$P^m\left\{\exists h \in H : \mathrm{er}_P(h) > (1+\alpha)\hat{\mathrm{er}}_z(h) + \eta^2(1+1/\alpha)\right\}$$
$$\leq 4\Pi_H(2m)\exp\left(\frac{-\eta^2 m}{4}\right).$$

Choosing $\alpha = 2\epsilon/(1-\epsilon)$ and $\eta^2 = 2\nu\epsilon^2/(1-\epsilon^2)$ gives the result.   □

The inequality in Theorem 5.8 can be made two-sided; the argument is similar. That theorem also implies a version of Theorem 4.3, with different constants. To see this, notice that $\mathrm{er}_P(h) \leq 1$ and $\hat{\mathrm{er}}_z(h) \leq 1$, so

$$P^m\left\{\exists h \in H : \mathrm{er}_P(h) - \hat{\mathrm{er}}_z(h) > \eta\right\}$$
$$\leq P^m\left\{\exists h \in H : \mathrm{er}_P(h) - \hat{\mathrm{er}}_z(h) > \frac{\mathrm{er}_P(h) + \hat{\mathrm{er}}_z(h) + \nu}{2+\nu}\eta\right\}.$$

5.6 Bibliographical Notes

The second part of the proof of Lemma 5.1 was suggested by Jon Baxter (see Theorem 12 in (Baxter, 1998)). The constants in that lemma improve on those in many similar results (see, for example, (Simon, 1996; Ben-David and Lindenbaum, 1997)). Lower bound results of the form of Theorem 5.2 have appeared in a number of papers; see (Vapnik and Chervonenkis, 1974; Devroye and Lugosi, 1995; Simon, 1996). The bounds in Theorem 5.2 improve (by constants) all previous bounds that we are aware of. The proof technique for the first inequality of the theorem uses ideas of Ehrenfeucht, Haussler, Kearns and Valiant (1989), who used a similar approach to give lower bounds for the restricted model (Theorem 5.6). The constants in the first inequality of Theorem 5.6 can be improved (from 32 to 12 and 100 to 20) at the expense of a more complicated proof; see (Devroye and Lugosi, 1995, Theorem 2).

Theorem 5.6 shows that, in the restricted model of learning, the rate at which the estimation error decreases as the sample size increases is essentially the same for every learnable function class. This does not imply that, for every target function, the estimation error decreases at this rate. In fact, it is possible for the rate to be considerably faster for every function in the class, but with different constants. See, for example, (Schuurmans, 1995).

Inequality (5.11), which we used to derive the relative uniform convergence results (Theorems 5.7 and 5.8) is an improvement on a result of Vapnik (1982) due to Anthony and Shawe-Taylor (1993b).

6

The VC-Dimension of Linear Threshold Networks

6.1 Feed-Forward Neural Networks

In this chapter, and many subsequent ones, we deal with feed-forward neural networks. Initially, we shall be particularly concerned with feed-forward linear threshold networks, which can be thought of as combinations of perceptrons.

To define a neural network class, we need to specify the architecture of the network and the parameterized functions computed by its components. In general, a feed-forward neural network has as its main components a set of *computation units*, a set of *input units*, and a set of *connections* from input or computation units to computation units. These connections are directed; that is, each connection is *from* a particular unit *to* a particular computation unit. The key structural property of a feed-forward network—the *feed-forward condition*—is that these connections do not form any loops. This means that the units can be labelled with integers in such a way that if there is a connection from the unit labelled i to the computation unit labelled j then $i < j$.

Associated with each unit is a real number called its *output*. The output of a computation unit is a particular function of the outputs of units that are connected to it. The feed-forward condition guarantees that the outputs of all units in the network can be written as an explicit function of the network inputs.

Often we will be concerned with *multi-layer* networks. For such networks, the computation units of the network may be grouped into *layers*, labelled $1, 2, \ldots, \ell$, in such a way that the input units feed into the computation units, and if there is a connection from a computation unit in layer i to a computation unit in layer j, then we must have $j > i$. Note, in particular, that there are no connections between any two units in

74

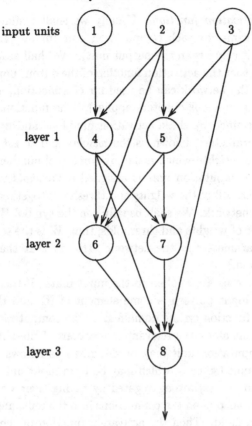

Fig. 6.1. A feed-forward network.

a given layer. Figure 6.1 shows a multi-layer network with three layers of computation units. This figure also illustrates the convention used to number the layers of computation units. Consistent with this numbering scheme, an 'ℓ-layer network' denotes a network with ℓ layers of computation units.

A feed-forward network is said to be *fully connected between adjacent layers* if it contains all possible connections between consecutive layers of computation units, and all possible connections from the input units to the first layer of computation units. For our purposes, one of the computation units in the final (highest) layer is designated as an *output unit*. (More generally, there may be more than one output unit.)

Associated with each computation unit is a fixed real function known as the unit's *activation function.* Usually we shall assume that this function is the same for each computation unit (or at least for each computation unit other than the output unit). We shall assume in this part of the book that the activation function of the output unit is binary-valued (so that the network can be used for classification, and so that the theory of the previous chapters applies). The functionality of the network is determined by these activation functions and by a number of adjustable parameters, known as the *weights* and *thresholds.* Each connection has a *weight*—which is simply some real number—assigned to it, and each computation unit is assigned a *threshold* value, again some real number. All of the weights and thresholds together constitute the *state* of the network. We shall usually use the symbol W to denote the total number of weights and thresholds; thus, W is the total number of adjustable parameters in the network. (Recall that the activation functions are fixed.)

The input patterns are applied to the input units. If there are n inputs then each input pattern is some element of $\mathbb{R}^n$ and the network computes some function on the domain $\mathbb{R}^n$. The computation units receive and transmit along the relevant connections of the network. The action of a computation unit may be described as follows. First, the inputs into the unit (some of which may be from input units and some from computation units) are aggregated by taking their weighted sum according to the weights on the connections into the unit, and then subtracting the threshold. Then the activation function of the unit takes this aggregation as its argument, the value computed being the output of the computation unit. Explicitly, suppose that the computation units and inputs are labelled with the integers $1, 2, \ldots, k$, and that the computation unit labelled r has activation function f_r. Suppose that this unit receives inputs $z_1, z_2, \ldots, z_d$ from d units, and that the weights on the corresponding connections are (respectively) $w_1, w_2, \ldots, w_d$. Then the output of r is

$$f_r \left(\sum_{j=1}^{d} w_j z_j - \theta \right),$$

where θ is the threshold assigned to unit r.

A feed-forward network is said to be a *linear threshold network* if each activation function is the step function,

$$f(y) = \mathrm{sgn}(y) = \begin{cases} 1 & \text{if } y \geq 0 \\ 0 & \text{otherwise.} \end{cases}$$

The simplest type of linear threshold network is the perceptron, discussed in earlier chapters. Later we shall look at sigmoid networks, which make use of the activation function $f(y) = 1/(1 + e^{-y})$, and also at networks with piecewise-polynomial activation functions.

6.2 Upper Bound

In this section we present upper bounds on the VC-dimension of feed-forward linear threshold networks (by which, to be precise, we mean the VC-dimension of the class of functions computed by the network). We already know one such result, from Chapter 3: the VC-dimension of a perceptron on n (real or binary) input units is $n + 1$, which equals W, the total number of weights and thresholds. The following result gives a general upper bound on the VC-dimension of any feed-forward linear threshold network, in terms of the total number W of weights and thresholds.

Theorem 6.1 *Suppose that N is a feed-forward linear threshold network having a total of W variable weights and thresholds, and k computation units. Let H be the class of functions computable by N on real inputs. Then for $m \geq W$ the growth function of H satisfies*

$$\Pi_H(m) \leq \left(\frac{emk}{W}\right)^W,$$

and hence VCdim $(H) < 2W \log_2(2k/\ln 2)$.

Proof Let k denote the number of computation units in the network. Since the network is a feed-forward network, we may label the computation units with the integers $1, 2, \ldots, k$ so that if the output of computation unit i is fed into unit j then $i < j$. We shall bound the growth function in an iterative manner, by considering in turn the action of each computation unit.

Recall that by a state of the network we mean an assignment of weights to the connections, and thresholds to the computation units. Suppose now that S is any set of m input patterns. We say that two states ω, ω' of N *compute different functions on S up to unit l* if there is some input pattern x in S such that, when x is input, the output of some computation unit labelled from 1 to l differs in the two states. (In other words, if one has access to the signals transmitted by units 1 to l only, then, using input patterns from S, one can differentiate between the two states.) We shall denote by $D_l(S)$ the maximum cardinality of a set of states that compute different functions on S up to unit l. Note that the number of functions computed by N on the set S is certainly bounded above by $D_k(S)$. (Two states that do not compute different functions up to unit k—the output unit—certainly yield the same function on S.) For l between 2 and k, we let ω^l denote the vector of weights and thresholds at units $1, 2, \ldots, l$. Thus ω^l describes the state of the network up to computation unit l. Crucial to the proof is the observation that the output of computation unit l depends only on the network inputs, the outputs of the computation units that feed into l, and the weights and thresholds at unit l. To exploit this, we 'decompose' ω^l into two parts, ω^{l-1} and ζ_l. The first of these describes the state of the network up to unit $l - 1$ (and hence determines the outputs of the computation units 1 to $l - 1$), while the second, ζ_l, denotes the threshold on unit l and the weights on the connections leading into l (from input units or previous computation units). Since computation unit l is a linear threshold unit, the set of functions computable by that unit (in isolation) has VC-dimension d_l, where d_l is the number of parameters associated with unit l (that is, the number of connections terminating at l, plus one for its threshold).

Consider first computation unit 1. Two states compute different functions up to unit 1 if and only if they result in different outputs at unit 1. Therefore, the number of such mutually different states is bounded simply by the number of dichotomies achievable by the perceptron determined by unit 1, on the sample S. The perceptron in question has VC-dimension d_1 and so, by Theorem 3.7, the number of dichotomies is no more than $(em/d_1)^{d_1}$, since $m \geq W \geq d_1$. In other words, $D_1(S) \leq (em/d_1)^{d_1}$.

We now consider a unit l, where $2 \leq l \leq k$. The decomposition of ω^l into ω^{l-1} and ζ_l shows that if two states compute different functions on S up to unit l, but do *not* compute different functions up to unit $l - 1$, then these states must be distinguished by the action of the unit l. Now, by Theorem 3.1, and the fact that l computes linear threshold functions of $d_l - 1$ inputs, if T is any set of m points of $\mathbb{R}^{d_l - 1}$, then the number of ways in which unit l can classify T, as the weight vector ζ_l varies, is at most $(em/d_l)^{d_l}$. Therefore, for each of the $D_{l-1}(S)$ different states up to unit $l - 1$, there are at most $(em/d_l)^{d_l}$ states that compute different functions up to unit l. Hence

$$D_l(S) \leq D_{l-1}(S) \, (em/d_l)^{d_l}.$$

It follows, by induction, that

$$D_k(S) \leq \prod_{l=1}^{k} \left(\frac{em}{d_l} \right)^{d_l}. \qquad (6.1)$$

As mentioned earlier, $\Pi_H(m)$ is bounded by the maximum of $D_k(S)$ over all S of cardinality m, so (6.1) implies

$$\ln \Pi_H(m) \leq \sum_{l=1}^{k} d_l \ln \left(\frac{em}{d_l} \right).$$

The expression on the right is reminiscent of the entropy of a discrete random variable. We may write

$$
\begin{aligned}
\frac{1}{W} \ln \Pi_H(m) + \ln \left(\frac{W}{em} \right) &\leq \sum_{l=1}^{k} \frac{d_l}{W} \ln \left(\frac{em}{d_l} \right) + \ln \left(\frac{W}{em} \right) \\
&= \sum_{l=1}^{k} \frac{d_l}{W} \ln \left(\frac{em}{d_l} \right) + \sum_{l=1}^{k} \frac{d_l}{W} \ln \left(\frac{W}{em} \right) \\
&= \sum_{l=1}^{k} \frac{d_l}{W} \ln \left(\frac{W}{d_l} \right),
\end{aligned}
$$

noting that $\sum_{l=1}^{k} d_l/W = 1$. Since $d_l/W > 0$, we see that the bound can indeed be expressed as an entropy. It is well known (and easy to show, using the convexity of the logarithm function) that entropy is maximized when the distribution is uniform, that is when $d_l/W = 1/k$ for $l = 1, 2, \ldots, k$. The fact that d_l is restricted to integer values can only decrease the sum. Hence,

$$\frac{1}{W} \ln \Pi_H(m) + \ln \left(\frac{W}{em} \right) \leq \ln k.$$

Rearranging, we have

$$\Pi_H(m) \leq \left(\frac{emk}{W} \right)^W.$$

To see that this gives the required bound on VCdim(H), notice that if $m > W \log_2(emk/W)$ then $2^m > \Pi_H(m)$, which implies VCdim(H) $\leq m$. Inequality (1.2) in Appendix 1 shows that for any $\alpha, x > 0$, $\ln x \leq \alpha x - \ln \alpha - 1$, with equality only if $\alpha x = 1$. Applying this inequality with $x = emk/W$ and $\alpha = \ln 2/(2ek)$ shows that it suffices to take $m = 2W \log_2(2k/\ln 2)$. $\qquad \square$

6.3 Lower Bounds

The following result shows that the VC-dimension of two-layer linear threshold networks is bounded below by a quantity of order W, the total number of weights.

Theorem 6.2 *Let N be a two-layer linear threshold network, fully connected between adjacent layers, with $n \geq 3$ input units, k computation units in the first layer (and one output unit in the second layer). Suppose that $k \leq 2^{n+1}/(n^2 + n + 2)$. Then the class H of functions computable by N on binary inputs is such that*

$$\mathrm{VCdim}(H) \geq nk + 1 \geq 3W/5,$$

where $W = nk + 2k + 1$ is the total number of weights and thresholds.

Proof We prove the result by constructing a shattered set of size $nk + 1$. Recall that the decision boundary of a linear threshold unit is a hyperplane, so that for all points on one side of the hyperplane, the unit outputs 0 and for all points on the other side, or on the hyperplane itself, it outputs 1. The idea of the proof is to choose appropriate values for the parameters of the network and then, for each of the k first layer units, to include in the shattered set n points that lie on its decision boundary. By adjusting the parameters of a first layer unit slightly, we can adjust the classification of each of the associated n points, without affecting the classification of the other points.

Now, a *three-packing* of $\{0,1\}^n$ is a subset T of $\{0,1\}^n$ such that for any two members of T, their Hamming distance (the number of entries on which they differ) is at least three. If we construct a three-packing in a greedy way, by iteratively adding to T some point that is at least Hamming distance three from all points in T, each new point added to the packing eliminates no more than $N = \binom{n}{2} + \binom{n}{1} + 1$ points from consideration. It follows that some three-packing T has

$$|T| \geq \frac{2^n}{N} = \frac{2^{n+1}}{n^2 + n + 2}.$$

So let $T = \{t_1, t_2, \ldots, t_k\}$ be a three-packing (recall that $k \leq 2^{n+1}/(n^2 + n + 2)$). For i between 1 and k, let S_i be the set of points in $\{0,1\}^n$ whose Hamming distance from t_i is 1. (Thus, S_i consists of all n points of $\{0,1\}^n$ differing from t_i in exactly one entry.) There is a single hyperplane passing through every point of S_i. (Without loss of generality, suppose t_i is the all-0 element of $\{0,1\}^n$, then S_i consists of all points with exactly one entry equal to 1, and the appropriate hyperplane is defined by the equation $x_1 + x_2 + \ldots + x_n = 1$.) Furthermore, because T is a three-packing no two of these k hyperplanes intersect in $[0,1]^n$. Let us set the weights and thresholds of the computation units in the first layer so that the decision boundary of the ith unit in the layer is the hyperplane passing through S_i, and for input t_i the output of the unit is 0. Assign weight 1 to each connection into the output unit, and assign threshold k to the output, so that the output of the network is 1 precisely when the output of all units in the first layer is 1.

Since the points of S_i sit on the hyperplanes described above, the weights and threshold corresponding to unit i may be perturbed—in other words, the planes moved slightly—so that for any given subset S_i' of S_i, unit i outputs 0 on inputs in S_i' and 1 on inputs in $S_i - S_i'$. Furthermore, because the hyperplanes do not intersect in the region $[0,1]^n$, such perturbations can be carried out independently for each of the k units in the first layer. The network can therefore achieve any desired classification of the points in $S = \bigcup_{j=1}^{k} S_j$. In other words, this set S is shattered.

Furthermore, by negating the weights and thresholds of the first layer units, and changing the threshold at the output unit to 1, the network can still shatter the set S by perturbing the first layer parameters. However, it now classifies each t_i as 1, where before they were classified as 0. So the set $S \cup \{t_1\}$ is shattered, and hence $\text{VCdim}(H) \geq nk + 1$.

The second inequality of the theorem follows from the fact that $n \geq 3$, which implies $W \leq nk + 2nk/3 + 1 < 5(nk + 1)/3$. $\qquad\square$

The lower bound just given is linear in the number W of weights and thresholds, while the upper bounds of the previous section indicate that the VC-dimension of a feed-forward linear threshold network is of order at most $W \log_2 W$. Moreover, we have already seen that the perceptron has VC-dimension W, so it is natural to ask whether the bound of Theorem 6.1 is of the best possible order or whether one should be able to prove that in this case the VC-dimension is really of order W. In other words, can it be true that some feed-forward linear threshold networks have VC-dimension *significantly* larger than W, the number of variable parameters? The answer is 'yes', as shown by the following results, which we state without proof. (See the Bibliographical Notes section at the end of the chapter.)

Theorem 6.3 *Let W be any positive integer greater than* 32. *Then there is a three-layer feed-forward linear threshold network N_W with at most W weights and thresholds, for which the following holds. If H is the class of functions computable by N_W on binary inputs, then* VCdim(H) > $(1/132)W \log_2 (k/16)$, *where k is the number of computation units.*

Theorem 6.3 refers to networks taking binary inputs. It is perhaps surprising that, even with this restriction, a network may have a 'superlinear' VC-dimension. The result shows that no upper bound better than order $W \log_2 k$ can be given: to within a constant, the bound of Theorem 6.1 is tight.

The networks of Theorem 6.3 have three layers. The following result shows that there are two-layer feed-forward linear threshold networks having superlinear VC-dimension on *real* inputs. These networks have fewer layers—and hence in a sense are less complex—than those of Theorem 6.3, but the result concerns real inputs, not binary inputs and hence is not immediately comparable with Theorem 6.3. For the same reason, the result is not directly comparable with Theorem 6.2.

Theorem 6.4 *Let N be a two-layer feed-forward linear threshold network, fully connected between adjacent layers, having k computation units and $n \geq 3$ inputs, where $k \leq 2^{n/2-2}$. Let H be the set of functions computable by N on $\mathbb{R}^n$. Then*

$$\text{VCdim}(H) \geq \frac{nk}{8} \log_2 \left(\frac{k}{4}\right) \geq \frac{W}{32} \log_2 \left(\frac{k}{4}\right),$$

where $W = nk + 2k + 1$ is the total number of weights and thresholds.

We omit the proof. (See the Bibliographical Notes section at the end of the chapter.) Theorem 6.4 should be compared to the upper bound of Theorem 6.1. The upper and lower bounds are within constant factors of each other.

Notice that Theorems 6.3 and 6.4 show that there are certain neural networks with VC-dimension growing at least as $W \log W$. Recall that the upper bound of Theorem 6.1 applies to feed-forward networks with an arbitrary number of layers. By embedding two- and three-layer networks in a network of any fixed depth, it is easy to show that there is a sequence of networks of that depth with VC-dimension increasing as $W \log W$. However this does not imply a similar result for arbitrary architectures. Given an arbitrary sequence of linear threshold networks of fixed depth with increasing W, it is clear that the VC-dimension cannot be forced to grow as $W \log W$ without some constraints on how the weights are distributed among the layers. A trivial example is a three-layer network with k_1 units in the first layer and $k_2 > 2^{k_1}$ units in the second layer. In this case, any weights associated with additional computation units in the second layer cannot lead to an increase in VC-dimension, since it is already possible to compute all boolean functions of the k_1 first layer outputs. However, in this case it is known that the VC-dimension is larger than some universal constant times W, provided that k_2 is smaller than a fixed exponential function of k_1. It is not known whether this bound can be improved without a stronger constraint on the number of second layer units.

6.4 Sigmoid Networks

Feed-forward *sigmoid networks* form an important and much-used class of neural network. In such networks, the output unit has the step function as its activation function, but the activation function of every other computation unit is the *standard sigmoid* function, σ, given by

$$\sigma(y) = \frac{1}{1 + e^{-y}}.$$

(A computation unit of this type is often called a *sigmoid unit*.) The graph of the function σ may be found in Chapter 1 as Figure 1.3. Note that the standard sigmoid network just defined has a binary-valued output, in contrast to the two-layer real-output sigmoid network discussed in Chapter 1.

The sigmoid function is, in a sense, a 'smoothed-out' version of the step function, sgn, since σ maps from $\mathbb{R}$ into the interval $(0, 1)$ and it has limits

$$\lim_{\alpha \to -\infty} \sigma(\alpha) = 0, \qquad \lim_{\alpha \to \infty} \sigma(\alpha) = 1.$$

As M increases, the graph of the function $\alpha \mapsto \sigma(M\alpha)$ becomes increasingly like that of the linear threshold step function $\text{sgn}(\alpha)$.

The VC-dimension upper bound results obtained in this chapter are specifically for linear threshold networks and cannot be applied to sigmoid networks. (We shall derive upper bounds on sigmoid networks in Chapter 8.) However, it is possible to use the lower bound results on the VC-dimension of multi-layer linear threshold networks to obtain lower bounds on the VC-dimension of multi-layer sigmoid networks, by means of the following observation.

Theorem 6.5 *Suppose* $s : \mathbb{R} \to \mathbb{R}$ *satisfies* $\lim_{\alpha \to \infty} s(\alpha) = 1$ *and* $\lim_{\alpha \to -\infty} s(\alpha) = 0$. *Let* N *be a feed-forward linear threshold network, and* N' *a network with the same structure as* N, *but with the threshold activation functions replaced by the activation function* s *in all non-output computation units. Suppose that* S *is any finite set of input patterns. Then, any function computable by* N *on* S *is also computable by* N'.

It is easy to see that the limits 1 and 0 can be replaced by any two distinct numbers.

Proof Consider a function h computable by N on S. Label the computation units with integers $1, 2, \ldots, k$ in such a way that unit j takes input from unit i only if $i < j$, and so that unit k is the output unit. Let $v_i(x)$ denote the *net input* to computation unit i in response to input pattern $x \in S$. (That is, if unit i has input vector z, weight vector w, and threshold w_0, $v_i(x) = w^T z + w_0$.) The proof uses the fact that we can multiply the argument of $s(\cdot)$ by a large constant and, provided the argument is not zero, the resulting function accurately approximates a threshold function.

First, define $\epsilon = \min_i \min_{x \in S} |v_i(x)|$. Suppose that $\epsilon > 0$. (Otherwise we can change the thresholds to ensure this, while keeping the function computed on S unchanged.) Now, we step through the network, replacing each threshold activation function $v \mapsto \mathrm{sgn}(v)$ by the function $v \mapsto s(Mv)$, where M is a positive real number. Let $v_{i,M}(x)$ denote the net input to computation unit i in response to $x \in S$ when the activation functions of units $1, \ldots, i-1$ have been changed in this way. Since S is finite and $\epsilon > 0$, the limiting property of s implies that

$$\lim_{M \to \infty} \max_{x \in S} |s(Mv_1(x)) - \mathrm{sgn}(v_1(x))| = 0.$$

Since the net input to a computation unit is a continuous function of the outputs of previous units, this implies that

$$\lim_{M \to \infty} \max_{x \in S} |v_{2,M}(x) - v_2(x)| = 0,$$

and so

$$\lim_{M \to \infty} \max_{x \in S} |s(Mv_{2,M}(x)) - \mathrm{sgn}(v_2(x))| = 0.$$

Proceeding in this way, we conclude that

$$\lim_{M \to \infty} \max_{x \in S} |v_{k,M}(x) - v_k(x)| = 0,$$

which shows that, for sufficiently large M,

$$\text{sgn}(v_{k,M}(x)) = \text{sgn}(v_k(x)) = h(x)$$

for all $x \in S$. Now, by scaling the weights and thresholds by M and replacing the activation function $v \mapsto s(Mv)$ by the function $v \mapsto s(v)$, we see that the function h on S is computable by N'. □

It follows immediately that any set of input patterns shattered by a network of linear threshold units is also shattered by a network of units each with an activation function s of the type described. Hence the lower bound results Theorem 6.2, Theorem 6.3 and Theorem 6.4 also hold for such networks, and in particular for standard sigmoid networks.

6.5 Bibliographical Notes

The proof of the upper bound of Theorem 6.1 is due to Baum and Haussler (1989). (For more on properties of the entropy function, which were used in that proof, see, for example, (Cover and Thomas, 1991).) This result was originally due to Cover (1968). A lower bound on the VC-dimension of two-layer networks that is linear in the number of weights was also presented in (Baum and Haussler, 1989). Theorem 6.2 gives a slight improvement (by a constant factor) of this result, with a simpler proof; see (Bartlett, 1993a). The corresponding result for real inputs (relying on the inputs being in general position, which is not the case for binary inputs) appears in (Baum, 1988), using a technique that appeared in (Nilsson, 1965). Lower bounds for networks with binary weights are given in (Ji and Psaltis, 1991). Theorem 6.3 is due to Maass (1994), and Theorem 6.4 is due to Sakurai (1993). General lower bounds for any smoothly parameterized function class are given in (Erlich, Chazan, Petrack and Levy, 1997) (see also (Lee, Bartlett and Williamson, 1995a)). The $\Omega(W)$ bound for arbitrary three-layer linear threshold networks with not too many computation units in the second layer was presented in (Bartlett, 1993a; Bartlett, 1993b). The fact that lower bounds for linear threshold networks imply lower bounds for sigmoid networks is proved, for example, in (Sontag, 1992; Koiran and Sontag, 1997).

7
Bounding the VC-Dimension using Geometric Techniques

7.1 Introduction

Results in the previous chapter show that the VC-dimension of the class of functions computed by a network of linear threshold units with W parameters is no larger than a constant times $W \log W$. These results cannot immediately be extended to networks of sigmoid units (with continuous activation functions), since the proofs involve counting the number of distinct outputs of all linear threshold units in the network as the input varies over m patterns, and a single sigmoid unit has an infinite number of output values. In this chapter and the next we derive bounds on the VC-dimension of certain sigmoid networks, including networks of units having the standard sigmoid activation function $\sigma(\alpha) = 1/(1 + e^{-\alpha})$. Before we begin this derivation, we study an example that shows that the form of the activation function is crucial.

7.2 The Need for Conditions on the Activation Functions

One might suspect that if we construct networks of sigmoid units with a well-behaved activation function, they will have finite VC-dimension. For instance, perhaps it suffices if the activation function is sufficiently smooth, bounded, and monotonically increasing. Unfortunately, the situation is not so simple. The following result shows that there is an activation function that has all of these properties, and even has its derivative monotonically increasing to the left of zero and decreasing to the right (so it is convex and concave in those regions), and yet is such that a two-layer network having only two computation units in the first layer, each with this activation function, has infinite VC-dimension. What is more, the activation function can be made arbitrarily close to

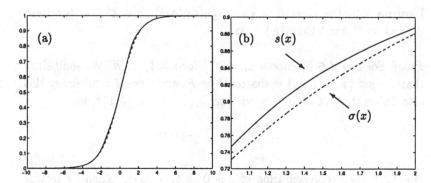

Fig. 7.1. The graphs of the functions $s(\cdot)$ (defined in Equation (7.1), with $c = 0.05$ and the standard sigmoid $\sigma(\cdot)$ (defined in Equation (1.1)), (a) in the interval $[-10, 10]$ and (b) in the interval $[1, 2]$.

the standard sigmoid, $\sigma(\alpha) = 1/(1 + e^{-\alpha})$. Clearly, then, finiteness of the VC-dimension of neural networks depends on more than simply the smoothness of the activation function.

Theorem 7.1 *Define*

$$s(x) = \frac{1}{1 + e^{-x}} + cx^3 e^{-x^2} \sin x \qquad (7.1)$$

for $c > 0$. Then $s(\cdot)$ is analytic, and for any sufficiently small $c > 0$, we have

$$\lim_{x \to \infty} s(x) = 1,$$

$$\lim_{x \to -\infty} s(x) = 0,$$

$$\frac{d^2}{dx^2} s(x) \begin{cases} < 0 & \text{if } x > 0 \\ > 0 & \text{if } x < 0. \end{cases}$$

Let N be a two-layer network with one real input, two first-layer computation units using this activation function, and one output unit, so that functions in H_N are of the form

$$x \mapsto \text{sgn}\,(w_0 + w_1 s(a_1 x) + w_2 s(a_2 x)),$$

with $x, w_0, w_1, w_2, a_1, a_2 \in \mathbb{R}$. Then $\text{VCdim}(H_N) = \infty$.

Figure 7.1 compares the graphs of $s(\cdot)$ and the standard sigmoid. The proof of Theorem 7.1 relies on the following lemma.

Lemma 7.2 *The class* $F = \{x \mapsto \mathrm{sgn}(\sin(ax)) : a \in \mathbb{R}^+\}$ *of functions defined on* $\mathbb{N}$ *has* $\mathrm{VCdim}(F) = \infty$.

Proof For any $d \in \mathbb{N}$, choose $x_i = 2^{i-1}$ for $i = 1, \ldots, d$. We shall show that the set $\{x_1, \ldots, x_d\}$ is shattered by F, and since d is arbitrary this establishes that $\mathrm{VCdim}(F) = \infty$. For $(b_1, \ldots, b_d) \in \{0,1\}^d$, let

$$c = \sum_{j=1}^{d} 2^{-j} b_j + 2^{-(d+1)}$$

(so the binary representation of c is $0 \cdot b_1 b_2 \cdots b_d 1$). Then by setting $a = 2\pi c$, we can use the function $\mathrm{sgn}(\sin(ax_i))$ to extract the bits b_i from c. That is,

$$
\begin{aligned}
\mathrm{sgn}(\sin(ax_i)) &= \mathrm{sgn}\left(\sin\left(2\pi \left(\sum_{j=1}^{d} 2^{-j} b_j + 2^{-(d+1)}\right) 2^{i-1}\right)\right) \\
&= \mathrm{sgn}\left(\sin\left(\sum_{j=1}^{i-1} (2^{i-j}\pi) b_j + \pi b_i \right.\right. \\
&\qquad\qquad \left.\left. + \sum_{j=i+1}^{d} (2^{i-j}\pi) b_j + 2^{i-d-1}\pi\right)\right) \\
&= \mathrm{sgn}\left(\sin\left(\pi\left(b_i + \sum_{j=1}^{d-i} 2^{-j} b_{i+j} + 2^{-(d-i+1)}\right)\right)\right),
\end{aligned}
$$

and the argument of $\sin(\cdot)$ in the last expression lies strictly between $b_i\pi$ and $(b_i + 1)\pi$, so $\mathrm{sgn}(\sin(ax_i)) = 1 - b_i$. Since this is true for any $i = 1, \ldots, d$, and any choice of the b_i, it follows that $\{x_1, \ldots, x_d\}$ is shattered. $\square$

It is now easy to verify the claims made in Theorem 7.1. The properties of $s(\cdot)$ are easy to check (although checking the properties of convexity to the left of zero and concavity to the right of zero is tedious). To show that the class H_N has infinite VC-dimension, we use the network N to compute $\mathrm{sgn}(\sin(ax))$. Specifically, for $a \in \mathbb{R}$, set the weights so that the network computes $\mathrm{sgn}(h_a(x))$, where

$$h_a(x) = s(ax) + s(-ax) - 1 = 2c(ax)^3 e^{-a^2 x^2} \sin(ax).$$

For $a > 0$ and $x > 0$, $\mathrm{sgn}(h_a(x)) = \mathrm{sgn}(\sin(ax))$, so Lemma 7.2 implies that $\mathrm{VCdim}(H_N) = \infty$.

7.3 A Bound on the Growth Function

In the remainder of this chapter, we consider classes of binary-valued functions that are obtained from parameterized real-valued functions by 'thresholding'. Classes defined in this way include the perceptron and the class of functions computed by thresholding the output of a multi-layer network of units having either the standard sigmoid activation function or a piecewise-polynomial activation function. In this definition, and in the remainder of this chapter, we assume that there are d real parameters; we use a to denote the vector of these parameters.

Definition 7.3 *Let H be a class of $\{0,1\}$-valued functions defined on a set X, and F a class of real-valued functions defined on $\mathbb{R}^d \times X$. We say that H is a k-combination of $\mathrm{sgn}(F)$ if there is a boolean function $g : \{0,1\}^k \to \{0,1\}$ and functions $f_1, \ldots, f_k$ in F so that for all h in H there is a parameter vector $a \in \mathbb{R}^d$ such that*

$$h(x) = g(\mathrm{sgn}(f_1(a,x)), \ldots, \mathrm{sgn}(f_k(a,x)))$$

for all x in X.

We say that a function f in F is continuous in its parameters *(C^p in its parameters†) if, for all x in X, $f(\cdot, x)$ is continuous (respectively, C^p).*

In this chapter we develop a technique for bounding the growth function of a class H of functions expressible as boolean combinations of parameterized real-valued functions in this way. Theorem 7.6 below provides a bound in terms of the number of connected components of the solution set in parameter space of certain systems of equations involving the real-valued functions that define H. (Recall that a connected component of a subset S of $\mathbb{R}^d$ is a maximal nonempty subset $A \subseteq S$ for which there is a continuous curve connecting any two points in A.) We can think of this as a generalization of the notion of the number of solutions of a system of equations. It turns out that we need only concern ourselves with systems of equations that are not degenerate in the following sense. (Here, for a function $f : \mathbb{R}^d \to \mathbb{R}^l$, if $f(a) = (f_1(a), \ldots, f_l(a))$, then the *Jacobian* of f at $a \in \mathbb{R}^d$, denoted $f'(a)$, is the $d \times l$ matrix with entry i,j equal to $D_i f_j(a)$, the partial derivative of $f_j(a)$ with respect to the ith component of $a = (a_1, \ldots, a_d)$.)

---

† that is, the first p derivatives of f are defined and are continuous functions.

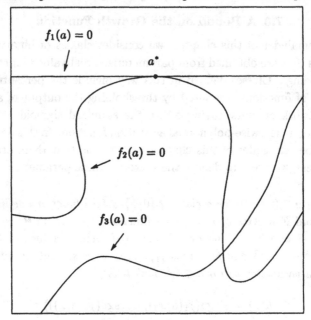

Fig. 7.2. An example illustrating Definition 7.4. The set $\{f_1, f_2, f_3\}$ does not have regular zero-set intersections, since the Jacobian of the function (f_1, f_2) : $\mathbb{R}^2 \to \mathbb{R}^2$ has rank 1 at a^*.

Definition 7.4 *A set $\{f_1, \dots, f_k\}$ of differentiable functions mapping from $\mathbb{R}^d$ to $\mathbb{R}$ is said to have* regular zero-set intersections *if, for all nonempty subsets $\{i_1, \dots, i_l\} \subseteq \{1, \dots, k\}$, the Jacobian of $(f_{i_1}, \dots, f_{i_l})$: $\mathbb{R}^d \to \mathbb{R}^l$ has rank l at every point a of the solution set*

$$\left\{ a \in \mathbb{R}^d : f_{i_1}(a) = \cdots = f_{i_l}(a) = 0 \right\}.$$

This definition forbids degenerate intersections of the zero-sets of the functions. For instance, if two zero-sets 'touch' at a point, so that the hyperplanes tangential to them at that point coincide, the functions do not have regular zero-set intersections (see Figure 7.2). More generally, when the zero-sets of more than two functions intersect at a point and the intersection of the tangent hyperplanes at that point has higher dimension than expected, the functions do not have regular zero-set intersections.

The main result of this chapter gives a growth function bound in terms of a *solution set components bound*. As in Chapter 3, we use the notation $CC(A)$ to denote the number of connected components of a set $A \subseteq \mathbb{R}^d$.

Definition 7.5 *Let G be a set of real-valued functions defined on $\mathbb{R}^d$. We say that G has* solution set components bound B *if for any $1 \leq k \leq d$ and any $\{f_1, \ldots, f_k\} \subseteq G$ that has regular zero-set intersections, we have*

$$CC \left(\bigcap_{i=1}^{k} \{a \in \mathbb{R}^d : f_i(a) = 0\} \right) \leq B.$$

Notice that the intersection of any $k > d$ zero-sets of functions with regular zero-set intersections must be empty (otherwise the rank condition in Definition 7.4 could not be satisfied). Hence we need only consider $k \leq d$ in the definition of the solution set components bound.

We shall always be concerned with classes F of real-valued functions defined on $\mathbb{R}^d \times X$, and with the solution set components bound for the class $G = \{a \mapsto f(a, x) : f \in F, x \in X\}$. We say that F has solution set components bound B when this is the case for the corresponding class G. Furthermore, we say that F is *closed under addition of constants* if, for any $c \in \mathbb{R}$, whenever $f \in F$, the function $(a, x) \mapsto f(a, x) + c$ is also in F.

With these definitions, we can present the main theorem of this chapter.

Theorem 7.6 *Suppose that F is a class of real-valued functions defined on $\mathbb{R}^d \times X$, and that H is a k-combination of $\mathrm{sgn}(F)$. If F is closed under addition of constants, has solution set components bound B, and functions in F are C^d in their parameters, then*

$$\Pi_H(m) \leq B \sum_{i=0}^{d} \binom{mk}{i} \leq B \left(\frac{emk}{d} \right)^d,$$

for $m \geq d/k$.

As an example, suppose H is the class of functions computed by the simple perceptron on $\mathbb{R}^d$. Then the parameter space is $\mathbb{R}^{d+1}$ and we can define F as the class of functions f satisfying

$$f(a, x) = \sum_{i=1}^{d} x_i a_i + a_0 + c,$$

for some c in $\mathbb{R}$, where $a = (a_0, a_1, \ldots, a_d)$. (We include the redundant constant c so that F is closed under addition of constants.) In this case, F has solution set components bound $B = 1$. Also, functions in F are

C^∞ in their parameters and H is a 1-combination of $\mathrm{sgn}(F)$, so

$$\Pi_H(m) \le \sum_{i=0}^{d+1} \binom{m}{i}.$$

Notice that

$$\sum_{i=0}^{d+1} \binom{m}{i} = 1 + \sum_{i=1}^{d+1} \left(\binom{m-1}{i} + \binom{m-1}{i-1} \right)$$

$$= 2 \sum_{i=0}^{d} \binom{m-1}{i} + \binom{m-1}{d+1},$$

so this bound is larger than the correct value (see Theorem 3.1) by $\binom{m-1}{d+1}$. However, the bound on the VC-dimension that is implied by Theorem 7.6 is tight.

7.4 Proof of the Growth Function Bound

The remainder of this chapter is more technical than most other parts of the book. The reader who is happy to accept Theorem 7.6 on trust can proceed to Chapter 8 (perhaps after reading the first paragraph of Section 7.5), without suffering much loss of continuity.

Growth function and connected components in parameter space

Recall that in the proof of the growth function bound for the perceptron, we first related the number of dichotomies of a set of input points x_i to the number of cells in the partition of the parameter space defined by the equations $w^T x_i - \theta = 0$ (Lemma 3.2). The following lemma shows that we can do this more generally, for any class that is a k-combination of thresholded real-valued functions. In this case, we relate the growth function to the number of connected components of the complement of certain zero-sets of functions that have regular zero-set intersections. (For the simple perceptron, this is equivalent to the condition that the examples are in general position.)

We first need the following lemma, which shows that almost all shifts of a set of functions result in a set that has regular zero-set intersections. We use this to show that we can always perturb the problem to give a new collection of zero-sets that have regular intersections, without decreasing the number of dichotomies.

Lemma 7.7 *Given a set $\{f_1, \ldots, f_k\}$ of C^d functions that map from $\mathbb{R}^d$ to $\mathbb{R}$, the set*

$$S = \{\lambda \in \mathbb{R}^k : \{f_1 - \lambda_1, \ldots, f_k - \lambda_k\} \text{ does not have}$$
$$\text{regular zero-set intersections}\}$$

has measure† 0.

Proof Consider a subset A of $\{f_1, \ldots, f_k\}$; without loss of generality suppose it is $\{f_1, \ldots, f_l\}$. If we define $f : \mathbb{R}^d \to \mathbb{R}^l$ as $f = (f_1, \ldots, f_l)$, Sard's Theorem (see Appendix 1) implies that the set

$$S_A = \{y \in \mathbb{R}^l : \exists x \in \mathbb{R}^d \text{ s.t. } f(x) = y \text{ and rank} f'(x) < l\}$$

has measure 0. Let $T_A = (\mathbb{R}^l - S_A) \times \mathbb{R}^{k-l}$. Clearly, the complement of T_A has measure 0. We can construct the corresponding set $T_A \subseteq \mathbb{R}^k$ of 'regular values' for any subset A. It is easy to see that, if we choose λ from the intersection over all subsets A of the T_A, then $\{f_1 - \lambda_1, \ldots, f_k - \lambda_k\}$ has regular zero-set intersections, so $S \subseteq \mathbb{R}^k - \bigcap_A T_A$. But we can write

$$\mathbb{R}^k - \bigcap_A T_A = \bigcup_A \left(\mathbb{R}^k - T_A\right),$$

which is a finite union of measure 0 sets, and hence has measure 0. So S has measure 0. $\square$

Lemma 7.8 *Let F be a class of real-valued functions defined on $\mathbb{R}^d \times X$ that is closed under addition of constants. Suppose that the functions in F are continuous in their parameters and let H be a k-combination of $\mathrm{sgn}(F)$. Then for some functions $f_1, \ldots, f_k$ in F and some examples $x_1, \ldots, x_m$ in X, the set*

$$\{a \mapsto f_i(a, x_j) : i = 1, \ldots, k, j = 1, \ldots, m\}$$

has regular zero-set intersections and the number of connected components of the set

$$\mathbb{R}^d - \bigcup_{i=1}^{k} \bigcup_{j=1}^{m} \{a \in \mathbb{R}^d : f_i(a, x_j) = 0\}$$

is at least $\Pi_H(m)$.

† See Section A1.3.

Proof Since H is a k-combination of sgn(F), we can fix functions $f_1, \ldots, f_k$ in F and $g : \{0,1\}^k \to \{0,1\}$ that give the parameterized representation

$$h(x) = g(\text{sgn}(f_1(a,x)), \ldots, \text{sgn}(f_k(a,x))))$$

for functions h in H. Fix arbitrary $x_1, \ldots, x_m$ in X. For each dichotomy computed by some function h in H, there must be a corresponding a in $\mathbb{R}^d$ satisfying

$$h(x_j) = g\left(\text{sgn}(f_1(a,x_j)), \ldots, \text{sgn}(f_k(a,x_j))\right)$$

for $j = 1, \ldots, m$. We want to relate the number of these dichotomies to the number of connected components of a certain set in the parameter space. To this end, consider the zero-sets in parameter space of the functions $a \mapsto f_i(a,x_j)$:

$$\left\{ a \in \mathbb{R}^d : f_i(a,x_j) = 0 \right\},$$

for $j = 1, 2, \ldots, m$ and $i = 1, 2, \ldots, k$. These sets split the parameter space into a number of cells, each of which is a connected component of the set

$$S = \mathbb{R}^d - \bigcup_{i=1}^{k} \bigcup_{j=1}^{m} \left\{ a \in \mathbb{R}^d : f_i(a,x_j) = 0 \right\}. \tag{7.2}$$

Figure 7.3 shows an example of the cells defined by these zero-sets, with $k = m = 2$.

If two parameters a_1 and a_2 in S give distinct dichotomies of the set $\{x_1, \ldots, x_m\}$, then a_1 and a_2 lie in distinct cells of S. (This is true because if a_1 and a_2 give distinct dichotomies, there must be some i and j such that one of $f_i(a_1, x_j)$ and $f_i(a_2, x_j)$ is positive and the other negative. Then the continuity of f_i with respect to its parameters implies that, for any continuous curve connecting a_1 and a_2, there must be a point on that curve where $f_i(a, x_j) = 0$.)

It is possible that we may be forced to consider parameters that lie on one of the zero-sets. In the case of the perceptron, we could adjust the offset parameter θ to ensure that any dichotomy can be computed with parameters that do not lie on any boundary set (where $w^T x_i - \theta = 0$ for some x_i), so we needed only to count the number of $(n+1)$-dimensional cells in parameter space. In the more general case we consider here, there might be dichotomies that can *only* be computed by parameters lying on some zero-set. In this case, we perturb the zero-sets by considering $f_i(a, x_j) - \lambda_{i,j} = 0$ for some small $\lambda_{i,j}$, instead of $f_i(a, x_j) = 0$. This

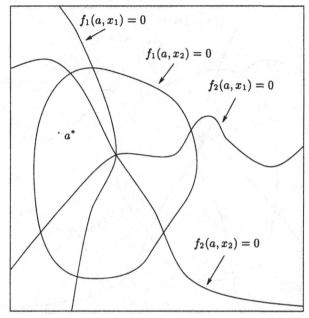

$f_1(a, x_1) = 0$

$f_1(a, x_2) = 0$

$f_2(a, x_1) = 0$

· a^*

$f_2(a, x_2) = 0$

Fig. 7.3. The connected components of the set S of Equation (7.2).

will ensure that dichotomies that previously could only be computed by parameters lying on the zero-set can be computed by parameters that lie strictly inside a distinct cell in the new (perturbed) partition of the parameter space.

For the example illustrated in Figure 7.3, the zero-sets of $f_1(a, x_1)$, $f_2(a, x_1)$, and $f_2(a, x_2)$ intersect at a single point. Suppose that the signs of these functions are such that the point a^* shown in the figure satisfies $f_1(a^*, x_1) > 0$, $f_2(a^*, x_1) < 0$, and $f_2(a^*, x_2) < 0$. Then the only parameter for which we have $\text{sgn}(f_1(\cdot, x_1)) = \text{sgn}(f_2(\cdot, x_1)) = \text{sgn}(f_2(\cdot, x_2)) = 1$—which corresponds to $f_1(a, x_1) \geq 0$, $f_2(a, x_1) \geq 0$, and $f_2(a, x_2) \geq 0$—is the intersection point of the three zero-sets. Figure 7.4 shows the situation when we replace $f_2(a, x_1)$ by $f_2(a, x_1) + \epsilon$; the shaded region in the figure marks parameters that do not lie on any of the zero-sets, but ensure that the three functions are nonnegative.

Now, suppose that $\left| H_{|\{x_1, \ldots, x_m\}} \right| = N$, and choose parameter vectors $a_1, \ldots, a_N$ from $\mathbb{R}^d$ so that for each distinct dichotomy there is a corresponding a_l. (Some of the a_l might lie in the zero-set of one of the

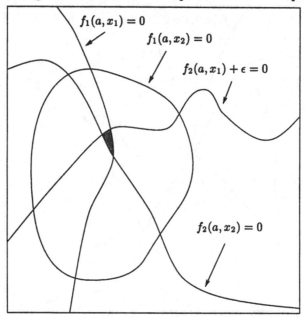

Fig. 7.4. A perturbed version of the arrangement of zero-sets in Figure 7.3. The shaded region is a new connected component that results from the perturbation.

functions $f_i(\cdot, x_j)$.) Choose ϵ strictly between 0 and

$$\min\{|f_i(a_l, x_j)| : f_i(a_l, x_j) < 0, 1 \le i \le k, 1 \le j \le m, 1 \le l \le N\}$$

(and choose any $\epsilon > 0$ if this set is empty). Then for any sequence $(\lambda_{1,1}, \ldots, \lambda_{k,m})$ from $(0, \epsilon)^{km}$, consider the sets

$$\{a \in \mathbb{R}^d : f_i(a, x_j) = -\lambda_{i,j}\}$$

for $i = 1, \ldots, k$ and $j = 1, \ldots, m$, and the complement of their union,

$$R = \mathbb{R}^d - \bigcup_{i=1}^{k} \bigcup_{j=1}^{m} \{a \in \mathbb{R}^d : f_i(a, x_j) = -\lambda_{i,j}\}.$$

Clearly, the choice of ϵ implies that all of the a_l's lie in R. In fact, each a_l must lie in a distinct connected component of R. To see this, notice that since a_1 and a_2 give rise to distinct dichotomies, there is some i and j such that $\text{sgn}(f_i(a_1, x_j)) \ne \text{sgn}(f_i(a_2, x_j))$. Without loss of generality, assume $f_i(a_1, x_j) \ge 0$ and $f_i(a_2, x_j) < 0$. Clearly, $f_i(a_1, x_j) > -\lambda_{i,j}$

and, by the choice of ϵ, $f_i(a_2, x_j) < -\epsilon < -\lambda_{i,j}$, which implies a_1 and a_2 are in distinct connected components of R.

It follows that, whatever the choice of the $\lambda_{i,j}$ (subject to $0 < \lambda_{i,j} < \epsilon$), for each dichotomy of $\{x_1, \ldots, x_m\}$ there corresponds at least one distinct connected component of R.

By Lemma 7.7, we can choose suitable values of $\lambda_{1,1}, \ldots, \lambda_{k,m}$ such that the set of functions

$$\left\{ \tilde{f}_i(\cdot, x_j) = f_i(\cdot, x_j) - \lambda_{i,j} : i = 1, \ldots, k, \ j = 1, \ldots, m \right\}$$

both has regular zero-set intersections and satisfies

$$\mathrm{CC}\left(\mathbb{R}^d - \bigcup_{i=1}^{k} \bigcup_{j=1}^{m} \left\{ a \in \mathbb{R}^d : \tilde{f}_i(a, x_j) = 0 \right\} \right) \geq N.$$

This is because the set of suitable $\lambda_{i,j}$ contains the intersection of a set of positive measure with the complement of a set of zero measure, and so is nonempty. The functions $\tilde{f}_i$ are in F because it is closed under addition of constants. The result follows. □

Bounding the number of connected components: the regular case

In the proof of the growth function bound for the simple perceptron, we used an inductive argument to count the number of cells in an arrangement of hyperplanes (Lemma 3.3). In this section, we use a very similar inductive argument to give a bound on the number of connected components of the set described in Lemma 7.8, in terms of the number of connected components of the solution set of a system of equations involving the functions $f_i(\cdot, x_j)$. (In the case of the simple perceptron, the number of connected components of the solution set is never more than one.) In this lemma, and in what follows, we use the convention that $\bigcap_{i \in \emptyset} S_i = \mathbb{R}^d$ for subsets $S_i \subseteq \mathbb{R}^d$.

Lemma 7.9 *Let $\{f_1, \ldots, f_k\}$ be a set of differentiable functions that map from $\mathbb{R}^d$ to $\mathbb{R}$, with regular zero-set intersections. For each i, define Z_i to be the zero-set of f_i: $Z_i = \{a \in \mathbb{R}^d : f_i(a) = 0\}$. Then*

$$\mathrm{CC}\left(\mathbb{R}^d - \bigcup_{i=1}^{k} Z_i \right) \leq \sum_{S \subseteq \{1, \ldots, k\}} \mathrm{CC}\left(\bigcap_{i \in S} Z_i \right).$$

The proof requires two lemmas. The first shows that if we take a connected component of a set defined by some of the zero-sets, and remove a connected component of its intersection with another of the zero-sets, the set is split into no more than two pieces. We omit the proof, which uses ideas from point set topology. (See the Bibliographic Notes section.)

Lemma 7.10 *Define a set of functions* $\{f_1, \dots, f_k\}$ *as in Lemma 7.9, and define sets* $S_1, \dots, S_{k-1}$ *so that for* $i = 1, \dots, k-1$, *either* $S_i = \{a \in \mathbb{R}^d : f_i(a) = 0\}$ *or* $S_i = \{a \in \mathbb{R}^d : f_i(a) \neq 0\}$. *Let* C *be a connected component of* $\cap_{i=1}^{k-1} S_i$, *and let* C' *be a connected component of* $C \cap \{a \in \mathbb{R}^d : f_k(a) = 0\}$. *Then* $C - C'$ *has no more than two connected components.*

The second lemma we need gives a result analogous to the induction step in the argument used to bound the growth function of the simple perceptron.

Lemma 7.11 *Define a set of functions* $\{f_1, \dots, f_k\}$ *and the zero-sets* $Z_1, \dots, Z_k$ *as in Lemma 7.9. Let* $I \subseteq \{1, \dots, k\}$ *and define* $M = \bigcap_{i \in I} Z_i$. *Define* $b = k - |I|$ *and let* $\{M_1, \dots, M_b\} = \{Z_i : i \notin I\}$. *Then*

$$\mathrm{CC}\left(M - \bigcup_{j=1}^{b} M_j\right) \leq \mathrm{CC}\left(M - \bigcup_{j=1}^{b-1} M_j\right) + \mathrm{CC}\left(M \cap M_b - \bigcup_{j=1}^{b-1} M_j\right).$$

Figure 7.5 illustrates the case in which $M = \mathbb{R}^3$ ($I = \emptyset$), and M_1, M_2, and M_3 are planes. Here, $M - \bigcup_{j=1}^{3} M_j$ consists of eight cells, bounded by the three planes, $M - \bigcup_{j=1}^{2} M_j$ consists of four cells, and $M \cap M_3 - \bigcup_{j=1}^{2} M_j$ consists of four cells, bounded by the bold lines in the figure. (Compare Figure 7.5 with Figure 3.2.)

Proof Let $S = M - \bigcup_{j=1}^{b-1} M_j$. Suppose that $\mathrm{CC}(S) = N$. We wish to show that removing M_b from S increases the number of connected components from N to no more than

$$N + \mathrm{CC}\left(M \cap M_b - \bigcup_{j=1}^{b-1} M_j\right).$$

Let $\{C_1, \dots, C_N\}$ be the connected components of S. Consider one of these components, C_j. Let A_1 be a connected component of $C_j \cap M_b$.

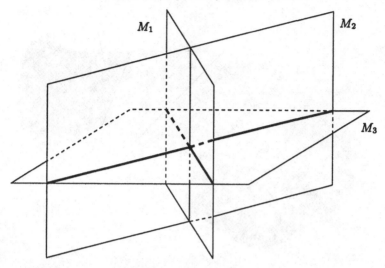

Fig. 7.5. An example of zero-sets M_1, M_2, and M_3 in $M = \mathbb{R}^3$. (See Lemma 7.11.) The intersections of M_3 ($= M \cap M_3$) with M_1 and M_2 are shown as bold lines.

(See Figure 7.6.) By Lemma 7.10 (with $C = C_j$ and $C' = A_1$), removing A_1 splits C_j into no more than two connected components. Consider a second component A_2 of $C_j \cap M_b$. Since it is disjoint from A_1, it lies entirely within one connected component of $C_j - A_1$. We have established that $C_j - A_1$ has at most two components. Let us suppose that its components are D_1 and D_2 (where we take $D_1 = \emptyset$ if in fact $C_j - A_1$ has just one component), and choose the labels of D_1 and D_2 so that $A_2 \cap D_1 = \emptyset$. (See Figure 7.6.) By Lemma 7.10 (with $C = D_2$ and $C' = A_2$), $CC(D_2 - A_2) \leq 2$, and so

$$
\begin{aligned}
CC(C_j - (A_1 \cup A_2)) &= CC((C_j - A_1) - A_2) \\
&= CC((D_1 - A_2) \cup (D_2 - A_2)) \\
&= CC(D_1 \cup (D_2 - A_2)) \\
&\leq 1 + CC(D_2 - A_2) \leq 3.
\end{aligned}
$$

Continuing in this way, considering in turn further components of $C_j \cap M_b$, we obtain

$$
CC(C_j - M_b) \leq CC(C_j \cap M_b) + 1.
$$

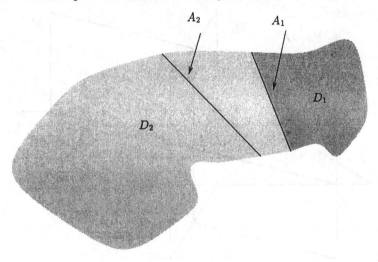

Fig. 7.6. A connected component C_j of S, as described in the proof of Lemma 7.11. The bold lines, A_1 and A_2, are connected components of $C_j \cap M_b$. The shaded regions, D_1 and D_2, are the two components of $C_j - A_1$.

Hence, writing S as a disjoint (and disconnected) union of the C_j, we have

$$
\begin{aligned}
\mathrm{CC}\left(M - \bigcup_{j=1}^{b} M_j \right) &= \mathrm{CC}\left(S - M_b \right) \\
&= \mathrm{CC}\left(\bigcup_{j=1}^{N} C_j - M_b \right) \\
&= \sum_{j=1}^{N} \mathrm{CC}\left(C_j - M_b \right) \\
&\leq \sum_{j=1}^{N} \left(\mathrm{CC}\left(C_j \cap M_b \right) + 1 \right) \\
&= \mathrm{CC}\left(\bigcup_{j=1}^{N} \left(C_j \cap M_b \right) \right) + N \\
&= \mathrm{CC}\left(S \cap M_b \right) + \mathrm{CC}(S),
\end{aligned}
$$

which is what we require.   □

Proof (of Lemma 7.9)

We shall prove that the following proposition, (P_b), is true for any $b \in \mathbb{N} \cup \{0\}$. The lemma will follow from the case $b = k$.

(P_b) Suppose $k \geq b$. Define functions $\{f_1, \ldots, f_k\}$ and their zero-sets $Z_1, \ldots, Z_k$ as in Lemma 7.9. Let $I \subseteq \{1, \ldots, k\}$ such that $|I| = k - b$. Define $M = \bigcap_{i \in I} Z_i$ (and recall that we define $\bigcap_{i \in \emptyset} Z_i = \mathbb{R}^d$), and let $\{M_1, \ldots, M_b\} = \{Z_i : i \notin I\}$. Then

$$\text{CC}\left(M - \bigcup_{i=1}^{b} M_i\right) \leq \sum_{S \subseteq \{1,\ldots,b\}} \text{CC}\left(M \cap \bigcap_{i \in S} M_i\right),$$

where, if $b = 0$, the right-hand side is to be interpreted as $\text{CC}(M)$.

Clearly, (P_0) is true, since it states that $\text{CC}(M) \leq \text{CC}(M)$ for $M = \bigcap_{i=1}^{k} Z_i$. Suppose that (P_b) is true, and consider $k \geq b + 1$ and $I \subseteq \{1, \ldots, k\}$ with $|I| = k - (b+1)$. Let $M = \bigcap_{i \in I} Z_i$, and define the zero sets $\{M_1, \ldots, M_{b+1}\} = \{Z_i : i \notin I\}$. Then Lemma 7.11 and (P_b) imply that

$$\text{CC}\left(M - \bigcup_{i=1}^{b+1} M_i\right)$$
$$\leq \text{CC}\left(M - \bigcup_{i=1}^{b} M_i\right) + \text{CC}\left(M \cap M_{b+1} - \bigcup_{i=1}^{b} M_i\right)$$
$$\leq \sum_{S \subseteq \{1,\ldots,b\}} \text{CC}\left(M \cap \bigcap_{i \in S} M_i\right) +$$
$$\sum_{S \subseteq \{1,\ldots,b\}} \text{CC}\left(M \cap M_{b+1} \cap \bigcap_{i \in S} M_i\right).$$

Notice that the first sum in this expression includes all subsets of the set $\{1, \ldots, b+1\}$ that do not contain $b+1$, and the second can be written as a sum of the same form over all subsets that contain $b+1$. It follows that

$$\text{CC}\left(M - \bigcup_{i=1}^{b+1} M_i\right) \leq \sum_{S \subseteq \{1,\ldots,b+1\}} \text{CC}\left(M \cap \bigcap_{i \in S} M_i\right),$$

and hence (P_{b+1}) is true. $\square$

Proof of Theorem 7.6

The proof of Theorem 7.6 is now immediate. The first inequality follows from Lemmas 7.8, and 7.9, taking the zero-sets Z_i in Lemma 7.9 to be those of the mk functions $a \mapsto f_i(a, x_j)$ defined on the parameter space $\mathbb{R}^d$, for $i = 1, 2, \ldots, k$ and $j = 1, 2, \ldots, m$. This gives the bound

$$\Pi_H(m) \leq \max_{Z_i} \sum_{S \subseteq \{1, \ldots, mk\}} \mathrm{CC} \left(\bigcap_{i \in S} Z_i \right)$$

$$\leq B \sum_{j=0}^{d} \binom{mk}{j},$$

where the maximum is over the zero-sets Z_i that have regular intersections, and the second inequality follows from the definition of the solution set components bound and the fact that the intersection of more than d such zero-sets is always empty.

The second inequality of Theorem 7.6 follows from Theorem 3.7, provided $m \geq d/k$.

7.5 More on Solution Set Components Bounds

In finding a solution set components bound for a set G of functions, it is often convenient to express the functions in G as functions of additional variables representing the result of intermediate calculations. For example, if, while computing $f(a)$, we calculate b_1, then b_2, and so on up to b_n, and we use these to calculate $f(a)$, then we can write f in the form

$$f(a) = \tilde{f}(a, b_1, \ldots, b_n),$$

where each b_i is a function only of a and $b_1, \ldots, b_{i-1}$. The theorem in this section shows that we can consider the variables $b_1, \ldots, b_n$ as extra parameters, and that we can obtain a solution set components bound for G from a bound for the class of functions involving these extra parameters. The situation is, however, not quite so simple: in calculating solution set components bounds for a function class, we need to consider simultaneously $k \leq d$ functions f of this form, and we must expect each to compute its own independent intermediate variables b_i. Hence, using n intermediate variables to compute each function f corresponds to the addition of dn new parameters, n for each of the d functions. (Typically, more parameters corresponds to a larger solution set components bound.) To simplify notation in the theorem and proof, when we write a function of these $dn + d$ arguments as a function of fewer arguments, it indicates that the function does not depend on the other arguments.

First, we formalize the notion of using additional, or 'intermediate', variables. In this definition, an intermediate calculation is expressed as $b = \phi(a)$ for some function ϕ. To ensure that the intermediate variables take the appropriate values, we use the trick of defining a function g for which the constraint $b = \phi(a)$ is satisfied when $g(a, b) = 0$. This implicit definition of the intermediate variables is convenient, since we are only interested in the behaviour of functions around their zero-sets.

Definition 7.12 *For a set G of differentiable real-valued functions defined on $\mathbb{R}^d$ and a set $\tilde{G}$ of differentiable real-valued functions defined on $\mathbb{R}^{d(n+1)}$, we say that $\tilde{G}$ computes G with n intermediate variables if, for any $1 \le k \le d$ and $\{f_1, \ldots, f_k\} \subseteq G$, there is a set*

$$\left\{ \tilde{f}_1, g_{1,1}, \ldots, g_{1,n}, \ldots, \tilde{f}_k, g_{k,1}, \ldots, g_{k,n} \right\} \subseteq \tilde{G}$$

that satisfies the following conditions.

(i) *For $i = 1, \ldots, k$, there are differentiable functions $\phi_{i,1}, \ldots, \phi_{i,n}$: $\mathbb{R}^{d(n+1)} \to \mathbb{R}$ which can be written*

$$\phi_{i,1}(a, b) = \phi_{i,1}(a)$$
$$\phi_{i,j}(a, b) = \phi_{i,j}(a, b_{i,1}, \ldots, b_{i,j-1}) \text{ for } j = 2, \ldots, n$$

where $a \in \mathbb{R}^d$, and $b = (b_{1,1}, \ldots, b_{1,n}, \ldots, b_{d,n}) \in \mathbb{R}^{dn}$. (The function $\phi_{i,j}$ defines the intermediate variable $b_{i,j}$, and the $\phi_{i,j}$ are ordered so that their values depend only on previously computed intermediate variables.)

(ii) *For $i = 1, \ldots, k$, the functions $g_{i,1}, \ldots, g_{i,n}$ can be written as $g_{i,j}(a, b) = g_{i,j}(a, b_{i,1}, \ldots, b_{i,j})$ for all a, b, and $j = 1, \ldots, n$. (That is, the function $g_{i,j}$ depends only on previously computed intermediate variables, and on $b_{i,j}$.)*

(iii) *For $i = 1, \ldots, k$, and $l = 1, \ldots, n$, if $b_{i,j} = \phi_{i,j}(a, b)$ for all a, b, and $j < l$, then for all a and b we have*

$$g_{i,l}(a, b) = 0 \text{ if and only if } b_{i,l} = \phi_{i,l}(a, b)$$

and

$$D_{b_{i,l}} g_{i,l}(a, \phi_{i,1}(a, b), \ldots, \phi_{i,l}(a, b)) \neq 0.$$

(That is, the function $g_{i,j}$ implicitly defines the intermediate variable $b_{i,j}$. The derivative condition ensures that the zero-set intersections remain regular.)

(iv) *For all* $a \in \mathbb{R}^d$ *and* $b \in \mathbb{R}^{dn}$, *if* $b_{i,j} = \phi_{i,j}(a,b)$ *for* $i = 1, \ldots, k$ *and* $j = 1, \ldots, n$ *then*

$$f_i(a) = \tilde{f}_i\left(a, \phi_{1,1}(a,b), \ldots, \phi_{k,n}(a,b)\right)$$

for $i = 1, \ldots, n$.

Theorem 7.13 *For function classes G and $\tilde{G}$ and a positive integer n, if $\tilde{G}$ computes G with n intermediate variables, then any solution set components bound for $\tilde{G}$ is also a solution set components bound for G.*

The following lemma will be used in the inductive proof of Theorem 7.13. It shows that adding a single intermediate variable preserves both the number of connected components and the regularity of the zero-set intersections. As explained above, we specify the value of the intermediate variable $b \in \mathbb{R}$ implicitly through the equation $g(a,b) = 0$, which implies $b = \phi(a)$ in the zero-set intersection.

Lemma 7.14 *Suppose $f_1, \ldots, f_k : \mathbb{R}^d \to \mathbb{R}$, $\tilde{f}_1, \ldots, \tilde{f}_k : \mathbb{R}^{d+1} \to \mathbb{R}$, and $\phi : \mathbb{R}^d \to \mathbb{R}$ are differentiable functions satisfying $f_i(a) = \tilde{f}_i(a, \phi(a))$ for all $a \in \mathbb{R}^d$. Let $g : \mathbb{R}^{d+1} \to \mathbb{R}$ be a differentiable function such that, for all $a \in \mathbb{R}^d$,*

$$g(a,b) = 0 \qquad \text{if and only if} \qquad b = \phi(a),$$

and

$$D_b g(a, \phi(a)) \neq 0.$$

Define

$$Z = \bigcap_{i=1}^{k} \{a : f_i(a) = 0\},$$

$$\tilde{Z} = \{(a,b) : g(a,b) = 0\} \cap \bigcap_{i=1}^{k} \left\{(a,b) : \tilde{f}_i(a,b) = 0\right\}.$$

Then we have:

(i) $\mathrm{CC}(Z) = \mathrm{CC}(\tilde{Z})$, *and*

(ii) *for $a \in Z$, the Jacobian of $(f_1, \ldots, f_k)$ at a has rank k if and only if the Jacobian of $(\tilde{f}_1, \ldots, \tilde{f}_k, g)$ at $(a, \phi(a))$ has rank $k+1$.*

Proof

1. The transformation $a \mapsto (a, \phi(a))$ is a one-to-one function mapping from Z to $\tilde{Z}$. Clearly, this transformation preserves connectedness, so $CC(Z) = CC(\tilde{Z})$.

2. Define $f = (f_1, \ldots, f_k)$ and $\tilde{f} = (\tilde{f}_1, \ldots, \tilde{f}_k)$. Fix a point $(a, \phi(a))$ in $\tilde{Z}$. In what follows, we consider the Jacobians of f and $(\tilde{f}, g)$ at a and $(a, \phi(a))$ respectively, but to simplify notation we write these as f' and $(\tilde{f}, g)'$, dropping the a and $(a, \phi(a))$.

We can write the Jacobian of $(\tilde{f}, g)$ as

$$(\tilde{f}, g)' = \left(\begin{array}{cc} D_a \tilde{f} & D_a g \\ D_b \tilde{f} & D_b g \end{array} \right).$$

Let $\rho(J)$ denote the rank of a matrix J. Then, since $D_b g \neq 0$ and

$$\left(\begin{array}{cc} I_k & 0 \\ -\frac{D_b \tilde{f}}{D_b g} & 1 \end{array} \right)$$

is a full rank $(k+1) \times (k+1)$ matrix (where I_k is the $k \times k$ identity matrix), we have

$$
\begin{aligned}
\rho((\tilde{f}, g)') &= \rho \left(\begin{array}{cc} D_a \tilde{f} & D_a g \\ D_b \tilde{f} & D_b g \end{array} \right) \\
&= \rho \left(\left(\begin{array}{cc} D_a \tilde{f} & D_a g \\ D_b \tilde{f} & D_b g \end{array} \right) \left(\begin{array}{cc} I_k & 0 \\ -\frac{D_b \tilde{f}}{D_b g} & 1 \end{array} \right) \right) \\
&= \rho \left(\begin{array}{cc} D_a \tilde{f} - \frac{D_b \tilde{f}}{D_b g} D_a g & D_a g \\ 0 & D_b g \end{array} \right) \\
&= \rho \left(D_a \tilde{f} - \frac{D_b \tilde{f}}{D_b g} D_a g \right) + 1.
\end{aligned}
$$

Now, since $g(a, \phi(a)) = 0$ for all a, $D_a g + D_b g \, \phi' = 0$. It follows that $\phi' = -D_a g / D_b g$, and hence

$$f' = D_a \tilde{f} + D_b \tilde{f} \, \phi' = D_a \tilde{f} - \frac{D_b \tilde{f}}{D_b g} D_a g,$$

so $\rho((\tilde{f}, g)') = \rho(f') + 1$, as required. $\square$

We can now prove Theorem 7.13.

Proof (of **Theorem 7.13**) Suppose $S_1 = \{f_1, \ldots, f_k\} \subseteq G$ has regular zero-set intersections in $\mathbb{R}^d$. Let

$$S_2 = \left\{ \tilde{f}_1, \ldots, \tilde{f}_k, g_{1,1}, \ldots, g_{k,n} \right\}$$

be the corresponding functions in $\tilde{G}$ satisfying Definition 7.12. We prove by induction that S_1 has regular zero-set intersections if and only if S_2 does, and that the numbers of connected components in their zero-set intersections are the same, from which the theorem follows.

The induction proceeds over a sequence of function classes, involving successively more of the additional variables $b_{i,j}$. To start with, define $G_0 = \{\tilde{f}_1^0, \ldots, \tilde{f}_k^0\}$, with $\tilde{f}_i^0 = f_i$. (So $G_0 = S_1$.) Now, define the set G_1 of functions mapping from $\mathbb{R}^{d+1}$ to $\mathbb{R}$ to be $G_1 = \left\{ \tilde{f}_1^1, \ldots, \tilde{f}_k^1, g_{1,1} \right\}$, with

$$\tilde{f}_i^1(a, b) = f_i(a)$$

for $i = 2, \ldots, k$ and all a, and

$$\tilde{f}_1^1(a, \phi_{1,1}(a)) = f_1(a),$$

for all a. Notice that we can think of $g_{1,1}$ as a function defined on $\mathbb{R}^{d+1}$. Lemma 7.14 implies that G_0 has regular zero-set intersections if and only if the same is true of G_1, and that the zero-set intersections have the same number of connected components. We proceed in this fashion, iteratively adding a parameter $(b_{i,j})$, modifying a function $(\tilde{f}_i^l)$ to depend on the new parameter, and adding another function $(g_{i,j})$ that implicitly defines the value of the new parameter in its zero-set. Finally, we obtain the set G_{kn}, which is the set of restrictions of functions in S_2 to $\mathbb{R}^{d+kn}$, so the result follows.   □

7.6 Bibliographical Notes

Several examples are known of well-behaved activation functions giving rise to small networks with infinite VC-dimension. The first was given by Sontag (1992). See also (Macintyre and Sontag, 1993). Sontag's example has the added feature that, for any set of points in $\mathbb{R}$, and any desired dichotomy, it is easy to find parameters for a two-layer network with two computation units in the first layer, so that the network computes the desired dichotomy of the points. (This implies that proving lower bounds on the computational complexity of learning two-layer sigmoid networks requires some strong conditions on the sigmoid functions—see Chapter 25. Of course, results from Chapter 5 show that such computational difficulties are irrelevant in this case, since the VC-dimension of the function class is infinite.) Krzyżak, Linder and Lugosi (1996) give a similar example for radial basis function networks. Devroye et al. (1996) give an example of a sigmoid network in which the activation function is again analytic and monotonically increasing, but also convex to the left of zero and concave to the right. They showed that a two-layer network with eight first-layer units of this kind has infinite VC-dimension. The example we give in Section 7.2 is simpler. The elegant proof of Lemma 7.2 was suggested by Jon Baxter and Phil Long.

The techniques for bounding the growth function that are described in the remainder of the chapter and in Chapter 8 are mainly due to Goldberg and Jerrum (1995). These ideas have a long history. The idea of counting the number of connected components in the partition of parameter space defined by the input points goes back to the growth function calculations for the simple perceptron. (See the bibliographical notes at the end of Chapter 3.) Goldberg and Jerrum gave bounds on the VC-dimension of function classes that are polynomial in their parameters; the idea of Lemma 7.8 arose in the proof of their result. A similar idea was independently suggested at the same time (and reported at the same conference, COLT'93) by Ben-David and Lindenbaum (1993). Both Ben-David and Lindenbaum's paper and an early version of Goldberg and Jerrum's paper used a result of Milnor (1964) that implies a bound on the number of connected components of the complement of the solution of a system of polynomial equations. Later versions of the Goldberg and Jerrum paper used the slightly stronger results of Warren (1968), who was studying approximation properties of polynomials, and apparently was unaware of Milnor's result. Following Goldberg and Jerrum, Karpinski and Macintyre (1997) noticed that a result developed by Warren as a tool could be used more generally: Lemma 7.9 was essentially in (Warren, 1968), and the proof of Lemma 7.10 is in (Warren, 1968). Karpinski and Macintyre showed how to tie these results together and use Sard's Theorem to reduce the problem to the regular case for C^∞ functions. They then used solution set components bounds for sets of functions involving exponentials to give VC-dimension bounds for sigmoid networks (we shall encounter these results in the next chapter). The idea of representing the computation of intermediate variables as the solution of another equation in an augmented set of parameters is also due to Karpinski and Macintyre.

8
Vapnik-Chervonenkis Dimension Bounds for Neural Networks

8.1 Introduction

In this chapter we apply the theory developed in the previous chapter to derive bounds on the VC-dimension for a number of specific types of neural network classes, including standard sigmoid networks.

8.2 Function Classes that are Polynomial in their Parameters

We first consider classes of functions that can be expressed as boolean combinations of thresholded real-valued functions, each of which is polynomial in its parameters. To apply Theorem 7.6 to obtain bounds on the VC-dimension for these classes, we need a solution set components bound (that is, a bound on the number of connected components in the intersection of zero-sets of polynomials). The following result will be useful for this. It follows from Bezout's Theorem (which describes the number of solutions of a non-degenerate system of polynomial equations). Here, the degree of a polynomial f of d variables is the maximum, over monomials appearing in f, of the sum of the exponents in the monomial.

Lemma 8.1 *Suppose $f : \mathbb{R}^d \to \mathbb{R}$ is a polynomial of degree l. Then the number of connected components of $\{a \in \mathbb{R}^d : f(a) = 0\}$ is no more than $l^{d-1}(l+2)$.*

Corollary 8.2 *For $l \in \mathbb{N}$, the set of degree l polynomials defined on $\mathbb{R}^d$ has solution set components bound $B = 2(2l)^d$.*

Proof Suppose $1 \leq k \leq d$ and that $f_1, \ldots, f_k$ are degree l polynomials defined on $\mathbb{R}^d$. Then the polynomial $\sum_{i=1}^{k} f_i^2$ has degree no more than

$2l$, and its zero-set is the intersection of the zero-sets of $\{f_1, \ldots, f_k\}$. Applying Lemma 8.1 gives the result. $\qquad\square$

Theorem 8.3 *Let F be a class of functions mapping from $\mathbb{R}^d \times X$ to $\mathbb{R}$ so that, for all $x \in X$ and $f \in F$, the function $a \mapsto f(a, x)$ is a polynomial on $\mathbb{R}^d$ of degree no more than l. Suppose that H is a k-combination of $\mathrm{sgn}(F)$. Then if $m \geq d/k$,*

$$\Pi_H(m) \leq 2 \left(\frac{2emkl}{d} \right)^d,$$

and hence $\mathrm{VCdim}(H) \leq 2d \log_2(12kl)$.

Proof From Theorem 7.6 and Corollary 8.2, we have

$$\Pi_H(m) \leq \sum_{i=0}^{d} \binom{mk}{i} 2(2l)^d,$$

and if $mk \geq d$, Theorem 3.7 shows that

$$\Pi_H(m) \leq 2(2l)^d \left(\frac{emk}{d} \right)^d = 2 \left(\frac{2emkl}{d} \right)^d.$$

To prove the bound on the VC-dimension, recall that if $\Pi_H(m) < 2^m$ then we have $\mathrm{VCdim}(H) < m$. Now, $2(2emkl/d)^d < 2^m$ if and only if $d(\log_2 m + \log_2(2ekl/d)) < m - 1$. But $\log_2 m \leq m/(2d) + \log_2(2d/(e \ln 2))$ (see (1.2) in Appendix 1), so it suffices to have $m > 2(d \log_2(4kl/\ln 2) + 1)$, which is implied by $m > 2d \log_2(12kl)$. $\qquad\square$

Theorem 8.3 is a powerful result; it can be used to give bounds on the VC-dimension of a function class in terms of the number of arithmetic operations required to compute the functions, as the following result demonstrates.

Theorem 8.4 *Suppose h is a function from $\mathbb{R}^d \times \mathbb{R}^n$ to $\{0, 1\}$ and let*

$$H = \left\{ x \mapsto h(a, x) : a \in \mathbb{R}^d \right\}$$

be the class determined by h. Suppose that h can be computed by an algorithm that takes as input the pair $(a, x) \in \mathbb{R}^d \times \mathbb{R}^n$ and returns $h(a, x)$ after no more than t operations of the following types:

- *the arithmetic operations $+$, $-$, $\times$, and $/$ on real numbers,*
- *jumps conditioned on $>$, $\geq$, $<$, $\leq$, $=$, and $\neq$ comparisons of real numbers, and*

- *output* 0 *or* 1.

Then $\text{VCdim}(H) \leq 4d(t+2)$.

Proof Let A denote the algorithm that computes h. We first show that any comparison that A makes can be expressed as a comparison of bounded degree polynomials in the parameters a. Then we show that the output of A can be expressed as a boolean function of the results of comparisons involving a bounded number of these polynomials. Theorem 8.3 then gives the result.

The degree of a rational function (a ratio of polynomials) is the sum of the degrees of the numerator and denominator polynomials. The result of an arithmetic operation on two rational functions can be expressed as a rational function with degree no more than the sum of the degrees. Furthermore, a comparison of two rational functions is equivalent to a comparison of two polynomials, with degree no more than the sum of the degrees of the rational functions. It follows that any comparison performed by A can be expressed as a comparison of polynomials of degree no more than 2^t.

The algorithm A can be expressed as a computation tree of depth no more than t, with each node corresponding to a comparison between polynomials, and each leaf corresponding to an output operation. There can be no more than $2^{t-1} - 1$ comparison nodes in this tree, so the number of distinct polynomials that are examined by the algorithm is no more than $2^{t-1} - 1$.

To invoke Theorem 8.3, we must express h as a fixed boolean combination of functions of the form $\text{sgn}(p_i(a))$ (where p_i is a polynomial). This involves only comparisons of the form $p_i(a) \geq 0$, so we may need to use a negated copy of each polynomial to allow the computation of the $>$, $\leq$, $=$, and $\neq$ comparisons using just the $\text{sgn}(\cdot)$ function. It follows that we can express h as a $(2^t - 2)$-combination of $\text{sgn}(F)$, where F is the class of polynomials of degree no more than 2^t. Theorem 8.3 shows that $\text{VCdim}(H) \leq 2d(2t + \log_2 12) < 4dt + 8d$. $\qquad \square$

This theorem has interesting consequences. If we consider a model of computing that only allows the standard arithmetic operations and comparisons with real numbers, then any class consisting of functions that are specified by a finite number of parameters and can be computed in finite time on such a computer has finite VC-dimension. Furthermore, if we consider a sequence of function classes computed in this way, with increasing dimension n of the input domain ($X = \mathbb{R}^n$), and with the number of parameters and the computation time growing only polynomially with n, then the VC-dimension also grows only polynomially. It follows that any class containing functions computable in time polynomial in the input dimension n has VC-dimension polynomial in n. The main result in Chapter 4 (Theorem 4.2) shows that this implies the sample complexity grows only polynomially with the input dimension.

The following result shows that the bound of Theorem 8.4 cannot be improved by more than a constant factor.

Theorem 8.5 *For all $d, t \geq 1$, there is a class H of functions, parameterized by d real numbers, that can be computed in time $O(t)$ (using the model of computation defined in Theorem 8.4), and that has* VCdim$(H) \geq dt$.

Proof The idea of the proof is to show that we can extract one of up to t bits from any of the d parameters in time $O(t)$ (with the input value specifying which parameter and which bit in that parameter). This means that we can shatter a set of dt input points.

More specifically, the algorithm we consider computes a function $h : \mathbb{R}^d \times \mathbb{R}^2 \to \{0, 1\}$. We shall define this function only for certain values of $a \in \mathbb{R}^d$ and $x \in \mathbb{R}^2$; it is easy to ensure that the algorithm halts in time $O(t)$ and outputs something for other parameter and input values.

Consider $x = (l, m) \in \{1, \dots, d\} \times \{1, \dots, t\}$. Let $a = (a_1, \dots, a_d)$ be a sequence of t-bit numbers in $[0, 1)$; explicitly, suppose $a_i = \sum_{j=1}^{t} a_{i,j} 2^{-j}$ for $a_{i_1}, \dots, a_{i,t} \in \{0, 1\}$. Then define

$$h(a, (l, m)) = a_{l,m}.$$

Clearly, h can be computed in time $O(t)$ by iteratively doubling, comparing with 1, and conditionally subtracting 1 from a_l. (We assume that $t = \Omega(d)$, since otherwise no algorithm can read the d parameters.) Since we can choose the $a_{i,j}$ arbitrarily, the set $\{1, \dots, d\} \times \{1, \dots, t\}$ (of size dt) is shattered by H. $\qquad\Box$

It is interesting to observe that Theorem 8.4 would no longer be true if we allowed computation of the floor function, $\lfloor \cdot \rfloor$, in unit time. In that case, there would be an algorithm to compute the function h of Theorem 8.5 in time† $O(\log_2(t))$, which would imply that there is a class H

---

† In fact, this observation and Theorem 8.4 show that in the model of computation defined in Theorem 8.4, taking the floor function of t-bit numbers takes time $\Omega(t/\log_2 t)$.

of functions that can be computed in time T and involving d parameters with $\text{VCdim}(H) = \Omega(2^T d)$. Similarly, if we allowed computation of the $\sin(\cdot)$ function in unit time, a constant time program could compute a class of functions defined by a single parameter but having infinite VC-dimension (see Lemma 7.2).

8.3 Piecewise-Polynomial Networks

As an easy example of the application of Theorem 8.4, we may consider the class of feed-forward linear threshold networks. Recall that Theorem 6.1 implies that the VC-dimension of the class of functions computed by a linear threshold network with W parameters (weights and thresholds) is $O(W \ln W)$. Since computing the output of a linear threshold network takes time $O(W)$, Theorem 8.4 immediately gives the following (slightly worse) bound.

Theorem 8.6 *Suppose N is a feed-forward linear threshold network with a total of W weights, and let H be the class of functions computed by this network. Then* $\text{VCdim}(H) = O(W^2)$.

This theorem can easily be generalized to networks with activation functions that are piecewise-polynomial. A piecewise-polynomial function $f : \mathbb{R} \to \mathbb{R}$ can be written as $f(\alpha) = \sum_{i=1}^{p} 1_{A(i)}(\alpha) f_i(\alpha)$, where $A(1), \ldots, A(p)$ are disjoint real intervals whose union is $\mathbb{R}$, and $f_1, \ldots, f_p$ are polynomials. We say that f has p pieces, and we define the degree of f as the largest degree of the polynomials f_i. Figure 8.1 shows a piecewise-polynomial activation function, which has three pieces and degree one. (In fact, Figure 1.3, which we described as the graph of the standard sigmoid function, illustrates a piecewise-polynomial activation function with 100 pieces and degree one, because this function was plotted using 100 line segments.)

Theorem 8.7 *Suppose N is a feed-forward network with a total of W weights and k computation units, in which the output unit is a linear threshold unit and every other computation unit has a piecewise-polynomial activation function with p pieces and degree no more than l. Then, if H is the class of functions computed by N, $\text{VCdim}(H) = O(W(W + kl \log_2 p))$.*

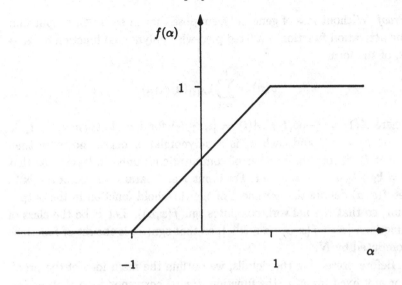

Fig. 8.1. A piecewise-linear activation function.

Proof To compute an activation function, we can determine the appropriate piece with $\lceil \log_2 p \rceil$ comparisons. Computing the value of the function takes an additional $O(l)$ steps. Hence, the total computation time is $O(W + kl \log_2 p)$, and Theorem 8.4 implies the result. $\square$

If the number of layers in the network is restricted, the following bound is better.

Theorem 8.8 *Suppose N is a feed-forward network of the form described in Theorem 8.7, with W weights, k computation units, and all non-output units having piecewise-polynomial activation functions with p pieces and degree no more than l. Suppose in addition that the computation units in the network are arranged in L layers, so that each unit has connections only from units in earlier layers. Then if H is the class of functions computed by N,*

$$\Pi_H(m) \le 2^L \left(2emkp(l+1)^{L-1} \right)^{WL},$$

and

$$\mathrm{VCdim}(H) \le 2WL\log_2(4WLpk/\ln 2) + 2WL^2\log_2(l+1) + 2L.$$

For fixed p and l, $\mathrm{VCdim}(H) = O(WL\log_2 W + WL^2)$.

Proof Without loss of generality, suppose that in each non-output unit the activation function is a fixed piecewise-polynomial function $\sigma : \mathbb{R} \to \mathbb{R}$, of the form

$$\sigma(u) = \sum_{i=1}^{p} 1_{A(i)}(u)\phi_i(u),$$

where $A(1) = (-\infty, t_1)$, $A(i) = [t_{i-1}, t_i)$ for $i = 2, \ldots, p$, $t_1 < t_2 < \cdots < t_p = \infty$, and each ϕ_i is a polynomial of degree no more than l. Let k_i denote the number of computational units in layer i, so that $k = k_1 + k_2 + \cdots + k_{L-1} + 1$. For input x and parameter vector $a \in \mathbb{R}^W$, let $f(x, a)$ denote the argument of the threshold function in the output unit, so that the network computes $\text{sgn}(f(x, a))$. Let F be the class of functions $\{x \mapsto f(x, a) : a \in \mathbb{R}^W\}$, so that $\text{sgn}(F)$ is the set of functions computed by N.

Before presenting the details, we outline the main idea of the proof. For any fixed input x, the function $f(x, a)$ corresponds to a piecewise-polynomial function in the parameters a, of bounded degree. Thus, the parameter domain $\mathbb{R}^W$ can be split into regions, and in each of these regions the function $f(x, \cdot)$ is polynomial. Theorem 8.3 shows that each region does not contribute much to the growth function. Taking the sum of these bounds over all regions gives the result.

Now, fix arbitrary $x_1, x_2, \ldots, x_m$ in X. We wish to bound

$$K = \left| \{ (\text{sgn}(f(x_1, a)), \ldots, \text{sgn}(f(x_m, a))) : a \in \mathbb{R}^W \} \right|.$$

Consider a partition $S = \{S_1, S_2, \ldots, S_N\}$ of the parameter domain $\mathbb{R}^W$. (So, $\bigcup_{i=1}^{N} S_i = \mathbb{R}^W$ and $S_i \cap S_j = \emptyset$ if $i \neq j$.) Clearly

$$K \leq \sum_{i=1}^{N} |\{ (\text{sgn}(f(x_1, a)), \ldots, \text{sgn}(f(x_m, a))) : a \in S_i \}|.$$

We choose the partition so that within each region S_i, the functions $f(x_1, \cdot), \ldots, f(x_m, \cdot)$ are all fixed polynomials of degree no more than $(l+1)^{L-1}$. Then, by Theorem 8.3, each term in this sum is no more than

$$2 \left(\frac{2em(l+1)^{L-1}}{W} \right)^W. \tag{8.1}$$

In the remainder of the proof, we define the partition and show that it is not too large. The partition is constructed recursively, through a sequence $S_1, S_2, \ldots, S_{L-1}$ of successive refinements. These partitions are constructed so that for any parameter value within a fixed element of partition S_n and for any unit in the first n layers, the net input to the unit lies within some fixed piece of the piecewise-polynomial activation function. In this way, we recursively construct the partition S_{L-1}, which defines regions of parameter space where the function f is polynomial in the parameters.

Let S_1 be a partition of $\mathbb{R}^W$ such that, for all $S \in S_1$, there are constants $b_{h,i,j} \in \{0, 1\}$ for which

$$\text{sgn}(p_{h,x_j}(a) - t_i) = b_{h,i,j} \qquad \text{for all } a \in S, \tag{8.2}$$

where $j \in \{1, \ldots, m\}$, $h \in \{1, \ldots, k_1\}$ and $i \in \{1, \ldots, p\}$, and where p_{h,x_j} is the affine function describing the net input to the h-th first layer unit, in response to x_j. Recall that t_i are the break-points of the piecewise-polynomial activation functions. Clearly, for any fixed S, any first layer unit, and any x_j, as a ranges over S the output of the first layer unit in response to x_j is a fixed polynomial in a. Note that the partition S_1 only distinguishes weights in the first layer of computation units. If we define H_1 as the set of functions

$$\left\{ (h, i, j) \mapsto \text{sgn}(p_{h,x_j}(a) - t_i) : a \in \mathbb{R}^W \right\},$$

then we can choose S_1 so that its size is no larger than $\Pi_{H_1}(mk_1p)$. If W_1 is the number of weights in the first layer, the functions in H_1 are thresholded versions of functions that are affine in these W_1 parameters, and so Theorem 8.3 implies that

$$|S_1| \le 2 \left(\frac{2emk_1p}{W_1} \right)^{W_1}.$$

(Notice that we can obtain a better bound from Theorem 3.1, but using the weaker consequence of Theorem 8.3 simplifies subsequent calculations, and only affects the final result by a constant factor.)

Now, let $W_1, \ldots, W_L$ be the number of variables used in computing the unit outputs up to layer $1, \ldots, L$ respectively (so $W_L = W$), and let $k_1, \ldots, k_L$ be the number of computation units in layer $1, \ldots, L$ respectively (recall that $k_L = 1$). Define S_n (for $n > 1$) as follows. Assume that for all S in S_{n-1} and all x_j, the net input of every unit in layer n in response to x_j is a fixed polynomial function of $a \in S$, of degree no more than $(l + 1)^{n-1}$. Let S_n be a partition of A that is a refinement of S_{n-1} (that is, for all $S \in S_n$, there is an $S' \in S_{n-1}$ with $S \subseteq S'$), such that for all $S \in S_n$ there are constants $b_{h,i,j} \in \{0, 1\}$ such that

$$\text{sgn}(p_{h,x_j}(a) - t_i) = b_{h,i,j} \qquad \text{for all } a \in S, \tag{8.3}$$

where p_{h,x_j} is the polynomial function describing the net input of the h-th unit in the n-th layer, in response to x_j, when $a \in S$. Since $S \subseteq S'$ for some $S' \in \mathcal{S}_{n-1}$, (8.3) implies that, within S, the output of each nth layer unit in response to an x_j is a fixed polynomial in a of degree no more than $l(l+1)^{n-1}$. If we define H_n as the set of functions

$$\left\{ (h,i,j) \mapsto \operatorname{sgn}(p_{h,x_j}(a) - t_i) : a \in \mathbb{R}^W \right\},$$

then we can choose $\mathcal{S}_n$ such that, for all $S' \in \mathcal{S}_{n-1}$ the number of subsets $|\{S \in \mathcal{S}_n : S \subseteq S'\}|$ is no more than $\Pi_{H_n}(mk_np)$. Since H_n contains thresholded functions that are polynomial in W_n parameters, with degree no more than $(l+1)^{n-1}$, Theorem 8.3 implies that for $S' \in \mathcal{S}_{n-1}$,

$$|\{S \in \mathcal{S}_n : S \subseteq S'\}| \le 2 \left(\frac{2emk_np(l+1)^{n-1}}{W_n} \right)^{W_n}.$$

Notice also that the net input of every unit in layer $n+1$ in response to x_j is a fixed polynomial function of $a \in S \in \mathcal{S}_n$ of degree no more than $(l+1)^n$.

Proceeding in this way we obtain a partition $\mathcal{S}_{L-1}$ of A such that for $S \in \mathcal{S}_{L-1}$ the network output in response to any x_j is a fixed polynomial of $a \in S$ of degree no more than $l(l+1)^{L-2}$. Furthermore,

$$
\begin{aligned}
|\mathcal{S}_{L-1}| &\le 2 \left(\frac{2emk_1p}{W_1} \right)^{W_1} \prod_{i=2}^{L-1} 2 \left(\frac{2emk_ip(l+1)^{i-1}}{W_i} \right)^{W_i} \\
&\le \prod_{i=1}^{L-1} 2 \left(\frac{2emk_ip(l+1)^{i-1}}{W_i} \right)^{W_i}.
\end{aligned}
$$

Multiplying by the bound (8.1) shows that

$$K \le \prod_{i=1}^{L} 2 \left(\frac{2emk_ip(l+1)^{i-1}}{W_i} \right)^{W_i}.$$

Since the points $x_1, \ldots, x_m$ were chosen arbitrarily, this gives the required upper bound on the growth function of H.

Taking logarithms to base two of this bound shows that the VC-dimension d of H satisfies

$$
\begin{aligned}
d &\le L + \sum_{i=1}^{L} W_i \log_2 \left(\frac{2edpk_i(l+1)^{i-1}}{W_i} \right) \\
&< L \left[1 + (L-1)W \log_2(l+1) + W \log_2(2edpk) \right].
\end{aligned}
$$

Applying Inequality (1.2), Appendix 1, shows that

$$\text{VCdim}(F) \le 2L\left[(L-1)W\log_2(l+1) + W\log_2(4WLpk/\ln 2) + 1\right].$$

The second statement in the theorem follows from the fact that $L \le k \le W$. □

This theorem implies that if we approximate an activation function with a piecewise-polynomial function, the resulting network has bounded VC-dimension. Suppose the activation function f increases monotonically and takes values between 0 and 1. Then there is a piecewise-constant function $\hat{f}$ with $O(1/\Delta)$ pieces that approximates f within Δ everywhere. (Using higher order polynomials instead of constants also allows the approximating function to match derivatives of f.) Then a feed-forward network with W parameters, L layers, and computation units with activation function $\hat{f}$ has VC-dimension $O(WL(L + \log_2(WL/\Delta)))$. So even though Theorem 7.1 shows that, for certain sigmoidal activation functions, small networks of units with these activation functions have infinite VC-dimension, there are many sigmoid functions (including the function defined in Theorem 7.1) for which networks of units with activation functions that accurately approximate these sigmoid functions have small VC-dimension. The class of functions that can be approximated accurately using piecewise-polynomial functions is large, and includes, for example, functions of bounded variation.

The bounds given by Theorems 8.7 and 8.8 are nearly optimal. For networks with a fixed number of layers and a piecewise-polynomial activation function with a fixed number of pieces of fixed degree, Theorem 6.3 shows that, in the case of binary inputs and at least three layers, the VC-dimension grows as $W\log_2 W$, and so Theorem 8.8 cannot be improved by more than a constant factor. Similarly, Theorem 6.4 shows this in the case of real inputs and at least two layers. If we also consider the number of layers, Theorem 8.7 gives better bounds than Theorem 8.8 when $W = o(L^2)$. The following theorem shows that the $O(W^2)$ bound of Theorem 8.7 cannot be improved by more than a constant factor if we allow an arbitrary number of layers. In fact, the result applies to a rich class of activation functions, including the standard sigmoid function, as well as piecewise-polynomial functions.

Theorem 8.9 *Suppose $s : \mathbb{R} \to \mathbb{R}$ has the following properties:*

(i) $\lim_{\alpha \to \infty} s(\alpha) = 1$ *and* $\lim_{\alpha \to -\infty} s(\alpha) = 0$, *and*

(ii) *s is differentiable at some point $\alpha_0 \in \mathbb{R}$, with $s'(\alpha_0) \neq 0$.*

For any $L \geq 1$ and $W \geq 10L - 14$, there is a feed-forward network with L layers and a total of W parameters, where every computation unit but the output unit has activation function s, the output unit being a linear threshold unit, and for which the set H of functions computed by the network has

$$\mathrm{VCdim}(H) \geq \left\lfloor \frac{L}{2} \right\rfloor \left\lfloor \frac{W}{2} \right\rfloor.$$

Clearly, the constants 1 and 0 in this theorem can be replaced by any two distinct numbers.

In the proof of Theorem 8.9, we construct a network of linear threshold units and linear units (that is, computation units with the identity activation function) that exhibits the lower bound, and then use the following result to show that we can replace these units by units with activation function s.

Lemma 8.10 *Let N be a feed-forward network of linear units and linear threshold units, with the output unit a linear threshold unit. Let N' be a feed-forward network identical to N, but with all computation units except the output unit replaced by computation units with activation function $s : \mathbb{R} \to \mathbb{R}$, where s has properties 1 and 2 of Theorem 8.9. Then for any finite set S of input patterns, every function on S computed by N can be computed by N'.*

Proof The proof is similar to the proof of Theorem 6.5: we show that we can accurately approximate a threshold function by multiplying the argument of $s(\cdot)$ by a large constant, and we can accurately approximate the identity function by concentrating on a neighbourhood of the differentiable point α_0 of s.

Consider a function g computed by N on S. Suppose that N contains k computation units, and label these units so that unit j takes input from unit i only if $i < j$. Let $v_i(x)$ denote the net input to computation unit i in response to input pattern $x \in S$, for $1 \leq i \leq k$. Defining

$$\epsilon = \min \left\{ \min_{x \in S} |v_i(x)| : i \text{ is a linear threshold unit} \right\},$$

we can assume without loss of generality that $\epsilon > 0$. Now, we step through the network, replacing each threshold activation function $v \mapsto$

sgn(v) by the function

$$v \mapsto s(Mv), \tag{8.4}$$

and replacing each identity activation function by

$$v \mapsto (s(v/M + \alpha_0) - s(\alpha_0)) \, M/s'(\alpha_0), \tag{8.5}$$

where M is a positive real number. For $1 \le i \le k$, let $v_{i,M}(x)$ denote the net input to computation unit i in response to $x \in S$ when the activation functions of units $1, \ldots, i-1$ have been changed in this way. If unit 1 is a linear threshold unit, the finiteness of S and the fact that $\epsilon > 0$ implies that

$$\lim_{M \to \infty} \max_{x \in S} |s(Mv_1(x)) - \mathrm{sgn}(v_1(x))| = 0.$$

If unit 1 is a linear unit, we have

$$\lim_{M \to \infty} \max_{x \in S} |(s(v_1(x)/M + \alpha_0) - s(\alpha_0)) \, M/s'(\alpha_0) - v_1(x)| = 0.$$

In either case, we have that

$$\lim_{M \to \infty} \max_{x \in S} |v_{2,M}(x) - v_2(x)| = 0.$$

Proceeding in this way, we conclude that

$$\lim_{M \to \infty} \max_{x \in S} |v_{k,M}(x) - v_k(x)| = 0,$$

and so, for sufficiently large M,

$$\mathrm{sgn}(v_{k,M}(x)) = \mathrm{sgn}(v_k(x)) = g(x).$$

By scaling the weights and adjusting the thresholds of units in the network, we can replace the activation functions (8.4) and (8.5) by $v \mapsto s(v)$, which shows that the function g on S is computable by N'. □

Proof **(of Theorem 8.9)** The proof follows that of Theorem 8.5; we show how the functions described there can be computed by a network, and keep track of the number of parameters and layers required. (It is not surprising that the dependence on time in the proof of Theorem 8.5 corresponds to the dependence on depth in this proof.)

Fix $M, N \in \mathbb{N}$. Let $a_i = \sum_{j=1}^{M} a_{i,j} 2^{-j}$ for $a_{i,j} \in \{0,1\}$, so $a_i \in [0,1)$ for $i = 1, \ldots, N$. We will consider inputs in $B_N \times B_M$, where

$$B_N = \{e_i : 1 \le i \le N\},$$

$e_i \in \{0,1\}^N$ has ith bit 1 and all other bits 0, and B_M is defined similarly.

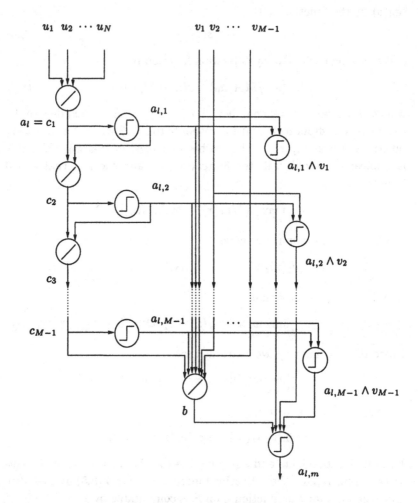

Fig. 8.2. The network of linear threshold units and linear units constructed to prove the VC-dimension lower bound of Theorem 8.9.

As in the proof of Theorem 8.5, we show how to extract the bits of the a_i, so that for input $x = (e_l, e_m)$ the network outputs $a_{l,m}$. (We use this encoding of the integers l, m to simplify the network computation and reduce the number of layers required.)

The construction is illustrated in Figure 8.2. Suppose the network input is $x = ((u_1, \ldots, u_N), (v_1, \ldots, v_M)) = (e_l, e_m)$. Then using one linear unit we can compute $\sum_{i=1}^{N} u_i a_i = a_l$. This involves $N + 1$ parameters and one computation unit in one layer. (In fact, we only need N parameters, but we need the extra parameter when we apply Lemma 8.10.)

Define

$$c_k = \sum_{j=k}^{M} 2^{k-1-j} a_{l,j},$$

for $k = 1, \ldots, M$. Then

$$a_{l,k} = \text{sgn}(c_k - 1/2)$$

for all k. Also, $c_1 = a_l$ and

$$c_k = 2c_{k-1} - a_{l,k-1}$$

for $k = 2, \ldots, M$. Clearly, we can compute the bits $a_{l,1}, \ldots, a_{l,M-1}$ and the numbers $c_2, \ldots, c_{M-1}$ in another $2(M-2) + 1$ layers, using $5(M-2) + 2$ parameters in $2(M-2) + 1$ computation units (see Figure 8.2).

Now set

$$b = \text{sgn}\left(2c_{M-1} - a_{l,M-1} - \sum_{i=1}^{M-1} v_i\right).$$

If $m = M$ then $b = a_{l,M}$, otherwise $b = 0$. This, and the computation of

$$a_{l,m} = b \vee \bigvee_{i=1}^{M-1} (a_{l,i} \wedge v_i)$$

involves another $5M$ parameters in $M + 1$ computation units, and adds another 2 layers. (Here, we are using the standard notation for describing boolean functions in terms of the OR connective $\vee$ and the AND connective $\wedge$, and we interpret 0 as FALSE and 1 as TRUE.)

In total, there are $2M$ layers and $10M + N - 7$ parameters, and the network shatters a set of size NM. Notice that we can add parameters and layers without affecting the function of the network. So for any $L, W \in \mathbb{N}$, we can set $M = \lfloor L/2 \rfloor$ and $N = W + 7 - 10M$, which is at least $\lfloor W/2 \rfloor$ provided $W \geq 10L - 14$. In that case, the VC-dimension is at least

$$\left\lfloor \frac{L}{2} \right\rfloor \left\lfloor \frac{W}{2} \right\rfloor.$$

Lemma 8.10 implies the result. $\qquad\qquad\qquad\qquad\qquad\qquad\qquad\square$

8.4 Standard Sigmoid Networks

Discrete inputs and bounded fan-in

In this section we consider networks with the standard sigmoid activation function, $\sigma(\alpha) = 1/(1 + e^{-\alpha})$. The first result is for two-layer networks with discrete inputs. We define the fan-in of a computation unit to be the number of input units or computation units that feed into it.

Theorem 8.11 *Consider a two-layer feed-forward network with input domain $X = \{-D, -D+1, \ldots, D\}^n$ (for $D \in \mathbb{N}$) and k first-layer computation units, each with the standard sigmoid activation function (the output unit being a linear threshold unit). Let W be the total number of parameters in the network, and suppose that the fan-in of each first-layer unit is no more than N. Then the class H of functions computed by this network has $\mathrm{VCdim}(H) \leq 2W \log_2(60ND)$.*

This theorem implies that if the fan-in of the first-layer units in a two-layer network is bounded by a fixed number N, and the inputs are restricted to a fixed discrete set of this kind, then the VC-dimension increases only linearly with the number of parameters. It is easy to see that, even for binary inputs, the VC-dimension of these networks is $\Theta(W)$. (The lower bound is exhibited by a two-layer linear threshold network with k first-layer units and Nk inputs, with each input connected to only one first-layer unit. The argument used to prove Theorem 6.2 easily extends to show that this network shatters a set of size $Nk = \Omega(W)$. Theorem 6.5 shows that this lower bound also applies to sigmoid networks.) In contrast, Theorem 8.9 shows that standard sigmoid networks with discrete inputs ($|X| = O(W^2)$) but fan-in $\Omega(W)$ and depth $\Omega(W)$ have VC-dimension $\Omega(W^2)$. Theorem 8.11 implies that there is a similar gap for linear threshold networks, because we can apply Theorem 6.5 (and the observation above) to give the following result.

Theorem 8.12 *Consider a two-layer feed-forward linear threshold network that has W parameters and whose first-layer units have fan-in no more than N. If H is the set of functions computed by this network on binary inputs, then $\mathrm{VCdim}(H) \leq 2W \log_2(60N)$. Furthermore, there is a constant c such that for all W there is a network with W parameters that has $\mathrm{VCdim}(H) \geq cW$.*

This result shows that there is a gap between the VC-dimension of these networks and the $\Omega(W \log_2 W)$ VC-dimension for both deeper networks with arbitrary fan-in (Theorem 6.3) and two-layer networks (even with constant fan-in) with richer input domains (Theorem 6.4).

Proof (of **Theorem 8.11**) The proof involves a simple transformation of the parameters in such a way that, for each input vector x, the network computes the sgn function of a polynomial in the transformed parameters. We can then apply Theorem 8.3.

Consider a first-layer unit, and suppose (without loss of generality) that it has connections from the first N input components, $x_1, \ldots, x_N$. Let $w_1, \ldots, w_N$ be the corresponding weights, and let θ be the threshold, so the unit computes

$$
\begin{aligned}
f(x) &= \frac{1}{1 + \exp\left(-\sum_{j=1}^{N} w_j x_j + \theta\right)} \\
&= \frac{\prod_{j=1}^{N} (e^{-w_j})^D}{\prod_{j=1}^{N} (e^{-w_j})^D + \left(\prod_{j=1}^{N} (e^{-w_j})^{D+x_j}\right) e^{\theta}}.
\end{aligned}
$$

Now, if we set $a_j = e^{-w_j}$ for $j = 1, \ldots, N$, and $a_0 = e^{\theta}$, we have

$$
f(x) = \frac{\prod_{j=1}^{N} a_j^D}{\prod_{j=1}^{N} a_j^D + \left(\prod_{j=1}^{N} a_j^{D+x_j}\right) a_0},
$$

which, for $x_j \in \{-D, \ldots, D\}$, is the ratio of a polynomial of degree ND and a polynomial of degree no more than $2ND + 1$. (Notice that such a transformation cannot decrease the VC-dimension.)

Since the network has a linear threshold output, it computes the sgn function of an affine combination of k of these rational functions, or of inputs. For a fixed input vector, this is equivalent to the sgn function of a polynomial of degree no more than $3ND + 2$ in the transformed first layer weights and the second layer weights. Theorem 8.3 shows that $\text{VCdim}(H) \leq 2W \log_2(36ND + 24) \leq 2W \log_2(60ND)$. $\qquad \square$

Notice that the proof technique of Theorem 8.11 is specific to the particular form of the standard sigmoid activation function. It apparently cannot be extended to arbitrary finite domains, since the proof requires elements of X to be small integral multiples of some number.

General standard sigmoid networks

The following result provides a general VC-dimension bound for standard sigmoid networks.

Theorem 8.13 *Let H be the set of functions computed by a feed-forward network with W parameters and k computation units, in which each computation unit other than the output unit has the standard sigmoid activation function (the output unit being a linear threshold unit). Then*

$$\Pi_H(m) \leq 2^{(Wk)^2/2}(18Wk^2)^{5Wk} \left(\frac{em}{W}\right)^W$$

provided $m \geq W$, and

$$\text{VCdim}(H) \leq (Wk)^2 + 11Wk\log_2(18Wk^2).$$

There is a considerable gap between this $O((kW)^2)$ bound and the best known lower bound of $\Omega(W^2)$, which is exhibited by a network with $k = \Theta(W)$ computation units (see Theorem 8.9).

The following result is analogous to Theorem 8.4, which gives bounds on the VC-dimension of a function class in terms of the number of arithmetic operations required to compute the functions. In this case, we also allow the computation of the exponential function to be one of the basic operations.

Theorem 8.14 *Let h be a function from $\mathbb{R}^d \times \mathbb{R}^n$ to $\{0,1\}$, determining the class*

$$H = \left\{x \mapsto h(a,x) : a \in \mathbb{R}^d\right\}.$$

Suppose that h can be computed by an algorithm that takes as input the pair $(a,x) \in \mathbb{R}^d \times \mathbb{R}^n$ and returns $h(a,x)$ after no more than t of the following operations:

- *the exponential function $\alpha \mapsto e^\alpha$ on real numbers,*
- *the arithmetic operations $+$, $-$, $\times$, and $/$ on real numbers,*
- *jumps conditioned on $>$, $\geq$, $<$, $\leq$, $=$, and $\neq$ comparisons of real numbers, and*
- *output 0 or 1.*

Then $\text{VCdim}(H) \leq t^2d(d + 19\log_2(9d))$. Furthermore, if the t steps include no more than q in which the exponential function is evaluated, then

$$\Pi_H(m) \leq 2^{(d(q+1))^2/2}(9d(q+1)2^t)^{5d(q+1)} \left(\frac{em(2^t-2)}{d}\right)^d,$$

and hence $\text{VCdim}(H) \leq (d(q+1))^2 + 11d(q+1)(t + \log_2(9d(q+1)))$.

This result immediately implies a bound on the VC-dimension for feed-forward standard sigmoid networks that is only a constant factor worse than the bound of Theorem 8.13. Notice that, for $q = 0$ (which corresponds to the function classes described by Theorem 8.4, defined in terms of arithmetic operations), this result is only a constant factor worse than Theorem 8.4, since $O(d(d + t + \log_2 d)) = O(dt)$ when we assume that the program makes use of all d parameters.

Proof of VC-dimension bounds for sigmoid networks and algorithms

The proofs of Theorems 8.13 and 8.14 use the following solution set components bound for polynomials of certain exponential functions.

Lemma 8.15 *Let $f_1, \ldots, f_q$ be fixed affine functions of $a_1, \ldots, a_d$, and let G be the class of polynomials in $a_1, \ldots, a_d, e^{f_1(a)}, \ldots, e^{f_q(a)}$ of degree no more than l. Then G has solution set components bound*

$$B = 2^{q(q-1)/2}(l+1)^{2d+q}(d+1)^{d+2q}.$$

Because the affine functions f_i in this lemma must be fixed, we cannot apply Theorem 7.6 directly (not even for the case of two-layer networks). The following lemma shows how we can apply Theorem 7.13 to get around this problem. Recall that the degree of a rational function (a ratio of two polynomials) is the sum of the degrees of the numerator and denominator polynomials.

Lemma 8.16 *Suppose G is the class of functions defined on $\mathbb{R}^d$ computed by a circuit satisfying the following conditions: the circuit contains q gates, the output gate computes a rational function of degree no more than $l \geq 1$, each non-output gate computes the exponential function of a rational function of degree no more than l, and the denominator of each rational function is never zero. Then G has solution set components bound $2^{(qd)^2/2}(9qdl)^{5qd}$.*

Proof The idea of the proof is to include extra variables to represent the value of the rational function computed at each gate and the value of the output of each gate. This shows that the class defined in Lemma 8.15 computes G with intermediate variables, so we can apply Theorem 7.13.

Fix a set of k functions $f_1, \ldots, f_k$ from G, where $k \leq d$. Define polynomials $n_{i,j}$ and $d_{i,j}$ (for $i = 1, \ldots, k$ and $j = 1, \ldots, q$) so that each f_i can be defined recursively in terms of $v_{i,1}, \ldots, v_{i,q-1}$, by

$$f_i(a) = \frac{n_{i,q}(a, v_{i,1}(a), \ldots, v_{i,q-1}(a))}{d_{i,q}(a, v_{i,1}(a), \ldots, v_{i,q-1}(a))}$$

and, for $j = 1, \ldots, q-1$,

$$v_{i,j}(a) = \exp\left(\frac{n_{i,j}(a, v_{i,1}(a), \ldots, v_{i,j-1}(a))}{d_{i,j}(a, v_{i,1}(a), \ldots, v_{i,j-1}(a))}\right).$$

(That is, $f_i(a)$ is the output of circuit i, and $v_{i,j}(a)$ is the output of gate j in circuit i.) Now, consider the functions

$$
\begin{aligned}
\tilde{f}_i(a, b, c) &= c_{i,q}, \\
g_{i,j}(a, b, c) &= c_{i,j} d_{i,j}(a, b_{i,1}, \ldots, b_{i,j-1}) - n_{i,j}(a, b_{i,1}, \ldots, b_{i,j-1}),
\end{aligned}
$$

for $i = 1, \ldots, k$ and $j = 1, \ldots, q$, and

$$h_{i,j}(a, b, c) = \exp(c_{i,j}) - b_{i,j}$$

for $i = 1, \ldots, k$ and $j = 1, \ldots, q-1$.

Let F be the set of polynomials in the variables (a, b, c) and $\exp(c_{i,j})$, for $i = 1, \ldots, k$ and $j = 1, \ldots, q-1$, of degree no more than $l + 1$. Clearly, the functions $\tilde{f}_i$, $g_{i,j}$, and $h_{i,j}$ are in F. Lemma 8.15 shows that F has solution set components bound

$$
\begin{aligned}
B &= 2^{d(q-1)(d(q-1)-1)/2}(l+2)^{d(5q-1)}(2qd+1)^{2d(2q-1)+1} \\
&< 2^{(qd)^2/2}(9qdl)^{5qd}.
\end{aligned}
$$

It is easy to check that F computes G with $2q - 1$ intermediate variables (the derivative condition is satisfied because the denominators of the rational functions are never zero), so Theorem 7.13 shows that this implies the same solution set components bound for G. $\square$

Proof (of **Theorem 8.13**) For a standard sigmoid network with W parameters and k computation units, and a fixed input vector x, there is an equivalent circuit of the kind defined in Lemma 8.16. To see this, notice that we can distribute the computation of the standard sigmoid function, so that the exponential function is computed at the output of one gate, and the function $\alpha \mapsto 1/(1 + \alpha)$ is computed by the gates to which this gate is connected. In this way, every gate in the circuit (except the output gate) computes a function of the form

$$\exp\left(-\sum_i \frac{w_i}{1+v_i} - \sum_j w_j x_j\right),$$

where v_i is the output of gate i and x_j is a component of the input vector. Since there are no more than k variables v_i in the denominators, we can compute a common denominator and express the argument of the exponential function as a rational function (of the weights w_j and gate outputs v_i) of degree no more than $2k$. Lemma 8.16 (with $d = W$, $q = k$, and $l = 2k$), together with Theorem 7.6 shows that

$$\Pi_H(m) \le 2^{(Wk)^2/2}(18Wk^2)^{5Wk}(em/W)^W$$

for $m \ge W$. For this number to be less than 2^m we require

$$m > (Wk)^2/2 + 5Wk\log_2(18Wk^2) + W\log_2(em/W).$$

Inequality (1.2) in Appendix 1 implies that

$$W\log_2 m \le m/2 + W\log_2(2W/(e\ln 2)),$$

so it suffices if

$$m > (Wk)^2 + 10Wk\log_2(18Wk^2) + 2W\log_2(2/\ln 2),$$

and this is implied by $m \ge (Wk)^2 + 11Wk\log_2(18Wk^2)$. ☐

Proof (of Theorem 8.14) We start with the growth function bound. The proof closely follows that of Theorem 8.4.

First, by the same argument as in the proof of Theorem 8.4, any rational function computed by the algorithm has degree no more than 2^t. Furthermore, the number of distinct circuits of the kind described in Lemma 8.16 (call these rational/exponential circuits) that are examined by the algorithm can be no more than $2^{t-1} - 1$, but to express this as a boolean combination of sgn functions, we may need to use a negated copy of each. Also, each rational/exponential circuit contains no more than $q+1$ gates. It follows that we can express h as a (2^t-2)-combination of $\mathrm{sgn}(F)$, where F is the class of rational/exponential circuits of size $q + 1$. Lemma 8.16 and Theorem 7.6 imply that

$$\Pi_H(m) \le 2^{(d(q+1))^2/2}(9d(q+1)2^t)^{5d(q+1)}\left(\frac{em(2^t - 2)}{d}\right)^d$$

(provided $m \geq d/(2^t - 2)$), and this is less than 2^m when

$$m > \frac{(d(q+1))^2}{2} + 5d(q+1)(t + \log_2(9d(q+1))) + d\log_2(e/d) + dt + d\log_2 m.$$

Applying Inequality (1.2) from Appendix 1 shows that

$$m > (d(q+1))^2 + 10d(q+1)(t + \log_2(9d(q+1))) + d(t + \log_2(2/\ln 2)),$$

will suffice, and this is implied by $m \geq (d(q+1))^2 + 11d(q+1)(t + \log_2(9d(q+1)))$. It follows that VCdim$(H) \leq (d(q+1))^2 + 11d(q+1)(t + \log_2(9d(q+1)))$.

If we allow up to $q = t - 1$ exponential functions in the computation, we have

$$\begin{aligned} \text{VCdim}(H) \quad &\leq \quad (dt)^2 + 11dt(t + \log_2(9dt)) \\ &< \quad t^2 d(d + 19\log_2(9d)), \end{aligned}$$

which is the first inequality of the theorem. $\square$

8.5 Remarks

The techniques used in this chapter to establish VC-dimension bounds for sigmoid networks are considerably more generally applicable. For instance, in *radial basis function networks*, the computation units compute a function of their input vector $x \in \mathbb{R}^n$ of the form $\phi((x - c)^T \Sigma(x - c))$, where $c \in \mathbb{R}^n$ and Σ is an $n \times n$ matrix. A common choice for $\phi(\cdot)$ is the function $\alpha \mapsto e^{-\alpha}$. In this case, Theorem 8.14 immediately implies bounds on the VC-dimension of these radial basis function networks, or even networks that combine piecewise-polynomial activation functions, the standard sigmoid, and radial basis functions. Other choices for ϕ include various rational functions, such as the function $\alpha \mapsto 1/(1 + \alpha)$. In this case, the more specific result, Theorem 8.4, implies slightly better bounds on the VC-dimension.

Another example of a function class for which the bounds of Theorem 8.14 are applicable is the *mixture of experts* model. In this model, the network computes the function

$$f(x) = \frac{\sum_{i=1}^{k} e^{g_i(x)} f_i(x)}{\sum_{i=1}^{k} e^{g_i(x)}},$$

where $f_1, \ldots, f_k$ and $g_1, \ldots, g_k$ are functions computed by sigmoid networks. The idea of the model is that each of the functions f_i gives a good approximation to the desired mapping in some region of the input space (f_i is an 'expert', with specialized expertise in that region), and the value at some x of each corresponding function g_i indicates the confidence in that expert's accuracy at the point x. Clearly, Theorem 8.14 gives bounds on the VC-dimension of the class of functions computed by these networks.

8.6 Bibliographical Notes

Bezout's Theorem is given, for example, in (Benedetti and Risler, 1990, Theorem 4.4.1, p. 206). The upper bounds on the VC-dimension of polynomially parameterized function classes, and of classes computed by bounded time algorithms (Theorems 8.3 and 8.4) are slight improvements (by constant factors) of the main results of Goldberg and Jerrum (1995). The lower bound (Theorem 8.5) is also due to Goldberg and Jerrum.

Koiran and Sontag (1997) showed that the functions that Goldberg and Jerrum used to establish the lower bound of Theorem 8.5 can be computed by sigmoid networks, which shows that there is a net with VC-dimension $\Omega(W^2)$. Lemma 8.10, which shows that linear units and linear threshold units can be simulated by sigmoids satisfying two mild conditions, is also due to Koiran and Sontag. They also showed that the $\Omega(W^2)$ lower bound applies to any activation function s that is C^2 but not essentially a linear function. The construction of Theorem 8.9 (which is from (Bartlett, Maiorov and Meir, 1998)), shows how the VC-dimension depends on the number of layers in the network (and also improves the constants from Koiran and Sontag's bound). Theorem 8.8— the upper bound for shallow networks of units with piecewise-polynomial activation functions—is also from (Bartlett et al., 1998). Sakurai (1999) independently obtained related (and in some cases improved) results.

The observation that Goldberg and Jerrum's bound for polynomial functions can be applied to give a bound on the VC-dimension of two-layer sigmoid networks with discrete inputs was made in (Bartlett and Williamson, 1996). Theorems 8.11 and 8.12 improve their result by showing the dependence of the bound on the fan-in of the first-layer units.

The solution set components bound of Lemma 8.15, for functions that are polynomial in the parameters and in exponentials of fixed affine functions of the parameters, is an immediate consequence of a result of Khovanskii (1991) (see also (Benedetti and Risler, 1990)). Khovanskii gives a general approach which is applicable to any functions that are solutions of certain first order differential equations. These functions are known as *Pfaffian functions*; the exponential function is an example. Lemma 8.15 can be expressed in this more general form, in terms of an arbitrary fixed Pfaffian function, but we do not know of any commonly used neural network classes for which this generalization would be useful. On the other hand, it would be interesting to establish conditions on activation functions that are necessary and sufficient for finiteness of the VC-dimension of the network. The Pfaffian condition is certainly not necessary.

Macintyre and Sontag (1993) used results from model theory to show that the VC-dimension of feed-forward sigmoid networks with the standard sigmoid activation function is finite. Karpinski and Macintyre (1997) showed how the techniques of Goldberg and Jerrum could be combined with the results of Khovanskii (through the application of Sard's Theorem described in the last chapter) to give a bound on the VC-dimension of feed-forward sigmoid networks with activation functions that are rational functions of Pfaffian functions. Theorem 8.13 is a special case of this result for the standard sigmoid. Theorem 8.14 uses the same techniques, and the ideas of Theorem 8.4 to give an analogous result for computations involving exponentials.

The mixture of experts model is described in (Jacobs, Jordan, Nowlan and Hinton, 1991), and radial basis function networks are described in (Powell, 1987). See also (Krzyżak et al., 1996). The techniques presented in this chapter can also be used to give bounds for the VC-dimension of certain classes of functions computed by recurrent neural networks (with feedback connections); see (DasGupta and Sontag, 1996; Koiran and Sontag, 1998).

Part two

Pattern Classification with Real-Output Networks

9

Classification with Real-Valued Functions

The general upper and lower bounds on sample complexity described in Chapters 4 and 5 show that the VC-dimension determines the sample complexity of the learning problem for a function class H. The results of Chapters 6 and 8 show that, for a variety of neural networks, the VC-dimension grows with the number of parameters. In particular, the lower bounds on the VC-dimension of neural networks described in Section 6.3, together with Theorem 6.5, show that with mild conditions on the architecture of a multi-layer network and the activation functions of its computation units, the VC-dimension grows at least linearly with the number of parameters.

These results do not, however, provide a complete explanation of the sample size requirements of neural networks for pattern classification problems. In many applications of neural networks the network parameters are adjusted on the basis of a small training set, sometimes an order of magnitude smaller than the number of parameters. In this case, we might expect the network to 'overfit', that is, to accurately match the training data, but predict poorly on subsequent data. Indeed, the results from Part 1 based on the VC-dimension suggest that the estimation error could be large, because VCdim(H)/m is large. Nonetheless, in many such situations these networks seem to avoid overfitting, in that the training set error is a reliable estimate of the error on subsequent examples. Furthermore, Theorem 7.1 shows that an arbitrarily small modification to the activation function can make the VC-dimension infinite, and it seems unnatural that such a change should affect the statistical behaviour of networks in applications.

One possible explanation of such discrepancies between theory and

133

practice is that in the theoretical model we have discussed, a learning algorithm is required to perform well for *any* probability distribution. In particular, in proving lower bounds on sample complexity, we used carefully constructed probability distributions, and it seems unlikely that these distributions are accurate models for applications. It could well be the case that learning problems that occur commonly in applications are easier than the 'distribution-free' theory indicates. However, it is not clear how we can take advantage of this, since, as argued in Section 2.1, in many applications of neural networks we have little knowledge of the process generating the data.

Another inadequacy of the learning model investigated in Part 1 is that it is not appropriate for many neural network learning algorithms. For instance, suppose we wish to use a real-output sigmoid network for binary classification. It is natural to threshold the real output of the network to obtain a binary classification label. This is the approach taken implicitly in Part 1 of this book, and the theoretical results obtained there apply. However, many learning algorithms for real-output sigmoid networks take into account the value of the real number that is computed by the network, and not simply its binary thresholded value. Such algorithms typically do not minimize the number of misclassifications over the training examples, but instead minimize the squared error of the real-valued outputs, a procedure that can lead to very different behaviour. An algorithm of this type is unlikely to return a function whose thresholded version makes a small number of classification errors on a sample but has its function values all close to the threshold. (Such a function would have real output values that, on the training sample, mostly fall on the correct side of the threshold, but not by much. Algorithms that minimize squared error, as we shall see, tend not to produce such 'indecisive' functions.) Therefore, we cannot expect that algorithms of this type will produce a function whose thresholded version has near-minimal sample error. For this reason, the theory of Part 1 cannot be readily used to guarantee a nearly optimal misclassification probability.

In the next seven chapters, we investigate an alternative model of learning that is more applicable to situations where a real-output neural network is used for binary classification, but in a way other than by simple thresholding. As described above, if one simply thresholds real-valued functions in some class and applies the theory of Part 1, then all that matters is whether a function gives a real number output lying on the correct side of the threshold. In the modified approach, we take into consideration the 'margin' by which the function value lies on the correct side; that is, we take into account the distance between the threshold value and the real number output by the network. Such an approach enables us to exploit the fact that learning algorithms commonly used for neural networks (such as gradient descent algorithms that locally minimize squared error) tend to produce classifiers having a large margin on most of the training examples. In the new model of learning, we shall require that the output hypothesis of the algorithm has misclassification probability nearly as small as the smallest error of a 'large margin' classifier in the class. We shall see that this approach eliminates some of the peculiarities of the results obtained in Part 1.

The new model is, in effect, a 'relaxation' of the learning model studied in Part I, in the sense that we weaken the requirement on the misclassification error of the output hypothesis. By measuring error using the margins, we obtain bounds on misclassification probability of the form

$$\text{error} \leq (\text{estimate of error}) + (\text{complexity penalty}),$$

where the error estimate is measured using margins and the complexity penalty depends, for instance, on the size of the parameters in the network, rather than on the number of parameters. In many cases, this new model explains how overfitting may be avoided even with training sets that are considerably smaller than the number of parameters. This does not contradict the lower bounds of Chapter 5: the complexity penalty can be smaller in the new model, because in situations where overfitting might occur in the old model, the new error estimate would be large. Loosely speaking, the limitations of the learning algorithms (that they cannot find functions with few errors on the training data, since those functions do not have large margins) effectively counter the deficiency in the amount of training data. Since the new model more accurately describes the types of learning algorithm used in practice, the results in this part are likely to give a more accurate explanation of the performance of these learning algorithms.

9.2 Large Margin Classifiers

Suppose F is a class of functions defined on the set X and mapping to the interval $[0,1]$, such as the class of all functions computable by a real-output sigmoid network, for example. One way to use such a class for binary classification is to use 'thresholded' versions of its functions; that is, to work with the class of binary-valued functions of the form $h(x) = \text{sgn}(f(x) - 1/2)$, and then to apply the theory of Part 1. Here, however, we take a different approach, in which we are interested in functions that classify examples correctly, but with a large margin. In this definition, f can be viewed as a function that maps to the interval $[0, 1]$; we define the notion of margin more generally because it will be useful later.

Definition 9.1 *Let $Z = X \times \{0, 1\}$. If f is a real-valued function in F, the* margin *of f on $(x, y) \in Z$ is*

$$\text{margin}(f(x), y) = \begin{cases} f(x) - 1/2 & \text{if } y = 1 \\ 1/2 - f(x) & \text{otherwise.} \end{cases}$$

Suppose γ is a nonnegative real number and P is a probability distribution on Z. We define the error $\text{er}_P^\gamma(f)$ *of f with respect to P and γ as the probability*

$$\text{er}_P^\gamma(f) = P\left\{\text{margin}(f(x), y) < \gamma\right\},$$

and the misclassification probability *of f as*

$$\text{er}_P(f) = P\left\{\text{sgn}(f(x) - 1/2) \neq y\right\}.$$

Clearly, if $\text{sgn}(f(x) - 1/2)$ correctly classifies y, the margin is nonnegative. We can interpret a large positive margin as a 'confident' correct classification. Notice that $\text{er}_P(f) \leq \text{er}_P^\gamma(f)$ for all $\gamma > 0$, and that inequality can hold.

Recall that a learning algorithm for a class H of binary-valued functions is a function taking a training sample $z \in Z^m$ and returning a function h in H that, with high probability over Z^m, has error satisfying

$$\text{er}_P(h) < \inf_{g \in H} \text{er}_P(g) + \epsilon.$$

We can define a *classification learning algorithm* for a class F of real-valued functions in an analogous way.

Definition 9.2 *Suppose that F is a class of functions mapping from X into $\mathbb{R}$ and that Z denotes $X \times \{0, 1\}$. A* classification learning algorithm *L for F takes as input a margin parameter $\gamma > 0$ and a sample $z \in \bigcup_{i=1}^\infty Z^i$, and returns a function in F such that, for any $\epsilon, \delta \in (0, 1)$ and any $\gamma > 0$, there is an integer $m_0(\epsilon, \delta, \gamma)$ such that if $m \geq m_0(\epsilon, \delta, \gamma)$ then, for any probability distribution P on $Z = X \times \{0, 1\}$,*

$$P^m\left\{\text{er}_P(L(\gamma, z)) < \inf_{g \in F} \text{er}_P^\gamma(g) + \epsilon\right\} \geq 1 - \delta.$$

We define the *sample complexity* function $m_L(\epsilon, \delta, \gamma)$ of L as the smallest integer that can be taken to be $m_0(\epsilon, \delta, \gamma)$ in this definition, and the *inherent sample complexity* $m_F(\epsilon, \delta, \gamma)$ of the classification learning problem for F as the minimum over all learning algorithms L of $m_L(\epsilon, \delta, \gamma)$. As in the definition of the binary classification problem, we say that an algorithm L has *estimation error bound* $\epsilon(m, \delta, \gamma)$ if, for all m, δ, γ, and P, with probability at least $1 - \delta$ over $z \in Z^m$ chosen according to P^m,

$$\mathrm{er}_P(L(\gamma, z)) < \inf_{g \in F} \mathrm{er}_P^\gamma(g) + \epsilon(m, \delta, \gamma).$$

The estimation error of L, denoted $\epsilon_L(m, \delta, \gamma)$, is the smallest possible estimation error bound.

Clearly, if F is a class of $\{0, 1\}$-valued functions, Definition 9.2 and the analogous Definition 2.1 for learning binary-valued function classes are equivalent. In deriving the results for neural network classes in the previous chapters, we have, in effect, considered the binary-valued class $H = \{\mathrm{sgn}(f - 1/2) : f \in F\}$. By considering directly the real-valued class F, Definition 9.2 gives a potentially easier learning problem, since now the learning algorithm needs only to find a function with misclassification probability close to the best error 'at margin γ'.

This definition of learning is well-motivated for neural networks. In particular, learning algorithms for real-output sigmoid networks typically attempt to find a function in F that approximately minimizes the squared error on the training sample. The following proposition shows that when there is a function with small squared error, that function is also a large margin classifier. In order to state the result, we need one further definition: for a function f in F and $\gamma > 0$, the *sample error of f with respect to γ* on the sample z is

$$\hat{\mathrm{er}}_z^\gamma(f) = \frac{1}{m} |\{i : \mathrm{margin}(f(x_i), y_i) < \gamma\}|.$$

Proposition 9.3 *For any function $f : X \to \mathbb{R}$ and any sequence of labelled examples $((x_1, y_1), \ldots, (x_m, y_m))$ in $(X \times \{0, 1\})^m$, if*

$$\frac{1}{m} \sum_{i=1}^m (f(x_i) - y_i)^2 < \epsilon$$

then

$$\hat{\mathrm{er}}_z^\gamma(f) < \epsilon/(1/2 - \gamma)^2$$

for all $0 \le \gamma < 1/2$.

Proof If $\text{margin}(f(x_i), y_i) < \gamma$, then $|f(x_i) - y_i| > 1/2 - \gamma$. So $\hat{\text{er}}_z^\gamma(f) \geq \epsilon/(1/2 - \gamma)^2$ implies

$$\frac{1}{m} \sum_{i=1}^{m} (f(x_i) - y_i)^2 \geq \epsilon.$$

$\square$

It is possible to obtain a result analogous to Theorem 2.4 that provides a bound on the sample complexity of classification learning with a finite class of real-valued functions. However, in this case there is no advantage to considering the real-valued nature of the class. We shall see in the following chapters that there can be a considerable advantage if the function class is infinite.

9.3 Remarks

When using a $[0, 1]$-valued function for pattern classification, we can interpret the value of the function as an estimate of the probability that the correct label is 1. This provides extra information that would be ignored if we simply thresholded the function, and this is frequently valuable in applications. For instance, in predicting outcomes of a medical procedure, it seems sensible to allow a classifier to return a 'don't know' value, rather than forcing it to predict either a 0 or a 1. In such cases, we can consider two kinds of errors: those where the classifier says 'don't know', and those in which it makes a prediction, but is wrong. For a class of $[0, 1]$-valued functions, it is reasonable to interpret a value near the threshold (say, within γ) as a 'don't know' value. In that case, er^γ measures the sum of the probabilities of these two kinds of errors. Although the results described in the following chapters give bounds on er_P in terms of the infimum over F of $\text{er}_P^\gamma(f)$, it is easy to extend these results to obtain bounds on er_P^γ.

9.4 Bibliographical Notes

The idea that studying margins might provide an explanation of the surprisingly good generalization performance of neural network classifiers was first described in (Bartlett, 1998), but the definition of learning presented in this chapter is new. This work builds on a large collection of results and intuition for linear classifiers. Many authors (see, for example, (Duda and Hart, 1973)) have suggested building linear classifiers with large margins; part of the motivation seems to have been robustness to noise in the input variables. Vapnik (1982) studied combinatorial properties of large margin classifiers. Boser, Guyon and Vapnik (1992) proposed algorithms for large margin linear classifiers. Shawe-Taylor, Bartlett, Williamson and Anthony (1996) gave an analysis of linear classifiers with large margins. The results in (Bartlett, 1998) also have technical ancestors in (Lee, Bartlett and Williamson, 1996; Lee, Bartlett and Williamson, 1995b) (see also (Koiran, 1994)) and in (Anthony and Bartlett, 1995), as well as in (Shawe-Taylor et al., 1996)—we shall meet some of these results in later chapters.

The observation (Proposition 9.3) that minimizing squared error gives good margins was made in (Bartlett, 1998). (But see (Sontag and Sussmann, 1989) for an illustration that minimizing squared error using gradient descent can be problematic, even for simple problems.)

The model described in this chapter is related to the problem of learning *probabilistic concepts* (see (Kearns and Schapire, 1994)). A probabilistic concept is a function defined on an input domain X mapping to the interval $[0, 1]$. The value of the function at a point $x \in X$ is an estimate of the probability that the label associated with x is 1. In this model, a learning algorithm aims to produce a probabilistic concept from some class that approximately minimizes the expected value of some loss function. Typical loss functions studied include the quadratic loss function, $(f(x), y) \mapsto (f(x) - y)^2$, and the absolute loss function $(f(x), y) \mapsto |f(x) - y|$. The quantity er_P^γ defined in this chapter is the expected value of the loss function $(f(x), y) \mapsto 1_{|f(x)-y|>1/2-\gamma}(x, y)$.

10

Covering Numbers and Uniform Convergence

10.1 Introduction

Just as in Chapter 4, we shall show that in many cases an algorithm returning a function with small sample error will constitute a learning algorithm (where, in the present context, the sample error is measured with respect to a certain margin). The details will be given in Chapter 13. As in the theory developed earlier for the case of classes of functions mapping into $\{0, 1\}$, we first obtain a 'uniform convergence' result, analogous to Theorem 4.3. The notion of *covering numbers* will prove crucial in our analysis.

10.2 Covering Numbers

Measuring the extent of a function class

Theorem 4.3 concerns a class of functions that map from some set X into $\{0, 1\}$, and it involves the growth function $\Pi_H(m)$. Recall that if S is a finite subset of X, then $H_{|s}$ denotes the restriction of H to S, and that the growth function Π_H is given by

$$\Pi_H(m) = \max\left\{ \left| H_{|s} \right| : S \subseteq X \text{ and } |S| = m \right\}.$$

Since H maps into $\{0, 1\}$, $H_{|s}$ is finite for every finite S. However, if we consider a class F of real-valued functions, we encounter the problem that even for finite S, $F_{|s}$ may be infinite. Thus we cannot make use of the cardinality of $F_{|s}$ in obtaining a uniform convergence result for real function classes. In fact, we only need the set $F_{|s}$ to have not too many elements that are very different; instead of cardinality, we use the notion of *covers* to measure the 'extent' of $F_{|s}$.

140

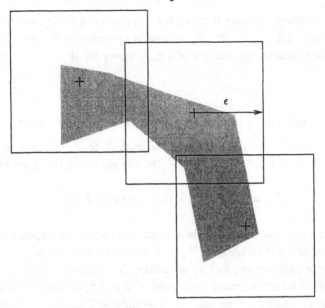

Fig. 10.1. The centres of the d_∞ balls form an ϵ-cover of the shaded region, $F_{|_\bullet} \subset \mathbb{R}^2$.

Covering numbers for subsets of Euclidean space

Given $W \subseteq \mathbb{R}^k$ and a positive real number ϵ, we say that $C \subseteq \mathbb{R}^k$ is a d_∞ ϵ-*cover for* W if $C \subseteq W$ and for every $w \in W$ there is a $v \in C$ such that

$$\max\{|w_i - v_i| : i = 1, \ldots, k\} < \epsilon.$$

In other words, given any vector w in W, there is some vector in C whose distance from w is less than ϵ, where distance is measured using the metric d_∞ on $\mathbb{R}^k$, defined by

$$d_\infty((x_1, x_2, \ldots, x_k), (y_1, y_2, \ldots, y_k)) = \max_i |x_i - y_i|.$$

For $v \in \mathbb{R}^k$ and $\epsilon > 0$, define the open d_∞ ball at v of radius ϵ to be the set

$$\{u \in \mathbb{R}^k : d_\infty(u, v) < \epsilon\}.$$

Then we could also define an ϵ-cover for $W \subseteq \mathbb{R}^k$ as a subset C of W for which W is contained in the union of the set of open d_∞ balls of radius ϵ centred at the points in C. Figure 10.1 illustrates this idea. We say

142   Covering Numbers and Uniform Convergence

that W is *totally bounded* if for each $\epsilon > 0$ there is a *finite* ϵ-cover for W. In this case, we define† the d_∞ ϵ-*covering number of* W, $\mathcal{N}(\epsilon, W, d_\infty)$, to be the minimum cardinality of a d_∞ ϵ-cover for W.

Uniform covering numbers for a function class

Suppose that F is a class of functions from X to $\mathbb{R}$. Given a sequence $x = (x_1, x_2, \ldots, x_k) \in X^k$, we let $F|_x$ be the subset of $\mathbb{R}^k$ given by

$$F|_x = \{(f(x_1), f(x_2), \ldots, f(x_k)) : f \in F\}.$$

(If the x_i are distinct, there is a clear one-to-one correspondence between $F|_x$ and the restriction $F|_S$ of F to the set $S = \{x_1, x_2, \ldots, x_n\} \subseteq X$.) For a positive number ϵ, we define the *uniform covering number* $\mathcal{N}_\infty(\epsilon, F, k)$ to be the maximum, over all $x \in X^k$, of the covering number $\mathcal{N}(\epsilon, F|_x, d_\infty)$ (and we take it to be infinite if there is no bound on these covering numbers); that is,

$$\mathcal{N}_\infty(\epsilon, F, k) = \max\left\{\mathcal{N}(\epsilon, F|_x, d_\infty) : x \in X^k\right\}.$$

The covering number $\mathcal{N}_\infty(\epsilon, F, k)$ can be interpreted as a measure of the richness of the class F at the scale ϵ. For a fixed value of ϵ, this covering number—and in particular how rapidly it grows with k—indicates how much the set $F|_x$ 'fills up' $\mathbb{R}^k$, when we examine it at the scale ϵ. For example, suppose that functions in F map to the interval $[0, 1]$. If there is a vector x in X^k with $F|_x = [0, 1]^k$, then $\mathcal{N}_\infty(\epsilon, F, k)$ grows roughly as $(1/\epsilon)^k$, and this is the fastest growth possible. However, we shall see that if functions in F are bounded and $F|_x$ is always contained in a linear subspace of $\mathbb{R}^k$ of dimension d, then $\mathcal{N}_\infty(\epsilon, F, k)$ grows roughly as $(k/\epsilon)^d$, which is polynomial in k. We shall see in the next section that the rate of growth of these covering numbers with k is crucial, just as the rate of growth of $\Pi_H(k)$ with k was crucial for binary classification.

In fact, the uniform covering number is a generalization of the growth function. To see this, suppose that functions in H map into $\{0, 1\}$. Then, for all $x \in X^k$, $H|_x$ is finite and, for all $\epsilon < 1$, $\mathcal{N}(\epsilon, H|_x, d_\infty) = |H|_x|$, so $\mathcal{N}_\infty(\epsilon, H, k) = \Pi_H(k)$.

---

† We explicitly write d_∞ in the definition since we shall see that it is useful to be able to define covering numbers in terms of other notions of distance.

10.3 A Uniform Convergence Result

In this section we present and prove a uniform convergence result for a class of real-valued functions. (Strictly speaking, it is not a uniform convergence result, since it gives uniform one-sided bounds on error probabilities.) The proof of this result is in many ways similar to the proof of the corresponding result in Chapter 4, Theorem 4.3, although the technical details are slightly more intricate.

Theorem 10.1 *Suppose that F is a set of real-valued functions defined on the domain X. Let P be any probability distribution on $Z = X \times \{0, 1\}$, ϵ any real number between 0 and 1, γ any positive real number, and m any positive integer. Then*

$$P^m \left\{ \mathrm{er}_P(f) \geq \hat{\mathrm{er}}_z^\gamma(f) + \epsilon \text{ for some } f \text{ in } F \right\}$$
$$\leq 2 \mathcal{N}_\infty \left(\gamma/2, F, 2m \right) \exp\left(-\frac{\epsilon^2 m}{8} \right).$$

Notice how this compares with Theorem 4.3: that bound involves the growth function, whereas this involves the covering number. Since the covering number is a generalization of the growth function, this result is, in a sense, a generalization of a one-sided version of Theorem 4.3. Recall that Theorem 4.3 is useful when $\Pi_H(m)$ increases polynomially with m, and this is guaranteed when the VC-dimension of H is finite. In the same way, Theorem 10.1 shows that the probability that the sample error does not provide a uniformly accurate error estimate decreases to zero as the training sample size m increases, provided that the covering number $\mathcal{N}_\infty(\gamma/2, F, 2m)$ does not grow too rapidly with m. In particular, if the covering number grows only polynomially with m, this probability goes to zero exponentially quickly as a function of m.

We now embark on the proof of Theorem 10.1. This uses the same key techniques as the proof of Theorem 4.3, namely symmetrization, permutation, and reduction to a finite class. Having presented some high-level justification for these techniques in Chapter 4, and having given many of the essential definitions, we proceed a little faster with the present proof.

Symmetrization

First, we have the following result, which allows us to consider a sample-based estimate of $\mathrm{er}_P(f)$.

Lemma 10.2 *With the notation as above, let*

$$Q = \{z \in Z^m : some\ f\ in\ F\ has\ \mathrm{er}_P(f) \geq \hat{\mathrm{er}}_z^\gamma(f) + \epsilon\}$$

and

$$R = \{(r, s) \in Z^m \times Z^m : some\ f\ in\ F\ has\ \hat{\mathrm{er}}_s(f) \geq \hat{\mathrm{er}}_r^\gamma(f) + \epsilon/2\}.$$

Then for $m \geq 2/\epsilon^2$,

$$P^m(Q) \leq 2P^{2m}(R).$$

Proof The proof closely follows the proof of Lemma 4.4.

If some $f \in F$ satisfies $\mathrm{er}_P(f) \geq \hat{\mathrm{er}}_r^\gamma(f) + \epsilon$ and $\hat{\mathrm{er}}_s(f) \geq \mathrm{er}_P(f) - \epsilon/2$, then it satisfies $\hat{\mathrm{er}}_s(f) \geq \hat{\mathrm{er}}_r^\gamma(f) + \epsilon/2$, so

$$
\begin{aligned}
P^{2m}(R) &\geq P^{2m} \{\exists f \in F,\ \mathrm{er}_P(f) \geq \hat{\mathrm{er}}_r^\gamma(f) + \epsilon\ \text{and} \\
&\qquad\qquad \hat{\mathrm{er}}_s(f) \geq \mathrm{er}_P(f) - \epsilon/2\} \\
&= \int_Q P^m \{s : \exists f \in F,\ \mathrm{er}_P(f) \geq \hat{\mathrm{er}}_r^\gamma(f) + \epsilon\ \text{and} \\
&\qquad\qquad \hat{\mathrm{er}}_s(f) \geq \mathrm{er}_P(f) - \epsilon/2\}\ dP^m(r). \qquad (10.1)
\end{aligned}
$$

As in the proof of Lemma 4.4, we can use Chebyshev's inequality to show that

$$P^m \{\hat{\mathrm{er}}_s(f) \geq \mathrm{er}_P(f) - \epsilon/2\} \geq 1/2$$

for all $f \in F$, provided that $m \geq 2/\epsilon^2$, and this, together with (10.1), shows that $P^{2m}(R) \geq P^m(Q)/2$. $\qquad\square$

Permutations

As in Chapter 4, we now bound the probability $P^{2m}(R)$ in terms of a probability involving permutations of the sample labels. Recall that Γ_m is the set of permutations σ on $\{1, 2, \ldots, 2m\}$ that switch elements from the first and second halves (that is, $\{\sigma(i), \sigma(i + m)\} = \{i, i + m\}$ for $i = 1, \ldots, m$). Recall also that we can regard a permutation σ as acting on an element of Z^{2m}, so that

$$\sigma z = \sigma(z_1, z_2, \ldots, z_{2m}) = (z_{\sigma(1)}, z_{\sigma(2)}, \ldots, z_{\sigma(2m)}).$$

Lemma 4.5 shows that

$$P^{2m}(R) = \mathbf{E}\Pr(\sigma z \in R) \leq \max_{z \in Z^{2m}} \Pr(\sigma z \in R), \qquad (10.2)$$

where the expectation is over z in Z^{2m} chosen according to P^{2m}, and the probability is over permutations chosen uniformly in Γ_m. So the problem reduces to estimating this latter probability.

Reduction to a finite class

In the analogous step of the proof of Theorem 4.3, we used the union bound to show that the probability that $\sigma z \in R$ is no more than the sum over all elements of $F_{|_z}$ of some probability involving an element. As noted earlier in this chapter, the corresponding restriction here is typically infinite, so instead we approximate $F_{|_z}$ by using a cover.

Lemma 10.3 *For the set $R \subseteq Z^{2m}$ defined in Lemma 10.2, and for a permutation σ chosen uniformly at random from Γ_m,*

$$\max_{z \in Z^{2m}} \Pr(\sigma z \in R) \leq \mathcal{N}_\infty \left(\gamma/2, F, 2m\right) \exp\left(-\frac{\epsilon^2 m}{8}\right).$$

Proof Fix $z = (z_1, \ldots, z_{2m})$ in Z^{2m}, where $z_i = (x_i, y_i)$. Let $x = (x_1, \ldots, x_{2m})$ and fix a minimal $\gamma/2$-cover T of $F_{|_x}$. Clearly, $|T| = \mathcal{N}(\gamma/2, F_{|_x}, d_\infty) \leq \mathcal{N}_\infty(\gamma/2, F, 2m)$. Then for all f in F there is an $\hat{f}$ in T with $|f(x_i) - \hat{f}_i| < \gamma/2$ for $1 \leq i \leq 2m$. Now, if $\sigma z \in R$ then, by definition, some f in F has $\hat{\text{er}}_s(f) \geq \hat{\text{er}}_r^\gamma(f) + \epsilon/2$, where $r = (z_{\sigma(1)}, \ldots, z_{\sigma(m)})$ and $s = (z_{\sigma(m+1)}, \ldots, z_{\sigma(2m)})$. By the definition of $\hat{\text{er}}_s(f)$ and $\hat{\text{er}}_r^\gamma(f)$, this f satisfies

$$\frac{1}{m} \left|\{m+1 \leq i \leq 2m : \text{sgn}\left(f(x_{\sigma(i)}) - 1/2\right) \neq y_{\sigma(i)}\}\right|$$

$$\geq \frac{1}{m} \left|\{1 \leq i \leq m : \text{margin}\left(f(x_{\sigma(i)}), y_{\sigma(i)}\right) < \gamma\}\right| + \frac{\epsilon}{2}.$$

Now, if $\text{sgn}(f(x) - 1/2) \neq y$ then $\text{margin}(f(x), y) \leq 0$, so this implies

$$\frac{1}{m} \left|\{m+1 \leq i \leq 2m : \text{margin}\left(f(x_{\sigma(i)}), y_{\sigma(i)}\right) \leq 0\}\right|$$

$$\geq \frac{1}{m} \left|\{1 \leq i \leq m : \text{margin}\left(f(x_{\sigma(i)}), y_{\sigma(i)}\right) < \gamma\}\right| + \frac{\epsilon}{2}. \quad (10.3)$$

Choose $\hat{f} \in T$ such that, for all i, $|\hat{f}_i - f(x_i)| < \gamma/2$. It follows that if $\text{margin}(\hat{f}_i, y_i) < \gamma/2$, then $\text{margin}(f(x_i), y_i) < \gamma$. Furthermore, if $\text{margin}(f(x_i), y_i) \leq 0$ then we have $\text{margin}(\hat{f}_i, y_i) < \gamma/2$. Combining these facts, we see that if $\sigma z \in R$ then there is some $\hat{f} \in T$ such that

$$\frac{1}{m} \left|\left\{m+1 \leq i \leq 2m : \text{margin}\left(\hat{f}_{\sigma(i)}, y_{\sigma(i)}\right) < \gamma/2\right\}\right|$$

$$\geq \frac{1}{m} \left| \left\{ 1 \leq i \leq m : \text{margin}\left(\hat{f}_{\sigma(i)}, y_{\sigma(i)}\right) < \gamma/2 \right\} \right| + \frac{\epsilon}{2}.$$

If we define

$$v(\hat{f}, i) = \begin{cases} 1 & \text{if } \text{margin}(\hat{f}_i, y_i) < \gamma/2 \\ 0 & \text{otherwise,} \end{cases}$$

then it follows that

$$\Pr(\sigma z \in R)$$

$$\leq \Pr\left(\exists \hat{f} \in T : \frac{1}{m} \sum_{i=1}^{m} \left(v(\hat{f}, \sigma(m+i)) - v(\hat{f}, \sigma(i)) \right) \geq \epsilon/2 \right).$$

The union bound then implies that this probability is no more than

$$|T| \max_{\hat{f} \in T} \Pr\left(\frac{1}{m} \sum_{i=1}^{m} \left(v(\hat{f}, \sigma(m+i)) - v(\hat{f}, \sigma(i)) \right) \geq \epsilon/2 \right)$$

$$= |T| \max_{\hat{f} \in T} \Pr\left(\frac{1}{m} \sum_{i=1}^{m} \left| v(\hat{f}, i) - v(\hat{f}, m+i) \right| \beta_i \geq \epsilon/2 \right),$$

where the final probability is over the β_i, which are independently and uniformly chosen from $\{-1, 1\}$. Hoeffding's inequality (see Appendix 1) shows that this probability is no more than $\exp(-\epsilon^2 m/8)$, which implies the result. □

Theorem 10.1 now follows from Lemma 10.2, Inequality (10.2), and Lemma 10.3. Indeed, it is trivially true for $m < 2/\epsilon^2$, because in that case the right-hand side of the bound is greater than 1, so we can apply Lemma 10.2.

In fact, Theorem 10.1 can be improved in the case that functions in F take values that are far from the threshold value of $1/2$. Clearly, the behaviour of a function in F is irrelevant in a region where its value is far from $1/2$. If functions in F are very complex in such regions, the covering number of F might be an overly pessimistic measure of the complexity of F. Instead of F, consider the class $\pi_\gamma(F)$, where $\pi_\gamma : \mathbb{R} \to [1/2 - \gamma, 1/2 + \gamma]$ satisfies

$$\pi_\gamma(\alpha) = \begin{cases} 1/2 + \gamma & \text{if } \alpha \geq 1/2 + \gamma \\ 1/2 - \gamma & \text{if } \alpha \leq 1/2 - \gamma \\ \alpha & \text{otherwise,} \end{cases} \tag{10.4}$$

(see Figure 10.2), and $\pi_\gamma(F) = \{\pi_\gamma \circ f : f \in F\}$, where $(g \circ f)(x) = g(f(x))$. It is clear that the analysis carried out in the above proof is still true when f is replaced by $\pi_\gamma \circ f$, and hence we can use a cover of $\pi_\gamma(F)$

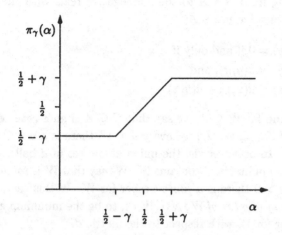

Fig. 10.2. The graph of the function $\pi_\gamma : \mathbb{R} \to [1/2 - \gamma, 1/2 + \gamma]$.

rather than F. Clearly, the covering numbers of $\pi_\gamma(F)$ are no larger than those of F, and can be considerably smaller. For example, if there is a point $x \in X$ for which the set $\{f(x) : f \in F\} \subseteq \mathbb{R}$ is unbounded, then $\mathcal{N}_\infty\,(\gamma/2, F, 1) = \infty$ for all $\gamma > 0$, whereas $\mathcal{N}_\infty\,(\gamma/2, \pi_\gamma(F), 1) \le 4$. Thus, the following theorem is an improvement of Theorem 10.1.

Theorem 10.4 *Suppose that F is a set of real-valued functions defined on a domain X. Let P be any probability distribution on $Z = X \times \{0, 1\}$, ϵ any real number between 0 and 1, γ any positive real number, and m any positive integer. Then*

$$P^m \left\{ \mathrm{er}_P(f) \ge \hat{\mathrm{er}}_z^\gamma(f) + \epsilon \text{ for some } f \text{ in } F \right\}$$
$$\le 2 \mathcal{N}_\infty \left(\frac{\gamma}{2}, \pi_\gamma(F), 2m \right) \exp\left(-\frac{\epsilon^2 m}{8} \right).$$

10.4 Covering Numbers in General

The notion of covering numbers can be defined quite generally, and in subsequent chapters we shall use several notions of covering numbers other than those discussed earlier in this chapter. We now give the general definition.

Recall that a *metric space* consists of a set A together with a *metric*,

d, a mapping from $A \times A$ to the nonnegative reals with the following properties, for all $x, y, z \in A$:

(i) $d(x, y) = 0$ if and only if $x = y$,

(ii) $d(x, y) = d(y, x)$, and

(iii) $d(x, z) \le d(x, y) + d(y, z)$.

For $\epsilon > 0$, and for $W \subseteq A$, we say that $C \subseteq A$ is an ϵ-*cover* of W with respect to d if $C \subseteq W$ and for every $w \in W$ there is a $v \in C$ such that $d(w, v) < \epsilon$. In other words, the union of the set of d balls of radius ϵ centred at the points in C contains W. We say that W is *totally bounded* if for each $\epsilon > 0$ there is a *finite* ϵ-cover for W. In this case, we define the ϵ-*covering number of* W, $\mathcal{N}(\epsilon, W, d)$, to be the minimum cardinality of an ϵ-cover for W with respect to the metric d.

Of course, the definition just given subsumes the one we used earlier in the chapter for $d = d_\infty$. There are many other metrics—and hence, types of covering number—on $\mathbb{R}^k$. Of particular relevance are the covering numbers corresponding to the metrics d_1 and d_2, given by

$$d_1(x, y) = \frac{1}{k} \sum_{i=1}^{k} |x_i - y_i|,$$

and

$$d_2(x, y) = \left(\frac{1}{k} \sum_{i=1}^{k} (x_i - y_i)^2 \right)^{1/2}.$$

In Section 10.2 we defined the uniform covering numbers $\mathcal{N}_\infty(\epsilon, F, k)$, for a function class F. In an analogous way, we may define uniform covering numbers corresponding to the d_1 and d_2 metrics: we define

$$\mathcal{N}_p(\epsilon, F, k) = \max \left\{ \mathcal{N}(\epsilon, F_{|_\bullet}, d_p) : x \in X^k \right\}$$

for $p = 1, 2, \infty$.

Jensen's inequality (see Appendix 1) shows that

$$d_1(x, y) \le d_2(x, y), \tag{10.5}$$

and it is immediate that

$$d_2(x, y) \le d_\infty(x, y). \tag{10.6}$$

Hence, we have the following result.

Lemma 10.5 *For any class F of real-valued functions defined on X, any $\epsilon > 0$, and any $k \in \mathbb{N}$,*

$$\mathcal{N}_1\left(\epsilon, F, k\right) \leq \mathcal{N}_2\left(\epsilon, F, k\right) \leq \mathcal{N}_\infty\left(\epsilon, F, k\right).$$

10.5 Remarks
Pseudo-metric spaces

It is possible to define general covering numbers with respect to a *pseudo-metric* rather than a metric. A pseudo-metric d satisfies the second and third conditions in the definition of a metric, but the first condition does not necessarily hold. Instead, $d(x, y) \geq 0$ for all x, y, and $d(x, x) = 0$, but we can have $x \neq y$ and $d(x, y) = 0$.

Improper coverings

Recall that, if (A, d) is a metric space and $W \subseteq A$, then, for $\epsilon > 0$, we say that $C \subseteq A$ is an ϵ-cover of W if $C \subseteq W$ and for every $w \in W$ there is a $v \in C$ such that $d(w, v) < \epsilon$. If we drop the requirement that $C \subseteq W$ then we say that C is an *improper cover*. (The type of cover we defined earlier is sometimes called a *proper* cover.) We use this definition of cover because it is often more convenient, but the following lemma shows that the corresponding definition of covering number is closely related to the one used in this chapter.

Lemma 10.6 *Suppose that W is a totally bounded subset of a metric space (A, d). For $\epsilon > 0$, let $\mathcal{N}'(\epsilon, W, d)$ be the minimum cardinality of a finite improper ϵ-cover for W. Then,*

$$\mathcal{N}(2\epsilon, W, d) \leq \mathcal{N}'(\epsilon, (W, d) \leq \mathcal{N}(\epsilon, W, d)$$

for all $\epsilon > 0$.

Proof The second inequality is immediate since any proper cover is also an improper cover. For the first inequality, suppose that C' is an improper ϵ-cover for W of mimimum cardinality. Then, since no element of C' can be removed (since it is minimal) without leaving some element of W 'uncovered', it must be the case that for each $v' \in C'$ there is $c(v') \in W$ with $d(c(v'), v') < \epsilon$. Consider the set $C = \{c(v') : v' \in C'\}$. We claim C is a proper 2ϵ-cover for W. Certainly, $C \subseteq W$. Furthermore, for $w \in W$, there is $v' \in C'$ such that $d(w, v') < \epsilon$, and by the triangle inequality, $d(w, c(v')) \leq d(w, v') + d(v', c(v')) < \epsilon + \epsilon$. The result follows.

$\square$

10.6 Bibliographical Notes

Theorems 10.1 and 10.4 are from (Bartlett, 1998). The proofs of these theorems use ideas due to Vapnik and Chervonenkis (1971) (see also Section 4.7) and Pollard (1984). Kolmogorov and Tihomirov (1961) give many useful properties of covers, including Lemma 10.6.

11
The Pseudo-Dimension and Fat-Shattering Dimension

11.1 Introduction

Chapters 4 and 5 show that the Vapnik-Chervonenkis dimension is crucial in characterizing learnability by binary-output networks, and that it can be used to bound the growth function. Chapter 10 shows that covering numbers are a generalization of the growth function useful for analysing classification by real-output neural networks (or, more generally, by real-valued function classes). We see later in the book that covering numbers are also important in analysing other models of learning. It is natural to ask whether there is a 'combinatorial' measure analogous to the VC-dimension that can be used to bound the covering numbers of a class of real-valued functions, and hence to quantify the sample complexity of classification learning. This is largely true, although the definitions and proofs are more complicated than for the binary classification case. In this chapter we introduce the key 'dimensions' that we use in our analysis of learning with real function classes and establish some associated basic results and useful properties. In the next chapter we show how these dimensions may be used to bound the covering numbers.

11.2 The Pseudo-Dimension

The definition of the pseudo-dimension

To introduce the first of the new dimensions, we first present a slightly different formulation of the definition of the VC-dimension. For a set of functions H mapping from X to $\{0, 1\}$, recall that a subset $S = \{x_1, x_2, \ldots x_m\}$ of X is *shattered* by H if $H_{|s}$ has cardinality 2^m. This means that for any binary vector $b = (b_1, b_2, \ldots, b_m) \in \{0, 1\}^m$, there is

151

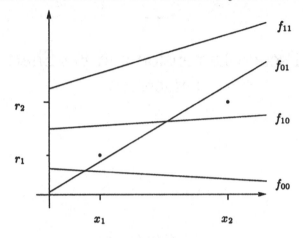

Fig. 11.1. The set $\{x_1, x_2\} \subset \mathbf{R}$ is shattered by the class F of affine functions on $\mathbf{R}$, $F = \{x \mapsto ax + b : a, b \in \mathbf{R}\}$. The points r_1, r_2 witness the shattering.

some corresponding function h_b in H such that

$$(h_b(x_1), h_b(x_2), \ldots, h_b(x_m)) = b,$$

or, in other words, such that $h_b(x_i) = b_i$ for all i.

For a class F of real-valued function, we may modify this definition of shattering as follows. (Recall that $\mathrm{sgn}(\alpha)$ takes value 1 if $\alpha \geq 0$ and 0 otherwise.)

Definition 11.1 *Let F be a set of functions mapping from a domain X to $\mathbf{R}$ and suppose that $S = \{x_1, x_2, \ldots, x_m\} \subseteq X$. Then S is pseudo-shattered by F if there are real numbers $r_1, r_2, \ldots, r_m$ such that for each $b \in \{0, 1\}^m$ there is a function f_b in F with $\mathrm{sgn}(f_b(x_i) - r_i) = b_i$ for $1 \leq i \leq m$. We say that $r = (r_1, r_2, \ldots, r_m)$ witnesses the shattering.*

Thus, S is pseudo-shattered if there are numbers $r_1, r_2, \ldots, r_m$ and 2^m functions f_b that achieve all possible 'above/below' combinations with respect to the r_i. (See Figure 11.1.) Often we will simply write 'shattered' when we mean 'pseudo-shattered'. Corresponding to this notion of shattering, we have the *pseudo-dimension*.

Definition 11.2 *Suppose that F is a set of functions from a domain X to $\mathbf{R}$. Then F has pseudo-dimension d if d is the maximum cardinality of a subset S of X that is pseudo-shattered by F. If no such*

*maximum exists, we say that F has infinite pseudo-dimension. The
pseudo-dimension of F is denoted* Pdim(F).

Other interpretations of pseudo-dimension

There are at least two other useful ways of defining pseudo-shattering
and the pseudo-dimension.

First, for any $f \in F$, let B_f be the indicator function of the region
below or on the graph of f; that is,

$$B_f(x,y) = \text{sgn}(f(x) - y).$$

Then the pseudo-dimension of F is precisely the VC-dimension of the
subgraph class $B_F = \{B_f : f \in F\}$.

Second, for any $x \in X^m$, define

$$F_{|_\mathbf{z}} = \{(f(x_1), f(x_2), \ldots, f(x_m)) : f \in F\} \subseteq \mathbb{R}^m.$$

Then the set $\{x_1, x_2, \ldots, x_m\}$ is pseudo-shattered if this subset of $\mathbb{R}^m$ is
sufficiently 'extensive' in the following geometrical sense. Suppose that
for a given $r \in \mathbb{R}^m$ and $W \subseteq \mathbb{R}^m$,

$$W + r = \{w + r : w \in W\}$$

denotes the *translate* of W by r, and define the 2^m *orthants* of $\mathbb{R}^m$ to
be the sets of points $(y_1, y_2, \ldots, y_m)$ defined by m inequalities, with inequality i being either $y_i \geq 0$ or $y_i < 0$. Then the set $\{x_1, x_2, \ldots, x_m\}$
is pseudo-shattered by F if and only if some translate $F_{|_\mathbf{z}} + r$ of $F_{|_\mathbf{z}}$ in-
tersects all 2^m orthants of $\mathbb{R}^m$. This interpretation of pseudo-dimension
is useful in some proofs.

Pseudo-dimension and compositions with non-decreasing functions

The following theorem shows that composing the function computed by
a neural network with a non-decreasing function (such as the standard
sigmoid, or the step function) does not increase its pseudo-dimension.

Theorem 11.3 *Suppose F is a class of real-valued functions and σ :
$\mathbb{R} \to \mathbb{R}$ is a non-decreasing function. Let $\sigma(F)$ denote the class $\{\sigma \circ f :
f \in F\}$. Then* Pdim$(\sigma(F)) \leq$ Pdim(F).

Proof For $d \leq \text{Pdim}(\sigma(F))$, suppose

$$\{\sigma \circ f_b : b \in \{0,1\}^d\} \subseteq \sigma(F)$$

pseudo-shatters a set $S = \{x_1, \ldots, x_d\} \subseteq X$, witnessed by $(r_1, \ldots, r_d)$. Then, by suitably relabelling the f_b, for all $b \in \{0,1\}^d$ and $i \in \{1, \ldots, d\}$, we have $\text{sgn}\,(\sigma(f_b(x_i)) - r_i) = b_i$. Take

$$y_i = \min\left\{f_b(x_i) : \sigma(f_b(x_i)) \geq r_i, b \in \{0,1\}^d\right\}$$

for $i = 1, \ldots, d$. (Notice that the minimum exists, since the set is finite.) Then, since σ is non-decreasing, it is straightforward to verify that $\text{sgn}\,(f_b(x_i) - y_i) = b_i$ for $b \in \{0,1\}^d$ and $i \in \{1, \ldots, d\}$. □

Pseudo-dimension and linear dimension

We now present a quite general result that is useful in estimating the pseudo-dimension of many function classes. Recall that a class F of real-valued functions is a *vector space* if for all $f, g \in F$ and any two real numbers λ and μ, the function $\lambda f + \mu g$ belongs to F. The following result links the pseudo-dimension to the linear dimension.

Theorem 11.4 *If F is a vector space of real-valued functions then* $\text{Pdim}(F) = \dim(F)$.

Proof For the class B_F of 'below-the-graph' indicator functions defined above, $\text{Pdim}(F) = \text{VCdim}(B_F)$. But

$$B_F = \{(x,y) \mapsto \text{sgn}(f(x) - y) : f \in F\},$$

so the functions in B_F are of the form $\text{sgn}(f + g)$, where f is a function from the vector space and g is the fixed function $g(x,y) = -y$. Theorem 3.5 now shows that $\text{VCdim}(B_F) = \dim(F)$. □

Many of the function classes discussed in this book contain functions that map into some bounded range, and hence cannot be a vector space. However, if the class is a subset of a vector space, the following immediate corollary can be applied.

Corollary 11.5 *If F is a subset of a vector space F' of real-valued functions then* $\text{Pdim}(F) \leq \dim(F')$.

Linear computation units and polynomial transformations

Theorem 11.4 immediately enables us to calculate the pseudo-dimension of many function classes. In this section, we consider linear functions of certain fixed transformations of the inputs.

Suppose that F is the class of *affine combinations* of n real inputs of the form

$$f(x) = w_0 + \sum_{i=1}^{n} w_i x_i,$$

where $w_i \in \mathbb{R}$ and $x = (x_1, \ldots, x_n) \in \mathbb{R}^n$ is the input pattern. We can think of F as the class of functions computable by a *linear computation unit*, which has the identity function as its activation function.

Theorem 11.6 *Let F be the class of real functions computable by a linear computation unit on $\mathbb{R}^n$. Then* $\mathrm{Pdim}(F) = n + 1$.

Proof It is easy to check that F is a vector space. Furthermore, if 1 denotes the identically-1 function and, f_i is the ith co-ordinate projection, $f_i(x) = x_i$, for $1 \leq i \leq n$, then $B = \{f_1, f_2, \ldots, f_n, 1\}$ is a basis of F. To see this, notice that any function in F is a linear combination of the elements of B, so it remains only to show that these functions are linearly independent. Suppose, then, that the constants $\alpha_1, \alpha_2, \ldots, \alpha_{n+1}$ are such that $f = \alpha_1 f_1 + \alpha_2 f_2 + \cdots + \alpha_n f_n + \alpha_{n+1} 1$ is the identically-0 function. Then, $f(0) = 0$ implies that $\alpha_{n+1} = 0$ and $f(e_1) = f(e_2) = \cdots = f(e_n) = 0$ imply that $\alpha_1 = \cdots = \alpha_n = 0$, where e_i has entry i equal to 1 and all other entries 0. It follows that $\dim(F) = n + 1$ and hence, by Theorem 11.4, $\mathrm{Pdim}(F) = n + 1$. ☐

We saw earlier in the book that the VC-dimension of the class of (binary-valued) functions computed by the boolean perceptron is the same as that computed on real inputs. The following theorem shows that the corresponding statement is true of pseudo-dimension.

Theorem 11.7 *Let F be the class of real functions computable by a linear computation unit on $\{0, 1\}^n$. Then* $\mathrm{Pdim}(F) = n + 1$.

Proof We need only note that in the proof of the previous theorem, the proof of the linear independence of the functions $f_1, f_2, \ldots, f_n, 1$ involved values of x (the all-0 vector and the e_i) that are in $\{0, 1\}^n$. Thus the functions form a basis of the space of functions computed by the linear computation unit on $\{0,1\}^n$. This space therefore has linear dimension and pseudo-dimension $n+1$.   □

As a generalization of the class of functions computable by a linear computation unit, we can consider the class of *polynomial transformations*. A polynomial transformation of $\mathbb{R}^n$ is a function of the form

$$f(x) = w_0 + w_1\phi_1(x) + w_2\phi_2(x) + \cdots + w_l\phi_l(x),$$

for $x \in \mathbb{R}^n$, where l is some integer and for each i between 1 and l, the function ϕ_i is defined on $\mathbb{R}^n$ by

$$\phi_i(x) = \prod_{j=1}^{n} x_j^{r_{ij}}$$

for some nonnegative integers r_{ij}. The *degree* of ϕ_i is $r_{i1}+r_{i2}+\cdots+r_{in}$. We say that the polynomial transformation f is of degree at most k when the largest degree of any ϕ_i is at most k. Thus the polynomial transformations of degree at most one are precisely the functions computed by a linear computation unit and, for example, the polynomial transformations of degree at most two on $\mathbb{R}^3$ are the functions of the form

$$\begin{aligned} f(x) \; = \; & w_0 + w_1x_1 + w_2x_2 + w_3x_3 + w_4x_1^2 + w_5x_2^2 + w_6x_3^2 + \\ & w_7x_1x_2 + w_8x_1x_3 + w_9x_2x_3. \end{aligned}$$

Theorem 11.8 *Let F be the class of all polynomial transformations on $\mathbb{R}^n$ of degree at most k. Then*

$$\mathrm{Pdim}(F) = \binom{n+k}{k}.$$

Proof It is easy to see that F is a vector space, so to prove the result we exhibit a basis for F of size $\binom{n+k}{k}$.

Let us denote the set $\{1,2,\ldots,n\}$ by $[n]$, and denote by $[n]^k$ the set of all selections of at most k objects from $[n]$ where repetition is allowed. Thus, $[n]^k$ may be thought of as a collection of 'multisets'. For example, $[3]^2$ consists of the multisets

$$\emptyset, \{1\}, \{2\}, \{3\}, \{1,1\}, \{2,2\}, \{3,3\}, \{1,2\}, \{1,3\}, \{2,3\}.$$

For each $T \in [n]^k$, and for any $x = (x_1, x_2, \ldots, x_n) \in \mathbb{R}^n$, ϕ^T denotes the function

$$\phi^T(x) = \prod_{i \in T} x_i,$$

with repetitions as required, and with the convention that $\prod_{i\in\emptyset} x_i = 1$. For example, $\phi^{\{1,2,3\}}(x) = x_1 x_2 x_3$, $\phi^{\{1,1,2\}}(x) = x_1^2 x_2$, and $\phi^\emptyset(x) = 1$.

It is clear that the functions ϕ_i used in the definition of the polynomial transformations may be written in the form $\phi_i = \phi^T$ for some multiset T. Therefore a function defined on $\mathbb{R}^n$ is a polynomial transformation of degree at most k if and only if there are constants w_T, one for each $T \in [n]^k$, such that

$$f(x) = \sum_{T\in[n]^k} w_T \phi^T(x).$$

It follows that F is a vector space of functions, spanned by the set $B(n,k) = \{\phi^T : T \in [n]^k\}$. We prove by induction that this set is linearly independent. The base case $(n = 1)$ follows from the fact that the functions $1, x, x^2, x^3, \ldots, x^k$ are linearly independent. Suppose now that the assertion is true for a value of $n \geq 1$ and let k be any positive integer. By the inductive assumption, the set $\{\phi^T : T \in [n]^k\}$ is a linearly independent set. For $0 \leq j \leq k$, let $T_j \subseteq [n+1]^k$ be the set of selections containing $n + 1$ exactly j times. Suppose that for some constants α_T, for all $x \in \mathbb{R}^{n+1}$,

$$\sum_{T\in[n+1]^k} \alpha_T \phi^T(x) = 0.$$

Then,

$$\sum_{j=0}^{k} x_{n+1}^j \sum_{T\in T_j} \alpha_T \phi_*^T(x) = 0$$

for all x, where, for $T \in T_j$, $\phi_*^T(x)$ is $\phi^T(x)$ with the j factors equal to x_{n+1} deleted. (So, $\phi_*^T \in B(n,k)$.) It follows, from the linear independence of the functions $1, x_{n+1}, x_{n+1}^2, \ldots, x_{n+1}^k$, that for all $x_1, x_2, \ldots, x_n$, we have

$$\sum_{T\in T_j} \alpha_T \phi_*^T(x) = 0$$

for each j. But the inductive assumption then implies that for all j and for all $T \in T_j$, $\alpha_T = 0$; that is, all the coefficients α_T are zero. Hence the functions are linearly independent. It follows that $\dim(F) = |B(n,k)| = |[n]^k|$.

It remains to show that $[n]^k$ consists of $\binom{n+k}{k}$ multisets. To see this, let us represent a multiset having k_i copies of element i as a binary vector consisting of k_1 ones, then a zero, then k_2 ones, then a zero,

..., then k_n ones, then a zero, then $(k - \sum_{i=1}^{n} k_i)$ ones. (For example, $\{1, 1, 2, 4, 4, 5\} \in [5]^6$ is encoded as 11010011010.) This defines a one-to-one correspondence between $[n]^k$ and the subset of vectors in $\{0, 1\}^{n+k}$ with exactly k ones. It follows that

$$|[n]^k| = \binom{n+k}{k}.$$

□

The following result shows that for $k > 1$, the pseudo-dimension of the class of polynomial transformations defined on $\{0, 1\}^n$ is strictly less than that of the class defined on $\mathbb{R}^n$. (We have seen above that these dimensions are equal when $k = 1$.)

Theorem 11.9 *Let F be the class of all polynomial transformations on $\{0, 1\}^n$ of degree at most k. Then*

$$\text{Pdim}(F) = \sum_{i=0}^{k} \binom{n}{i}.$$

Proof The proof involves showing that a subset of the set $B(n, k)$ defined in the proof of the previous theorem is a basis for F. If we restrict attention to binary inputs, then any terms ϕ^T in which T contains a repetition are redundant, simply because for $x = 0$ or 1, $x^r = x$ for all r. We shall denote the set of all subsets of at most k objects from $[n]$ by $[n]^{(k)}$. Any $T \in [n]^{(k)}$ contains no repetitions. For example, $[3]^{(2)}$ consists of the sets

$$\emptyset, \{1\}, \{2\}, \{3\}, \{1, 2\}, \{1, 3\}, \{2, 3\},$$

Clearly, $[n]^{(k)}$ consists of $\sum_{i=0}^{k} \binom{n}{i}$ sets. In view of the redundancy of repetitions in the binary-input case, the class F of polynomial transformations on $\{0, 1\}^n$ is generated by the set

$$C(n, m) = \{\phi^T : T \in [n]^{(k)}\}.$$

To show that this is a basis, suppose that for some constants α_T and for all $x \in \{0, 1\}^n$,

$$A(x) = \sum_{T \in [n]^{(k)}} \alpha_T \phi^T(x) = 0.$$

Set x to be the all-0 vector to deduce that $\alpha_\emptyset = 0$. Let $1 \le l \le k$ and assume, inductively, that $\alpha_T = 0$ for all $T \subseteq [n]$ with $|T| < l$. Let

$T \subseteq [n]$ with $|T| = l$. Setting x_i equal to 1 if $i \in T$ and 0 if $i \notin T$, we deduce that $A(x) = \alpha_T = 0$. Thus for all T of cardinality l, $\alpha_T = 0$. Hence $\alpha_T = 0$ for all T, and the functions are linearly independent. □

11.3 The Fat-Shattering Dimension

Definition of the fat-shattering dimension

Recall that a set $S = \{x_1, x_2, \ldots, x_m\}$ is shattered by a function class F if there are numbers $r_1, r_2, \ldots, r_m$ such that all 2^m 'above/below' combinations with respect to the r_i are possible. We can make this condition more stringent by requiring not merely that the function values on the x_i be either above r_i or below r_i, but above or below by at least a certain 'clearance'. The following definition formalizes this.

Definition 11.10 *Let F be a set of functions mapping from a domain X to $\mathbb{R}$ and suppose that $S = \{x_1, x_2, \ldots, x_m\} \subseteq X$. Suppose also that γ is a positive real number. Then S is γ-shattered by F if there are real numbers $r_1, r_2, \ldots, r_m$ such that for each $b \in \{0,1\}^m$ there is a function f_b in F with*

$$f_b(x_i) \geq r_i + \gamma \text{ if } b_i = 1, \text{ and } f_b(x_i) \leq r_i - \gamma \text{ if } b_i = 0, \text{ for } 1 \leq i \leq m.$$

We say that $r = (r_1, r_2, \ldots, r_m)$ witnesses the shattering.

Thus, S is γ-shattered if it is shattered with a 'width of shattering' of at least γ. (See Figure 11.2.) This notion of shattering leads to the following dimension.

Definition 11.11 *Suppose that F is a set of functions from a domain X to $\mathbb{R}$ and that $\gamma > 0$. Then F has γ-dimension d if d is the maximum cardinality of a subset S of X that is γ-shattered by F. If no such maximum exists, we say that F has infinite γ-dimension. The γ-dimension of F is denoted $\text{fat}_F(\gamma)$. This defines a function $\text{fat}_F : \mathbb{R}^+ \to \mathbb{N} \cup \{0, \infty\}$, which we call the fat-shattering dimension of F. We say that F has finite fat-shattering dimension whenever it is the case that for all $\gamma > 0$, $\text{fat}_F(\gamma)$ is finite.*

Since this dimension depends on the scale γ, it is often described as a *scale-sensitive dimension*. To illustrate the fat-shattering dimension, we consider classes of functions of bounded variation. We say that a function $f : [0,1] \to \mathbb{R}$ is of *bounded variation* if there is V such that

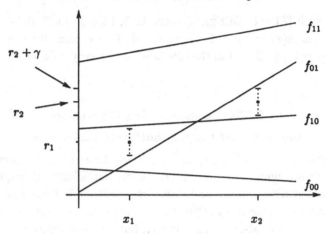

Fig. 11.2. The set $\{x_1, x_2\} \subset \mathbb{R}$ is γ-shattered by the class F of affine functions on $\mathbb{R}$, $F = \{x \mapsto ax + b : a, b \in \mathbb{R}\}$. The points r_1, r_2 witness the shattering.

for every integer n and every sequence $y_1, y_2, \ldots, y_n$ of numbers with $0 \leq y_1 < y_2 < \cdots < y_n \leq 1$, we have

$$\sum_{i=1}^{n-1} |f(y_{i+1}) - f(y_i)| \leq V.$$

In this case, we say that f has *total variation* at most V.

Theorem 11.12 *Let F be the set of all functions mapping from the interval $[0,1]$ to the interval $[0,1]$ and having total variation at most V. Then*

$$\mathrm{fat}_F(\gamma) = 1 + \left\lfloor \frac{V}{2\gamma} \right\rfloor.$$

Proof Suppose that $\gamma > 0$ and that the set $S = \{x_1, x_2, \ldots, x_m\}$ is γ-shattered, witnessed by $r = (r_1, r_2, \ldots, r_m)$. Assume, without loss of generality, that $x_1 < x_2 < \cdots < x_m$. (Clearly, no two of the x_i can be equal.) Since S is γ-shattered, there are two functions $f_1, f_2 \in F$ with the following properties:

$$\begin{aligned} f_1(x_i) &\geq r_i + \gamma &&\text{for } i \text{ odd,} \\ f_1(x_i) &< r_i - \gamma &&\text{for } i \text{ even,} \end{aligned}$$

and

$$f_2(x_i) < r_i - \gamma \qquad \text{for } i \text{ odd,}$$
$$f_2(x_i) \geq r_i + \gamma \qquad \text{for } i \text{ even.}$$

Suppose that m is odd. Then the total variation V_1 of f_1 satisfies

$$V_1 \geq \sum_{i=1}^{m-1} |f_1(x_i) - f_1(x_{i+1})|$$

$$= \sum_{l=1}^{(m-1)/2} (|f_1(x_{2l-1}) - f_1(x_{2l})| + |f_1(x_{2l+1}) - f_1(x_{2l})|)$$

$$\geq \sum_{l=1}^{(m-1)/2} (f_1(x_{2l-1}) - 2f_1(x_{2l}) + f_1(x_{2l+1}))$$

$$\geq \sum_{l=1}^{(m-1)/2} (r_{2l-1} - 2r_{2l} + r_{2l+1}) + 2(m-1)\gamma.$$

Similarly, the total variation V_2 of f_2 satisfies

$$V_2 \geq \sum_{l=1}^{(m-1)/2} (-r_{2l-1} + 2r_{2l} - r_{2l+1}) + 2(m-1)\gamma.$$

Clearly, $\max(V_1, V_2) \geq 2(m-1)\gamma$. If m is even, the same argument shows that

$$\max(V_1, V_2)$$
$$\geq \left| \sum_{l=1}^{m/2-1} (r_{2l-1} - 2r_{2l} + r_{2l+1}) + r_{m-1} - r_m \right| + 2(m-1)\gamma$$
$$\geq 2(m-1)\gamma.$$

But, since f_1 and f_2 have total variation at most V, it follows that $m \leq 1 + V/(2\gamma)$, and so

$$\text{fat}_F(\gamma) \leq 1 + \left\lfloor \frac{V}{2\gamma} \right\rfloor.$$

Now, let $d = \lfloor V/2\gamma \rfloor$ and let $S = \{i/d : i = 0, 1, 2, \ldots, d\}$, which has cardinality $d + 1$. Let G consist of 2^{d+1} functions $g : [0,1] \to \{0, 2\gamma\}$ that are piecewise-constant on the intervals

$$\left[0, \frac{1}{2d}\right), \left[\frac{1}{2d}, \frac{3}{2d}\right), \ldots, \left[\frac{2d-3}{2d}, \frac{2d-1}{2d}\right), \left[\frac{2d-1}{2d}, 1\right].$$

Then it is clear that S is shattered by G, witnessed by the all-γ vector $r = (\gamma, \gamma, \ldots, \gamma)$. Furthermore, $G \subseteq F$, since each $g \in G$ has total variation at most $2\gamma d = 2\gamma \lfloor V/2\gamma \rfloor \leq V$. It follows that F γ-shatters S and hence

$$\mathrm{fat}_F(\gamma) \geq |S| = 1 + \left\lfloor \frac{V}{2\gamma} \right\rfloor,$$

as required.   □

Relating fat-shattering dimension and pseudo-dimension

Given that the notion of γ-shattering is a refinement of that of pseudo-shattering, some relationships between the fat-shattering dimension and the pseudo-dimension can be given.

Theorem 11.13 *Suppose that F is a set of real-valued functions. Then:*

(i) *For all $\gamma > 0$, $\mathrm{fat}_F(\gamma) \leq \mathrm{Pdim}(F)$.*

(ii) *If a finite set S is pseudo-shattered then there is γ_0 such that for all $\gamma < \gamma_0$, S is γ-shattered.*

(iii) *The function fat_F is non-increasing with γ.*

(iv) $\mathrm{Pdim}(F) = \lim_{\gamma \downarrow 0} \mathrm{fat}_F(\gamma)$ *(where both sides may be infinite).*

Proof For (i), we need only note that if a finite set S is γ-shattered for some $\gamma > 0$ then it is pseudo-shattered. For (ii), suppose the finite set $S = \{x_1, x_2, \ldots, x_m\}$ is pseudo-shattered by F, witnessed by $r = (r_1, r_2, \ldots, r_m)$. With the functions $f_b \in F$ as in the definition of pseudo-shattering, let

$$\gamma_0 = \frac{1}{2} \min \left\{ r_i - f_b(x_i) : 1 \leq i \leq m,\ b \in \{0,1\}^m,\ f_b(x_i) < r_i \right\}.$$

Then for all $\gamma < \gamma_0$, S is γ-shattered, witnessed by r', where $r'_i = r_i - \gamma_0/2$. To prove (iii), we observe that if $\gamma < \gamma'$ then any γ'-shattered set is also γ-shattered. Part (iv) follows immediately.   □

It should be noted that it is possible for the pseudo-dimension to be infinite, even when the fat-shattering dimension is finite for all positive γ. Indeed, by Theorem 11.12 and part (iv) of Theorem 11.13, this is true for the class of functions on $[0, 1]$ of total variation at most V (for any V).

We say that a function class is *closed under scalar multiplication* if for all $f \in F$ and all real numbers λ, the function λf belongs to F. Any vector space of functions is certainly closed under scalar multiplication, so the class of functions computable by the linear computation unit, for instance, has this property. (Note, however, that any set of functions mapping into a bounded range does not have this property.)

Theorem 11.14 *Suppose that a set F of real-valued functions is closed under scalar multiplication. Then, for all positive γ,*

$$\text{fat}_F(\gamma) = \text{Pdim}(F).$$

In particular, F has finite fat-shattering dimension if and only if it has finite pseudo-dimension.

Proof Suppose that a finite set $S = \{x_1, x_2, \ldots, x_m\}$ is pseudo-shattered and that γ is some arbitrary positive number. Part (ii) of Theorem 11.13 shows that there is a $\gamma_0 > 0$ such that S is γ_0-shattered. Suppose the shattering is witnessed by $(r_1, r_2, \ldots, r_m)$, and let the functions $\{f_b\}$ be as in the definition of γ_0-shattering. Then the functions $\{(\gamma/\gamma_0)f_b\}$ γ-shatter S, witnessed by $((\gamma/\gamma_0)r_1, \ldots, (\gamma/\gamma_0)r_m)$. But these functions are also in F, since F is closed under scalar multiplication, and so for all $\gamma > 0$, $\text{fat}_F(\gamma) \geq \text{Pdim}(F)$. Combining this with part (i) of Theorem 11.13 gives the result. □

11.4 Bibliographical Notes

The pseudo-dimension was introduced by Pollard (1984; 1990), who also observed that Theorem 11.4 follows from the corresponding result for VC-dimension. Several closely related dimensions have been considered; see, for example, the definition of VC-major classes in (Dudley, 1987). Theorem 11.3 is from (Haussler, 1992); see also Proposition 4.2 in (Dudley, 1987)). The results on classes of polynomial transformations may be found in (Anthony, 1995; Anthony and Holden, 1993; Anthony and Holden, 1994).

The fat-shattering dimension was introduced by Kearns and Schapire (1994), who used it to prove lower bounds in a related learning problem (that of learning probabilistic concepts—see Section 9.4). Closely related quantities were used earlier in approximation theory (Lorentz, 1986, p. 113), and attributed in (Tikhomirov, 1969) to Kolmogorov. The calculation of the fat-shattering dimension of bounded variation functions

164   *The Pseudo-Dimension and Fat-Shattering Dimension*

(Theorem 11.12) is due to Simon (1997). (In fact, Simon calculates a slightly different dimension, but the calculation is essentially identical.)

12

Bounding Covering Numbers with Dimensions

12.1 Introduction

Having introduced the pseudo-dimension and fat-shattering dimension, we now show how these can be used to bound the covering numbers of a function class. Given that these dimensions are generalizations of the VC-dimension and that the covering numbers are generalizations of the growth function, this is analogous to bounding the growth function in terms of the VC-dimension. The details are, as one might expect, rather more complicated.

12.2 Packing Numbers

In computing upper bounds on covering numbers, it is often useful to bound related measures of 'richness' known as *packing numbers*. Since several different packing numbers are also useful later in the book, we define them for a general metric space.

Suppose that A is a set and that d is a metric on A. Given $W \subseteq A$ and a positive number ϵ, a subset $P \subseteq W$ is said to be ϵ-*separated*, or to be *an ϵ-packing of W*, if for all distinct $x, y \in P$, $d(x, y) \geq \epsilon$. Figure 12.1 shows a subset of $\mathbb{R}^2$ that is ϵ-separated with respect to the d_2 metric.

We define the ϵ-*packing number of W*, $\mathcal{M}(\epsilon, W, d)$, to be the maximum cardinality of an ϵ-separated subset of W. (If there is no upper bound on the cardinality of ϵ-separated subsets of W, we say that the packing number is infinite.) We are particularly interested in the cases where A is $\mathbb{R}^k$ for some k and the metric d is either the d_∞ metric, the d_1 metric, or the d_2 metric. As for covering numbers, we are concerned with cases where $W = H_{|_x}$ for a function class H and a sample x of length k. We define the *uniform packing numbers* as

$$\mathcal{M}_p(\epsilon, H, k) = \max\left\{ \mathcal{M}(\epsilon, H_{|_x}, d_p) : x \in X^k \right\}$$

165

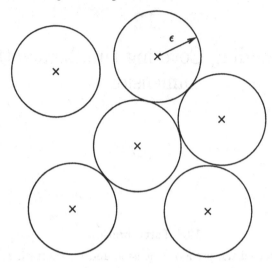

Fig. 12.1. The crosses form an ϵ-separated subset of $\mathbb{R}^2$ with respect to the d_2 metric.

for $p = 1, 2, \infty$.

It turns out that packing numbers are intimately related to covering numbers, as the following result shows.

Theorem 12.1 *Let (A, d) be a metric space. Then for all positive ϵ, and for every subset W of A, the covering numbers and packing numbers satisfy*

$$\mathcal{M}(2\epsilon, W, d) \le \mathcal{N}(\epsilon, W, d) \le \mathcal{M}(\epsilon, W, d). \qquad (12.1)$$

Proof For the first inequality in (12.1), suppose that C is an ϵ-cover for W and that P is a 2ϵ-packing of W of maximum cardinality, $\mathcal{M}(2\epsilon, W, d)$. We show that $|P| \le |C|$, from which the inequality follows. Now, for each $w \in P$, since C is an ϵ-cover for W, there is some $v \in C$ such that $d(w, v) < \epsilon$. If $|P| > |C|$, then (by a simple application of the 'pigeonhole† principle') there must be some $v \in C$ such that for two points w_1, w_2 of P, $d(w_1, v) < \epsilon$ and $d(w_2, v) < \epsilon$. Then, since d is a metric,

$$d(w_1, w_2) \le d(w_1, v) + d(w_2, v) < 2\epsilon.$$

† The pigeonhole principle states that if n pigeons are distributed over fewer than n pigeonholes, some pigeonhole must contain more than one pigeon.

But this contradicts the fact that the points of P are 2ϵ-separated, and we obtain the desired result.

To prove the second inequality, suppose that P is an ϵ-packing of maximal cardinality, $\mathcal{M}(\epsilon, W, d)$. Then for any $w \in W$, there must be a $v \in P$ with $d(v, w) < \epsilon$; otherwise w is not an element of P and $P \cup \{w\}$ is an ϵ-packing, which contradicts the assumption that P is a maximal ϵ-packing. It follows that any maximal ϵ-packing is an ϵ-cover. $\quad\square$

12.3 Bounding with the Pseudo-Dimension

In this section we bound the d_∞-covering numbers by a quantity involving the pseudo-dimension.

Theorem 12.2 *Let F be a set of real functions from a domain X to the bounded interval $[0, B]$. Let $\epsilon > 0$ and suppose that the pseudo-dimension of F is d. Then*

$$\mathcal{N}_\infty (\epsilon, F, m) \leq \sum_{i=1}^{d} \binom{m}{i} \left(\frac{B}{\epsilon}\right)^i,$$

which is less than $(emB/(\epsilon d))^d$ for $m \geq d$.

Quantization

Integral to the proof of Theorem 12.2 is the technique of *quantizing* the function class. This is a method that we employ several times in the book.

Suppose that F is a class of functions mapping from a domain X into a bounded interval in $\mathbb{R}$. We assume that this interval is $[0, 1]$; by shifting and scaling, everything that follows can be modified to deal with the case where functions in F map into some other bounded interval.

Let α be any positive real number. For any real number u, the *quantized version of u, with quantization width α* is

$$Q_\alpha(u) = \alpha \left\lfloor \frac{u}{\alpha} \right\rfloor .$$

In other words, $Q_\alpha(u)$ is the largest integer multiple of α less than or equal to u. (See Figure 12.2.) For a function $f \in F$, the function $Q_\alpha(f)$ is defined on X as

$$(Q_\alpha(f))(x) = Q_\alpha(f(x)) .$$

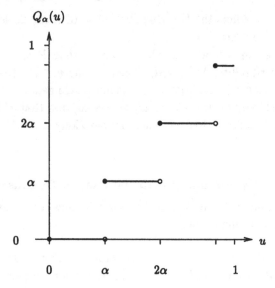

Fig. 12.2. The quantization function $Q_\alpha : \mathbb{R} \to \mathbb{R}$.

This function maps from X into the finite subset $\{0, \alpha, 2\alpha, \ldots, \lfloor 1/\alpha \rfloor \alpha\}$ of $[0, 1]$. We denote by $Q_\alpha(F)$ the function class $\{Q_\alpha(f) : f \in F\}$.

Proof of Theorem 12.2

Packing numbers and the quantized class

To derive upper bounds on covering numbers, we bound the corresponding packing numbers and appeal to Theorem 12.1. (This approach is typical; it seems to be easier to show that there cannot be too many well-separated functions than to show directly that a small cover exists.) The first step in bounding the packing numbers of a function class is to reduce the problem to one involving a quantized version of F, as expressed by the following lemma.

Lemma 12.3 *For a set F of real-valued functions mapping from X into the interval $[0, 1]$, we have*

$$\mathcal{M}_\infty \left(\epsilon, F, m \right) \leq \mathcal{M}_\infty \left(\alpha \left\lfloor \frac{\epsilon}{\alpha} \right\rfloor, Q_\alpha(F), m \right)$$

for all positive integers m, *all* $\epsilon > 0$, *and all* $0 < \alpha \leq \epsilon$. *Hence,*

$$\mathcal{M}_\infty\left(\epsilon, F, m\right) \leq \max_{x \in X^m} \left| Q_\epsilon(F)_{|_\bullet} \right|.$$

Proof We use the following inequality, which holds for any real numbers a, b.

$$|Q_\alpha(a) - Q_\alpha(b)| \geq Q_\alpha(|a - b|).$$

To see this, notice that

$$\left\lfloor \frac{|a-b|}{\alpha} \right\rfloor = \left\lfloor \left| \left\lfloor \frac{a}{\alpha} \right\rfloor - \left\lfloor \frac{b}{\alpha} \right\rfloor + \frac{a}{\alpha} - \left\lfloor \frac{a}{\alpha} \right\rfloor - \left(\frac{b}{\alpha} - \left\lfloor \frac{b}{\alpha} \right\rfloor\right) \right| \right\rfloor$$

$$\leq \left| \left\lfloor \frac{a}{\alpha} \right\rfloor - \left\lfloor \frac{b}{\alpha} \right\rfloor \right| + \left\lfloor \left| \frac{a}{\alpha} - \left\lfloor \frac{a}{\alpha} \right\rfloor - \left(\frac{b}{\alpha} - \left\lfloor \frac{b}{\alpha} \right\rfloor\right) \right| \right\rfloor,$$

but the second term is zero since it is the floor function of the difference between two numbers in the interval $[0, 1)$.

Now, fix ϵ, m, and $x = (x_1, \ldots, x_m) \in X^m$. Consider any two functions $f, g \in F$, and let $f_{|_\bullet}$ denote $(f(x_1), f(x_2), \ldots, f(x_m))$. Then $d_\infty(f_{|_\bullet}, g_{|_\bullet}) \geq \epsilon$ implies that some $1 \leq i \leq m$ has $|f(x_i) - g(x_i)| \geq \epsilon$. By the inequality above, this implies that

$$|Q_\alpha f(x_i) - Q_\alpha g(x_i)| \geq \alpha \left\lfloor \frac{\epsilon}{\alpha} \right\rfloor.$$

Hence, the quantized versions of distinct elements of an ϵ-separated set are $\alpha\lfloor \epsilon/\alpha \rfloor$-separated. For $\alpha \leq \epsilon$, this gives the first inequality of the theorem. The second inequality follows on substituting $\alpha = \epsilon$, since

$$\mathcal{M}(\epsilon, Q_\epsilon(F)_{|_\bullet}, d_\infty) = \left| Q_\epsilon(F)_{|_\bullet} \right|.$$

$\square$

Now, since $Q_\epsilon(\cdot)$ is non-decreasing, Theorem 11.3 shows that the pseudo-dimension of the quantized class is no more than that of F,

$$\mathrm{Pdim}\left(Q_\epsilon(F)\right) \leq \mathrm{Pdim}(F) \qquad (12.2)$$

for all $\epsilon > 0$.

A combinatorial result

We now see that to bound the covering number, it is enough to bound the cardinality of $Q_\epsilon(F)_{|_\bullet}$. Fixing some $x \in X^m$, we may regard the class $Q_\epsilon(F)_{|_\bullet}$ as a set of functions mapping from the *finite* set S consisting of the entries of x to the finite range Y.

It is possible to bound the size of $Q_\epsilon(F)_{|s}$ using Theorem 3.6, by considering the corresponding subgraph class $B_{Q_\epsilon(F)}$ (see Section 11.2). To see this, notice that

$$\left| Q_\epsilon(F)_{|s} \right| \leq \left| B_{Q_\epsilon(F)_{|s \times Y}} \right|.$$

(Indeed, if we were to add a function to F so that $Q_\epsilon(F)_{|s}$ contained a new vector, this would lead to a new vector in $B_{Q_\epsilon(F)_{|s \times Y}}$.) Theorem 3.6 shows that

$$\left| Q_\epsilon(F)_{|s} \right| \leq \sum_{i=0}^{d} \binom{mN}{i}, \qquad (12.3)$$

where $N = |Y| = \lfloor 1/\epsilon \rfloor + 1$ and $d = \text{VCdim}\left(B_{Q_\epsilon(F)}\right)$. But then $d = \text{Pdim}\left(Q_\epsilon(F)\right) \leq \text{Pdim}(F)$, so we have a bound in terms of the pseudo-dimension of F. However, to prove Theorem 12.2 we need a slightly better bound. The following result is sufficient.

Theorem 12.4 *Suppose that H is a set of functions from a finite set X of cardinality m to a finite set $Y \subseteq \mathbb{R}$ of cardinality N and that H has pseudo-dimension at most d. Then*

$$|H| \leq \sum_{i=0}^{d} \binom{m}{i} (N-1)^i.$$

Notice that substituting $N = 1$ into this theorem gives Sauer's Lemma (Theorem 3.6). Theorem 12.4 follows from a more general result, which also applies to other notions of dimension. Before presenting this result, we require some definitions.

We can think of a subset T of $\{0,1\}^m$ as a set of $\{0,1\}$-valued functions defined on $\{1,\ldots,m\}$, each of which maps i to t_i for some $(t_1,\ldots,t_m) \in T$. Using this interpretation, we can define the VC-dimension of T as the VC-dimension of the class $\{i \mapsto t_i : (t_1,\ldots,t_m) \in T\}$ of functions defined on $\{1,\ldots,m\}$. For any finite subset $Y \subseteq \mathbb{R}$, a set $S \subseteq Y^m$ of m-vectors, and a set Φ of functions from Y to $\{0,1\}$, we define the Φ-*dimension* of S, denoted $\Phi\text{dim}(S)$, as the maximum over $\phi_1, \phi_2, \ldots, \phi_m \in \Phi$ of

$$\text{VCdim}\left(\{(\phi_1(y_1),\ldots,\phi_m(y_m)) : (y_1,\ldots,y_m) \in S\}\right).$$

To see how this general framework applies to the problem considered in Theorem 12.4, suppose that $X = \{x_1, x_2, \ldots, x_m\}$, $Y = \{y_1, y_2, \ldots, y_N\}$ where $y_1 < y_2 < \cdots < y_N$, and that we take

$$S = H_{|X} = \{(h(x_1), h(x_2), \ldots, h(x_m)) : h \in H\}$$

and $\Phi = \Phi_S = \{s_i : 1 \le i \le N\}$, where $s_i(\alpha) = \operatorname{sgn}(\alpha - y_i)$. Then it is straightforward to see that $\Phi\dim(S)$ is precisely $\operatorname{Pdim}(H)$.

The following theorem uses the notion of a *spanning set*. Recall that, for a subset $\{v_1, \ldots, v_N\}$ of a vector space V, we define the span of the subset as

$$\operatorname{span}\{v_1, \ldots, v_N\} = \left\{ \sum_{i=1}^{N} \alpha_i v_i : \alpha_i \in \mathbb{R} \right\},$$

and we say that the subset *spans* V if $\operatorname{span}\{v_1, \ldots, v_N\} = V$. For a finite set $Y = \{y_1, y_2, \ldots, y_N\}$ the set of real-valued functions defined on Y (denoted $\mathbb{R}^Y$) is a vector space of dimension N. In the following theorem, the condition that $\Phi_{|_Y}$ spans the vector space $\mathbb{R}^Y$ ensures that the set Φ is rich enough to capture the complexity of the set S.

Theorem 12.5 *For a finite set Y of cardinality N, and a set $S \subseteq Y^m$ with*

$$\Phi\dim(S) \le d,$$

if $\Phi_{|_Y}$ spans $\mathbb{R}^Y$ then

$$|S| \le \sum_{i=0}^{d} \binom{m}{i} (N-1)^i.$$

To see that this theorem implies Theorem 12.4, suppose that $Y = \{y_1, \ldots, y_N\}$ where $y_1 < y_2 < \cdots < y_N$, and that $s_1, s_2, \ldots, s_N$ are as defined above. Then, as we have noted, $\Phi\dim(S) = \operatorname{Pdim}(H)$. Furthermore, $\Phi_{|_Y}$ consists of the N vectors

$$(1, 1, 1, \ldots, 1), \ (0, 1, 1, \ldots, 1), \ (0, 0, 1, \ldots, 1), \ \ldots, (0, 0, \ldots, 0, 1).$$

These vectors span $\mathbb{R}^N$ and hence $\Phi_{|_Y}$ spans $\mathbb{R}^Y$.

The proof of Theorem 12.5 uses the following lemma, which shows that a certain class $\Phi^{(d)}$ has $\Phi^{(d)}_{|_S}$ spanning $\mathbb{R}^S$. The proof also uses the observation that any such class must have $|S| \le \dim(\operatorname{span}(\Phi^{(d)}))$. For a set of functions Φ as above, $\Phi^{(d)}$ denotes the following set of functions defined on Y^m. (These functions are 'monomials' evaluated by forming the products of the values of some of the functions in Φ at up to d of the y_i.)

$$\Phi^{(d)} = \left\{ (y_1, \ldots, y_m) \mapsto \prod_{i=1}^{d} \prod_{j=1}^{k} \phi_j(y_{l_i}) : k \ge 0, \ \phi_j \in \Phi, \ 1 \le l_i \le m \right\}.$$

We use the convention that $\prod_{i \in \emptyset} a_i = 1$.

Lemma 12.6 *Suppose Y is a finite set, Φ is a set of $\{0,1\}$-valued functions defined on Y, and $S \subseteq Y^m$ satisfies $\Phi\dim(S) = d$. If $\Phi|_Y$ spans $\mathbb{R}^Y$, then $\Phi^{(d)}|_S$ spans $\mathbb{R}^S$.*

Proof The proof is in two steps. First, we show that if $\Phi|_Y$ spans $\mathbb{R}^Y$ then $\Phi^{(m)}|_{Y^m}$ spans $\mathbb{R}^{Y^m}$. Then we show that this implies $\Phi^{(d)}|_S$ spans $\mathbb{R}^S$.

If $\Phi|_Y$ spans $\mathbb{R}^Y$, where $Y = \{y_1, y_2, \ldots, y_N\}$, then there are functions $\phi_1, \ldots, \phi_N$ in Φ for which the matrix

$$
M = \begin{pmatrix}
\phi_1(y_1) & \phi_1(y_2) & \cdots & \phi_1(y_N) \\
\phi_2(y_1) & \phi_2(y_2) & \cdots & \phi_2(y_N) \\
\vdots & \vdots & & \vdots \\
\phi_N(y_1) & \phi_N(y_2) & \cdots & \phi_N(y_N)
\end{pmatrix}
$$

is of full rank. The Kronecker product of two $N \times N$ matrices, $A = (a_{ij})$ and B, is given by

$$
A \otimes B = \begin{pmatrix}
a_{11}B & a_{12}B & \cdots & a_{1N}B \\
a_{21}B & a_{22}B & \cdots & a_{2N}B \\
\vdots & \vdots & & \vdots \\
a_{N1}B & a_{N2}B & \cdots & a_{NN}B
\end{pmatrix}.
$$

If A and B are of full rank, so is $A \otimes B$. (To see this, notice that $(A \otimes B)(C \otimes D) = (AC) \otimes (BD)$, so we have $(A \otimes B)(A^{-1} \otimes B^{-1}) = I_N \otimes I_N = I_{N^2}$, where I_N is the $N \times N$ identity matrix.) Therefore, the m-fold Kronecker product, $M \otimes M \otimes \cdots \otimes M$ is of full rank. Now, it is easy to see that this matrix is of the form

$$
\begin{pmatrix}
\psi_1(z_1) & \psi_1(z_2) & \cdots & \psi_1(z_{N^m}) \\
\psi_2(z_1) & \psi_2(z_2) & \cdots & \psi_2(z_{N^m}) \\
\vdots & \vdots & & \vdots \\
\psi_{N^m}(z_1) & \psi_{N^m}(z_2) & \cdots & \psi_{N^m}(z_{N^m})
\end{pmatrix},
$$

where the N^m functions $\psi_i : Y^m \to \mathbb{R}$ are all the functions of the form

$$
\psi((w_1, w_2, \ldots, w_m)) = \phi_{j_1}(w_1)\phi_{j_2}(w_2) \cdots \phi_{j_m}(w_m)
$$

where $1 \leq j_1, j_2, \ldots, j_m \leq N$, and where the z_i are all the elements of Y^m of the form $(y_{i_1}, y_{i_2}, \ldots, y_{i_m})$ for $1 \leq i_1, i_2, \ldots, i_m \leq N$. It follows that $\Phi^{(m)}|_{Y^m}$ spans $\mathbb{R}^{Y^m}$.

For the second part of the proof, we show that this implies that $\Phi^{(d)}|_S$ spans $\mathbb{R}^S$. Consider a monomial in $\Phi^{(m)}$ involving $k > d$ components of y. We show that, for all $y \in S$, this is equivalent to some linear combination of monomials each of which involves no more than $k - 1$ components. Without loss of generality, we shall consider the monomial $\prod_{i=1}^{k} \phi_i(y_i)$, with $k > d$. Since

$$\mathrm{VCdim}\,\{(\phi_1(y_1),\ldots,\phi_k(y_k)) : y \in Y\} \le d,$$

there is some k-vector $(b_1,\ldots,b_k) \in \{0,1\}^k$ such that, for all $y \in S$, some $1 \le i \le k$ has $\phi_i(y_i) \ne b_i$. If we define

$$z_i(y) = \begin{cases} 1 - \phi_i(y_i) & \text{if } b_i = 0, \\ \phi_i(y_i) & \text{otherwise,} \end{cases}$$

then $\prod_{i=1}^{k} z_i(y) = 0$ for all $y \in S$. Expanding the product in this equation to a sum, and noticing that $\prod_{i=1}^{k} \phi_i(y_i)$ appears in only one term shows that we can write

$$\prod_{i=1}^{k} \phi_i(y_i) = p\,(\phi_1(y_1),\ldots,\phi_k(y_k))$$

for all $y \in S$, where p is a polynomial involving only monomials with no more than $k - 1$ of the variables $\phi_i(y_i)$. Applying this result iteratively to every monomial involving more than d components shows that any monomial in $\Phi^{(m)}$ is equivalent on S to a linear combination of monomials in $\Phi^{(d)}$. Combining this with the first part of the proof, we see that $\Phi^{(d)}|_S$ spans $\mathbb{R}^S$. $\qquad\square$

Proof (of Theorem 12.5) Since Φ spans $\mathbb{R}^Y$, Lemma 12.6 implies that any function on S can be represented as a linear combination of elements of $\Phi^{(d)}$. But any function $\phi : Y \to \mathbb{R}$—and, in particular, any function in Φ—can be represented as a polynomial of degree no more than $N - 1$,

$$\phi(y) = \sum_{i=1}^{N} \frac{\phi(i)}{\prod_{j \ne i}(i - j)} \prod_{j \ne i}(y - j).$$

It follows that any function on S can be represented as a linear combination of elements of the set M_d^{N-1} of monomials with up to d variables, each with exponent no more than $N - 1$,

$$M_d^{N-1} = \left\{ y \mapsto \prod_{i=1}^{l} y_{j_i}^{k_i} : 0 \le l \le d,\ 1 \le j_i \le m,\ 0 \le k_i \le N - 1 \right\},$$

where, as above, we use the convention that $\prod_{i \in \emptyset} y_{j_i}^{k_i} = 1$. That is, $M_d^{N-1}\big|_s$ spans $\mathbb{R}^S$, and so $|S| \leq \dim\left(\text{span}\left(M_d^{N-1}\right)\right)$. The proof of Theorem 11.8 shows that the set of all monomials of bounded degree is linearly independent, which implies that

$$|S| \leq \left|M_d^{N-1}\right| = \sum_{i=0}^{d} \binom{m}{i}(N-1)^i.$$

$\square$

Obtaining Theorem 12.2

Theorem 12.2 follows immediately. Fix any x and let H be the restriction of $Q_\epsilon(F)$ to the set consisting of the m entries of X. Then H maps into the finite set Y of cardinality $N = 1 + \lfloor 1/\epsilon \rfloor$ and, by Lemma 12.3, Theorem 12.1, and Theorem 12.4,

$$\mathcal{N}_\infty(\epsilon, F, m) \leq \max_{x \in X^m} \left|Q_\epsilon(F)_{|_x}\right| = |H| \leq \sum_{i=0}^{d} \binom{m}{i} \left\lfloor \frac{1}{\epsilon} \right\rfloor^i,$$

where $d = \text{Pdim}(H) \leq \text{Pdim}(F)$. The first inequality of the theorem now follows, on rescaling F and ϵ by a factor of B. The second inequality follows from Theorem 3.7.

12.4 Bounding with the Fat-Shattering Dimension

A general upper bound

We now present one of the key results of this chapter, in which we bound the packing numbers (and hence the covering numbers) by an expression involving the fat-shattering dimension.

Theorem 12.7 *Suppose that F is a set of real functions from a domain X to the bounded interval $[0, B]$ and that $\epsilon > 0$. Then*

$$\mathcal{M}_\infty(\epsilon, F, m) < 2\left(mb^2\right)^{\lceil \log_2 y \rceil},$$

where $b = \lfloor 2B/\epsilon \rfloor$, and, with $d = \text{fat}_F(\epsilon/4)$,

$$y = \sum_{i=1}^{d} \binom{m}{i} b^i.$$

The proof of this result is given below, but first we state a useful corollary, which follows from the relationships between covering numbers and packing numbers expressed by Theorem 12.1.

Theorem 12.8 *Let F be a set of real functions from a domain X to the bounded interval $[0, B]$. Let $\epsilon > 0$ and let $d = \mathrm{fat}_F(\epsilon/4)$. Then for all $m \geq d$,*

$$\mathcal{N}_\infty(\epsilon, F, m) < 2 \left(\frac{4mB^2}{\epsilon^2} \right)^{d \log_2(4eBm/(d\epsilon))}.$$

Proof Theorem 12.1 and Theorem 12.7 imply that

$$\mathcal{N}_\infty(\epsilon, F, m) < 2 \left(\frac{4mB^2}{\epsilon^2} \right)^{\lceil \log_2(\sum_{i=1}^d \binom{m}{i}(2B/\epsilon)^i) \rceil}.$$

By Theorem 3.7, for $m \geq d \geq 1$,

$$y = \sum_{i=1}^d \binom{m}{i} \left(\frac{2B}{\epsilon} \right)^i < \left(\frac{2B}{\epsilon} \right)^d \sum_{i=1}^d \binom{m}{i} < \left(\frac{2B}{\epsilon} \right)^d \left(\frac{em}{d} \right)^d,$$

and hence

$$\lceil \log_2 y \rceil \leq \lceil d \log_2(2eBm/(d\epsilon)) \rceil.$$

If $d \geq 1$, this is no more than $d \log_2(4eBm/(d\epsilon))$, from which the result follows. If $d = 0$, it is easy to see that $\mathcal{N}_\infty(\epsilon, F, m) \leq 1$.   □

Proof of Theorem 12.7

As in the proof of Theorem 12.2, Theorem 12.7 is proved by relating the packing numbers and dimension of F to those of $Q_\alpha(F)$, for appropriate α. In this case we bound the packing numbers using combinatorial techniques, much as we bounded the growth function in Theorem 3.6.

Relating packing numbers and dimensions to those of the quantized class

For a function class F, if $\epsilon > 0$, Lemma 12.3 shows that

$$\mathcal{M}_\infty(\epsilon, F, m) \leq \mathcal{M}_\infty(\epsilon, Q_{\epsilon/2}(F), m).$$

If $\alpha < 2\epsilon$ then

$$\mathrm{fat}_{Q_\alpha(F)}(\epsilon) \leq \mathrm{fat}_F(\epsilon - \alpha/2), \tag{12.4}$$

which implies

$$\mathrm{fat}_{Q_{\epsilon/2}(F)}(\epsilon/2) \leq \mathrm{fat}_F(\epsilon/4).$$

To see (12.4), suppose that $Q_\alpha(F)$ ϵ-shatters $\{x_1, \ldots, x_d\} \subseteq X$, witnessed by the vector $(r_1 \ldots, r_d) \in \mathbb{R}^d$. Then for all $b = (b_1, \ldots, b_d) \in \{0,1\}^d$ there is a function $f_b \in F$ with

$$Q_\alpha f_b(x_i) - r_i \geq \epsilon \quad \text{if } b_i = 1$$
$$Q_\alpha f_b(x_i) - r_i \leq -\epsilon \quad \text{if } b_i = 0.$$

It follows that

$$f_b(x_i) - r_i \geq \epsilon \quad \text{if } b_i = 1$$
$$f_b(x_i) - r_i < -\epsilon + \alpha \quad \text{if } b_i = 0.$$

So F $(\epsilon - \alpha/2)$-shatters $\{x_1, \ldots, x_d\} \subseteq X$, witnessed by the sequence $(r_1 + \alpha/2, \ldots, r_d + \alpha/2)$. This implies (12.4).

A finite combinatorial problem

Fix $x \in X^m$, let H denote $Q_{\epsilon/2}(F)_{|_x}$, and let $d = \text{fat}_{Q_{\epsilon/2}(F)}(\epsilon/2)$. By a simple rescaling, the following lemma shows that

$$\mathcal{M}(\epsilon, H, d_\infty) \leq 2(mb^2)^{\lceil \log_2 y \rceil},$$

where $b = \lfloor 2B/\epsilon \rfloor$ and y is as defined in the lemma. This implies Theorem 12.7.

Lemma 12.9 *Let* $Y = \{0, 1, \ldots, b\}$, *and suppose* $|X| = m$ *and* $H \subseteq Y^X$ *has* $\text{fat}_H(1) = d$. *Then*

$$\mathcal{M}(2, H, d_\infty) \leq 2(mb^2)^{\lceil \log_2 y \rceil},$$

with $y = \sum_{i=1}^d \binom{m}{i} b^i$.

As in the proof of Theorem 3.6, the proof of this lemma uses a counting argument, although the proof here is more complicated. The proof hinges on using an inductive argument to bound, for 2-separated classes of functions, the number of distinct pairs consisting of a 1-shattered set and a witness for the shattering.

Proof We can assume that $b \geq 3$. (The result holds trivially if $b \leq 2$ since in that case a maximal 2-packing of H has cardinality 1 or 2.)

For $k \geq 2$ and $m \geq 1$, define $t(k, m)$ as

$$\min\Big\{ |\{(A, r) : G \text{ 1-shatters } A \subseteq X, \text{ witnessed by } r : A \to Y, A \neq \emptyset\}| :$$

$$|X| = m, G \subseteq Y^X, |G| = k, \text{ and } G \text{ is 2-separated}\Big\},$$

or take $t(k, m)$ to be infinite if the minimum is over the empty set.

Notice that the number of pairs (A, r) with $A \neq \emptyset$ and $|A| \leq d$ is less than

$$y = \sum_{i=1}^{d} \binom{m}{i} b^i,$$

since for each fixed A of positive cardinality $i \leq d$, there are at most $(b-1)^i < b^i$ possible functions r that witness the 1-shattering of A. (The definition of 1-shattering shows that we cannot have $r(x) = 0$ or $r(x) = b$.) It follows from the definition of t that if $t(k, m) \geq y$, then every 2-separated set $G \subseteq Y^X$ of cardinality k 1-shatters some A with $|A| > d$. But $\mathrm{fat}_H(1) = d$, so if $t(k, m) \geq y$ then $\mathcal{M}(2, H, d_\infty) < k$. Hence, it suffices to show that

$$t\left(2(mb^2)^{\lceil \log_2 y \rceil}, m\right) \geq y \qquad (12.5)$$

for all $d \geq 1$ and $m \geq 1$.

Now, if there is no 2-separated subset of Y^X of cardinality $k = 2(mb^2)^{\lceil \log_2 y \rceil}$, then $t(2(mb^2)^{\lceil \log_2 y \rceil}, m) = \infty$ and we are done. So assume that such a set G of functions exists. Split G arbitrarily into $k/2$ pairs. (Note that k is divisible by 2.) Since the functions in G are 2-separated, for each such pair (g_1, g_2), we can choose some $x \in X$ such that $|g_1(x) - g_2(x)| \geq 2$. By the pigeonhole principle, there is an $x_0 \in X$ such that we choose $x = x_0$ for at least $k/(2m)$ of these pairs. (Otherwise, the number of functions in G would be less than $2mk/(2m) = k$, a contradiction.) The number of possible $\{i, j\} \subseteq Y$ with $j \geq i + 2$ is $\binom{b+1}{2} - b$. We can apply the pigeonhole principle again to deduce that there exist $i, j \in Y$ with $j \geq i + 2$ such that for at least

$$\frac{k/(2m)}{\binom{b+1}{2} - b} > \frac{k}{mb^2}$$

pairs (g_1, g_2), we have $\{g_1(x_0), g_2(x_0)\} = \{i, j\}$. Thus, there are two subsets G_1, G_2 of G such that $|G_1| = |G_2| > k/(mb^2)$ and, for some $x_0 \in X$ and some $i, j \in Y$ with $j \geq i + 2$, $g_1(x_0) = i$ for $g_1 \in G_1$ and $g_2(x_0) = j$ for $g_2 \in G_2$. Clearly the functions in G_1 are 2-separated on $X - \{x_0\}$, since they are 2-separated on X but equal on x_0. The same is true of G_2. Hence, by the definition of the function t, there are at least $t\left(\lfloor k/mb^2 \rfloor, m - 1\right)$ pairs (A, r) such that G_1 1-shatters $A \subseteq X - \{x_0\}$, witnessed by $r : A \to Y$, and the same is true of G_2. Moreover, if both G_1 and G_2 1-shatter A witnessed by r, then G 1-shatters $A \cup \{x_0\}$, witnessed by r', where r' equals r on A and $r'(x_0) = \lfloor (i+j)/2 \rfloor$. It follows that

$$t(k,m) \geq 2t\left(\left\lfloor \frac{k}{mb^2} \right\rfloor, m-1\right).\tag{12.6}$$

Since the total number of functions in H is bounded by $(b+1)^m$, we have $|G| = 2(mb^2)^{\lceil \log_2 y \rceil} \leq (b+1)^m$, from which it follows that $m > \lceil \log_2 y \rceil$. Applying (12.6) $\lceil \log_2 y \rceil$ times shows that

$$t\left(2(mb^2)^{\lceil \log_2 y \rceil}, m\right) \geq 2t\left(2(mb^2)^{\lceil \log_2 y \rceil - 1}, m-1\right)$$
$$\geq 2^{\lceil \log_2 y \rceil} t(2, m - \lceil \log_2 y \rceil),\tag{12.7}$$

but the definition of t shows that $t(2,m) = 1$ for all $m \geq 1$. Combining this with (12.7) gives (12.5), and this completes the proof. $\qquad\square$

A general lower bound

Recall that the d_1-metric on $\mathbb{R}^k$ is defined as follows:

$$d_1((x_1, x_2, \ldots, x_k), (y_1, y_2, \ldots, y_k)) = \frac{1}{k}\sum_{i=1}^{k}|x_i - y_i|.$$

Recall also that, for all $x, y \in \mathbb{R}^k$, $d_1(x,y) \leq d_\infty(x,y)$, so that for any function class F, any ϵ, and any m, $\mathcal{N}_1(\epsilon, F, m) \leq \mathcal{N}_\infty(\epsilon, F, m)$ (see Lemma 10.5). The following result gives a lower bound on the d_1-covering numbers (and hence on the d_∞-covering numbers).

Theorem 12.10 *Let F be a set of real functions and let $\epsilon > 0$. Then,*

$$\mathcal{N}_\infty(\epsilon, F, m) \geq \mathcal{N}_1(\epsilon, F, m) \geq e^{\text{fat}_F(16\epsilon)/8}$$

for $m \geq \text{fat}_F(16\epsilon)$.

Proof We first show that if $d = \text{fat}_F(16\epsilon)$ then $\mathcal{N}_1(2\epsilon, F, d) \geq e^{d/8}$. Fix a sample x of length d that is 16ϵ-shattered. Then, by the definition of 16ϵ-shattering, there is a vector $r \in \mathbb{R}^d$ such that the following holds: for any $b \in \{0,1\}^d$, there is $f_b \in F$ such that $f_b(x_i) \geq r_i + 16\epsilon$ if $b_i = 1$ and $f_b(x_i) \leq r_i - 16\epsilon$ if $b_i = 0$. Let $G = \{f_b : b \in \{0,1\}^d\} \subseteq F$ be such a set of 2^d functions. For $b, c \in \{0,1\}^d$, let $\Delta(b,c)$ be the number of entries on which b and c differ (that is, the Hamming distance between them). For $g \in G$, denote by $g_{|_\bullet}$ the element $(g(x_1), g(x_2), \ldots, g(x_d))$ of $\mathbb{R}^d$. Then it is clear that for any $b, c \in \{0,1\}^d$,

$$d_1\left(f_{b|_\bullet}, f_{c|_\bullet}\right) \geq \frac{32\epsilon\Delta(b,c)}{d}.$$

Therefore, if $d_1\left(f_{b|_s}, f_{c|_s}\right) < 4\epsilon$ then $\Delta(b,c) < d/8$. It follows that, for any fixed $f_b \in G$, the number of functions $f_c \in G$ for which the distance $d_1\left(f_{b|_s}, f_{c|_s}\right)$ is *less than* 4ϵ is no more than

$$\sum_{l=0}^{\lfloor d/8 \rfloor} \binom{d}{l}.$$

But, by a Chernoff bound (see Appendix 1), this sum of binomial coefficients is at most

$$2^d \, \mathrm{LE}(1/2, d, d/8) \le 2^d \, e^{-9d/64} < 2^d \, e^{-d/8}.$$

That is, every function in G has no more than $2^d e^{-d/8}$ functions from G at d_1 distance less than 4ϵ.

Suppose C is a 2ϵ-cover for $F|_s$. For each element $c \in C$, if some $g \in G$ satisfies $d_1\left(c|_s, g|_s\right) < 2\epsilon$, we have

$$\left\{g' \in G : d_1\left(g'|_s, c|_s\right) < 2\epsilon\right\} \subseteq \left\{g' \in G : d_1\left(g'|_s, g|_s\right) < 4\epsilon\right\},$$

by the triangle inequality. But this set has cardinality no more than $2^d e^{-d/8}$, so every element of the cover C accounts for no more than $2^d e^{-d/8}$ elements of G. Since C covers G, we must have

$$|C| \ge \frac{|G|}{2^d \, e^{-d/8}} = e^{d/8}.$$

This shows that

$$\mathcal{N}_1\left(2\epsilon, F, d\right) \ge \exp\left(\mathrm{fat}_F\left(16\epsilon\right)/8\right).$$

Now we bound $\mathcal{N}_1\left(\epsilon, F, m\right)$ for $m \ge d$. Suppose that $m \ge d$ and let $m = kd + r$ where k, r are integers, with $k \ge 1$ and $0 \le r < d$. Let z be the sample of length m obtained by concatenating k copies of x and adjoining the first r entries, $x_1, x_2, \ldots, x_r$ of x. Now, for $f, g \in F$,

$$
\begin{aligned}
d_1\left(f|_z, g|_z\right) &= \frac{1}{m}\sum_{i=1}^{m} |f(z_i) - g(z_i)| \\
&= \frac{k}{kd+r}\left(\sum_{i=1}^{d} |f(x_i) - g(x_i)|\right) + \\
&\qquad \frac{1}{kd+r}\sum_{j=1}^{r} |f(x_j) - g(x_j)|
\end{aligned}
$$

$$\geq \frac{kd}{kd+r}\left(\frac{1}{d}\sum_{i=1}^{d}|f(x_i)-g(x_i)|\right)$$

$$\geq \frac{m-r}{m}d_1\left(f_{|_{s}}, g_{|_{s}}\right).$$

Since $m \geq d$, we have $m = kd + r < (k+1)d \leq 2kd$ and hence $r = m - kd < m/2$. Hence, if $d_1\left(f_{|_{s}}, g_{|_{s}}\right) < \epsilon$ then $d_1\left(f_{|_{s}}, g_{|_{s}}\right) < 2\epsilon$. As a result, given any ϵ-cover of $F_{|_{s}}$, there is a 2ϵ-cover of $F_{|_{s}}$ of the same cardinality. Therefore

$$\mathcal{N}_1\left(\epsilon, F, m\right) \geq \mathcal{N}_1\left(2\epsilon, F, d\right) \geq \exp\left(\text{fat}_F\left(16\epsilon\right)/8\right),$$

as required.   □

Fat-shattering dimension characterizes covering numbers

The upper and lower bound results Theorem 12.8 and Theorem 12.10 show that the fat-shattering dimension determines in a fairly precise manner the covering numbers of a function class. The following theorem (which follows immediately from the preceding ones) makes this clear.

Theorem 12.11 *If F is a class of functions mapping from a set X into the interval $[0, B]$, then for any ϵ, if $m \geq \text{fat}_F\left(\epsilon/4\right) \geq 1$,*

$$\frac{\log_2 e}{8}\text{fat}_F\left(16\epsilon\right) \leq \log_2 \mathcal{N}_1\left(\epsilon, F, m\right)$$

$$\leq \log_2 \mathcal{N}_\infty\left(\epsilon, F, m\right) \leq 3\,\text{fat}_F\left(\epsilon/4\right)\log_2^2\left(\frac{4eBm}{\epsilon}\right).$$

This shows, in particular, that if a class has finite fat-shattering dimension, then the covering number $\mathcal{N}_\infty\left(\epsilon, F, m\right)$ is a sub-exponential function of m.

An example

To illustrate the application of these results, consider again the class F of functions from $[0, 1]$ to $[0, 1]$ of total variation at most V. We have seen (Theorem 11.12) that $\text{fat}_F\left(\gamma\right) = 1+\lfloor V/(2\gamma)\rfloor$. From Theorem 12.8, we obtain the following upper bound on the covering numbers of this class.

Theorem 12.12 *Let F be the class of functions of total variation at most V, mapping from the interval $[0,1]$ into $[0,1]$. Then, for any $\epsilon > 0$,*

$$\mathcal{N}_\infty(\epsilon, F, m) < 2\left(\frac{4m}{\epsilon^2}\right)^{(1+2V/\epsilon)\log_2(2em/V)}$$

for all m.

In Chapter 10 it was noted that the appropriate covering numbers for analysing classification by real function classes are those of the class $\pi_\gamma(F)$, which maps into a bounded interval of length 2γ. Indeed, in Theorem 10.4, the key covering number is $\mathcal{N}_\infty(\gamma/2, \pi_\gamma(F), 2m)$. The following result applies.

Theorem 12.13 *Suppose that F is a set of real functions and that $\gamma > 0$. If $d = \text{fat}_F(\gamma/8)$ then*

$$\mathcal{N}_\infty(\gamma/2, \pi_\gamma(F), 2m) \le 2(128m)^{d\log_2(32em/d)}.$$

Proof By a trivial translation, we may assume $\pi_\gamma(F)$ maps into $[0, 2\gamma]$. Then, by Theorem 12.8, taking $B = 2\gamma$ and $\epsilon = \gamma/2$, we have

$$\mathcal{N}_\infty(\gamma/2, \pi_\gamma(F), m) \le 2(64m)^{d\log_2(16em/d)},$$

from which the result follows. □

12.5 Comparing the Two Approaches

We have seen that if F is uniformly bounded and has finite pseudo-dimension then there is a constant c_1 such that the covering numbers satisfy

$$\mathcal{N}_\infty(\epsilon, F, m) \le \left(\frac{c_1 m}{\epsilon d}\right)^d,$$

where $d = \text{Pdim}(F)$. More generally, if F is uniformly bounded and has finite fat-shattering dimension, then there are constants c_2, c_3 such that

$$\mathcal{N}_\infty(\epsilon, F, m) \le \left(\frac{c_2 m}{\epsilon^2}\right)^{d\log_2(c_3 m/(d\epsilon))},$$

where $d = \text{fat}_F(\epsilon/4)$. Certainly, $d = \text{fat}_F(\epsilon/4) \le \text{Pdim}(F)$, and if the two are equal then the first bound is better. However, it is possible for $\text{fat}_F(\epsilon/4)$ to be *significantly* less than $\text{Pdim}(F)$. For example, for the class F of bounded variation functions considered in Theorem 12.12, $\text{Pdim}(F)$ is infinite, but $\text{fat}_F(\epsilon/4)$ is finite for all $\epsilon > 0$. It follows that there can be no characterization of the rate of growth of the covering numbers (as in Theorem 12.11) in terms of the pseudo-dimension. Nonetheless, the first bound is sometimes useful. For instance, if a function class F has finite pseudo-dimension then, for all sufficiently small ϵ, the fat-shattering dimension $\text{fat}_F(\epsilon/4)$ equals the pseudo-dimension, and then the covering number bound of Theorem 12.2 is better than that of Theorem 12.8.

12.6 Remarks

A large family of dimensions, defined in terms of a set of $\{0,1\}$-valued functions Φ, satisfy the conditions of Theorem 12.5. It can be shown that all of these dimensions are closely related. It is possible to extend the definition of these dimensions to include sets Φ of functions that map from Y to $\{0,*,1\}$, and the fat-shattering dimension emerges as a special case. Then a generalization of Lemma 12.9 can be obtained in terms of any such dimension, provided the set Φ satisfies a weaker version of the spanning condition. This weaker condition is that, for any two elements of Y that are separated by a gap of a certain size, there is a function in Φ that labels one of these elements as a 0 and the other as a 1. (This is weaker than the condition that $\Phi_{|Y}$ spans $\mathbb{R}^Y$, since that condition is equivalent to the condition that, for any two elements of Y, there is a function in Φ that labels those elements distinctly.)

Theorem 12.11 cannot be significantly improved: there are examples of function classes that show that the lower bound cannot be improved by more than a constant factor, and that the upper bound cannot be improved by more than a log factor. However, there is one aspect of this theorem that can be loose. For any non-decreasing function f from $\mathbb{R}^+$ to $\mathbb{N} \cup \{\infty\}$, it is easy to construct a function class F that has $\text{fat}_F(\gamma) = f(\gamma)$. In particular, the fat-shattering dimension can increase at an arbitrary rate as its argument approaches zero. It follows that the constant in the argument of the fat-shattering function can be important. It is known that if fat_F is finite at a scale slightly smaller than $\epsilon/2$, then the logarithms of these ϵ-covering numbers ($\ln \mathcal{N}_1(\epsilon, F, m)$, $\ln \mathcal{N}_\infty(\epsilon, F, m)$) grow 'acceptably slowly' with m (that is, slower than linearly), whereas they grow unacceptably quickly if fat_F is infinite at a scale slightly larger than ϵ. (See the Bibliographical Notes.) Notice that there is still an unexplained gap of a factor of two in our knowledge of the appropriate scale at which the fat-shattering dimension determines these covering numbers. It may be that this gap is inevitable. The intuition behind this conjecture is as follows. The proofs of upper bounds on these quantities naturally involve packing numbers, whereas the proofs of lower bounds involve covering numbers. Theorem 12.1 shows that

$$\mathcal{M}_\infty\left(2\epsilon, F, m\right) \leq \mathcal{N}_\infty\left(\epsilon, F, m\right) \leq \mathcal{M}_\infty\left(\epsilon, F, m\right).$$

There is an upper bound on $\mathcal{M}_\infty\left(\epsilon, F, m\right)$ in terms of some fat-shattering dimension at a scale of roughly ϵ. To avoid violating this upper bound, if it is possible that $\mathcal{N}_\infty\left(\epsilon, F, m\right)$ is close to $\mathcal{M}_\infty\left(2\epsilon, F, m\right)$ in the inequality above, any lower bound on $\mathcal{N}_\infty\left(\epsilon, F, m\right)$ must be in terms of the fat-shattering dimension at a scale of roughly 2ϵ.

12.7 Bibliographical Notes

Theorem 12.1, relating coverings to packings, is due to Kolmogorov and Tihomirov (1961). Theorems 12.2 (the bound on covering numbers in terms of pseudo-dimension) and 12.4 (the generalization of Sauer's Lemma—Theorem 3.6—to classes of functions that map to a finite domain) are due to Haussler and Long (1995). The latter result improves on a result due to Natarajan (1991b) which uses a slightly different notion of dimension. Theorem 12.5, the generalization of Sauer's Lemma in terms of Φ-dimensions, is due to Gurvits (1997a). The linear algebraic proof technique appears in (Babai and Frankl, 1992), and the idea of Φ-dimensions is due to Ben-David, Cesa-Bianchi, Haussler and Long (1995). That paper studied the problem of learning classes of functions that take values in a finite set. It also showed that a large family of the Φ-dimensions are close to each other (see Section 12.6). The extension of these results to $\{0, *, 1\}$-valued families Φ, described in Section 12.6, was in (Anthony and Bartlett, 1995). See also (Cesa-Bianchi and Haussler, 1998).

Theorem 12.7, giving covering number bounds in terms of the fat-shattering dimension, is due to Alon, Ben-David, Cesa-Bianchi and Haussler (1993). The corresponding lower bound, Theorem 12.10, is from (Bartlett, Kulkarni and Posner, 1997). (That paper also gave tighter bounds than Theorem 12.12 for covering numbers of the class of functions of bounded variation.) The calculation of covering number bounds for classes $\pi_\gamma(F)$ (Theorem 12.13) is from (Bartlett, 1998). The investigation of the scales at which finiteness of the fat-shattering dimension is necessary and sufficient for learning is described in (Bartlett and Long, 1995; Bartlett and Long, 1998). The conjecture that the gap in these scales is inevitable is due to Phil Long.

13
The Sample Complexity of Classification Learning

13.1 Large Margin SEM Algorithms

After our digression into covering numbers, pseudo-dimension and fat-shattering dimension, we now return to the central learning problem of this part of the book. In this chapter, we use the results of the last few chapters to construct classification learning algorithms and to determine bounds on the sample complexity of these algorithms.

In Chapter 4 we saw that for binary classification, it was appropriate to use an algorithm that, given a training sample, returns as output hypothesis some function which minimizes sample error; that is, we considered SEM algorithms L, which have the property that for all z,

$$\hat{\mathrm{er}}_z \left(L(z) \right) = \min_{h \in H} \hat{\mathrm{er}}_z(h).$$

In analysing classification learning algorithms for real-valued function classes, it is useful to consider algorithms that, given a sample and a parameter γ, return hypotheses minimizing the sample error *with respect to γ*. Recall that, for a sample $z = ((x_1, y_1), \ldots, (x_m, y_m)) \in Z^m$, a function $f : X \to \mathbb{R}$, and $\gamma > 0$, the sample error of f with respect to γ is defined as

$$\hat{\mathrm{er}}_z^\gamma(f) = \frac{1}{m} |\{i : \mathrm{margin}(f(x_i), y_i) < \gamma\}|.$$

(See Definition 9.1.)

Definition 13.1 *Suppose that F is a set of real-valued functions defined on the domain X. Then a large margin sample error minimization algorithm (or large margin SEM algorithm) L for F takes as input a margin parameter $\gamma > 0$ and a sample $z \in \bigcup_{m=1}^{\infty} Z^m$, and returns a function* *from F such that for all $\gamma > 0$, all m, and all $z \in Z^m$,*

$$\hat{\mathrm{er}}_z^\gamma \left(L(\gamma, z) \right) = \min_{f \in F} \hat{\mathrm{er}}_z^\gamma (f).$$

13.2 Large Margin SEM Algorithms as Classification Learning Algorithms

Chapter 4 establishes that SEM algorithms are learning algorithms for binary-valued classification when the class H has finite VC-dimension. We show now that, analogously, the large margin SEM algorithms for a function class F are classification learning algorithms when F has finite fat-shattering dimension. It is useful to recall the definition of a classification learning algorithm for a real function class F. For any probability distribution P on Z, such an algorithm L takes as input a number $\gamma \in (0, 1/2]$ and a random binary-labelled sample z, and returns a function $f \in F$. If $m \geq m_L(\epsilon, \delta, \gamma)$, then with probability at least $1-\delta$, f satisfies

$$\mathrm{er}_P(f) < \mathrm{opt}_P^\gamma(F) + \epsilon,$$

where $\mathrm{opt}_P^\gamma(F) = \inf_{f \in F} \mathrm{er}_P^\gamma(f)$. (Here, $m_L(\epsilon, \delta, \gamma)$ denotes the sample complexity of L.)

In Chapter 4, we made use of a uniform convergence result (Theorem 4.3) which tells us that, provided H has finite VC-dimension and m is large, then with high probability

$$\hat{\mathrm{er}}_z(h) - \epsilon < \mathrm{er}_P(h) < \hat{\mathrm{er}}_z(h) + \epsilon$$

for all $h \in H$. In this chapter, we make use of Theorem 10.4, which, as we shall see, establishes that for many function classes F,

$$\mathrm{er}_P(f) < \hat{\mathrm{er}}_z^\gamma(f) + \epsilon$$

for all $f \in F$ with high probability (provided m is large enough). We use this to obtain the following result.

Theorem 13.2 *Suppose that F is a set of real-valued functions defined on X and that L is a large margin SEM algorithm for F. Suppose that $\epsilon \in (0,1)$ and $\gamma > 0$. Then, given any probability distribution P on Z, for all m, we have*

$$P^m \left\{ \mathrm{er}_P \left(L(\gamma, z) \right) \geq \mathrm{opt}_P^\gamma(F) + \epsilon \right\} \leq 2 \mathcal{N}_\infty \left(\gamma/2, \pi_\gamma(F), 2m \right) e^{-\epsilon^2 m/72} + e^{-2\epsilon^2 m/9}.$$

It should be noted that Theorem 10.4 is not 'two-sided' in the way that Theorem 4.3 is, for it does not bound the probability that $\mathrm{er}_P(f) \geq \mathrm{\hat{e}r}_z^\gamma(f) - \epsilon$. For this reason, we prove Theorem 13.2 using a slightly different approach from that taken in Chapter 4. In proving Theorem 4.2, we used the uniform lower bound on $\mathrm{er}_P(f)$ to show that a near-optimal function in the class is likely to have small sample error. However, since we need only show this for a single such near-optimal function, we do not need a *uniform* lower bound. In the analogous step in the proof of Theorem 13.2, we use instead the following simple consequence of Hoeffding's inequality (see Appendix 1).

Lemma 13.3 *Suppose that f is a real-valued function defined on X, P is a probability distribution on Z, ϵ, γ are real numbers with $\epsilon > 0$ and $\gamma > 0$, and m is a positive integer. Then*

$$P^m \left\{ \mathrm{\hat{e}r}_z^\gamma(f) \geq \mathrm{er}_P^\gamma(f) + \epsilon \right\} \leq e^{-2\epsilon^2 m}.$$

Proof **(of Theorem 13.2)** Let $f^* \in F$ satisfy $\mathrm{er}_P^\gamma(f^*) < \mathrm{opt}_P^\gamma(F) + \epsilon/3$. By Lemma 13.3,

$$\mathrm{\hat{e}r}_z^\gamma(f^*) < \mathrm{opt}_P^\gamma(F) + \frac{2\epsilon}{3} \qquad (13.1)$$

with probability at least $1 - e^{-2\epsilon^2 m/9}$. By Theorem 10.4, with probability at least $1 - 2\mathcal{N}_\infty \left(\gamma/2, \pi_\gamma(F), 2m \right) e^{-\epsilon^2 m/72}$,

$$\mathrm{er}_P(f) < \mathrm{\hat{e}r}_z^\gamma(f) + \epsilon/3 \text{ for all } f \in F. \qquad (13.2)$$

Thus, with probability at least

$$1 - e^{-2\epsilon^2 m/9} - 2\mathcal{N}_\infty \left(\gamma/2, \pi_\gamma(F), 2m \right) e^{-\epsilon^2 m/72}$$

we have both (13.1) and (13.2), and in that case

$$
\begin{aligned}
\mathrm{er}_P(L(\gamma, z)) \quad &< \quad \mathrm{\hat{e}r}_z^\gamma(L(\gamma, z)) + \frac{\epsilon}{3} \\
&\leq \quad \mathrm{\hat{e}r}_z^\gamma(f^*) + \frac{\epsilon}{3} \\
&< \quad \mathrm{opt}_P^\gamma(F) + \epsilon.
\end{aligned}
$$

(The second inequality follows from the fact that L is a large margin SEM algorithm, and so $\mathrm{\hat{e}r}_z^\gamma(L(\gamma, z)) = \min_{f \in F} \mathrm{\hat{e}r}_z^\gamma(f) \leq \mathrm{\hat{e}r}_z^\gamma(f^*)$.) $\square$

Combining this result with Theorem 12.8, which bounds the covering numbers in terms of the fat-shattering dimension, gives the following result.

Theorem 13.4 *Suppose that F is a set of real-valued functions with finite fat-shattering dimension, and that L is a large margin SEM algorithm for F. Then L is a classification learning algorithm for F. Given $\delta \in (0,1)$ and $\gamma > 0$, suppose $d = \text{fat}_{\pi_\gamma(F)}(\gamma/8) \geq 1$. Then the estimation error of L satisfies*

$$\epsilon_L(m,\delta,\gamma) \leq \left(\frac{72}{m} \left(d \log_2 \left(\frac{32em}{d} \right) \ln(128m) + \ln \left(\frac{6}{\delta} \right) \right) \right)^{1/2}.$$

Furthermore, the sample complexity of L satisfies

$$m_L(\epsilon,\delta,\gamma) \leq m_0(\epsilon,\delta,\gamma) = \frac{144}{\epsilon^2} \left(27d \ln^2 \left(\frac{3456d}{\epsilon^2} \right) + \ln \left(\frac{6}{\delta} \right) \right)$$

for all $\epsilon \in (0,1)$.

Proof By Theorem 13.2 and Theorem 12.13,

$$P^m \left\{ \text{er}_P \left(L(\gamma, z) \right) \geq \text{opt}_P^\gamma(F) + \epsilon \right\}$$
$$\leq 2 \mathcal{N}_\infty \left(\gamma/2, \pi_\gamma(F), 2m \right) e^{-\epsilon^2 m/72} + e^{-2\epsilon^2 m/9}$$
$$\leq 3 \max \left(\mathcal{N}_\infty \left(\gamma/2, \pi_\gamma(F), 2m \right), 1 \right) e^{-\epsilon^2 m/72}$$
$$< 6(128m)^{d \log_2(32em/d)} e^{-\epsilon^2 m/72}, \tag{13.3}$$

for $d = \text{fat}_{\pi_\gamma(F)}(\gamma/8) \geq 1$. Clearly, this last quantity is no more than δ when

$$\epsilon \geq \left(\frac{72}{m} \left(d \log_2 \left(\frac{32em}{d} \right) \ln(128m) + \ln \left(\frac{6}{\delta} \right) \right) \right)^{1/2}.$$

We now consider the sample complexity. The expression (13.3) is no more than δ if

$$\frac{\epsilon^2 m}{72} \geq \ln \left(\frac{6}{\delta} \right) + 7d \ln \left(\frac{32e}{d} \right) + d \log_2 \left(\frac{2^{12}e}{d} \right) \ln m + \frac{d}{\ln 2} \ln^2 m,$$

and for this it suffices if

$$m \geq \frac{72}{\epsilon^2} \left(\ln \left(\frac{6}{\delta} \right) + 7d \ln \left(\frac{32e}{d} \right) + 14d \ln m + \frac{d}{\ln 2} \ln^2 m \right).$$

To proceed from here, we bound $\ln m$ and $\ln^2 m$ from above by expressions that are linear in m. For the $\ln m$ term, we use Inequality (1.2) (in Appendix 1), which implies

$$\frac{72 \cdot 14d}{\epsilon^2} \ln m \leq \frac{m}{4} + \frac{1008d}{\epsilon^2} \ln \left(\frac{4032d}{e\epsilon^2} \right).$$

For the $\ln^2 m$ term we make use of Inequality (1.3) (in Appendix 1). Taking $b = 1728d/(\epsilon^2 \ln 2)$ and supposing that $m \geq 1/b$, this inequality shows that

$$\frac{72d}{\epsilon^2 \ln 2} \ln^2 m \leq \frac{m}{4} + \frac{216d}{\epsilon^2 \ln 2} \ln^2 \left(\frac{1728d}{\epsilon^2 \ln 2}\right),$$

so it suffices to have $m/2$ at least

$$\frac{72}{\epsilon^2} \left(\ln\left(\frac{6}{\delta}\right) + 7d\ln\left(\frac{32e}{d}\right) + 14d\ln\left(\frac{4032d}{e\epsilon^2}\right) + \frac{3d}{\ln 2} \ln^2\left(\frac{1728d}{\epsilon^2 \ln 2}\right)\right).$$

Some straightforward approximations yield the result.   □

13.3 Lower Bounds for Certain Function Classes

Theorem 13.4 provides an upper bound on the sample complexity of any large margin SEM classification learning algorithm in terms of the fat-shattering dimension. For many function classes, it can be shown that the sample complexity of *any* classification learning algorithm is bounded below by a quantity involving the fat-shattering dimension.

Recall that a function class F is closed under addition of constants if for every $f \in F$ and every real number c, the function $x \mapsto f(x) + c$ also belongs to F. For instance, if F is the set of functions computable by a linear computation unit, then F is closed under addition of constants: we simply adjust the threshold.

Theorem 13.5 *Suppose that F is a set of functions mapping into the interval $[0,1]$ and that F is closed under addition of constants. Then, if L is any classification learning algorithm for F, the sample complexity of L satisfies*

$$m_L(\epsilon, \delta, \gamma) \geq \max\left(\frac{d}{320\epsilon^2}, 2\left\lfloor\frac{1-\epsilon^2}{2\epsilon^2}\ln\frac{1}{8\delta(1-2\delta)}\right\rfloor\right).$$

for $0 < \epsilon, \delta < 1/64$ and $\gamma > 0$, where $d = \text{fat}_{\pi_{4\gamma}(F)}(2\gamma) \geq 1$.

(Recall that $\pi_\gamma : \mathbb{R} \to [1/2 - \gamma, 1/2 + \gamma]$ is the squashing function defined in (10.4).)

Proof The idea of the proof is to construct a class H of $\{0,1\}$-valued functions (the definition of which depends on the parameter γ), and show that a classification learning algorithm for F can be used as a

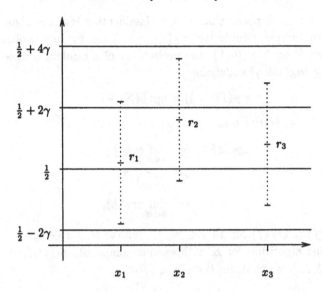

Fig. 13.1. Points $\{x_1, \ldots, x_3\}$ in the set T, with their associated witnesses r_i. The dotted lines extend 2γ above and below each r_i.

learning algorithm for H, and that the estimation errors (and hence sample complexities) of both are closely related.

The first step is to construct the class H. Fix $\gamma > 0$. Choose a set $S \subseteq X$ so that $|S| = d = \operatorname{fat}_{\pi_{4\gamma}(F)}(2\gamma)$ and S is 2γ-shattered by $\pi_{4\gamma}(F)$, witnessed by $r \in [1/2-2\gamma, 1/2+2\gamma]^d$. By the pigeonhole principle, either at least $d/2$ of the r_i fall in the interval $[1/2 - 2\gamma, 1/2]$, or at least that many fall in $[1/2, 1/2 + 2\gamma]$. Let $T \subseteq S$ contain the corresponding x_i, so $|T| \geq d/2$. Clearly, T is γ-shattered by $\pi_{2\gamma}(F)$, witnessed by either $(1/2 - \gamma, 1/2 - \gamma, \ldots, 1/2 - \gamma)$ or $(1/2 + \gamma, 1/2 + \gamma, \ldots, 1/2 + \gamma)$ (see Figure 13.1). Because F is closed under addition of constants, it follows also that T is γ-shattered, witnessed by $(1/2, \ldots, 1/2)$; we simply 'shift' all the relevant functions as necessary. Now let $F_0 \subseteq F$ be the set of functions f in F such that for all $x \in T$, $|f(x) - 1/2| \geq \gamma$. Clearly, the set H of $\{0, 1\}$-valued functions on T defined by

$$H = \{x \mapsto \operatorname{sgn}(f(x) - 1/2) : f \in F_0\}$$

is the set of all $\{0, 1\}$-valued functions on T, and hence $\operatorname{VCdim}(H) \geq d/2$.

The second step of the proof is to relate the problem of classification learning F to that of learning H, and to appeal to the lower bound results from Chapter 5. Suppose that L is a classification learning algorithm for F, with sample complexity $m_L(\epsilon, \delta, \gamma)$. Then for any probability distribution P on $X \times \{0, 1\}$, the probability of a random sample z of length $m \geq m_L(\epsilon, \delta, \gamma)$ satisfying

$$\mathrm{er}_P(L(\gamma, z)) < \mathrm{opt}_P^{\gamma}(F) + \epsilon$$

is at least $1 - \delta$. Notice that

$$
\begin{aligned}
\mathrm{opt}_P^{\gamma}(F) &= \inf_{f \in F} \mathrm{er}_P^{\gamma}(f) \\
&\leq \inf_{f \in F_0} \mathrm{er}_P^{\gamma}(f) \\
&= \inf_{h \in H} \mathrm{er}_P(h),
\end{aligned}
$$

since $\mathrm{er}_P^{\gamma}(f) = \mathrm{er}_P(f)$ for all $f \in F_0$. It follows that $z \mapsto \mathrm{sgn}(L(\gamma, z))$ is a learning algorithm for H with sample complexity $m_L(\epsilon, \delta, \gamma)$. But Theorem 5.2 shows that, for $0 < \epsilon, \delta < 1/64$,

$$m_L(\epsilon, \delta, \gamma) \geq \max\left(\frac{d}{320\epsilon^2}, 2 \left\lfloor \frac{1-\epsilon^2}{2\epsilon^2} \ln \frac{1}{8\delta(1-2\delta)} \right\rfloor \right).$$

$\square$

Theorems 13.4 and 13.5 show how the inherent sample complexity of a function class grows with the fat-shattering dimension and the accuracy parameter ϵ. In particular, they show that there are constants c_1 and c_2 for which

$$\frac{c_1 \mathrm{fat}_{\pi_{4\gamma}(F)}(2\gamma)}{\epsilon^2} \leq m_F(\epsilon, \delta, \gamma) \leq \frac{c_2 \mathrm{fat}_{\pi_{\gamma}(F)}(\gamma/8)}{\epsilon^2}$$

for suitably small ϵ and δ, provided that F is closed under addition of constants. Clearly, it is only the behaviour of functions in F near the threshold value of $1/2$ that influences the complexity of F for classification learning, whereas the fat-shattering dimension in these bounds measures the complexity of functions in $\pi_{\gamma}(F)$ over the whole of their $[1/2 - \gamma, 1/2 + \gamma]$ range. The condition that F is closed under addition of constants ensures that the complexity of functions in F is, in a sense, uniform over this range. For example, consider the following class of functions (which is not closed under addition of constants). Let α be a positive constant, and define F as the set of all functions mapping from $\mathbb{N}$ to $[1/2 + \alpha, \infty)$. Then $\mathrm{fat}_{\pi_{\gamma}(F)}(\gamma/8)$ is infinite for $\gamma \geq 4\alpha/3$, but there is a classification learning algorithm for F. (Indeed, since $\mathrm{sgn}(f)$ is identically 1 for all f in F, classification learning with F is trivial.) The class F is certainly complex, but the complexity of the functions in

F is restricted to a range that does not include the threshold, and hence this complexity is irrelevant for classification learning.

13.4 Using the Pseudo-Dimension

The analysis in the previous section uses an upper bound on covering numbers in terms of the fat-shattering dimension. However, we have also derived an upper bound (Theorem 12.2) on covering numbers in terms of the pseudo-dimension, and it is natural to investigate what this will tell us about the sample complexity of classification learning algorithms. Using Theorem 12.2 as it applies to $\pi_\gamma(F)$, the following result can easily be obtained.

Theorem 13.6 *If F is a set of real functions having finite pseudo-dimension, and L is a large margin SEM algorithm for F, then L is a classification learning algorithm for F. For all $\delta \in (0,1)$, all m, and $\gamma > 0$, its estimation error satisfies*

$$\epsilon_L(m,\delta,\gamma) \leq \epsilon_0(m,\delta,\gamma) = \left(\frac{72}{m} \left(d \ln \left(\frac{8em}{d} \right) + \ln \left(\frac{3}{\delta} \right) \right) \right)^{1/2},$$

where $d = \mathrm{Pdim}(F)$.

This result is, however, weaker than the VC-dimension results of Chapter 4. To see this, let $H = \{x \mapsto \mathrm{sgn}(f(x) - 1/2) : f \in F\}$, and notice that $\mathrm{VCdim}(H) \leq \mathrm{Pdim}(F)$ and $\mathrm{opt}_P(H) \leq \mathrm{opt}_P^\gamma(F)$. It follows that Theorem 4.2 implies a stronger version of Theorem 13.6 (with smaller constants). Thus, using the pseudo-dimension to analyse classification learning for classes of real-valued functions gives no improvement over the results of Chapter 4. However, using the fat-shattering dimension in a 'scale-sensitive' analysis of classification learning can give a significant improvement over the VC-dimension results of Part 1. In the next chapter, we see examples of neural network classes that have finite fat-shattering dimension, but whose thresholded versions have infinite VC-dimension.

13.5 Remarks

Relative uniform convergence results

Theorem 13.5 implies that, for function classes satisfying a mild "self-similarity" condition (the class is closed under addition of constants), the rate of uniform convergence of $\mathrm{er}_P(f)$ to $\hat{\mathrm{er}}_z^\gamma(f)$ can be no faster than $1/\sqrt{m}$. However, just as the relative uniform convergence results of Section 5.5 demonstrate for the learning model of Part 1, it turns out that $\mathrm{er}_P(f)$ converges more quickly to $(1+\alpha)\hat{\mathrm{er}}_z^\gamma(f)$ for any fixed $\alpha > 0$, as the following result shows.

Theorem 13.7 *Suppose that F is a set of real-valued functions defined on X, P is a probability distribution on Z, $\gamma > 0$, and $\alpha, \beta > 0$,*

$$P^m \left\{ \exists f \in F : \mathrm{er}_P(f) > (1+\alpha)\hat{\mathrm{er}}_z^\gamma(f) + \beta \right\}$$
$$\leq 4 \mathcal{N}_\infty \left(\gamma/2, \pi_\gamma(F), 2m \right) \exp \left(\frac{-\alpha\beta m}{4(1+\alpha)} \right).$$

The theorem follows from the inequality

$$P^m \left\{ \exists f \in F : \frac{\mathrm{er}_P(f) - \hat{\mathrm{er}}_z^\gamma(f)}{\sqrt{\mathrm{er}_P(f)}} > \epsilon \right\}$$
$$\leq 4 \mathcal{N}_\infty \left(\gamma/2, \pi_\gamma(F), 2m \right) \exp \left(\frac{-\epsilon^2 m}{4} \right) \quad (13.4)$$

in the same way that Theorem 5.7 follows from Inequality (5.11). We omit the proof of this inequality; it is closely related to the proof of Theorem 10.1.

13.6 Bibliographical Notes

Most of the results in this chapter have their origins in (Bartlett, 1998). Theorem 13.2 follows (using Hoeffding's inequality, as in Lemma 13.3) from a corresponding result in (Bartlett, 1998). Clearly, the proof uses ideas of Vapnik and Chervonenkis (1971) and Pollard (1984), but working with the d_∞ metric, as in (Anthony and Bartlett, 1995). The proof technique used for the lower bound, Theorem 13.5, is from (Bartlett, 1998). Similar techniques are used by Simon (1996) to give a lower bound for the sample complexity of learning probabilistic concepts (see Section 9.4), in terms of a different scale-sensitive dimension (that is smaller than the fat-shattering dimension). Inequality (13.4), and a slightly weaker version of Theorem 13.7 are also given in (Bartlett, 1998). Independent related work appears in (Horváth and Lugosi, 1998), relating the classification performance of a class of real-valued functions to a certain scale-sensitive dimension.

14

The Dimensions of Neural Networks

14.1 Introduction

In this chapter we bound the pseudo-dimension and the fat-shattering dimension of the function classes computed by certain neural networks. The pseudo-dimension bounds follow easily from VC-dimension bounds obtained earlier, so these shall not detain us for long. Of more importance are the bounds we obtain on the fat-shattering dimension. We derive these bounds by bounding certain covering numbers. Later in the book, we shall use these covering number bounds directly.

We bound the covering numbers and fat-shattering dimensions for networks that are fully connected between adjacent layers, that have units with a bounded activation function satisfying a Lipschitz constraint, and that have all weights (or all weights in certain layers) constrained to be small. We give two main results on the covering numbers and fat-shattering dimensions of networks of this type. In Section 14.3 we give bounds in terms of the number of parameters in the network. In contrast, Section 14.4 gives bounds on the fat-shattering dimension that instead grow with the bound on the size of the parameters and, somewhat surprisingly, are independent of the number of parameters in the network. This result is consistent with the intuition we obtain by studying networks of linear units (units with the identity function as their activation function). For a network of this kind, no matter how large, the function computed by the network is a linear combination of the input variables, and so its pseudo-dimension does not increase with the number of parameters. In a network of computation units in which the activation function satisfies a Lipschitz constraint, if the weights are constrained to be small then the function computed by the network is 'approximately linear' in the parameters. It makes sense, then, that the

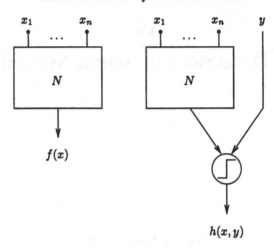

Fig. 14.1. The networks N and N' of Theorem 14.1; N computes $f \in F$ and N' computes $h \in H'$.

fat-shattering dimension in this case does not increase with the number of parameters. On the other hand, the closeness to linearity of the network function depends on the magnitude of the weights, the number of layers, and the scale of interest, and we shall see that the bound on $\mathrm{fat}_F(\gamma)$ increases with $1/\gamma$, with the weight bound, and with the number of layers.

These results suggest that there are two distinct notions of the complexity of a multi-layer network: we can restrict a network's complexity either by restricting the number of parameters or by restricting the size of the parameters.

14.2 Pseudo-Dimension of Neural Networks

We spent much effort in Part 1 in bounding the VC-dimension of various types of neural network. Fortunately, we can use our VC-dimension bounds to obtain bounds on the pseudo-dimension of real-output networks. The following result relates the pseudo-dimension of the set of functions computed by a real-output network to the VC-dimension of an augmented version of the same network. Figure 14.1 illustrates the networks described in the theorem.

Theorem 14.1 *Let N be any neural network with a single real-valued output unit, and form a neural network N' as follows. The network N' has one extra input unit and one extra computation unit. This additional computation unit is a linear threshold unit receiving input only from the output unit of N and from the new input unit, and it is the output unit of N'. If H' is the set of $\{0,1\}$-valued functions computed by N' and F the set of real-valued functions computed by N then $\mathrm{Pdim}(F) \leq \mathrm{VCdim}(H')$.*

Proof Any state of N' is of the form $\omega' = (\omega, w, \theta)$, where ω is a state of N, w is the weight on the connection from the new input to the new output unit, and θ is the threshold on the new computation unit. Any input pattern to N' is of the form (x, y) where x is an input pattern to N and y is the new input. If $h_{\omega'}$ is the function computed by N' when in state ω' then $h_{\omega'}(x, y) = \mathrm{sgn}\left(f_\omega(x) + wy - \theta\right)$, where f_ω is the function N computes in state ω. Thus, if a state ω' of N' has $\theta = 0$ and $w = -1$, then

$$h_{\omega'}(x, y) = \mathrm{sgn}\left(f_\omega(x) - y\right). \tag{14.1}$$

But then the VC-dimension of the subset of H' that corresponds to this choice of w and θ is the VC-dimension of the sub-graph class,

$$B_F = \{(x, y) \mapsto \mathrm{sgn}(f(x) - y) : f \in F\},$$

which is precisely the pseudo-dimension of F (see Section 11.2). The result follows. $\qquad\square$

It is clear that, in the notation of Theorem 14.1, the network N' has precisely two more parameters than N, one more computation unit, and one more input. In fact, if the activation function s of the output unit in the network N is non-decreasing and continuous from the right†, then we can write

$$\mathrm{sgn}\left(s(g(x)) - y\right) = \mathrm{sgn}\left(g(x) - s^{-1}(y)\right),$$

where $s^{-1}(y) = \inf\{a : s(a) > y\}$. It follows that we can compute the functions described in the proof of Theorem 14.1 using a network N' with the same number of computation units as N. Notice that the standard sigmoid function, the identity function, and the sgn function are all non-decreasing and continuous from the right.

---

† A function $s : \mathbb{R} \to \mathbb{R}$ is continuous from the right if, for all $x_0 \in \mathbb{R}$, $\lim_{x \downarrow x_0} s(x) = s(x_0)$.

We could give many specific pseudo-dimension bounds now by using earlier VC-dimension bounds. We give just one example, which follows from Theorem 8.13.

Theorem 14.2 *Let F be the set of functions computed by a feed-forward network with W parameters and k computation units, in which each computation unit (including the output) has the standard sigmoid activation function. Then*

$$\text{Pdim}(F) \leq ((W+2)k)^2 + 11(W+2)k \log_2(18(W+2)k^2).$$

14.3 Bounds on the Fat-Shattering Dimension in terms of Number of Parameters

Covering numbers of compositions of function classes

In this section we bound the covering numbers and fat-shattering dimension of multilayer networks by quantities depending on the number of adjustable parameters. To obtain these bounds, we use the fact that the functions computed by all units beyond the first layer can be approximated accurately by a finite set of such functions. The precise details of this follow, but the basic idea is quite simple: we form a grid in parameter space of the required fineness (depending on the level of approximation required) and we use functions corresponding to the grid points.

In the analysis of this section, we split the network into two parts: the first layer, and later layers. We bound certain covering numbers for the classes of functions computable by these parts, and then combine these covering number bounds.

In what follows, X is the input space $\mathbb{R}^n$, Y_1 is the output set of the first layer (so that, for example, $Y_1 = [0,1]^k$ if there are k units in the first layer, each of which maps to $[0,1]$), F_1 is the class of vector-valued functions that can be computed by the first layer, and G is the class of functions that can be computed by the remainder of the network. Then F_1 is a class of functions from X to Y_1, G is a class of functions from Y_1 to $\mathbb{R}$, and the set of functions computable by the network is the composition of these classes, $G \circ F_1$, given by $G \circ F_1 = \{g \circ f : g \in G, f \in F_1\}$ where $(g \circ f)(x) = g(f(x))$.

We define the *uniform*, or L_∞, *distance* between functions $f, g : Y_1 \to$

$\mathbb{R}$ by

$$d_{L_\infty}(g, h) = \sup_{y \in Y_1} |g(y) - h(y)|.$$

The following lemma bounds the d_∞ covering number of the composition of two function classes in terms of a d_∞ covering number of one class and an L_∞ covering number of the other. Recall, from Chapter 10, that $\mathcal{N}(\epsilon, F, d)$ denotes the ϵ-covering number of a function class F with respect to the metric d, and that, for a positive integer m,

$$\mathcal{N}_\infty(\epsilon, F, m) = \max\left\{\mathcal{N}(\epsilon, F_{|_x}, d_\infty) : x \in X^m\right\}.$$

Lemma 14.3 *Let X be a set and (Y_1, ρ) a metric space. Suppose that $L \geq 0$, F_1 is a class of functions mapping from X to Y_1, and G is a class of real-valued functions defined on Y_1 satisfying the following Lipschitz condition: for all g in G and all y, z in Y_1,*

$$|g(y) - g(z)| \leq L\rho(y, z).$$

For $y = (y_1, \ldots, y_m)$ and $z = (z_1, \ldots, z_m)$ from Y_1^m, let

$$d_\infty^\rho(y, z) = \max_{1 \leq i \leq m} \rho(y_i, z_i).$$

Then

$$\mathcal{N}_\infty(\epsilon, G \circ F_1, m) \leq \max_{x \in X^m} \mathcal{N}(\epsilon/(2L), F_{1|_x}, d_\infty^\rho) \, \mathcal{N}(\epsilon/2, G, d_{L_\infty}).$$

Proof Fix $x \in X^m$. Suppose that $\hat{F}_1$ is an $\epsilon/(2L)$-cover of $F_{1|_x}$ with respect to d_∞^ρ and $\hat{G}$ is an $\epsilon/2$-cover of G with respect to d_{L_∞}. Let

$$\hat{G}_{|_{\hat{F}_1}} = \left\{\left(\hat{g}(\hat{f}_1), \hat{g}(\hat{f}_2), \ldots, \hat{g}(\hat{f}_m)\right) : \hat{f} = (\hat{f}_1, \hat{f}_2, \ldots, \hat{f}_m) \in \hat{F}_1, \; \hat{g} \in \hat{G}\right\}.$$

We show that $\hat{G}_{|_{\hat{F}_1}}$ is an ϵ-cover of $(G \circ F_1)_{|_x}$ with respect to d_∞. Since $\hat{G}_{|_{\hat{F}_1}}$ has cardinality no more than $\mathcal{N}(\epsilon/(2L), F_{1|_x}, d_\infty)\mathcal{N}(\epsilon/2, G, d_{L_\infty})$, the result follows. To see that $\hat{G}_{|_{\hat{F}_1}}$ is a cover, choose $f \in F_1$ and $g \in G$, and pick $\hat{f} \in \hat{F}_1$ and $\hat{g} \in \hat{G}$ such that $d_\infty^\rho(f_{|_x}, \hat{f}) \leq \epsilon/(2L)$ and $d_{L_\infty}(g, \hat{g}) \leq \epsilon/2$, where $f_{|_x} = (f(x_1), \ldots, f(x_m))$. Then

$$\max_{1 \leq i \leq m} \rho(f(x_i), \hat{f}_i) \leq \epsilon/(2L),$$

and so

$$\max_{1 \leq i \leq m} |g(f(x_i)) - g(\hat{f}_i)| \leq L\left(\epsilon/(2L)\right) = \epsilon/2,$$

which implies

$$\max_{1 \leq i \leq m} |g(f(x_i)) - \hat{g}(\hat{f_i})| \leq \epsilon.$$

The result follows. □

It is clear that the existence of a finite L_∞-cover of a function class is a much stronger requirement than the existence of any of the other covers we considered in Chapter 12, because it implies that a finite set of functions approximates the function class accurately at *all points* of the input space. Even the class of functions computed by the real weight perceptron with a single input cannot be approximated in this strong sense, as the following proposition shows. In contrast, however, Theorem 3.1 (together with the observation that the covering number equals the growth function for $\{0,1\}$-valued functions—see Section 10.2) shows that we can find a d_∞-cover for this class whose cardinality grows linearly with m.

Proposition 14.4 *Let F be the class of functions computed by the real weight perceptron with a single real input. Then*

$$\mathcal{N}(\epsilon, F, d_{L_\infty}) = \infty$$

for $\epsilon < 1$.

Proof Suppose there is a finite ϵ-cover $\hat{F}$. Then each element of $\hat{F}$ is a function $f_a : \mathbb{R} \to \{0,1\}$ corresponding to a certain 'transition point' a, so that $f_a(x) = 0$ if and only if $x < a$. Let $S \subseteq \mathbb{R}$ be the set of all transition points of functions from the cover. Since S is finite, we can choose a function f in F that has a transition point not in S, and hence for all elements $\hat{f}$ of the cover there is some point in $\mathbb{R}$ at which f differs from $\hat{f}$ by 1. Hence $\epsilon \geq 1$, and the result follows. □

Even though the existence of a finite L_∞ cover for functions computed by all but the first layer of the network is a stringent requirement, if we bound the parameters and allow only smooth activation functions in that part of the network, we can approximate the class in this strong sense, as we shall see.

Covering numbers for neural network classes

For the remainder of this section, we consider the class F of functions computed by a feed-forward real-output multi-layer network. We assume that this network has the following properties:

- The network has $\ell \geq 2$ layers, with connections only between adjacent layers.

- There are W weights in the network.

- For some b, each computation unit maps into the interval $[-b, b]$, and each computation unit in the first layer has a non-decreasing activation function.

- There are constants $V > 0$ and $L > 1/V$, so that for each unit in all but the first layer of the network, the vector w of weights associated with that unit has $\|w\|_1 \leq V$, and the unit's activation function $s : \mathbb{R} \to [-b, b]$ satisfies the Lipschitz condition $|s(\alpha_1) - s(\alpha_2)| \leq L|\alpha_1 - \alpha_2|$ for all α_1, α_2 in $\mathbb{R}$. (Here, $\|w\|_1$ is the sum of absolute values of the entries of w.)

For convenience, we also assume that the computation units have no thresholds. It is straightforward to transform a network with thresholds to one without: we add a new input unit with a constant value, and a new computation unit in each non-output layer, with one connection from the new unit in the previous layer, and we replace the threshold in a computation unit with a connection from the new unit in the previous layer.

Theorem 14.5 *For the class F of functions computed by the network described above, if $\epsilon \leq 2b$, then*

$$\mathcal{N}_\infty(\epsilon, F, m) \leq \left(\frac{4embW(LV)^\ell}{\epsilon(LV - 1)} \right)^W.$$

The proof of this theorem uses Lemma 14.3. Suppose the network has k units in the first layer. We split the network so that $F = G \circ F_1$, where F_1 is the class of functions from X to $Y_1 = [-b, b]^k$ computed by the first layer units, and G is the class of functions from Y_1 to $[-b, b]$ computed by the later layers.

As a first step, we show that functions in G satisfy a Lipschitz condition. For $a = (a_1, \ldots, a_k) \in \mathbb{R}^k$, let $\|a\|_\infty = \max_i |a_i|$. (We will use the corresponding metric on Y_1, given by $\rho(a, b) = \|a - b\|_\infty$ for $a, b \in Y_1$.)

Lemma 14.6 *For the class G of functions computed by all but the first layer, as defined above, every g in G and y_1, y_2 in Y_1 satisfy*

$$|g(y_1) - g(y_2)| \leq (LV)^{(\ell-1)} \|y_1 - y_2\|_\infty.$$

Proof We decompose the function class G into functions computed by each layer of units. Let Y_i be the output space of units in layer i, so if there are k_i units in layer i, then $Y_i = [-b, b]^{k_i}$. Then we can write $G = G_\ell \circ G_{\ell-1} \circ \cdots \circ G_2$, where G_i is the class of functions from Y_{i-1} to Y_i computed by layer i. Then for any $g_i \in G_i$ and $y_1, y_2 \in Y_{i-1}$, by the Lipschitz condition on s,

$$\|g_i(y_1) - g_i(y_2)\|_\infty \leq L \max |w^T(y_1 - y_2)|,$$

where the maximum is over all weight vectors w associated with a unit in layer i. Clearly (see Inequality (1.8) in Appendix 1), $|w^T(y_1 - y_2)| \leq \|w\|_1 \|y_1 - y_2\|_\infty \leq V\|y_1 - y_2\|_\infty$. The result now follows by induction on i. $\qquad\square$

The second step of the proof of Theorem 14.5 is to bound the d_∞^ρ-covering numbers of $F_{1|_s}$, where ρ is the absolute difference metric on $\mathbb{R}$, $\rho(a, b) = |a - b|$.

Lemma 14.7 *For the class F_1 of functions computed by the first layer defined as above, and for $x \in X^m$,*

$$\mathcal{N}(\epsilon, F_{1|_s}, d_\infty^\rho) \leq \left(\frac{2emb}{\epsilon}\right)^{W - W_G},$$

where W_G is the number of weights in all but the first layer.

Proof Fix $x \in X^m$. For $f \in F_1$, (noting that F_1 is a class of vector-valued functions), write $f(x) = (f_1(x), \dots, f_k(x)) \in [-b, b]^k$, and define

$$F_{1,i} = \{f_i : (f_1, \dots, f_k) \in F_1\}$$

for $i = 1, \dots, k$. Clearly, $F_{1|_s} \subseteq F_{1,1|_s} \times \cdots \times F_{1,k|_s}$, and so we can construct a cover of $F_{1|_s}$ with respect to d_∞^ρ by taking the product of covers of $F_{1,i|_s}$ with respect to d_∞. This implies

$$\mathcal{N}(\epsilon, F_{1|_s}, d_\infty^\rho) \leq \prod_{i=1}^k \mathcal{N}(\epsilon, F_{1,i|_s}, d_\infty).$$

Suppose $X \subseteq \mathbb{R}^n$. Since the activation function of each first-layer computation unit is a non-decreasing function, we can apply Theorems 11.3, 11.6 and 12.2 to show that

$$\max_{x \in X^m} \mathcal{N}(\epsilon, F_{1,i|_a}, d_\infty) \leq \left(\frac{2emb}{\epsilon n}\right)^n$$

for any i. Since $kn = W - W_G$, the result follows. $\qquad\square$

The final step in the proof of Theorem 14.5 is to show that there is a small L_∞ cover of G.

Lemma 14.8 *With notation as defined above, if $\epsilon \leq 2b$ and $LV > 1$ then*

$$\mathcal{N}(\epsilon, G, d_{L_\infty}) \leq \left(\frac{2LVW_G b(LV)^{\ell-1}}{\epsilon(LV-1)}\right)^{W_G}.$$

Proof We construct a fine grid of points in parameter space, and show that the set of functions corresponding to these parameter values forms an ϵ-cover of the class G with respect to d_{L_∞}. To this end, let $\Delta = 2V/N$ for some integer N (which will be chosen later), and consider the set

$$S = \{-V, -V + \Delta, \dots, V - \Delta, V\}^{W_G},$$

regarded as a subset of the parameter space. Clearly $|S| = (N+1)^{W_G}$. Let S_G be the subset consisting of the points of S that satisfy the weight constraints described in the definition of the network. Consider a function g in G, and its corresponding vector w of parameter values. Clearly, there is a point $\hat{w}$ in S (corresponding to a function $\hat{g}$ in G) such that every component of $\hat{w}$ is within Δ of the corresponding component of w. Now, as in the proof of Lemma 14.6, write $G = G_\ell \circ G_{\ell-1} \circ \cdots \circ G_2$. Define $g_2 \in G_2, \dots, g_\ell \in G_\ell$ so that $g = g_\ell \circ \cdots \circ g_2$, and define $\hat{g}_2, \dots, \hat{g}_\ell$ similarly. Consider $y_1 \in Y_1$, and let $y_{i+1} = g_{i+1}(y_i)$ for $i = 1, \dots, \ell-1$. Similarly, let $\hat{y}_1 = y_1$, and define $\hat{y}_{i+1} = \hat{g}_{i+1}(\hat{y}_i)$. Now, we prove by induction that

$$\|y_i - \hat{y}_i\|_\infty \leq L\Delta W_G b \frac{(LV)^{i-1} - 1}{LV - 1}. \tag{14.2}$$

First, notice that this is trivially true for $i = 1$. Next, assume that (14.2) is true for $i \geq 1$. We have

$$\begin{aligned}
\|y_{i+1} - \hat{y}_{i+1}\|_\infty &= \|g_{i+1}(y_i) - \hat{g}_{i+1}(\hat{y}_i)\|_\infty \\
&\leq \|g_{i+1}(y_i) - g_{i+1}(\hat{y}_i)\|_\infty + \|g_{i+1}(\hat{y}_i) - \hat{g}_{i+1}(\hat{y}_i)\|_\infty.
\end{aligned}$$

By the same argument as in the proof of Lemma 14.6, the first term in this expression is no more than $LV\|y_i - \hat{y}_i\|_\infty$. To bound the second term, consider a unit in layer $(i+1)$ of the network, and let the relevant components of w and $\hat{w}$ be v and $\hat{v}$ respectively, so the unit computes $s(v^T \hat{y}_i)$ in calculating $g_{i+1}(\hat{y}_i)$ and $s(\hat{v}^T \hat{y}_i)$ in calculating $\hat{g}_{i+1}(\hat{y}_i)$. Then it is clear that

$$|s(v^T \hat{y}_i) - s(\hat{v}^T \hat{y}_i)| \leq L\|v - \hat{v}\|_1 \|\hat{y}_i\|_\infty \leq L\Delta W_G b.$$

It follows that

$$\|y_{i+1} - \hat{y}_{i+1}\|_\infty \leq L\Delta W_G b \left(\frac{(LV)^{i-1} - 1}{LV - 1} LV + 1 \right)$$

$$= L\Delta W_G b \left(\frac{(LV)^i - 1}{LV - 1} \right).$$

Hence,

$$d_{L_\infty}(g, \hat{g}) \leq L\Delta W_G b \frac{(LV)^{\ell-1} - 1}{LV - 1},$$

and so S_G corresponds to a d_{L_∞} ϵ-cover of G if this quantity is less than ϵ. For this, it suffices if we choose

$$N \geq \frac{2LVW_G b((LV)^{\ell-1} - 1)}{\epsilon(LV - 1)} + 1,$$

and we have $\mathcal{N}(\epsilon, G, d_{L_\infty}) \leq (N + 1)^{W_G}$, which implies the result. $\qquad \square$

Theorem 14.5 follows immediately from Lemmas 14.3, 14.6, 14.7, and 14.8 (with the L of Lemma 14.3 taken to be $(LV)^{\ell-1}$).

A bound on the fat-shattering dimension

As a corollary of Theorem 14.5, we can obtain a bound on the fat-shattering dimension of the neural networks under consideration.

Theorem 14.9 *For the class F of functions computed by the network described above,*

$$\text{fat}_F(\epsilon) \leq 16W \left(\ell \ln(LV) + 2\ln(32W) + \ln \left(\frac{b}{\epsilon(LV - 1)} \right) \right).$$

Proof Theorem 14.5 establishes that

$$\mathcal{N}_\infty(\epsilon, F, m) \leq \left(\frac{4embW(LV)^\ell}{\epsilon(LV - 1)} \right)^W.$$

By Theorem 12.10,

$$\mathcal{N}_\infty\left(\epsilon, F, m\right) \geq e^{\mathrm{fat}_F(16\epsilon)/8}$$

for $m \geq \mathrm{fat}_F(16\epsilon)$. Setting $d = \mathrm{fat}_F(\epsilon)$, replacing ϵ by $\epsilon/16$, taking $m = d$ in the lower bound just stated, and using Inequality (1.2) from Appendix 1 shows that

$$
\begin{aligned}
\frac{d}{8} &\leq \ln\left(\mathcal{N}_\infty\left(\epsilon/16, F, d\right)\right) \\
&\leq W \ln\left(\frac{64edbW(LV)^\ell}{\epsilon(LV-1)}\right) \\
&= W \ln d + W \ln\left(\frac{64ebW(LV)^\ell}{\epsilon(LV-1)}\right) \\
&\leq \frac{d}{16} + W \ln\left(\frac{16W}{e}\right) + W \ln\left(\frac{64ebW(LV)^\ell}{\epsilon(LV-1)}\right),
\end{aligned}
$$

from which the result follows.   □

For fixed depth, the bound of Theorem 14.9 is $O(W \ln(VW/\epsilon))$. Thus, the rate of growth with the number of parameters W is essentially the same as the corresponding results for linear threshold networks and for piecewise-polynomial networks (Theorems 6.1 and 8.8). Both the bound V on the size of the parameters and the scale ϵ enter only logarithmically.

14.4 Bounds on the Fat-Shattering Dimension in terms of Size of Parameters

In this section, we bound the fat-shattering dimension of sigmoid networks by quantities that do not depend on the number of parameters in the network. The key idea is to approximate a network with bounded weights by one with few weights. There are two steps in the derivation, outlined in the next two sections: the first presents an approximation result for convex combinations of bounded functions, and the second uses this to bound the covering numbers of the class of convex combinations of basis functions in terms of covering numbers of the basis function class.

An approximation result

The following result shows that a convex combination of bounded functions can be approximated by some small convex combination. The measure of approximation error is defined in terms of a scalar product†. For a subset S of a vector space H, the convex hull of S, $\mathrm{co}(S) \subseteq H$, is defined as

$$\mathrm{co}(S) = \left\{ \sum_{i=1}^{N} \alpha_i s_i : N \in \mathbb{N}, s_i \in S, \alpha_i > 0, \sum_{i=1}^{N} \alpha_i = 1 \right\}.$$

Theorem 14.10 *Let F be a vector space with a scalar product and let $\|f\| = \sqrt{(f,f)}$ be the induced norm on F. Suppose $G \subseteq F$ and that, for some $B > 0$, $\|g\| \le B$ for all $g \in G$. Then for all $f \in \mathrm{co}(G)$, all $k \in \mathbb{N}$, and all $c > B^2 - \|f\|^2$, there are elements $g_1, \ldots, g_k$ of G satisfying*

$$\left\| \frac{1}{k} \sum_{i=1}^{k} g_i - f \right\|^2 \le \frac{c}{k}.$$

Proof The proof uses the probabilistic method. The idea is to show that, for a suitable random choice of the g_i, the expectation of the squared norm is bounded by c/k, from which it follows that there must exist some g_i's for which the squared norm is no larger than this. Write $f \in \mathrm{co}(G)$ as $\sum_{i=1}^{N} \alpha_i f_i$ for $f_i \in G$ and suppose the g_i's are chosen independently such that $\Pr(g_i = f_j) = \alpha_j$. Then we have

$$\mathrm{E} \left\| \frac{1}{k} \sum_{i=1}^{k} g_i - f \right\|^2 = \mathrm{E} \frac{1}{k^2} \sum_{i=1}^{k} \sum_{j=1}^{k} (g_i - f, g_j - f)$$

$$= \mathrm{E} \frac{1}{k^2} \sum_{i=1}^{k} \left(\|g_i - f\|^2 + \sum_{j \neq i} (g_i - f, g_j - f) \right).$$

The second term inside the sum is zero, since the independence of g_i and g_j implies

$$\mathrm{E}(g_i - f, g_j - f) = \mathrm{E} \left(\sum_{l=1}^{N} \alpha_l f_l - f, g_j - f \right) = \mathrm{E}(0, g_j - f) = 0.$$

For the first term, notice that

$$\mathrm{E}\|g_i - f\|^2 = \mathrm{E}\|g_i\|^2 + \|f\|^2 - 2\mathrm{E}(g_i, f)$$
$$= \mathrm{E}\|g_i\|^2 - \|f\|^2$$
$$< c.$$

† If F is a vector space, a scalar product on F is a function defined for all f_1, f_2 in F and denoted (f_1, f_2) with the properties: (1) $(f_1, f_1) > 0$ for $f_1 \neq 0$, (2) $(f_1, f_2) = (f_2, f_1)$, (3) $(\lambda f_1, f_2) = \lambda(f_1, f_2)$, and (4) $(f_1, f_2 + f_3) = (f_1, f_2) + (f_1, f_3)$.

Combining shows that

$$\mathbf{E}\left\| \frac{1}{k}\sum_{i=1}^{k} g_i - f \right\|^2 \le \frac{1}{k^2}\sum_{i=1}^{k} c = \frac{c}{k}.$$

$\square$

Relating covering numbers

Recall the definition of the metric d_2: for any $x = (x_1,\ldots,x_n)$ and $y = (y_1,\ldots,y_n)$ in $\mathbb{R}^n$,

$$d_2(x,y) = \left(\frac{1}{n}\sum_{i=1}^{n}(x_i - y_i)^2\right)^{1/2}.$$

Notice that d_2 is the metric induced by the scalar product $(a,b) = (1/n)\sum_{i=1}^{n} a_i b_i$ on $\mathbb{R}^n$. The following theorem uses the previous result to bound covering numbers (with respect to d_2) of bounded linear combinations of functions.

Theorem 14.11 *Suppose $b > 0$ and that F is a class of $[-b,b]$-valued functions defined on a set X, and $\mathcal{N}_2(\epsilon, F, m)$ is finite for all $m \in \mathbb{N}$ and $\epsilon > 0$. Then provided $\epsilon_1 + \epsilon_2 \le \epsilon$,*

$$\log_2 \mathcal{N}_2(\epsilon, \mathrm{co}(F), m) \le \left\lceil \frac{b^2}{\epsilon_1^2} \right\rceil \log_2 \mathcal{N}_2(\epsilon_2, F, m).$$

Proof Suppose $\mathcal{N}_2(\epsilon_2, F, m) = N$. Then for any $x = (x_1,\ldots,x_m) \in X^m$ there is an ϵ_2-cover S of $F_{|_{\mathbf{x}}}$ such that $|S| = N$. We use Theorem 14.10 to show that we can approximate vectors in the restriction of $\mathrm{co}(F)$ to x using small convex combinations of functions in S. To this end, define $T_k \subseteq \mathbb{R}^m$ as

$$T_k = \left\{ \frac{1}{k}\sum_{i=1}^{k} s_i : s_i \in S \right\}.$$

Clearly $|T_k| \le N^k$. Choose any $f \in \mathrm{co}(F)$, and suppose $f = \sum_{i=1}^{l} \alpha_i f_i$ with $\alpha_i > 0$, $\sum_{i=1}^{l} \alpha_i = 1$, and $f_i \in F$. Using the notation $g_{|_{\mathbf{x}}} = (g(x_1),\ldots,g(x_m))$, let $f_{i|_{\mathbf{x}}} = (f_i(x_1),\ldots,f_i(x_m)) \in \mathbb{R}^m$. Since S is an ϵ_2-cover of $F_{|_{\mathbf{x}}}$ with respect to the d_2 metric, there are vectors $\hat{f}_1,\ldots,\hat{f}_l$ in S such that

$$d_2(f_{i|_{\mathbf{x}}}, \hat{f}_i) \le \epsilon_2.$$

It follows that

$$d_2\left(f_{|_\bullet}, \sum_{i=1}^l \alpha_i \hat{f}_i\right) \le \epsilon_2.$$

But Theorem 14.10 shows that there are $g_1, \ldots, g_k$ in S such that

$$d_2\left(\frac{1}{k}\sum_{i=1}^k g_i, \sum_{i=1}^l \alpha_i \hat{f}_i\right) \le \frac{b}{\sqrt{k}},$$

and the triangle inequality for d_2 then implies that

$$d_2\left(\frac{1}{k}\sum_{i=1}^k g_i, f_{|_\bullet}\right) \le \epsilon_2 + \frac{b}{\sqrt{k}}.$$

Since this is true for any $f \in \mathrm{co}(F)$, T_k is an $(\epsilon_2 + b/\sqrt{k})$-cover of $\mathrm{co}(F)_{|_\bullet}$. Choosing $k = \lceil b^2/\epsilon_1^2 \rceil$ gives the desired result. $\qquad\square$

We use the following two simple results in deriving the covering number and fat-shattering dimension bounds for neural networks. The first concerns covering numbers of scaled versions of a function class. For a real number α and a subset F of a normed vector space, we define $\alpha F = \{\alpha f : f \in F\}$.

Lemma 14.12 *If G is a normed vector space with induced metric d and F is a subset of G, then $\mathcal{N}(\epsilon, F, d) = \mathcal{N}(|\alpha|\epsilon, \alpha F, d)$, for any $\epsilon > 0$ and $\alpha \in \mathbb{R}$.*

Proof If $\hat{F}$ is a minimal ϵ-cover of F, then for all $f \in F$ there is an $\hat{f}$ in $\hat{F}$ with $d(f, \hat{f}) < \epsilon$. Since d is induced by a norm, it satisfies the property $d(\alpha f, \alpha \hat{f}) = |\alpha| d(f, \hat{f})$. It follows that $\alpha \hat{F}$ is an $|\alpha|\epsilon$-cover of αF, which implies $\mathcal{N}(|\alpha|\epsilon, \alpha F, d) \le \mathcal{N}(\epsilon, F, d)$. The reverse inequality is proved similarly. $\qquad\square$

Finally, the following lemma shows that taking the composition of a fixed function with functions from a class does not significantly increase the covering number, provided the fixed function satisfies a Lipschitz condition.

Lemma 14.13 *Suppose F is a class of real-valued functions defined on a set X, and the function $\phi : \mathbb{R} \to \mathbb{R}$ satisfies the Lipschitz condition $|\phi(x) - \phi(y)| \le L|x - y|$ for all $x, y \in \mathbb{R}$. Let $\phi \circ F = \{\phi \circ f : f \in F\}$. Then $\mathcal{N}_2(\epsilon, \phi \circ F, m) \le \mathcal{N}_2(\epsilon/L, F, m)$.*

The proof is similar to the proof of Lemma 14.12, but uses the fact that

$$|(\phi \circ f)(x) - (\phi \circ g)(x)| \leq L|f(x) - g(x)|.$$

Covering numbers for two-layer networks

We first consider two-layer networks in which the first-layer units compute arbitrary functions from some set. The following theorem follows easily from Theorem 14.11. In the theorem statement, $-F_1$ denotes $(-1)F_1$.

Theorem 14.14 *Suppose $b > 0$ and that F_1 is a class of $[-b, b]$-valued functions defined on a set X and satisfying the following conditions:*

(i) $F_1 = -F_1$,

(ii) F_1 *contains the identically zero function, and*

(iii) $\mathcal{N}_2(\epsilon, F_1, m)$ *is finite for all $m \in \mathbb{N}$ and $\epsilon > 0$.*

For $V \geq 1$, define

$$F = \left\{ \sum_{i=1}^{N} w_i f_i : N \in \mathbb{N}, f_i \in F_1, \sum_{i=1}^{N} |w_i| \leq V \right\}.$$

Then for $\epsilon_1 + \epsilon_2 \leq \epsilon$,

$$\log_2 \mathcal{N}_2(\epsilon, F, m) \leq \left\lceil \frac{V^2 b^2}{\epsilon_1^2} \right\rceil \log_2 \mathcal{N}_2 \left(\frac{\epsilon_2}{V}, F_1, m \right).$$

Proof The conditions on F_1 imply that $F = V\mathrm{co}(F_1)$. Theorem 14.11 and Lemma 14.12 give the result. $\square$

We can apply this result to give covering number bounds for two-layer networks. The following corollary gives a bound that depends on the input dimension, and is applicable to a network with non-decreasing activation functions in the first layer units.

Corollary 14.15 *Suppose that $b > 0$ and $s : \mathbb{R} \to [-b, b]$ is a non-decreasing function. Let $V \geq 1$ and suppose that F is the class of functions from $\mathbb{R}^n$ to $\mathbb{R}$ given by*

$$F = \left\{ x \mapsto \sum_{i=1}^{N} w_i s(v_i^T x + v_{i0}) + w_0 : N \in \mathbb{N}, v_i \in \mathbb{R}^n, v_{i0} \in \mathbb{R}, \right.$$

$$\left. \sum_{i=0}^{N} |w_i| \le V \right\}.$$

Then for $0 < \epsilon \le b$ and $m \ge n + 1$,

$$\log_2 \mathcal{N}_2\left(\epsilon, F, m\right) \le \frac{5V^2 b^2 (n+3)}{\epsilon^2} \log_2 \left(\frac{4embV}{\epsilon(n+1)} \right).$$

Proof Define F_1 as the class of functions computed by units in the first layer,

$$F_1 = \left\{ x \mapsto s(v_i^T x + v_{i0}) : v_i = (v_{i1}, \dots, v_{in}) \in \mathbb{R}^n, v_{i0} \in \mathbb{R} \right\}.$$

Theorem 11.4 shows that the pseudo-dimension of the class of affine combinations is $n + 1$. Theorem 11.3 shows that this is not increased by composing with the activation function, and Theorem 12.2 shows that

$$\mathcal{N}_2\left(\epsilon, F_1, m\right) \le \mathcal{N}_\infty\left(\epsilon, F_1, m\right) \le \left(\frac{2emb}{\epsilon(n+1)} \right)^{n+1}$$

for $m \ge d$. Lemma 14.12 shows that $\mathcal{N}_2\left(\epsilon, -F_1, m\right) = \mathcal{N}_2\left(\epsilon, F_1, m\right)$, and so the class $F_1 \cup -F_1 \cup \{0, 1\}$ (where 0 and 1 are the identically zero and identically one functions) has covering number

$$\mathcal{N}_2\left(\epsilon, F_1 \cup -F_1 \cup \{0, 1\}, m\right) \le 2\mathcal{N}_2\left(\epsilon, F_1, m\right) + 2.$$

Theorem 14.14 shows that

$$\log_2 \mathcal{N}_2\left(\epsilon, F, m\right) \le \left\lceil \frac{V^2 b^2}{\epsilon_1^2} \right\rceil \log_2 \left(2 \left(\frac{2embV}{\epsilon_2(n+1)} \right)^{n+1} + 2 \right).$$

Substituting $\epsilon_1 = \epsilon_2 = \epsilon/2$ gives the result.   ☐

The second corollary gives a bound on the logarithm of the covering number that increases only logarithmically with the input dimension, but it requires smooth activation functions in the first layer units and a bound on the first layer weights.

Corollary 14.16 *Suppose that $b, L > 0$ and $s : \mathbb{R} \to [-b, b]$ satisfies $|s(\alpha_1) - s(\alpha_2)| \le L|\alpha_1 - \alpha_2|$ for all $\alpha_1, \alpha_2 \in \mathbb{R}$. For $V \ge 1$ and $B \ge 1$, let*

$$F = \left\{ \sum_{i=1}^{N} w_i f_i + w_0 : N \in \mathbb{N}, f_i \in F_1, \sum_{i=0}^{N} |w_i| \le V \right\}$$

where

$$F_1 = \left\{ x \mapsto s \left(\sum_{i=1}^{n} v_i x_i + v_0 \right) : v_i \in \mathbb{R}, x \in [-B, B]^n, \sum_{i=0}^{n} |v_i| \leq V \right\}.$$

Then for $\epsilon \leq V \min\{BL, b\}$,

$$\log_2 \mathcal{N}_2 (\epsilon, F, m) \leq 50 \left(\frac{V^3 L^2 b B}{\epsilon^2} \right)^2 \log_2(2n + 2).$$

Proof Applying Theorem 14.14 (as in the proof of Corollary 14.15) as well as Lemma 14.13 shows that

$$
\begin{aligned}
\log_2 \mathcal{N}_2 (\epsilon, F_1, m) &\leq \left\lceil \frac{V^2 B^2 L^2}{\epsilon_1^2} \right\rceil \log_2 \mathcal{N}_2 \left(\frac{\epsilon_2}{VL}, G \cup -G \cup \{0, 1\}, m \right) \\
&\leq \left\lceil \frac{V^2 B^2 L^2}{\epsilon_1^2} \right\rceil \log_2 \left(2 \mathcal{N}_2 \left(\frac{\epsilon_2}{VL}, G, m \right) + 2 \right),
\end{aligned}
$$

provided $B \geq 1$ and $\epsilon_1 + \epsilon_2 \geq \epsilon$, where $G = \{x \mapsto x_i : i \in \{1, \ldots, n\}\}$. Clearly, for all $\epsilon > 0$, $\mathcal{N}_2 (\epsilon, G, m) \leq |G| = n$. Since $\lceil V^2 B^2 L^2 / \epsilon_1^2 \rceil < 2V^2 B^2 L^2 / \epsilon_1^2$, we can choose $\epsilon_1 < \epsilon$ such that

$$\left\lceil \frac{V^2 B^2 L^2}{\epsilon_1^2} \right\rceil \leq \frac{2V^2 B^2 L^2}{\epsilon^2}.$$

Hence,

$$\log_2 \mathcal{N}_2 (\epsilon, F_1, m) \leq \frac{2V^2 B^2 L^2}{\epsilon^2} \log_2(2n + 2).$$

Similarly, if $b \geq 1$,

$$\log_2 \mathcal{N}_2 (\epsilon, F, m) \leq \left\lceil \frac{V^2 b^2}{\epsilon_1^2} \right\rceil \log_2 \left(2 \mathcal{N}_2 \left(\frac{\epsilon_2}{V}, F_1, m \right) + 2 \right)$$

for $\epsilon_1 + \epsilon_2 \leq \epsilon$. Setting $\epsilon_1 = \epsilon_2 = \epsilon/2$ gives

$$
\begin{aligned}
\log_2 \mathcal{N}_2 (\epsilon, F, m) &\leq \frac{5V^2 b^2 L^2}{\epsilon^2} \left(2 + \log_2 \mathcal{N}_2 \left(\frac{\epsilon}{2V}, F_1, m \right) \right) \\
&\leq \frac{5V^2 b^2 L^2}{\epsilon^2} \left(2 + \frac{8V^4 B^2 L^2}{\epsilon^2} \log_2(2n + 2) \right) \\
&\leq \frac{50 V^6 L^4 b^2 B^2}{\epsilon^4} \log_2(2n + 2),
\end{aligned}
$$

and the result follows. $\qquad\square$

Covering numbers for deeper networks

We can use a similar approach to give bounds for deeper networks. For convenience, we assume that the bound B on the magnitude of the input values is equal to the maximum magnitude b of the activation function. Define

$$F_0 = \{x \mapsto x_i : x = (x_1, \ldots, x_n) \in [-b, b]^n, i \in \{1, \ldots, n\}\} \cup \{0, 1\},$$

where 0 and 1 are the identically zero and identically one functions, respectively. For $i \geq 1$, define

$$F_i = \left\{ s\left(\sum_{j=1}^{N} w_j f_j\right) : N \in \mathbb{N}, f_j \in \bigcup_{k=0}^{i-1} F_k, \sum_{j=1}^{N} |w_j| \leq V \right\}. \quad (14.3)$$

Thus, F_ℓ is the class of functions that can be computed by an ℓ-layer feed-forward network in which each unit has the sum of the magnitudes of its weights bounded by V. We assume as above that the activation function $s : \mathbb{R} \to [-b, b]$ satisfies the Lipschitz condition $|s(\alpha_1) - s(\alpha_2)| \leq L|\alpha_1 - \alpha_2|$ for all $\alpha_1, \alpha_2 \in \mathbb{R}$.

Theorem 14.17 *For $\ell \geq 1$, the class F_ℓ defined above satisfies*

$$\log_2 \mathcal{N}_2(\epsilon, F_\ell, m) \leq \frac{1}{2}\left(\frac{2b}{\epsilon}\right)^{2\ell} (2VL)^{\ell(\ell+1)} \log_2(2n + 2),$$

provided $b \geq 1$, $V \geq 1/(2L)$, and $\epsilon \leq VbL$.

Proof As in the proof of Corollary 14.16,

$$\log_2 \mathcal{N}_2(\epsilon, F_1, m) \leq \frac{2V^2 b^2 L^2}{\epsilon^2} \log_2(2n + 2). \quad (14.4)$$

Theorem 14.14 and Lemma 14.13 imply that

$$\log_2 \mathcal{N}_2(\epsilon, F_i, m) \leq \frac{5V^2 b^2 L^2}{\epsilon^2} \log_2 \mathcal{N}_2\left(\frac{\epsilon}{2VL}, G_{i-1}, m\right) \quad (14.5)$$

for $i \geq 1$, where $G_{i-1} = \bigcup_{k=0}^{i-1} F_k$. Clearly, $G_i = G_{i-1} \cup F_i$, so for $i \geq 2$,

$$\log_2 \mathcal{N}_2(\epsilon, G_i, m)$$

$$\leq \log_2\left(\mathcal{N}_2(\epsilon, G_{i-1}, m) + \mathcal{N}_2\left(\frac{\epsilon}{2VL}, G_{i-1}, m\right)^{(5V^2 b^2 L^2/\epsilon^2)}\right)$$

$$\leq 1 + \frac{5V^2 b^2 L^2}{\epsilon^2} \log_2 \mathcal{N}_2\left(\frac{\epsilon}{2VL}, G_{i-1}, m\right)$$

$$\leq \frac{6V^2 b^2 L^2}{\epsilon^2} \log_2 \mathcal{N}_2\left(\frac{\epsilon}{2VL}, G_{i-1}, m\right). \quad (14.6)$$

We now prove by induction that this implies

$$\log_2 \mathcal{N}_2\left(\epsilon, G_i, m\right) \leq \left(\frac{6V^2b^2L^2}{\epsilon^2}\right)^{i-1} (2VL)^{(i-1)(i-2)} \times$$
$$\log_2 \mathcal{N}_2\left(\frac{\epsilon}{(2VL)^{i-1}}, G_1, m\right) (14.7)$$

Clearly, this is true for $i = 1$. If it is true for $1 \leq i \leq j-1$, (14.6) implies

$$\log_2 \mathcal{N}_2\left(\epsilon, G_j, m\right)$$
$$\leq \frac{6V^2b^2L^2}{\epsilon^2} \log_2 \mathcal{N}_2\left(\frac{\epsilon}{2VL}, G_{j-1}, m\right)$$
$$\leq \frac{6V^2b^2L^2}{\epsilon^2} \left(\frac{6V^2b^2L^2(2VL)^2}{\epsilon^2}\right)^{j-2} (2VL)^{(j-2)(j-3)} \times$$
$$\log_2 \mathcal{N}_2\left(\frac{\epsilon}{(2VL)^{j-1}}, G_1, m\right)$$
$$= \left(\frac{6V^2b^2L^2}{\epsilon^2}\right)^{j-1} (2VL)^{(j-1)(j-2)} \log_2 \mathcal{N}_2\left(\frac{\epsilon}{(2VL)^{j-1}}, G_1, m\right),$$

as desired. Now, Inequality (14.4) shows that

$$\log_2 \mathcal{N}_2\left(\epsilon, G_1, m\right) \leq \log_2\left((2n+2)^{(2V^2b^2L^2/\epsilon^2)} + 2n + 2\right)$$
$$\leq \frac{3V^2b^2L^2}{\epsilon^2} \log_2(2n+2). \qquad (14.8)$$

Combining (14.5), (14.7), and (14.8) shows that

$$\log_2 \mathcal{N}_2\left(\epsilon, F_\ell, m\right)$$
$$\leq \frac{5V^2b^2L^2}{\epsilon^2} \log_2 \mathcal{N}_2\left(\frac{\epsilon}{2VL}, G_{\ell-1}, m\right)$$
$$\leq \frac{5V^2b^2L^2}{\epsilon^2} \left(\frac{6V^2b^2L^2(2VL)^2}{\epsilon^2}\right)^{\ell-2} (2VL)^{(\ell-2)(\ell-3)} \times$$
$$\log_2 \mathcal{N}_2\left(\frac{\epsilon}{(2VL)^{\ell-1}}, G_1, m\right)$$
$$\leq \frac{5V^2b^2L^2}{\epsilon^2} \left(\frac{6V^2b^2L^2(2VL)^2}{\epsilon^2}\right)^{\ell-2} (2VL)^{(\ell-2)(\ell-3)} \times$$
$$\frac{3V^2b^2L^2(2VL)^{2(\ell-1)}}{\epsilon^2} \log_2(2n+2)$$
$$< \frac{1}{2}\left(\frac{6V^2b^2L^2}{\epsilon^2}\right)^\ell (2VL)^{\ell(\ell-1)} \log_2(2n+2),$$

which implies the result. $\qquad\qquad\qquad\qquad\qquad\qquad\square$

A bound on the fat-shattering dimension

Using the covering number bounds of Corollary 14.15, together with
Theorem 12.10, straightforward calculations (similar to those used to
prove Theorem 14.9) give the following bound on the fat-shattering dimension of two-layer networks with bounded weights.

Theorem 14.18 *Suppose that $b \geq 1$ and $s : \mathbb{R} \to [-b,b]$ is a non-
decreasing function. Let $V \geq 1$ and suppose that F is the class of functions from $\mathbb{R}^n$ to $\mathbb{R}$ given by*

$$F = \left\{ x \mapsto \sum_{i=1}^{N} w_i s(v_i^T x + v_{i0}) + w_0 : N \in \mathbb{N}, v_i \in \mathbb{R}^n, v_{i0} \in \mathbb{R}, \right.$$

$$\left. \sum_{i=0}^{N} |w_i| \leq V \right\}.$$

Then for $0 < \epsilon \leq b$,

$$\mathrm{fat}_F(\epsilon) \leq 2^{16}(n+3) \left(\frac{bV}{\epsilon}\right)^2 \ln\left(\frac{2^8 bV}{\epsilon}\right).$$

Using the proof techniques from Theorem 14.17, this result can easily be extended to networks of any fixed depth, with bounded non-
decreasing activation functions in the first layer and bounded, smooth
(Lipschitz) activation functions in later layers. As mentioned at the be-
ginning of this chapter, these bounds show that when the parameters in
all except the first layer are not too large relative to the relevant scale
(that is, V is small relative to ϵ), the fat-shattering dimension of the
network grows linearly with the input dimension n. Hence, when the
computation units in all except the first layer are operating in their 'approximately linear' region, the dimension grows just as it would if the
network contained only linear computation units.

When the units in the first layer also have smooth activation functions
and small weights, Theorems 14.17 and 12.10 immediately imply the
following result. In this case, when the weights are small relative to the
relevant scale, the fat-shattering dimension can be even smaller than the
dimension of a network of linear units.

Theorem 14.19 *Suppose that F_ℓ is defined recursively by (14.3). Then*

$$\mathrm{fat}_{F_\ell}(\epsilon) \leq 4 \left(\frac{32b}{\epsilon}\right)^{2\ell} (2VL)^{\ell(\ell+1)} \ln(2n+2),$$

provided $b \geq 1$, $V \geq 1/(2L)$, and $\epsilon \leq 16VbL$.

Note that both this bound and that of Theorem 14.18 depend on the bound V on the size of the weights, but do not involve W, the number of weights. For a fixed number of layers ℓ, both bounds are independent of the size of the network.

14.5 Remarks

Because the pseudo-dimension gives a bound on the fat-shattering dimension, the VC-dimension bounds of Chapter 8, together with Theorem 14.1, imply bounds for several networks, including those with piecewise-polynomial activation functions and the standard sigmoid activation function. These bounds are in terms of the number of parameters in the network, and have the advantage over Theorem 14.5 that they do not require a bound on the magnitude of the parameters. However, for networks of units with the standard sigmoid activation function, these bounds grow more quickly with the size of the network.

The techniques used in Section 14.4 can be applied to any function classes that can be expressed as compositions of bounded linear combinations and bounded scalar functions satisfying a Lipschitz condition. For example, there are straightforward analogues of Theorems 14.18 and 14.19 for radial basis function networks with bounded parameters. (See Section 8.5.)

Linear classifiers

Techniques from Section 14.4 give the following result for the class of linear functions with bounded inputs and bounded weights. We assume that the inputs have bounded infinity-norm, defined by $\|x\|_\infty = \max_i |x_i|$, for $x = (x_1, \ldots, x_n) \in \mathbb{R}^n$, and that the weights have bounded 1-norm, defined by $\|w\|_1 = \sum_{i=1}^n |w_i|$, for $w = (w_1, \ldots, w_n) \in \mathbb{R}^n$. The proof follows from the bound on the covering numbers of F_1 in the proof of Corollary 14.16, together with Theorem 12.10.

Theorem 14.20 *For the class $F_V = \left\{ x \mapsto w^T x : \|x\|_\infty \leq 1, \|w\|_1 \leq V \right\}$ we have*

$$\mathrm{fat}_{F_V}(\epsilon) \leq 2^{12} \left(\frac{V}{\epsilon} \right)^2 \ln(2n + 2).$$

Since the 1-norm and the infinity-norm are dual norms, the bounds on these norms ensure that functions in F are bounded. A similar result to Theorem 14.20 can be obtained for another pair of dual norms, the 2-norm of x and the 2-norm of w.

Theorem 14.21 *For the class $F_V = \{x \mapsto w^T x : \|x\|_2 \leq 1, \|w\|_2 \leq V\}$ we have*

$$\mathrm{fat}_{F_V}(\epsilon) \leq \left(\frac{V}{\epsilon}\right)^2.$$

These results are especially interesting because of the attractive computational properties of these function classes. A problem closely related to large margin sample error minimization for the class defined in Theorem 14.21 (namely, the problem of maximizing γ so that $\hat{\mathrm{er}}_z^\gamma(f) = 0$) can be expressed as a quadratic optimization problem with convex constraints. This problem can be solved in polynomial time using interior point methods. As a result, these function classes have been studied extensively. The bounds of Theorems 14.20 and 14.21, together with the results of Chapter 13, explain why the generalization performance of these classifiers does not have a significant dependence on the input dimension n.

The proof of Theorem 14.21 involves two lemmas. The first shows that the sum of any subset of a shattered set is far from the sum of the remainder of that set. The second shows that these sums cannot be too far apart when the 2-norms of the input vectors are small. Comparing the results gives the bound on the fat-shattering dimension.

Lemma 14.22 *Let $F_V = \{x \mapsto w^T x : \|x\|_2 \leq 1, \|w\|_2 \leq V\}$. If S is ϵ-shattered by F_V, then every subset $S_0 \subseteq S$ satisfies*

$$\left\| \sum S_0 - \sum (S - S_0) \right\|_2 \geq |S|\epsilon/V.$$

(Here, for a finite set T, $\sum T$ denotes the sum of the members of T.)

Proof Suppose that $S = \{x_1, \ldots, x_d\}$ is ϵ-shattered by F_V, witnessed by $r_1, \ldots, r_d \in \mathbb{R}$. Then for all $b = (b_1, \ldots, b_d) \in \{-1, 1\}^d$ there is a w_b with $\|w_b\| \leq V$ such that, for all i, $b_i(w_b^T x_i - r_i) \geq \epsilon$. Fix a subset $S_0 \subseteq S$. We consider two cases. If

$$\sum \{r_i : x_i \in S_0\} \geq \sum \{r_i : x_i \in S - S_0\}, \qquad (14.9)$$

then fix $b_i = 1$ if and only if $x_i \in S_0$. In that case we have $w_b^T x_i \geq r_i + \epsilon$ if $x_i \in S_0$, and $w_b^T x_i \leq r_i - \epsilon$ otherwise. It follows that

$$w_b^T \left(\sum S_0 \right) \geq \sum \{r_i : x_i \in S_0\} + |S_0|\epsilon.$$

Similarly,

$$w_b^T \left(\sum (S - S_0) \right) \leq \sum \{r_i : x_i \in S - S_0\} - |S - S_0|\epsilon.$$

Hence,

$$w_b^T \left(\sum S_0 - \sum (S - S_0) \right) \geq |S|\epsilon.$$

But since $\|w\|_2 \leq V$, the Cauchy-Schwarz inequality (Inequality (1.7) in Appendix 1) implies that

$$\left\| \sum S_0 - \sum (S - S_0) \right\|_2 \geq |S|\epsilon/V.$$

In the other case (if (14.9) is not satisfied), we fix $b_i = 1$ if and only if $x_i \in S - S_0$, and use an identical argument. $\qquad\square$

Lemma 14.23 *For all $S \subseteq \mathbb{R}^n$ with $\|x\|_2 \leq 1$ for $x \in S$, some $S_0 \subseteq S$ satisfies*

$$\left\| \sum S_0 - \sum (S - S_0) \right\|_2 \leq \sqrt{|S|}.$$

Proof The proof uses the probabilistic method. Fix any finite set $S = \{x_1, \ldots, x_d\}$ satisfying the conditions of the lemma. We choose S_0 randomly, by defining $S_0 = \{x_i \in S : b_i = 1\}$, where $b_1, \ldots, b_d \in \{-1, 1\}$ are independent and uniform random variables. Then

$$\mathbf{E} \left\| \sum S_0 - \sum (S - S_0) \right\|_2^2 = \mathbf{E} \left\| \sum_{i=1}^d b_i x_i \right\|_2^2$$

$$= \sum_{i=1}^d \mathbf{E} \left(b_i x_i^T \left(\sum_{j=1}^d b_j x_j \right) \right)$$

$$= \sum_{i=1}^d \left(\sum_{j \neq i} \mathbf{E}(b_i b_j x_i^T x_j) + \mathbf{E}\|b_i x_i\|_2^2 \right)$$

$$= \sum_{i=1}^d \mathbf{E}\|b_i x_i\|_2^2$$

$$\leq |S|,$$

where the last equality follows from the fact that the b_i's have zero mean and are independent. Since the expected value of this squared norm is no more than $|S|$, there must be a set S_0 for which this quantity is no more than $|S|$. □

Theorem 14.21 follows immediately: if S is ϵ-shattered, then $|S|\epsilon/V \leq \sqrt{|S|}$, so $|S| \leq (V/\epsilon)^2$.

14.6 Bibliographical Notes

Theorem 14.1, the observation that the pseudo-dimension of a neural network can be bounded by the VC-dimension of a related network, appears in (Vidyasagar, 1997).

The techniques of Theorem 14.5—relating covering numbers of compositions of function classes to covering numbers of the classes—have been used by a number of authors; see, for example, (White, 1990; Haussler, 1992; Barron, 1994; McCaffrey and Gallant, 1994).

Theorem 14.10, the approximation result on which the results of Section 14.4 are based, is attributed in (Dudley, 1987) to Maurey (see (Pisier, 1981; Carl, 1982)), and was used by Jones (1992), and Barron (1993) to obtain approximation rates for two layer neural networks. Makovoz (1996) gives an improvement of this result that is significantly better when the subset G has small covering numbers, and shows that his result is optimal (see also (Dudley, 1987, Theorem 5.1)). If, in deriving a bound on covering numbers for two-layer networks (like Corollary 14.15), we use Makovoz' result in place of Theorem 14.10, we obtain a slight improvement: for input dimension n, the new bound on the log covering number grows as $\epsilon^{-2n/(1+n)}$, ignoring log factors. Comparing this with the old bound, which is roughly of the form $1/\epsilon^2$, shows that the improvement is significant for $n = 1$, but as the input dimension n becomes large, the new bound approaches the old. Typically, we are interested in problems with large input dimension, where the improvement is not significant. However, the difference is significant if we are interested in the asymptotic distribution of the largest difference between expected error and sample error of functions in the class. See, for example, (van der Vaart and Wellner, 1996).

Theorem 14.11 and its proof were in (Lee et al., 1996), and Corollary 14.15 is a more general version of a result there. See (Dudley, 1987, Theorem 5.1) for a similar, but weaker, result. Using uniform approximation techniques due to Barron (1992), Gurvits and Koiran (1997) give a bound on the fat-shattering dimension for these networks that implies a weaker result than Corollary 14.15. Corollary 14.16 and Theorem 14.17 are from (Bartlett, 1998), as are the corresponding bounds on the fat-shattering dimension (Theorems 14.18 and 14.19). Theorem 14.20, the fat-shattering dimension bound for convex combinations of points in an l_∞ ball in $\mathbb{R}^n$, is an immediate consequence of these results. A shorter proof of the uniform convergence implications of that theorem is given in (Schapire, Freund, Bartlett and Lee, 1998). A similar result for this class—with an even shorter proof—is given in (Mason, Bartlett and Baxter, 1999).

Vapnik and Chervonenkis (see (Vapnik, 1982)) gave a result that can be used to give a weaker version of Theorem 14.21 (see (Shawe-Taylor et al., 1996; Shawe-Taylor, Bartlett, Williamson and Anthony, 1998)). For details of the quadratic optimization problem for support vector machines mentioned after that theorem, see (Boser et al., 1992; Cortes and Vapnik, 1995; Wahba, 1990; Vapnik, 1995). (See also (Schölkopf, Burges and Smola, 1999; Smola, Bartlett, Schölkopf and Schuurmans, 1999).) Gurvits (1997b) gave a simple proof of a weaker version of Theorem 14.21, using random approximation ideas similar to those used for Theorem 14.10. The proof given here uses the same ideas, but is simpler again, and gives a better constant. See (Bartlett and Shawe-Taylor, 1999). That theorem can be significantly improved for support vector machines, where the variables x are themselves fixed non-linear functions of input variables; see (Williamson, Smola and Schölkopf, 1999; Guo, Bartlett, Shawe-Taylor and Williamson, 1999).

15
Model Selection

15.1 Introduction

The first two parts of this book have considered the following three step approach to solving a pattern classification problem.

(i) Choose a suitable class of functions.

(ii) Gather data.

(iii) Choose a function from the class.

In this formulation, the class is fixed before the data is gathered, and the aim is to select a function that is nearly optimal in the class. The results presented so far show how the estimation error depends on the complexity of this fixed class and the amount of data. For example, consider a two-layer network N_W with input set X, W parameters, a linear threshold output unit, and first-layer units with a fixed bounded piecewise-linear activation function (such as the activation function illustrated in Figure 8.1). Theorem 8.8, Theorem 4.3, and the proof of Theorem 4.2 together imply the following result. For convenience in what follows, we split the result into the key results that imply it.†

Theorem 15.1 *There are constants c_1, c_2, c_3 such that the following holds. For any W, let H_W be the class of functions computed by the two-layer network N_W with piecewise-linear first-layer units, as defined above. Suppose P is a probability distribution on $X \times \{0, 1\}$, and $z \in Z^m$ is chosen according to P^m. Then with probability at least $1 - \delta$, every h*

---

† In fact, we did not use Inequality (15.1) to derive Theorem 4.2. We include it here for uniformity. It is easy to obtain, using an identical argument to the proof of Lemma 13.3.

in H_W satisfies

$$\mathrm{er}_P(h) < \hat{\mathrm{er}}_z(h) + \left(\frac{c_1}{m}\left(W\ln(Wm) + \ln\left(\frac{1}{\delta}\right)\right)\right)^{1/2}.$$

For any fixed h^* (in particular, for $h^* \in H_W$ satisfying $\mathrm{er}_P(h^*) < \inf_{h \in H_W}\mathrm{er}_P(h) + 1/m$), with probability at least $1 - \delta$ we have

$$\hat{\mathrm{er}}_z(h^*) < \mathrm{er}_P(h^*) + \left(\frac{c_2}{m}\ln\left(\frac{1}{\delta}\right)\right)^{1/2}. \tag{15.1}$$

Hence, if L_W is a SEM algorithm for H_W (so that $L_W(z)$ has $\hat{\mathrm{er}}_z$ minimal over H_W), then with probability at least $1 - \delta$ we have

$$\mathrm{er}_P(L_W(z)) < \inf_{h \in H_W}\mathrm{er}_P(h) + \left(\frac{c_3}{m}\left(W\ln(Wm) + \ln\left(\frac{1}{\delta}\right)\right)\right)^{1/2}.$$

Unfortunately, this result is applicable only if we fix the complexity of our class (that is, the number of first-layer units, and hence the number W of parameters) *before* seeing any data. This is rather unsatisfactory; we would prefer that, after seeing the data, a learning system could choose automatically a suitable level of complexity that gives the smallest possible error. This problem is known as *model selection*.

As a second example, Theorem 14.18, Theorem 13.2, and the proof of Theorem 13.4 together imply the following result. Here, the class F_V of functions computed by the two-layer network N_V is defined by

$$F_V = \left\{ x \mapsto \sum_{i=1}^{k} w_i s(v_i^T x + v_{i0}) + w_0 : k \in \mathbb{N}, \sum_{i=0}^{k}|w_i| \le V \right\}, \tag{15.2}$$

where V is a positive constant, $x \in \mathbb{R}^n$, and the activation function $s : \mathbb{R} \to [-1, 1]$ associated with each first-layer unit is a non-decreasing function.

Theorem 15.2 *There are constants c_1, c_2, c_3 such that the following holds. For any V and n, let F_V be the function class defined by (15.2). Fix $\gamma \in (0, 1]$ and suppose that P is a probability distribution on $X \times \{0, 1\}$, and that $z \in Z^m$ is chosen according to P^m. Then with probability at least $1 - \delta$, every $f \in F_V$ satisfies*

$$\mathrm{er}_P(f) < \hat{\mathrm{er}}_z^\gamma(f) + \left(\frac{c_1}{m}\left(\frac{V^2 n}{\gamma^2}\ln^2(m)\ln\left(\frac{V}{\gamma}\right) + \ln\left(\frac{1}{\delta}\right)\right)\right)^{1/2}.$$

For any fixed f^*, with probability at least $1 - \delta$ we have

$$\hat{\mathrm{er}}_z^\gamma(f^*) < \mathrm{er}_P^\gamma(f^*) + \left(\frac{c_2}{m}\ln\left(\frac{1}{\delta}\right)\right)^{1/2}.$$

In particular, this is true for $f^* \in F_V$ with $\mathrm{er}_P^\gamma(f^*) < \inf_{f \in F_V} \mathrm{er}_P^\gamma(f) + 1/m$. Hence, if L_V is a large margin sample error minimization algorithm for F_V (so that $\hat{\mathrm{er}}_z^\gamma(L_V(z,\gamma)) = \min_{f \in F_V} \hat{\mathrm{er}}_z^\gamma(f))$, then with probability at least $1 - \delta$ we have

$$\mathrm{er}_P(L_V(z,\gamma))$$

$$< \inf_{f \in F_V} \mathrm{er}_P^\gamma(f) + \left(\frac{c_3}{m}\left(\frac{V^2 n}{\gamma^2}\ln^2(m)\ln\left(\frac{V}{\gamma}\right) + \ln\left(\frac{1}{\delta}\right)\right)\right)^{1/2} \quad (15.3)$$

In this case, there are two complexity parameters, the weight bound V and the margin γ, that must be fixed in advance. Again, it would be preferable to choose these parameters automatically.

15.2 Model Selection Results

The lower bound results of Chapter 5 show that we cannot hope to find a function whose error is nearly minimal over the set of networks with any number and size of parameters. However, in both cases the above results show how to trade complexity for estimation error. For instance, increasing γ in (15.3) decreases the estimation error term, but may increase the error term. An obvious approach here is to choose the complexity parameters (and hence function class) to minimize these upper bounds on misclassification probability. However the bounds of Theorems 15.1 and 15.2 are applicable only if the complexity parameters are fixed in advance. The following results are versions of these theorems that allow the complexity parameters to be chosen after the data has been seen. The estimation error bounds increase by only a log factor.

In the first of these theorems, let H_W be the class of functions computed by two-layer networks with W parameters, as in Theorem 15.1. Let L^c be a learning algorithm that returns $h \in \bigcup_W H_W$ corresponding to a pair (h, W) with $h \in H_W$ that minimizes

$$\hat{\mathrm{er}}_z(h) + \left(\frac{c}{m}\left(W\ln(Wm) + \ln\left(\frac{W}{\delta}\right)\right)\right)^{1/2}, \quad (15.4)$$

over all values of $W \in \mathbb{N}$ and $h \in H_W$. (Since in (15.4) we can always restrict our consideration to a finite set of values of W, the quantity to be minimized takes values in a finite set, and so the minimum always exists.) Notice that, if L_W is a sample error minimization algorithm for H_W, then a suitable algorithm L^c is the one which returns the function $L_W(z)$ corresponding to the value of W for which

$$\hat{\mathrm{er}}_z(L_W(z)) + \left(\frac{c}{m} \left(W \ln(Wm) + \ln \left(\frac{W}{\delta} \right) \right) \right)^{1/2}$$

is minimized. Here, $c \in \mathbb{R}$ is a parameter of the algorithm.

Theorem 15.3 *There are constants c, c_1 for which the following holds. Suppose P is a probability distribution on $X \times \{0,1\}$, and $z \in Z^m$ is chosen according to P^m. For the two-layer network learning algorithm L^c described above, with probability at least $1 - \delta$ we have*

$$\mathrm{er}_P(L^c(z))$$

$$< \inf_W \left(\inf_{h \in H_W} \mathrm{er}_P(h) + \left(\frac{c_1}{m} \left(W \ln(Wm) + \ln \left(\frac{W}{\delta} \right) \right) \right)^{1/2} \right).$$

Define $H = \bigcup_W H_W$ to be the class of functions computed by two-layer networks with any number of parameters. Then we can think of the algorithm L^c as minimizing an expression of the form

$$(\text{sample error of } h) + (\text{complexity penalty for } h)$$

over H, where the complexity penalty involves the number W of parameters in the network that computes the function h. This optimization problem involves an explicit trade-off between the number of parameters and the sample error. The results of Chapter 5 show that, if we minimize only the sample error over the class H, we cannot always hope to obtain small error. Theorem 15.3 shows that if we include the complexity penalty term, we can be confident that we will obtain a function with small error. Furthermore, this approach is nearly optimal in the sense that the resulting classification function minimizes the sum of error and a complexity penalty term.

For the second theorem, let F_V be the class of functions computed by the two-layer network with bounded output weights as described in Theorem 15.2, for any positive real number V. Let L^c be a learning algorithm that returns $f \in \bigcup_V F_V$ corresponding to a triple (f, V, γ) that has $f \in F_V$ and

$$\hat{\mathrm{er}}_z^\gamma(f) + \left(\frac{c}{m} \left(\frac{V^2 n}{\gamma^2} \ln^2(m) \ln \left(\frac{V}{\gamma} \right) + \ln \left(\frac{V}{\gamma \delta} \right) \right) \right)^{1/2} \qquad (15.5)$$

within $1/m$ of its infimum over all values of $\gamma \in (0,1]$, $V \in \mathbb{R}^+$, and

$f \in F_V$. (We need to consider an algorithm that approximately minimizes this error criterion, since we cannot be sure that the minimum always exists.) Notice that, if L_V is a large margin sample error minimization algorithm for F_V, a suitable L^c is that which returns the function $L_V(z, \gamma)$ corresponding to the values of V and γ for which

$$\hat{\text{er}}_z^\gamma(L_V(z, \gamma)) + \left(\frac{c}{m} \left(\frac{V^2 n}{\gamma^2} \ln^2(m) \ln \left(\frac{V}{\gamma} \right) + \ln \left(\frac{V}{\gamma \delta} \right) \right) \right)^{1/2}$$

is within $1/m$ of its infimum over all values of $\gamma \in (0, 1]$ and $V \in \mathbb{R}^+$.

Theorem 15.4 *There are constants c, c_1 such that the following holds. Suppose P is a probability distribution on $X \times \{0, 1\}$, and $z \in Z^m$ is chosen according to P^m. For the two-layer network learning algorithm L^c described above, with probability at least $1 - \delta$ we have*

$$\text{er}_P(L^c(z))$$

$$< \inf_{V, \gamma} \left(\inf_{f \in F_V} \text{er}_P^\gamma(f) + \left(\frac{c_1}{m} \left(\frac{V^2 n}{\gamma^2} \ln^2(m) \ln \left(\frac{V}{\gamma} \right) + \ln \left(\frac{V}{\gamma \delta} \right) \right) \right)^{1/2} \right).$$

In the same way as for Theorem 15.3, if we define $F = \bigcup_V F_V$ to be the class of functions computed by two-layer networks with unbounded parameters, we can think of the algorithm described by Theorem 15.4 as minimizing over F an expression of the form

(sample error of f) + (complexity penalty for f),

where the complexity penalty involves both the scale parameter γ and the size V of the parameters in the network that computes the function f. The theorem shows that including the complexity penalty term in the optimization will probably result in a function that has error no more than the minimum of the sum of the error $\text{er}_P^\gamma(f)$ (with respect to γ) and a penalty term that depends on the complexity of the network at scale γ. The quantity $\text{er}_P^\gamma(f)$ can be larger than the misclassification probability $\text{er}_P(\text{sgn}(f))$ of the thresholded function. This is the cost incurred by measuring complexity in terms of the size of the parameters rather than the number of parameters. On the other hand, this result and Theorem 15.3 are incomparable, since there are situations where each approach results in a smaller error than the other.

Theorems 15.3 and 15.4 are examples of more general results that bound the error of algorithms that minimize a sum of sample error and a complexity penalty term. We shall discuss these more general results in Section 15.4.

15.3 Proofs of the Results

The proofs of these theorems use the following lemma, which shows how to extend a probability statement that is true for any fixed value of a parameter $\alpha \in (0, 1]$ to one that is uniform over all values of α. In the application to Theorem 15.1 above, for example, α corresponds to the reciprocal of the complexity parameter W.

Lemma 15.5 *Suppose P is a probability distribution and*

$$\{E(\alpha_1, \alpha_2, \delta) : 0 < \alpha_1, \alpha_2, \delta \le 1\}$$

is a set of events such that:

(i) *For all $0 < \alpha \le 1$ and $0 < \delta \le 1$,*

$$P(E(\alpha, \alpha, \delta)) \le \delta.$$

(ii) *For all $0 < \alpha_1 \le \alpha \le \alpha_2 \le 1$ and $0 < \delta_1 \le \delta \le 1$,*

$$E(\alpha_1, \alpha_2, \delta_1) \subseteq E(\alpha, \alpha, \delta).$$

Then for $0 < a, \delta < 1$,

$$P\left(\bigcup_{\alpha \in (0,1]} E(\alpha a, \alpha, \delta \alpha(1 - a)) \right) \le \delta.$$

The idea of the proof is to split the interval of values of the parameter α into a countable collection of intervals that get exponentially smaller as α gets close to zero, and allocate an exponentially decreasing proportion of the probability δ to these sets. In a sense, we are penalizing small values of α, since the conditions of the theorem imply that the probability statements we make get weaker as α gets close to zero. In the application to Theorems 15.1 and 15.2 above, this implies that we make progressively weaker statements as the complexity parameters W, V, and $1/\gamma$ increase. However, in this case it is not a significant penalty, since it introduces only an extra logarithmic factor into the error bounds.

Proof We assume, of course, that for all $0 < a < 1$ and $0 < \delta < 1$, the event $\bigcup_{\alpha \in (0,1]} E(\alpha a, \alpha, \delta \alpha(1 - a))$ is measurable. Then we have

$$P\left(\bigcup_{\alpha \in (0,1]} E(\alpha a, \alpha, \delta \alpha(1 - a)) \right)$$

$$= P\left(\bigcup_{i=0}^{\infty} \{E(\alpha a, \alpha, \delta\alpha(1-a)) : \alpha \in (a^{i+1}, a^i]\}\right)$$

$$\leq P\left(\bigcup_{i=0}^{\infty} E(a^{i+1}, a^{i+1}, \delta a^i(1-a))\right)$$

$$\leq \sum_{i=0}^{\infty} P\left(E(a^{i+1}, a^{i+1}, \delta a^i(1-a))\right)$$

$$\leq \delta(1-a)\sum_{i=0}^{\infty} a^i = \delta.$$

$\square$

Proof (of Theorem 15.3) We combine the first inequality of Theorem 15.1 with Lemma 15.5, taking $E(\alpha_1, \alpha_2, \delta)$ to be the set of $z \in Z^m$ for which some h in H_{W_2} has

$$\mathrm{er}_P(h) \geq \hat{\mathrm{er}}_z(h) + \left(\frac{c_1}{m}\left(W_1 \ln m + \ln(1/\delta)\right)\right)^{1/2},$$

where $W_1 = \lfloor 1/\alpha_1 \rfloor$ and $W_2 = \lfloor 1/\alpha_2 \rfloor$. (In this proof, we do not take the trouble to evaluate any universal constants, but it is clear that suitable constants can be found.) Lemma 15.5 implies (on taking $a = 1/2$, say) that, with probability at least $1 - \delta$, every $h \in \bigcup_W H_W$ satisfies

$$\mathrm{er}_P(h) < \hat{\mathrm{er}}_z(h) + \left(\frac{c}{m}\left(W \ln(Wm) + \ln\left(\frac{W}{\delta}\right)\right)\right)^{1/2},$$

for some constant c, where W is the smallest value for which $h \in H_W$. In particular, if $L^c(z) \in H_W$, we have

$$\mathrm{er}_P(L^c(z)) < \hat{\mathrm{er}}_z(L^c(z)) + \left(\frac{c}{m}\left(W \ln(Wm) + \ln\left(\frac{W}{\delta}\right)\right)\right)^{1/2}$$

$$\leq \hat{\mathrm{er}}_z(h^*) + \left(\frac{c}{m}\left(W^* \ln(W^*m) + \ln\left(\frac{W^*}{\delta}\right)\right)\right)^{1/2} \quad (15.6)$$

for any W^* and $h^* \in H_{W^*}$, from the definition of the algorithm L^c. Now, let W^* and $h^* \in H_{W^*}$ be such that

$$\mathrm{er}_P(h^*) + \left(\frac{c}{m}\left(W^* \ln(W^*m) + \ln\left(\frac{W^*}{\delta}\right)\right)\right)^{1/2} + \left(\frac{c_2}{m}\ln\left(\frac{1}{\delta}\right)\right)^{1/2}$$

is within $1/m$ of its infimum over all W and $h \in H_W$. Then combining (15.6) with the second inequality of Theorem 15.1 shows that

$$\mathrm{er}_P(L^c(z))$$

$$< \inf_W \left(\inf_{h \in H_W} \mathrm{er}_P(h) + \left(\frac{c'}{m} \left(W \ln(Wm) + \ln \left(\frac{W}{\delta} \right) \right) \right)^{1/2} \right).$$

□

The proof of Theorem 15.4 is similar, except that Lemma 15.5 is applied twice. For the first application, we fix γ and define $E(\alpha_1, \alpha_2, \delta)$ to be the set of $z \in Z^m$ for which some f in F_{V_2} has

$$\mathrm{er}_P(f) \geq \hat{\mathrm{er}}_z^\gamma(f) + \left(\frac{c_1}{m} \left(\frac{V_1^2 n}{\gamma^2} \ln^2(m) \ln \left(\frac{V_1}{\gamma} \right) + \ln \left(\frac{1}{\delta} \right) \right) \right)^{1/2},$$

where $V_1 = 1/\alpha_1$ and $V_2 = 1/\alpha_2$. For the second application, we define $E(\alpha_1, \alpha_2, \delta)$ to be the set of $z \in Z^m$ for which some V and some f in F_V satisfy

$$\mathrm{er}_P(f) \geq \hat{\mathrm{er}}_z^{\gamma_2}(f) + \left(\frac{c_2}{m} \left(\frac{V^2 n}{\gamma_1^2} \ln^2(m) \ln \left(\frac{V}{\gamma_1} \right) + \ln \left(\frac{V}{\delta} \right) \right) \right)^{1/2},$$

where $\gamma_1 = \alpha_1$ and $\gamma_2 = \alpha_2$.

15.4 Remarks

The model selection methods described in this chapter are similar to a number of techniques that are commonly used by neural network practitioners. The learning algorithm L^c, described in Theorem 15.4, that approximately minimizes the quantity (15.5), is qualitatively similar to a popular technique known as *weight decay*. In this technique, the cost function (typically, total squared error on the training data) is augmented with a penalty term involving the sum of the squares of the parameters, and gradient descent is used to locally minimize this penalized cost function. In the same way, (15.5) is a combination of a sample error term and a penalty term that increases as the size of the weights increase. *'Early stopping'* is a related approach. Here, the gradient descent procedure is initialized near the origin of parameter space, and stopped after only a small number of steps have been taken. In this case, the final parameters are guaranteed to be small.

It is clear that the proof of the first main result of this chapter (Theorem 15.3) extends to give a similar result for any indexed family of function classes $\{H_t : t \in \mathbb{N}\}$ that have increasing VC-dimension. In this case, the penalty term involves the VC-dimension of the class containing the function. Similarly, Theorem 15.4 extends to give a similar result for any indexed family of function classes $\{F_t : t \in \mathbb{R}^+\}$ with increasing fat-shattering dimension, and the corresponding penalty term involves the fat-shattering dimension. One interpretation of these results is that in balancing the performance of a function on the sample and the complexity of the function, we should aim to minimize a combination of the error on the training data and the number of bits needed to accurately describe the function's behaviour on the training data (that is, the logarithm of the growth function, or the logarithm of the appropriate covering number.) This is similar to the philosophy behind the *minimum description length principle*, a model selection technique that advocates choosing a function providing the shortest description of the labels of the training points. Here, the length of the description is the total number of bits needed to specify both the identity of the function and the identity of the points on which it errs.

It is possible to derive slightly different versions of these results using the relative uniform convergence results of Theorems 5.7 and 13.7. These lead to error bounds of the form

$$\mathrm{er}_P(L^c(z)) < c_1 \inf_W \left(\inf_{h \in H_W} \mathrm{er}_P(h) + \frac{1}{m} \left(W \ln(Wm) + \ln\left(\frac{W}{\delta}\right) \right) \right)$$

and

$$\mathrm{er}_P(L^c(z))$$
$$< c_1 \inf_{V,\gamma} \left(\inf_{f \in F_V} \mathrm{er}_P^\gamma(f) + \frac{1}{m} \left(\frac{V^2 n}{\gamma^2} \ln^2(m) \ln\left(\frac{V}{\gamma}\right) + \ln\left(\frac{V}{\gamma\delta}\right) \right) \right)$$

for the two neural network classes considered here. (Of course, more general results are possible for indexed families of function classes with increasing VC-dimension or fat-shattering dimension.) These results have the attractive property that if some function in one of the classes has zero error, then the error of the algorithm's hypothesis approaches zero at essentially the optimal rate (see, for instance, Section 5.3). That is, for every algorithm, the estimation error could not decrease significantly faster, even if we knew in advance which function class contained the target function. This property of an algorithm is known as 'adaptivity': the algorithm automatically adapts to the complexity of the target function.

Although the rate of convergence of these methods is nearly optimal, they suffer from the drawback that they are based on *upper bounds* on error. While the upper bounds are tight in general (that is, there are probability distributions that illustrate that they cannot be improved), if those upper bounds are loose for a particular problem, and in particular if the complexity that minimizes the upper bound does not correspond to that which minimizes the error, then these methods may not give optimal results.

15.5 Bibliographical Notes

A general result of the form of Theorem 15.3 was given by Vapnik (1982), who named the approach *structural risk minimization*. Similar results, for a sequence of classes of bounded VC-dimension, have been presented by a number of authors, including Linial, Mansour and Rivest (1991), Lugosi (1995), Lugosi and Zeger (1996), and Shawe-Taylor et al. (1996; 1998). Related results are given by Faragó and Lugosi (1993) for linear threshold networks, and by Krzyżak et al. (1996) for radial basis function networks. Barron (1991) (see also (Barron, 1994)) has investigated the more general notion of *complexity regularization*, and gave general results of the flavour of Theorems 15.3. These ideas have been applied in a neural network context by Lugosi and Zeger (1996).

A large number of related model selection methods have been proposed. Rissanen's minimum description length (Rissanen, 1978) (see also (Rissanen, 1986; Rissanen, 1989)), Wallace's minimum message length (Wallace and Boulton, 1968), and Akaike's information criterion (Akaike, 1974) are some of the better known. Kearns, Mansour, Ng and Ron (1997) give a critique of a number of these methods, as well as of structural risk minimization.

The approach formalized in Lemma 15.5 is known as the *method of sieves*; see (Grenander, 1981). That lemma, as well as Theorem 15.4, appeared in (Bartlett, 1998).

Heuristic techniques that aim to keep the weights of a neural network small during training, such as weight decay, are described in (Hertz et al., 1991).

Part three
Learning Real-Valued Functions

16

Learning Classes of Real Functions

16.1 Introduction

This part of the book examines supervised learning problems in which we require a learning system to model the relationship between a pattern and a real-valued quantity. For example, in using a neural network to predict the future price of shares on the stock exchange, or to estimate the probability that a particular patient will experience problems during a surgical procedure, the predictions are represented by the real-valued output of the network.

In the pattern classification problems studied in Parts 1 and 2, the (x, y) pairs are generated by a probability distribution on the product space $X \times \{0, 1\}$. In a similar way, we assume in this part of the book that the data is generated by a probability distribution P on $X \times \mathbb{R}$. This is a generalization of the pattern classification model, and includes a number of other data-generating processes as special cases. For example, it can model a deterministic relationship between patterns and their labels, where each (x, y) pair satisfies $y = f(x)$ for some function f. It can model a deterministic relationship with additive independent observation noise, where $y_i = f(x_i) + \eta_i$, and the η_i are independent and identically distributed random variables. It can also model a noisy relationship in which the observation noise variables η_i are mutually independent, but the distribution of η_i depends on the pattern x_i.

In the pattern classification problem, we aim to find a function f that has $\Pr(f(x) \neq y)$ nearly minimal over a certain class of functions. When $f(x)$ and y are real-valued, this aim is typically too ambitious. Instead, it is more appropriate to take account of 'how far' $f(x)$ is from y and not simply whether or not it equals y. To measure how accurately $f(x)$ approximates y, we use the *quadratic loss*: the aim is to find a function

231

f for which the expected quadratic loss, $\mathbf{E}(f(x) - y)^2$, is nearly minimal over some function class. This is called the *real prediction problem*.

Many other choices of loss function are possible (and we examine some of these in Chapter 21), but quadratic loss has several desirable properties. In particular, for random $(x, y) \in X \times \mathbb{R}$, it is easy to show that

$$\mathbf{E}(f(x) - y)^2 = \mathbf{E}\left(\mathbf{E}(y|x) - f(x)\right)^2 + \mathbf{E}\left(\mathbf{E}(y|x) - y\right)^2, \qquad (16.1)$$

which implies that choosing a function f to minimize quadratic loss is equivalent to finding the best approximation of the conditional expectation of y given x.

Since quadratic loss is not bounded, we need to make some additional assumptions about the probability distribution P that generates the (x, y) pairs. To see why this is necessary, consider a distribution P that allocates a small probability (say, α) to some pair (x_0, y_0), where the magnitude of y_0 is large. Then unless a learning algorithm sees the pair (x_0, y_0) (and this can be made arbitrarily unlikely), we cannot hope that it will choose a function that gives a near-optimal prediction for the point x_0. Even though the probability of this point is small, the cost of an inaccurate prediction can be arbitrarily large. To avoid this difficulty, we assume that the random variable y falls in a bounded interval. This assumption is quite natural if y represents a physical quantity. We shall insist, however, that a learning algorithm can cope with any bound on the length of the interval. One reason for this requirement is that the range of y values may not be known in advance.

It is easy to construct a similar example to that above, showing that we also need some boundedness assumption on the real-valued functions used by a learning algorithm. Consequently, we assume that these functions map to a bounded interval. We concentrate on functions computed by a variety of neural networks, typically with a bounded activation function at the output or a bound on the magnitudes of the output parameters, so this constraint is not too restrictive.

16.2 The Learning Framework for Real Estimation

In the real prediction problem, we assume that training examples are generated at random according to some probability distribution on the set $X \times \mathbb{R}$. We define the *error* of a function $f : X \to \mathbb{R}$ with respect to P to be the expected value of $(f(x) - y)^2$, where the expectation is taken with respect to $z = (x, y)$ drawn according to P. We write this as

$$\mathrm{er}_P(f) = \mathbf{E}\left(f(x) - y\right)^2 = \mathbf{E}\,\ell_f,$$

where the loss function $\ell_f : X \times \mathbb{R} \to \mathbb{R}^+$ is given by $\ell_f(x, y) = (f(x) - y)^2$. Of course, if P is concentrated on $X \times \{0, 1\}$ and if f maps to $\{0, 1\}$ then the present definition of error coincides with that introduced in Chapter 2. We shall assume that the range of the functions in F is the bounded interval $[0, 1]$, and that P is such that y falls in a bounded interval, so that there is a bound $B \geq 1$ for which $(\hat{y} - y)^2 \leq B^2$ for all $\hat{y} \in [0, 1]$. That is, P is such that $1 - B \leq y \leq B$ with probability 1. Obviously, the particular intervals chosen are not crucial, since we can transform the problem by shifting and rescaling the functions and the y values.

A learning algorithm in the present context will take as input some sample $z \in (X \times \mathbb{R})^m$ and return some function in F. In learning a real function class, the aim is to produce, with high probability, a function whose error is close to the optimal error, $\mathrm{opt}_P(F) = \inf_{f \in F} \mathrm{er}_P(f)$. We formalize this as follows.

Definition 16.1 *Suppose that F is a set of functions mapping from a domain X into the real interval $[0, 1]$. A learning algorithm L for F is a function*

$$L : \bigcup_{m=1}^{\infty} (X \times \mathbb{R})^m \to H$$

with the following property:

- *given any $\epsilon \in (0, 1)$,*
- *given any $\delta \in (0, 1)$,*
- *given any $B \geq 1$,*

there is an integer $m_0(\epsilon, \delta, B)$ such that if $m \geq m_0(\epsilon, \delta, B)$ then,

- *for any probability distribution P on $X \times [1 - B, B]$,*

if z is a training sample of length m, drawn randomly according to the product probability distribution P^m, then, with probability at least $1 - \delta$, the function $L(z)$ output by L is such that

$$\mathrm{er}_P(L(z)) < \mathrm{opt}_P(F) + \epsilon$$

where

$$\mathrm{opt}_P(F) = \inf_{f \in F} \mathrm{er}_P(f).$$

That is, for $m \geq m_0(\epsilon, \delta, B)$,

$$P^m \left\{ \mathrm{er}_P(L(z)) < \mathrm{opt}_P(F) + \epsilon \right\} \geq 1 - \delta.$$

We say that F is learnable *if there is a learning algorithm for F.*

The *sample complexity* of a learning algorithm for F is defined in the obvious manner: for each ϵ, δ, and B, $m_L(\epsilon, \delta, B)$ is the least possible value $m_0(\epsilon, \delta, B)$ can take in Definition 16.1. It is easy to see that L is a learning algorithm if and only if there is a function $\epsilon_L(m, \delta, B)$ such that, for all $\delta \in (0, 1)$ and $B \geq 1$, $\epsilon_L(m, \delta, B) \to 0$ as $m \to \infty$, and such that for all m, δ, B, and P, with probability at least $1 - \delta$ over $z \in Z^m$ chosen according to P^m,

$$\mathrm{er}_P(L(z)) < \mathrm{opt}_P(H) + \epsilon_L(m, \delta, B).$$

In this case, the least possible $\epsilon_L(m, \delta, B)$ is the *estimation error* of the algorithm L. It is, as in the previous two learning models, a simple matter to interchange between estimation error bounds and sample complexity bounds.

We shall find it convenient to ignore the dependence on B in the sample complexity and estimation error bounds. In proving upper bounds on sample complexity in this and later chapters, we assume that $B = 1$, define $Z = X \times [0, 1]$, and assume that the support of the probability distribution is a subset of Z. Hence, the loss function ℓ_f maps from Z to $[0, 1]$. This simplifies the statements and proofs of the results. Also in the interests of conciseness, we define $m_L(\epsilon, \delta)$ as $m_L(\epsilon, \delta, 1)$, and similarly for ϵ_L. It is always straightforward to extend these proofs to arbitrary $B \geq 1$, without changing any of the algorithms. We shall indicate these extensions in the "Remarks" sections.

16.3 Learning Finite Classes of Real Functions

SEM algorithms learn finite classes

As with earlier learning problems, the 'empirical' error (sample error) of a function on the training sample is useful as an indication of its error. Given a function $f \in F$ and sample $z = ((x_1, y_1), (x_2, y_2), \ldots, (x_m, y_m))$ in Z^m, we define the *sample error* $\hat{\mathrm{er}}_z(f)$ of f on z to be

$$\hat{\mathrm{er}}_z(f) = \frac{1}{m} \sum_{i=1}^{m} (f(x_i) - y_i)^2.$$

With this definition of sample error, we can define a *sample error min-imization* (SEM) algorithm for a finite class F to be a function L from Z^m to F with the property that

$$\hat{\text{er}}_z(L(z)) = \min_{f \in F} \hat{\text{er}}_z(f).$$

Theorem 16.2 *Let F be a finite class of functions mapping from a set X into the interval $[0, 1]$ and suppose that L is a SEM algorithm for F. Then L is a learning algorithm for F, whose estimation error satisfies*

$$\epsilon_L(m, \delta) \leq \epsilon_0(m, \delta) = \left(\frac{2}{m} \ln \left(\frac{2|F|}{\delta} \right) \right)^{1/2}.$$

Proof Suppose $\epsilon = \epsilon_0(m, \delta)$. By Hoeffding's inequality, for any fixed $f \in F$,

$$P^m \left\{ |\hat{\text{er}}_z(f) - \text{er}_P(f)| \geq \frac{\epsilon}{2} \right\}$$

$$= P^m \left\{ \left| \sum_{i=1}^m \ell_f(z_i) - m\,\mathbf{E}\ell_f \right| \geq \frac{m\epsilon}{2} \right\}$$

$$\leq 2e^{-\epsilon^2 m/2}.$$

Hence

$$P^m \left\{ \exists f \in F, \ |\hat{\text{er}}_z(f) - \text{er}_P(f)| \geq \frac{\epsilon}{2} \right\} \leq 2|F|e^{-\epsilon^2 m/2},$$

which is δ, since $\epsilon = \epsilon_0(\epsilon, \delta)$. Denote by f^* any function in F for which

$$\text{er}_P(f^*) = \text{opt}_P(F) = \min_{f \in F} \text{er}_P(F).$$

(Note that such an f^* exists, since F is finite.) Then, with probability at least $1 - \delta$,

$$\begin{aligned}
\text{er}_P(L(z)) &< \hat{\text{er}}_z(L(z)) + \frac{\epsilon}{2} \\
&\leq \hat{\text{er}}_z(f^*) + \frac{\epsilon}{2} \\
&< \left(\text{er}_P(f^*) + \frac{\epsilon}{2} \right) + \frac{\epsilon}{2} \\
&= \text{opt}_P(F) + \epsilon.
\end{aligned}$$

$\square$

An application to neural networks

As a straightforward application of Theorem 16.2, we have the following learnability result for neural networks in which we restrict the allowable states to be those in which the weights and thresholds are expressible as a sequence of k binary digits. (We assume that for each weight and threshold, one of the k bits indicates whether the weight or threshold value is positive or negative.)

Theorem 16.3 *Suppose that N is a neural network with arbitrary activation functions and an output that takes values in $[0,1]$. Let F be the set of functions computable by N when each weight and threshold is represented using k bits. Then any SEM algorithm for F is a learning algorithm for F and the sample complexity of any such algorithm L is bounded as follows:*

$$m_L(\epsilon, \delta) \leq \frac{2}{\epsilon^2}\left(kW\ln 2 + \ln\left(\frac{2}{\delta}\right)\right),$$

where W is the total number of adjustable weights and thresholds.

Proof We need only note that since there are 2^k numbers expressible in the given form, the total number of possible states—that is, assignments of weights and thresholds—is $(2^k)^W$ since there are 2^k possibilities for each weight and threshold. Therefore, F is finite and $|F| \leq 2^{kW}$. The result follows immediately from Theorem 16.2.   □

16.4 A Substitute for Finiteness

When we studied classification by real function classes, we found it useful to use covering numbers, and to bound these using the fat-shattering dimension and pseudo-dimension. We shall carry out a similar analysis for the present framework in the next two chapters, but first we present a slightly less sophisticated way of extending to some infinite classes the type of analysis we have just carried out for finite function classes. This approach will, in a sense, be superseded by results in the next few chapters, but is worth pursuing at this stage since it enables us to introduce the notion of an *approximate-SEM* algorithm.

Suppose that F is some set of functions mapping from a domain X into the interval $[0,1]$. Recall from Chapter 14 that the L_∞ metric d_{L_∞}

on F is given by

$$d_{L_\infty}(f,g) = \sup_{x \in X} |f(x) - g(x)|,$$

for $f, g \in F$. We can obtain a result similar to Theorem 16.2, for function classes that are not necessarily finite but that are totally bounded with respect to the L_∞ metric. In this result, the learning algorithm makes use of what we shall call an *approximate-SEM algorithm*. Although total boundedness with respect to the L_∞ metric is a rather stringent condition, we shall nevertheless find approximate-SEM algorithms useful for real prediction when the function classes satisfy weaker conditions.

Definition 16.4 *An* approximate-SEM *algorithm $\mathcal{A}$ for a function class F takes as input a sample z in $\bigcup_{m=1}^{\infty} (X \times \mathbb{R})^m$ and an error bound ϵ in $\mathbb{R}^+$, and returns a function in F such that*

$$\hat{\text{er}}_z(\mathcal{A}(z,\epsilon)) < \inf_{f \in F} \hat{\text{er}}_z(f) + \epsilon$$

for all z and all ϵ.

Note that, since F may be infinite, then, unlike the error measure used in Part 1 of the book, the set of values of $\hat{\text{er}}_z(f)$, as f ranges through F, may be infinite. Thus, we use $\inf_{f \in F} \hat{\text{er}}_z(f)$ above, since there may be *no* minimum value of $\hat{\text{er}}_z(f)$. For example, consider the class

$$F = \left\{ x \mapsto \frac{1}{1 + e^{-wx}} : w \in \mathbb{R} \right\}$$

of functions defined on $\mathbb{R}$, and suppose that the training data z satisfies $x_i > 0$ and $y_i = 1$ for all i. Then $\inf_{f \in F} \hat{\text{er}}_z(f) = 0$, since

$$\lim_{w \to \infty} \frac{1}{1 + e^{-wx_i}} = y_i$$

for all i, but every $f \in F$ has $\hat{\text{er}}_z(f) > 0$.

The next theorem shows that if F has finite covering numbers with respect to the L_∞ metric, then any approximate-SEM algorithm for F can be used to construct a learning algorithm.

Theorem 16.5 *Suppose that F is a class of functions mapping to the interval $[0, 1]$ that is totally bounded with respect to d_{L_∞}. Suppose that $\mathcal{A}$ is an approximate-SEM algorithm for F and let L satisfy $L(z) = \mathcal{A}(z, \epsilon_0/12)$ for $z \in Z^m$, where $\epsilon_0 = \sqrt{72/m}$. Then L is a learning* algorithm for F and

$$m_L(\epsilon, \delta) \leq m_0(\epsilon, \delta) = \frac{72}{\epsilon^2} \ln \left(\frac{2\mathcal{N}(\epsilon/12, F, d_{L_\infty})}{\delta} \right).$$

Proof Suppose that $m \geq m_0(\epsilon, \delta)$, and that $z \in Z^m$. Then, since $\epsilon_0 = \sqrt{72/m}$, and $m \geq m_0(\epsilon, \delta) \geq 72/\epsilon^2$, we have $\epsilon_0 \leq \epsilon$. It follows that

$$\text{êr}_z(L(z)) = \text{êr}_z(A(z, \epsilon_0/12)) < \inf_{f \in F} \text{êr}_z(f) + \frac{\epsilon_0}{12} \leq \inf_{f \in F} \text{êr}_z(f) + \frac{\epsilon}{12}.$$

(Note that, since ϵ is not given as part of the input to the learning algorithm, we cannot simply ask that the algorithm returns a hypothesis with sample error within $\epsilon/12$ of optimal. Instead, we use ϵ_0, determined from the length m of the sample, and which turns out to be no more than ϵ provided $m \geq m_0(\epsilon, \delta)$. This idea will be useful in later chapters.)

We now note that if $f, g \in F$ are such that $d_{L_\infty}(f, g) < \alpha < 1$, then for any probability distribution P on $Z = X \times [0, 1]$,

$$|\text{er}_P(f) - \text{er}_P(g)| < 2\alpha.$$

To prove this, we first observe that for any $x \in X$,

$$\begin{aligned}
(f(x) - y)^2 &= (f(x) - g(x) + g(x) - y)^2 \\
&= (f(x) - g(x))(f(x) + g(x) - 2y) + (g(x) - y)^2 \\
&\leq 2\alpha + (g(x) - y)^2, \qquad (16.2)
\end{aligned}$$

where we have used the fact that $|f(x) - g(x)| < \alpha$. Therefore,

$$\text{er}_P(f) = \mathbf{E}(f(x) - y)^2 \leq \mathbf{E}\left(2\alpha + (g(x) - y)^2\right) = 2\alpha + \text{er}_P(g),$$

and since the same argument can be repeated with f and g interchanged, $|\text{er}_P(f) - \text{er}_P(g)| < 2\alpha$. Since P is arbitrary, we also have $|\text{êr}_z(f) - \text{êr}_z(g)| < 2\alpha$ for all z.

For $\epsilon > 0$, let $C_{\epsilon/12}$ be some fixed $\epsilon/12$-cover for F with respect to d_{L_∞}, of cardinality $\mathcal{N}(\epsilon/12, F, d_{L_\infty})$. Now, for any function $f \in F$ there is $\hat{f} \in C_{\epsilon/12}$ such that $d_{L_\infty}(f, \hat{f}) < \epsilon/12$ and so

$$|\text{er}_P(f) - \text{er}_P(\hat{f})| < \frac{\epsilon}{6} \qquad (16.3)$$

and

$$|\text{êr}_z(f) - \text{êr}_z(\hat{f})| < \frac{\epsilon}{6} \qquad (16.4)$$

for all z. Let P be any distribution on Z and let f^* be such that

$$\text{er}_P(f^*) < \text{opt}_P(F) + \frac{\epsilon}{12}.$$

Denote by $\hat{f}^*$ a function in $C_{\epsilon/12}$ such that

$$d_{L_\infty}(\hat{f}^*, f^*) < \frac{\epsilon}{12}.$$

From the proof of Theorem 16.2, since $m \geq m_0(\epsilon, \delta)$, we have that with probability at least $1 - \delta$, for all $g \in C_{\epsilon/12}$,

$$|\hat{\mathrm{er}}_z(g) - \mathrm{er}_P(g)| < \frac{\epsilon}{12}. \tag{16.5}$$

For convenience, we denote $L(z)$ by f_z. Choose $\hat{f}_z \in C_{\epsilon/12}$ such that $d_{L_\infty}(\hat{f}_z, f_z) < \epsilon/12$. Then the following chain of inequalities holds with probability at least $1 - \delta$:

$$
\begin{aligned}
\mathrm{er}_P(L(z)) &= \mathrm{er}_P(f_z) \\
&< \frac{\epsilon}{6} + \mathrm{er}_P(\hat{f}_z) && \text{by (16.3)} \\
&< \frac{\epsilon}{6} + \left(\hat{\mathrm{er}}_z(\hat{f}_z) + \frac{\epsilon}{12}\right) && \text{by (16.5)} \\
&< \frac{3\epsilon}{12} + \left(\hat{\mathrm{er}}_z(f_z) + \frac{\epsilon}{6}\right) && \text{by (16.4)} \\
&< \frac{5\epsilon}{12} + \left(\inf_{f \in F} \hat{\mathrm{er}}_z(f) + \frac{\epsilon}{12}\right) \\
&\leq \frac{\epsilon}{2} + \hat{\mathrm{er}}_z(f^*) \\
&< \frac{\epsilon}{2} + \left(\hat{\mathrm{er}}_z(\hat{f}^*) + \frac{\epsilon}{6}\right) && \text{by (16.4)} \\
&< \frac{2\epsilon}{3} + \left(\mathrm{er}_P(\hat{f}^*) + \frac{\epsilon}{12}\right) && \text{by (16.5)} \\
&< \frac{3\epsilon}{4} + \left(\mathrm{er}_P(f^*) + \frac{\epsilon}{6}\right) && \text{by (16.3)} \\
&< \frac{11\epsilon}{12} + \left(\mathrm{opt}_P(F) + \frac{\epsilon}{12}\right) \\
&= \mathrm{opt}_P(F) + \epsilon.
\end{aligned}
$$

The result follows.   □

16.5 Remarks

It is trivial to extend Theorem 16.2 to the case of an arbitrary bound B on $|f(x) - y|$; the bound on the random variables in Hoeffding's inequality is increased by a factor of B^2, which gives

$$\epsilon_L(m, \delta, B) \leq \left(\frac{2B^4}{m} \ln\left(\frac{2|F|}{\delta}\right)\right)^{1/2}.$$

Similarly, we can extend Theorem 16.5 to this case. Here, Inequality (16.2) relating $(f(x) - y)^2$ to $(g(x) - y)^2$ when $|f(x) - g(x)| < \alpha$ becomes

$$(f(x) - y)^2 \le 2B\alpha + (g(x) - y)^2.$$

Hence, as well as changing the constants in Hoeffding's inequality, we need to adjust the scale of the cover, which gives

$$m_L(\epsilon, \delta, B) \le \frac{72B^4}{\epsilon^2} \ln \left(\frac{2\mathcal{N}(\epsilon/(12B), F, d_{L_\infty})}{\delta} \right).$$

Learning with respect to a touchstone class

We mentioned in Chapter 2 that the learning model of binary classification may be weakened by asking only that the algorithm return a function with error close to the optimal error in a 'touchstone class'. The same modification may be made for real prediction. Explicitly, given the touchstone class T of real functions, we may modify Definition 16.1 by allowing the algorithm to return a function in a larger set $F \supset T$, and requiring only that, with high probability,

$$\mathrm{er}_P(L(z)) < \mathrm{opt}_P(T) + \epsilon = \inf_{f \in T} \mathrm{er}_P(f) + \epsilon.$$

Allowing an algorithm to choose a function from the larger set F in this way can make learning computationally easier. Furthermore, it can provide a significant reduction in the sample complexity, compared to learning the class T in the usual sense. Chapter 20 gives an example of this kind: if the function class T is finite, and F is the set of convex combinations of functions from T, the estimation error $\mathrm{er}_P(L(z)) - \inf_{f \in T} \mathrm{er}_P(f)$ of an approximate-SEM algorithm L decreases more quickly as a function of m than the estimation error of any learning algorithm that returns functions from T.

16.6 Bibliographical Notes

The model presented in this chapter is a special case of models that have been proposed by Vapnik (1982) and Haussler (1992). We shall encounter these more general models in Chapter 21.

Theorem 16.5 is an easy extension of Theorem 16.2. This result can be improved, to give a better convergence rate (Barron, 1994; McCaffrey and Gallant, 1994). In Chapter 20, we shall prove a result that implies this better result (Theorem 20.10).

17
Uniform Convergence Results for Real Function Classes

17.1 Uniform Convergence for Real Functions

In Chapter 19, we shall show that in many cases an approximate-SEM algorithm constitutes a learning algorithm. As in the development of the earlier learning models, we first derive a uniform convergence result for classes of real-valued functions. The following result and its proof are similar to those of Theorems 4.3 and 10.1.

Theorem 17.1 *Suppose that F is a set of functions defined on a domain X and mapping into the real interval $[0,1]$. Let P be any probability distribution on $Z = X \times [0,1]$, ϵ any real number between 0 and 1, and m any positive integer. Then*

$$P^m \left\{ some\ f\ in\ F\ has\ |\mathrm{er}_P(f) - \hat{\mathrm{er}}_z(f)| \geq \epsilon \right\}$$
$$\leq\ 4\mathcal{N}_1\left(\epsilon/16, F, 2m\right) \exp\left(-\epsilon^2 m/32\right).$$

Notice how this compares with Theorem 4.3: that bound involves the growth function, whereas this involves the covering number. As we have seen, the notion of error used here reduces to that of Chapter 4 when the functions are $\{0,1\}$-valued, and the covering number is a generalization of the growth function, so in a sense this result is a generalization of Theorem 4.3. Theorem 17.1 is also similar to Theorem 10.1, although (as noted in Chapter 10) that result is one-sided. (Another difference is that the present bound involves d_1 covering numbers rather than the larger d_∞ covering numbers.)

The proof of Theorem 17.1 uses the same key techniques as the proofs of Theorems 4.3 and Theorem 10.1, namely symmetrization, permutation, and reduction to a finite class.

241

Symmetrization

Lemma 17.2 *With the notation as above, let*

$$Q = \{z \in Z^m : \text{some } f \text{ in } F \text{ has } |\text{er}_P(f) - \hat{\text{er}}_z(f)| \geq \epsilon\}$$

and

$$R = \left\{(r, s) \in Z^m \times Z^m : \text{some } f \text{ in } F \text{ has } |\hat{\text{er}}_r(f) - \hat{\text{er}}_s(f)| \geq \frac{\epsilon}{2}\right\}$$

Then, for $m \geq 4/\epsilon^2$, $P^m(Q) \leq 2\,P^{2m}(R)$.

Proof The proof is similar to the proofs of Lemmas 4.4 and 10.2.

If some f in F satisfies $|\text{er}_P(f) - \hat{\text{er}}_r(f)| \geq \epsilon$ and $|\text{er}_P(f) - \hat{\text{er}}_s(f)| < \epsilon/2$, then it also satisfies $|\hat{\text{er}}_r(f) - \hat{\text{er}}_s(f)| \geq \epsilon/2$, so

$$\begin{aligned}
P^{2m}(R) &\geq P^{2m}\{\exists f \in F : |\text{er}_P(f) - \hat{\text{er}}_r(f)| \geq \epsilon \text{ and} \\
&\qquad\qquad |\text{er}_P(f) - \hat{\text{er}}_s(f)| < \epsilon/2\} \\
&= \int_Q P^m\{s : \exists f \in F, |\text{er}_P(f) - \hat{\text{er}}_r(f)| \geq \epsilon \text{ and} \\
&\qquad\qquad |\text{er}_P(f) - \hat{\text{er}}_s(f)| < \epsilon/2\}\, dP^m(r). \quad (17.1)
\end{aligned}$$

Hoeffding's inequality shows that

$$P^m\{|\text{er}_P(f) - \hat{\text{er}}_s(f)| < \epsilon/2\} \geq 1/2$$

for all $f \in F$, provided that $m \geq 4/\epsilon^2$, and this, together with (17.1), shows that $P^{2m}(R) \geq P^m(Q)/2$. □

Permutation and reduction to a finite class

Recall that Γ_m is the set of permutations on $\{1, 2, \ldots, 2m\}$ that switch elements i and $m+i$, for i in some subset of $\{1, \ldots, m\}$. By Lemma 4.5,

$$P^{2m}(R) = \mathbb{E}\Pr(\sigma z \in R) \leq \max_{z \in Z^{2m}} \Pr(\sigma z \in R),$$

where the expectation is over z in Z^{2m} chosen according to P^{2m}, and the probability is over permutations σ chosen uniformly in Γ_m. To bound this latter probability, we again use the notion of covering numbers. We first require two technical results concerning the covering numbers of ℓ_F and of F. The first concerns covers of $(\ell_F)_{|_z}$, and is the key to the reduction to a finite class. The second shows how a bound on the cardinality of such covers can be given in terms of the covering numbers of the class F itself.

Lemma 17.3 *Suppose that F is a set of functions mapping from a set X into $[0,1]$, and for $f \in F$ let $\ell_f : Z \to [0,1]$ be given by $\ell_f(x,y) = (f(x) - y)^2$. Denote by ℓ_F the collection $\{\ell_f : f \in F\}$. Let $z \in Z^{2m}$ and suppose that $(\ell_G)_{|_z}$ is an $\epsilon/8$-cover with respect to d_1 for $(\ell_F)_{|_z}$, where $G \subseteq F$. Define $r = (r_1, \dots, r_m) \in Z^m$ and $s = (s_1, \dots, s_m) \in Z^m$ so that $z = (r_1, \dots, r_m, s_1, \dots, s_m)$. Then, if $f \in F$ satisfies $|\hat{er}_r(f) - \hat{er}_s(f)| \geq \frac{\epsilon}{2}$, there is some $g \in G$ such that $|\hat{er}_r(g) - \hat{er}_s(g)| \geq \frac{\epsilon}{4}$.*

Proof Fix $z = (r_1, \dots, r_m, s_1, \dots, s_m) = (r, s) \in Z^{2m}$. Suppose that $f \in F$ satisfies

$$|\hat{er}_r(f) - \hat{er}_s(f)| \geq \frac{\epsilon}{2}$$

and let $g \in G$ be such that

$$\frac{1}{2m} \sum_{i=1}^{2m} |\ell_f(z_i) - \ell_g(z_i)| < \frac{\epsilon}{8}.$$

Then

$$
\begin{aligned}
&|\hat{er}_r(g) - \hat{er}_s(g)| \\
&= \left| \frac{1}{m} \sum_{i=1}^{m} \ell_g(z_i) - \frac{1}{m} \sum_{i=m+1}^{2m} \ell_g(z_i) \right| \\
&= \left| \frac{1}{m} \sum_{i=1}^{m} (\ell_g(z_i) - \ell_f(z_i)) \right. \\
&\qquad \left. - \frac{1}{m} \sum_{i=m+1}^{2m} (\ell_g(z_i) - \ell_f(z_i)) + \hat{er}_r(f) - \hat{er}_s(f) \right| \\
&\geq |\hat{er}_r(f) - \hat{er}_s(f)| \\
&\qquad - \left| \frac{1}{m} \sum_{i=1}^{m} (\ell_g(z_i) - \ell_f(z_i)) - \frac{1}{m} \sum_{i=m+1}^{2m} (\ell_g(z_i) - \ell_f(z_i)) \right| \\
&\geq |\hat{er}_r(f) - \hat{er}_s(f)| - \frac{1}{m} \sum_{i=1}^{2m} |\ell_g(z_i) - \ell_f(z_i)| \\
&> \epsilon/4.
\end{aligned}
$$

$\square$

Lemma 17.4 *For all positive integers m, for all positive numbers ϵ, and for all $z \in Z^m$, $\mathcal{N}(\epsilon, (\ell_F)_{|_z}, d_1) \leq \mathcal{N}_1(\epsilon/2, F, m)$.*

Proof Fix $z = ((x_1, y_1), (x_2, y_2), \ldots, (x_m, y_m))$ and $f, g \in F$. Then the d_1-distance between the vectors $\ell_{f_{|_z}} = (\ell_f(z_1), \ldots, \ell_f(z_m))$ and $\ell_{g_{|_z}}$ is

$$\frac{1}{m} \sum_{i=1}^{m} |\ell_f(z_i) - \ell_g(z_i)|$$

$$= \frac{1}{m} \sum_{i=1}^{m} |(f(x_i) - y_i)^2 - (g(x_i) - y_i)^2|$$

$$= \frac{1}{m} \sum_{i=1}^{m} |(f(x_i) - g(x_i))(f(x_i) + g(x_i) - 2y_i)|$$

$$\leq \frac{2}{m} \sum_{i=1}^{m} |f(x_i) - g(x_i)|,$$

where we have used the fact that, since f and g map into $[0, 1]$ and $y_i \in [0, 1]$, $|f(x_i) + g(x_i) - 2y_i| \leq 2$. It follows that, given any $\epsilon/2$-cover for $F_{|_z}$, there is an ϵ-cover for $(\ell_F)_{|_z}$, of the same cardinality. The result follows. □

We now use these results to bound $\max_{z \in Z^{2m}} \Pr(\sigma z \in R)$.

Lemma 17.5 *For the set $R \subseteq Z^{2m}$ defined in Lemma 17.2, and for a permutation σ chosen uniformly at random from Γ_m,*

$$\max_{z \in Z^{2m}} \Pr(\sigma z \in R) \leq 2\mathcal{N}_1\left(\epsilon/16, F, 2m\right) \exp\left(\frac{-\epsilon^2 m}{32}\right).$$

Proof Suppose that $z \in Z^{2m}$, where $z_i = (x_i, y_i)$, and let T be a minimal $\epsilon/8$-cover for $(\ell_F)_{|_z}$ with respect to the d_1 metric. Lemma 17.4 shows that

$$|T| = \mathcal{N}(\epsilon/8, (\ell_F)_{|_z}, d_1) \leq \mathcal{N}_1\left(\epsilon/16, F, 2m\right),$$

Pick $G \subseteq F$ such that $T = (\ell_G)_{|_z}$ and $|G| = |T|$. Lemma 17.3 shows that if $\sigma z = rs \in R$ then there is some $\hat{f} \in G$ such that

$$\left| \hat{\text{er}}_r(\hat{f}) - \hat{\text{er}}_s(\hat{f}) \right| \geq \epsilon/4.$$

Thus,

$$\Pr(\sigma z \in R)$$

$$\leq \Pr\left(\exists \hat{f} \in G : \left| \frac{1}{m} \sum_{i=1}^{m} \left(\ell_{\hat{f}}(z_{\sigma(i)}) - \ell_{\hat{f}}(z_{\sigma(m+i)}) \right) \right| \geq \epsilon/4 \right)$$

$$\leq \; |T| \max_{f \in G} \Pr \left(\left| \frac{1}{m} \sum_{i=1}^{m} \left(\ell_f(z_{\sigma(i)}) - \ell_f(z_{\sigma(m+i)}) \right) \right| \geq \epsilon/4 \right)$$

$$= \; |T| \max_{f \in G} \Pr \left(\left| \frac{1}{m} \sum_{i=1}^{m} \left| \ell_f(z_i) - \ell_f(z_{m+i}) \right| \beta_i \right| \geq \epsilon/4 \right),$$

where each β_i is independently and uniformly drawn from $\{-1, 1\}$. By Hoeffding's inequality, the probability in the last line is no more than $2\exp(-\epsilon^2 m/32)$, which implies the result. $\qquad\square$

Theorem 17.1 now follows. It is trivially true for $m < 4/\epsilon^2$, because the right-hand side of the bound is greater than 1 in that case. For $m \geq 4/\epsilon^2$, we have

$$P^m(Q) \leq 2 P^{2m}(R) \leq 4 \mathcal{N}_1 \left(\epsilon/16, F, 2m \right) e^{-\epsilon^2 m/32},$$

as required.

17.2 Remarks

The results in this chapter do not depend significantly on the choice of the quadratic loss function. In particular, except in the proof of Lemma 17.4, boundedness was the only property of this function that we used. An examination of the proof of that lemma reveals that we only use the fact that the loss function $\ell(f(x), y)$ varies slowly when the function value $f(x)$ varies. Indeed, it is easy to prove the following generalization of Lemma 17.4, which requires that the loss function satisfies a Lipschitz condition. (To see that it is a generalization, notice that the quadratic loss function satisfies this condition with $L = 2$ when the ranges of the functions and of y are restricted to the interval $[0, 1]$.)

Lemma 17.6 *Let Y be a real interval and $B \geq 1$, and suppose that the loss function $\ell : [0, 1] \times Y \to [0, B]$ satisfies the Lipschitz condition,*

$$|\ell(y_1, y_0) - \ell(y_2, y_0)| \leq L|y_1 - y_2|$$

for all y_0, y_1, y_2. Define $\ell_f(x, y) = \ell(f(x), y)$. Then for a class F of $[0, 1]$-valued functions,

$$\max_{z \in (X \times Y)^m} \mathcal{N}(\epsilon, \ell_{F|_z}, d_1) \leq \mathcal{N}_1 \left(\epsilon/L, F, m \right).$$

This implies the following generalization of Theorem 17.1. Its proof is essentially identical to that of Theorem 17.1, except that we need to take account of the changed bound on the loss function in applying Hoeffding's inequality.

Theorem 17.7 *Suppose that F is a set of functions defined on a domain X and mapping into the real interval $[0,1]$, $Y \subseteq \mathbb{R}$, and $B \geq 1$. Let P be any probability distribution on $Z = X \times Y$, ϵ any real number between 0 and 1, and m any positive integer. Then for a loss function $\ell : [0,1] \times Y \to [0, B]$ satisfying the Lipschitz condition of Lemma 17.6,*

$$P^m \left\{ \text{some } f \text{ in } F \text{ has } \left| \mathbf{E}\ell_f - \frac{1}{m} \sum_{i=1}^{m} \ell_f(z_i) \right| \geq \epsilon \right\}$$

$$\leq 4 \mathcal{N}_1 \left(\epsilon/(8L), F, 2m \right) \exp \left(-\epsilon^2 m/(32B^4) \right).$$

Notice that if ℓ is the quadratic loss and Y is such that ℓ maps to $[0, B]$, the Lipschitz condition is satisfied with $L = 2B$.

17.3 Bibliographical Notes

The techniques of this chapter go back to Vapnik and Chervonenkis (1971), and Pollard (1984) (see also (Haussler, 1992)). Lemma 17.6 is due to Natarajan (1993) (see also (Bartlett, Long and Williamson, 1996; Vidyasagar, 1997)).

18

Bounding Covering Numbers

18.1 Introduction

We have seen that, for the real prediction model of learning considered in this part of the book, the d_1-covering numbers are crucial. These covering numbers are always bounded above by the d_∞-covering numbers, the main object of study in Chapter 12, so the upper bounds for the d_∞-covering numbers obtained in that chapter are also upper bounds on the d_1-covering numbers. However, it is possible to obtain better bounds on the d_1-covering numbers using more direct arguments. As in Chapter 12, we present two bounds, one in terms of the fat-shattering dimension, and one in terms of the pseudo-dimension.

18.2 Bounding with the Fat-Shattering Dimension

This section gives a bound on the d_1-packing numbers in terms of the fat-shattering dimension. This bound, presented in the following theorem, uses a similar proof to that of Theorem 12.7, so some parts of the proof are only sketched.

Theorem 18.1 *Suppose that F is a set of real functions from a domain X to the bounded interval $[0, 1]$ and that $0 < \epsilon \le 1$. Then*

$$\mathcal{M}_1 (\epsilon, F, m) < 2b^{3(\lceil \log_2 y \rceil + 1)},$$

where $b = \lfloor 4/\epsilon \rfloor$ and, with $d = \mathrm{fat}_F (\epsilon/8) \ge 1$,

$$y = \sum_{i=1}^{d} \binom{m}{i} b^i.$$

We therefore obtain the following bound on the covering numbers.

Theorem 18.2 *Let F be a set of real functions from a domain X to the bounded interval $[0,1]$. Let $0 < \epsilon \leq 1$ and let $d = \mathrm{fat}_F(\epsilon/8)$. Then for $m \geq d \geq 1$,*

$$\mathcal{N}_1(\epsilon, F, m) < 2 \left(\frac{4}{\epsilon}\right)^{3d\log_2(16em/(d\epsilon))}.$$

Proof By Theorem 18.1 and the relationship between covering and packing numbers,

$$\mathcal{N}_1(\epsilon, F, m) \leq \mathcal{M}_1(\epsilon, F, m) < 2 \left(\frac{4}{\epsilon}\right)^{3(\lceil\log_2 y\rceil + 1)}.$$

By Theorem 3.7, for $m \geq d \geq 1$,

$$y \leq \sum_{i=1}^{d} \binom{m}{i} \left(\frac{4}{\epsilon}\right)^i < \left(\frac{em}{d}\right)^d \left(\frac{4}{\epsilon}\right)^d,$$

and hence

$$\lceil\log_2 y\rceil + 1 \leq d\log_2 \left(\frac{4em}{d\epsilon}\right) + 2 \leq d\log_2 \left(\frac{16em}{d\epsilon}\right).$$

The result follows. ☐

Proof of Theorem 18.1

As in the proof of Theorem 12.7, we first relate the packing number and dimension of F to the quantized version $Q_\alpha(F)$, for appropriate α. (Recall that $Q_\alpha(F) = \{Q_\alpha(f) : f \in F\}$, where $Q_\alpha(f)(x) = \alpha\lfloor f(x)/\alpha\rfloor$.) Fix $\epsilon, m, 0 < \alpha < \epsilon$, and $x = (x_1, \ldots, x_m) \in X^m$. Consider $f, g \in F$, and let $f_{|_\bullet}$ denote $(f(x_1), \ldots, f(x_m))$. Then, using the fact that

$$|Q_\alpha(a) - Q_\alpha(b)| \geq Q_\alpha(|a - b|)$$

for all $a, b \in \mathbb{R}$ (see the proof of Lemma 12.3), we have

$$
\begin{aligned}
d_1\left(Q_\alpha(f)_{|_\bullet}, Q_\alpha(g)_{|_\bullet}\right) &\geq \frac{1}{m}\sum_{i=1}^{m} Q_\alpha\left(|f(x_i) - g(x_i)|\right) \\
&> \frac{1}{m}\sum_{i=1}^{m} |f(x_i) - g(x_i)| - \alpha \\
&= d_1(f_{|_\bullet}, g_{|_\bullet}) - \alpha.
\end{aligned}
$$

Hence, given any ϵ-separated subset of $F|_a$, there is an $(\epsilon - \alpha)$-separated subset of $Q_\alpha(F)$. It follows that

$$\mathcal{M}_1(\epsilon, F, m) \leq \mathcal{M}_1(\epsilon - \alpha, Q_\alpha(F), m).$$

The proof of Theorem 12.7 also showed that

$$\text{fat}_{Q_\alpha(F)}(\epsilon) \leq \text{fat}_F(\epsilon - \alpha/2)$$

for $\alpha < 2\epsilon$ (see (12.4)).

Now, let H denote $Q_{\epsilon/4}(F)$, and let $d = \text{fat}_{Q_{\epsilon/4}(F)}(\epsilon/4)$. The following lemma shows that

$$\mathcal{M}(3\epsilon/4, H, d_1) \leq 2b^{3(\lceil \log_2 y \rceil + 1)},$$

where $b = \lfloor 4/\epsilon \rfloor$ and y is as defined in the lemma. This implies Theorem 18.1.

Lemma 18.3 *Let* $Y = \{0, 1, \ldots, b\}$ *with* $b \geq 3$, *and suppose that* $|X| = m$ *and* $H \subseteq Y^X$ *has* $\text{fat}_H(1) = d \geq 1$. *Then*

$$\mathcal{M}(3, H, d_1) \leq 2b^{3(\lceil \log_2 y \rceil + 1)},$$

with

$$y = \sum_{i=1}^{d} \binom{m}{i} b^i.$$

Proof By analogy with the proof of Theorem 12.7, for $k \geq 2$ and $m \geq 1$, define $t_1(k, m)$ as

$$\min \Big\{ |\{(A, r) : G \text{ 1-shatters } A \subseteq X, \text{ witnessed by } r : A \to Y, A \neq \emptyset\}| :$$

$$|X| = m, G \subseteq Y^X, |G| = k, \text{ and } G \text{ is 3-separated} \Big\},$$

or take $t_1(k, m)$ to be infinite if the minimum is over the empty set. Here, '3-separated' means with respect to d_1, and we regard d_1 as a metric on Y^X by defining $d_1(f, g) = (1/m) \sum_{x \in X} |f(x) - g(x)|$.

By the same argument as in the proof of Lemma 12.9, it suffices to show that

$$t_1 \left(2b^{3(\lceil \log_2 y \rceil + 1)}, m \right) \geq y$$

for all $d \geq 1$ and $m \geq 1$. Also as in the proof of Lemma 12.9, we shall demonstrate this by proving a lower bound on t using induction.

Choose a set G of $2b^{3(\lceil \log_2 y \rceil + 1)}$ pairwise 3-separated functions, and split G arbitrarily into $k/2$ pairs. Consider any pair (g_1, g_2) and let $l \leq m$ be the number of points x for which $|g_1(x) - g_2(x)| \geq 2$. Then

$$3 \leq d_1(g_1, g_2) = \frac{1}{m} \sum_{x \in X} |g_1(x) - g_2(x)| \leq \frac{1}{m} (bl + 2(m - l)),$$

from which we obtain $l > m/b$. (Note that $b > 2$.) It follows that there are $kl/2 > km/(2b)$ triples (g_1, g_2, x) with $|g_1(x) - g_2(x)| \geq 2$. By the pigeonhole principle there is some $x_0 \in X$ such that for more than $k/(2b)$ of the pairs (g_1, g_2), we have $|g_1(x_0) - g_2(x_0)| \geq 2$. By the pigeonhole principle again, there are $i, j \in Y$ with $j \geq i + 2$ such that for at least

$$\frac{k}{2b\left(\binom{b+1}{2} - b\right)} > \frac{k}{b^3}$$

of *these* pairs, we have $\{g_1(x_0), g_2(x_0)\} = \{i, j\}$. If we let G_1 denote these functions with $g(x_0) = i$ and G_2 denote the functions with $g(x_0) = j$, it is easy to see that, for any $g, g' \in G_1$,

$$\frac{1}{m-1} \sum_{x \in X - \{x_0\}} |g(x) - g'(x)| \geq \frac{3m}{m-1} > 3,$$

and a similar statement is true for G_2. It follows that G has two subsets, each of size at least k/b^3, and each 3-separated on $X - \{x_0\}$. Thus,

$$t_1(k, m) \geq 2 t_1 \left(\left\lfloor \frac{k}{b^3} \right\rfloor, m - 1\right).$$

An easy inductive proof, using the fact that $t_1(2, m) \geq 1$ for all m, together with the observation that $m > \lceil \log_2 y \rceil$ (obtained in a manner similar to the corresponding observation in the proof of Theorem 12.7), yields

$$t\left(2b^{3(\lceil \log_2 y \rceil + 1)}, m\right) \geq y,$$

completing the proof. □

18.3 Bounding with the Pseudo-Dimension

Since the fat-shattering dimension is always no more than the pseudo-dimension, if a function class F has finite pseudo-dimension, then Theorem 18.2 trivially yields an upper bound on covering numbers in terms of the pseudo-dimension. However, for classes of finite pseudo-dimension, a quite different bound can be obtained.

Theorem 18.4 *Let F be a nonempty set of real functions mapping from a domain X into the real interval $[0, 1]$ and suppose that F has finite pseudo-dimension d. Then*

$$\mathcal{N}_1(\epsilon, F, m) \leq \mathcal{M}_1(\epsilon, F, m) < e(d+1) \left(\frac{2e}{\epsilon} \right)^d$$

for all $\epsilon > 0$.

We omit the proof of this theorem, but prove the slightly weaker result,

$$\mathcal{M}_1(\epsilon, F, m) < 2 \left(\frac{2e}{\epsilon} \ln \left(\frac{8e}{\epsilon} \right) \right)^d. \tag{18.1}$$

The result is obtained as a corollary of a more general result on packing numbers of F. For a probability distribution P on X, we define the pseudo-metric $d_{L_1(P)}$ on the function class F by

$$d_{L_1(P)}(f, g) = \mathbf{E} \left(|f(x) - g(x)| \right) = \int |f(x) - g(x)| \, dP.$$

The packing numbers of F with respect to $d_{L_1(P)}$ are then denoted $\mathcal{M}(\epsilon, F, d_{L_1(P)})$. We shall prove the following result.

Theorem 18.5 *Let F be a nonempty set of real functions mapping from a domain X into the real interval $[0, 1]$, and suppose F has finite pseudo-dimension d. Then*

$$\mathcal{M}(\epsilon, F, d_{L_1(P)}) < 2 \left(\frac{2e}{\epsilon} \ln \left(\frac{8e}{\epsilon} \right) \right)^d$$

for any probability distribution P on X, and for all $0 < \epsilon \leq 1$.

To obtain Inequality (18.1), we can simply note that if $x \in X^m$ and if we take P_x to be the distribution that is uniform on the entries of x and vanishes elsewhere, then $\mathcal{M}(\epsilon, F_{|_x}, d_1) = \mathcal{M}(\epsilon, F, d_{P_x})$, and so

$$
\begin{aligned}
\mathcal{M}_1(\epsilon, F, m) &= \max \left\{ \mathcal{M}(\epsilon, F_{|_x}, d_1) : x \in X^m \right\} \\
&= \max \left\{ \mathcal{M}(\epsilon, F, d_{P_x}) : x \in X^m \right\} \\
&< 2 \left(\frac{2e}{\epsilon} \ln \left(\frac{8e}{\epsilon} \right) \right)^d,
\end{aligned}
$$

for all $\epsilon > 0$.

To proceed with the proof of Theorem 18.5, we first need a key lemma, and for this we shall need some additional notation. For any $z \in \mathbb{R}^k$, we define the element sgn(z) of $\{0,1\}^k$ to be

$$\text{sgn}(z) = (\text{sgn}(z_1), \text{sgn}(z_2), \ldots, \text{sgn}(z_k)),$$

and for $x \in X^k$ and $r \in \mathbb{R}^k$ let

$$\text{sgn}\left(F_{|_x} - r\right) = \{\text{sgn}\left(f_{|_x} - r\right) : f \in F\},$$

where, as usual, $f_{|_x} = (f(x_1), f(x_2), \ldots, f(x_k))$.

Lemma 18.6 *Let F be a set of functions from X to $[0,1]$, and suppose that P is a probability distribution on X. Let $x \in X^k$ be drawn according to the probability distribution P^k, and let r be a random element of $[0,1]^k$ where each entry of r is independently drawn according to the uniform probability distribution on $[0,1]$. Then for $0 < \epsilon < 1$,*

$$\mathbf{E}\left|\text{sgn}\left(F_{|_x} - r\right)\right| \geq \mathcal{M}(\epsilon, F, d_{L_1(P)})\left(1 - \mathcal{M}(\epsilon, F, d_{L_1(P)})e^{-\epsilon k}\right),$$

where the expectation is over the random choice of x and r.

Proof Let G be an ϵ-separated subset of F, with respect to $d_{L_1(P)}$, and suppose that G has maximum possible cardinality $\mathcal{M}(\epsilon, F, d_{L_1(P)})$. Then we have

$$\mathbf{E}\left|\text{sgn}\left(F_{|_x} - r\right)\right|$$
$$\geq \mathbf{E}\left|\text{sgn}\left(G_{|_x} - r\right)\right|$$
$$\geq \mathbf{E}\left|\{g \in G : \text{sgn}\left(g_{|_x} - r\right) \neq \text{sgn}\left(h_{|_x} - r\right) \, \forall h \in G, h \neq g\}\right|$$
$$= \sum_{g \in G} \text{Pr}\left(\text{sgn}\left(g_{|_x} - r\right) \neq \text{sgn}\left(h_{|_x} - r\right) \, \forall h \in G, h \neq g\right)$$
$$= \sum_{g \in G} \left(1 - \text{Pr}\left(\exists h \in G, h \neq g, \text{sgn}\left(g_{|_x} - r\right) = \text{sgn}\left(h_{|_x} - r\right)\right)\right)$$
$$\geq \sum_{g \in G} \left(1 - |G| \max_{h \in G, h \neq g} \text{Pr}\left(\text{sgn}\left(g_{|_x} - r\right) = \text{sgn}\left(h_{|_x} - r\right)\right)\right).$$

Now,

$$\text{Pr}\left(\text{sgn}\left(g_{|_x} - r\right) = \text{sgn}\left(h_{|_x} - r\right)\right)$$
$$= \prod_{i=1}^{k}\left(1 - \text{Pr}\left(r_i \text{ is between } h(x_i) \text{ and } g(x_i)\right)\right)$$
$$= \prod_{i=1}^{k}\left(1 - \mathbf{E}\left|h(x_i) - g(x_i)\right|\right)$$

$$\leq \ \exp\left(-\sum_{i=1}^{k} \mathbf{E}\,|h(x_i) - g(x_i)|\right)$$

$$\leq \ e^{-\epsilon k},$$

where the second last inequality follows from Inequality (1.4) in Appendix 1, and the last inequality follows from the fact that h and g are ϵ-separated. The result follows, since we now have

$$\mathbf{E}\,\left|\mathrm{sgn}\left(F_{|_x} - r\right)\right| \geq |G|\left(1 - |G|e^{-\epsilon k}\right)$$

and $|G| = \mathcal{M}(\epsilon, F, d_{L_1(P)})$. □

We also have the following bound on $\left|\mathrm{sgn}\left(F_{|_x} - r\right)\right|$ for any $x \in X^k$.

Lemma 18.7 *Let F be a set of functions mapping from X to $\mathbb{R}$ and having pseudo-dimension $d \geq 1$. Then, for all $k \geq d$, $\epsilon > 0$, $x \in X^k$, and $r \in \mathbb{R}^k$,*

$$\left|\mathrm{sgn}\left(F_{|_x} - r\right)\right| < \left(\frac{ek}{d}\right)^d.$$

Proof Let H be the set of $\{0,1\}$-valued functions defined on $X \times \mathbb{R}$ as follows.

$$H = \{(x,r) \mapsto \mathrm{sgn}(f(x) - r) : f \in F\}.$$

The definition of pseudo-dimension implies that $\mathrm{Pdim}(F) = \mathrm{VCdim}(H)$, and it is easy to see that

$$\max_{x \in X^k, r \in \mathbb{R}^k} \left|\mathrm{sgn}\left(F_{|_x} - r\right)\right| = \Pi_H(k).$$

The result follows immediately from Theorem 3.7. □

Theorem 18.5 now follows after some manipulation.

Proof **(of Theorem 18.5)** Clearly, if $d = \mathrm{Pdim}(F) = 0$, $\mathcal{M}_1\left(\epsilon, F, m\right) = 1$, so the result holds in that case. Assume then that $d \geq 1$. Let $\mathcal{M} = \mathcal{M}(\epsilon, F, d_{L_1(P)})$. By the lemmas just presented,

$$\mathcal{M}\left(1 - \mathcal{M}e^{-\epsilon k}\right) \leq \mathbf{E}\,\left|\mathrm{sgn}\left(F_{|_x} - r\right)\right| < \left(\frac{ek}{d}\right)^d, \qquad (18.2)$$

for $k \geq d$. We want to establish that

$$\mathcal{M} < 2\left(\frac{2e}{\epsilon}\ln\left(\frac{8e}{\epsilon}\right)\right)^d$$

for $0 < \epsilon \leq 1$. If $(1/\epsilon)\ln(2\mathcal{M}) \leq d$ and $0 < \epsilon \leq 1$ then the right-hand side of this bound is

$$2 \left(\frac{2e}{\epsilon} \ln \left(\frac{8e}{\epsilon} \right) \right)^d > \left(\frac{2e}{\epsilon} \right)^{\ln(2\mathcal{M})} = (2\mathcal{M})^{\ln(2e/\epsilon)} > \mathcal{M},$$

so the theorem holds in this case. Suppose now that $d < (1/\epsilon)\ln(2\mathcal{M})$. Taking $k = \lceil (1/\epsilon)\ln(2\mathcal{M}) \rceil$, we have $k \geq (1/\epsilon)\ln(2\mathcal{M})$, $\mathcal{M}e^{-\epsilon k} \leq 1/2$, and $k \geq d$. Thus,

$$\left(\frac{ek}{d} \right)^d > \mathcal{M}\left(1 - \mathcal{M}e^{-\epsilon k} \right) \geq \mathcal{M}/2.$$

Now,

$$\left(\frac{ek}{d} \right)^d \leq \left(\frac{e}{d} \left(\frac{1}{\epsilon}\ln(2\mathcal{M}) + 1 \right) \right)^d,$$

and so

$$(\mathcal{M}/2)^{1/d} \leq \frac{e}{d} \ln \left(4^{1/\epsilon}e \right) + \frac{e}{\epsilon} \ln \left((\mathcal{M}/2)^{1/d} \right).$$

Applying Inequality (1.2) from Appendix 1 implies

$$(\mathcal{M}/2)^{1/d} \leq \frac{2e}{\epsilon} \ln \left(\frac{2 \cdot 4^{1/d}e^{\epsilon/d}}{\epsilon} \right),$$

which gives the result.   □

18.4 Comparing the Different Approaches

It is useful to see how the bounds of this chapter compare with those implied by the results of Chapter 12.

Suppressing all multiplicative and additive constants (including those in the exponent) in order to emphasize the dependence on m and ϵ, the bound resulting from Theorem 12.8 takes the form

$$\mathcal{N}_1(\epsilon, F, m) \leq \mathcal{N}_\infty(\epsilon, F, m) \leq \left(\frac{\sqrt{m}}{\epsilon} \right)^{\mathrm{fat}_F(\epsilon/4)\log_2(m/(\epsilon\,\mathrm{fat}_F(\epsilon/4)))},$$

whereas the bound of Theorem 18.2 has the form

$$\mathcal{N}_1(\epsilon, F, m) \leq \left(\frac{1}{\epsilon} \right)^{\mathrm{fat}_F(\epsilon/8)\log_2(m/(\epsilon\,\mathrm{fat}_F(\epsilon/8)))}.$$

For a fixed value of ϵ, the second bound grows more slowly with m than the first. In this sense, the second bound is often better.

Consider now the bounds involving the pseudo-dimension. Suppressing again all multiplicative and additive constants, Theorem 12.2 implies a bound of the form

$$\mathcal{N}_1\left(\epsilon, F, m\right) \leq \mathcal{N}_\infty\left(\epsilon, F, m\right) \leq \left(\frac{m}{\epsilon}\right)^{\mathrm{Pdim}(F)},$$

whereas the bound of Theorem 18.4 has the form

$$\mathcal{N}_1\left(\epsilon, F, m\right) \leq \left(\frac{1}{\epsilon}\right)^{\mathrm{Pdim}(F)}.$$

The latter bound removes the dependence on m and hence is significantly better.

There are two bounds derived in this chapter: one involving the fat-shattering dimension and one involving the pseudo-dimension. Concerning which of these is more useful, we may make comments similar to those made in Section 12.5. Generally speaking, if a class has finite pseudo-dimension, then for small ϵ it is better to bound $\mathcal{N}_1\left(\epsilon, F, m\right)$ using Theorem 18.4 rather than Theorem 18.2. For larger values of ϵ, or for classes with infinite pseudo-dimension, Theorem 18.2 may give better results.

18.5 Remarks

All of the covering number bounds presented in this chapter assume that functions in the class map to the interval $[0,1]$. Lemma 14.12 shows that we can easily use these results to obtain covering number bounds for classes of functions that map to any bounded interval, simply by scaling and shifting the functions. A similar comment applies to packing numbers.

$L_2(P)$ *covering numbers*

The covering numbers discussed so far in this book are perhaps not the most natural. For example, if P is a probability distribution on X, consider the pseudo-metric $d_{L_2(P)}$ defined by

$$d_{L_2(P)}(f, g) = \left(\int_X (f(x) - g(x))^2 \, dP(x)\right)^{1/2}.$$

For the problem of learning to minimize squared error, this metric measures the distance between functions in some class F in the most direct way. If we have access to a small cover of F with respect to $d_{L_2(P)}$

for every P, then we can use it to construct a learning algorithm. The uniform convergence result for finite classes (that follows from Hoeffding's inequality and the union bound—see the proof of Theorem 16.2) shows that the element of the cover with smallest sample error will have expected error that is near-minimal over the cover, and the fact that every function in F is approximated by an element of the cover implies that this error is also nearly minimal over all of the class F. Of course, the fact that the learning algorithm does not know the probability distribution P—in general the cover will depend on the distribution—is a drawback to this approach.

In fact, it is possible to generate such a cover using training data, and its size can be bounded in terms of the fat-shattering dimension. For a sample $(x_1, \ldots, x_m)$ chosen according to a probability distribution P, choose a subset of F whose restriction to the sample forms a cover of F with respect to the metric d_2. It is straightforward to apply a uniform convergence result like Theorem 17.1 to show that, for sufficiently large m, with high probability this subset constitutes a cover with respect to the metric $d_{L_2(P)}$. Strictly speaking, instead of uniform convergence over all functions in F, we need that, for all *pairs* of functions in F, their distances under the metric d_2 and under the metric $d_{L_2(P)}$ are close, but this follows easily from Theorem 17.1. Thus, it is possible to prove the following result.

Theorem 18.8 *There are constants c_1, c_2, c_3 such that, for all probability distributions P on X,*

$$\ln\left(\mathcal{N}(\epsilon, F, d_{L_2(P)})\right) \leq c_1 \mathrm{fat}_F(c_2\epsilon) \ln^2\left(\frac{\mathrm{fat}_F(c_3\epsilon^2)}{\epsilon}\right).$$

A converse result is immediate from the lower bound on d_1 covers in terms of the fat-shattering dimension (Theorem 12.10). This shows that

$$\max_P \ln\left(\mathcal{N}(\epsilon, F, d_{L_2(P)})\right) \geq \max_P \ln\left(\mathcal{N}(\epsilon, F, d_{L_1(P)})\right) \geq \mathrm{fat}_F(16\epsilon)/8.$$

18.6 Bibliographical Notes

Theorem 18.1 is from (Bartlett and Long, 1995), and its proof uses ideas from (Alon et al., 1993). Theorem 18.4 is due to Haussler (1995). The proof we give for the weaker Inequality (18.1) comes from (Haussler, 1992), using techniques due to Pollard (1984) and Dudley (1978).

For a proof of a result analogous to Theorem 18.8, but for $L_1(P)$ covers, see (Bartlett et al., 1997). Buescher and Kumar (1991; 1992) used the approach of constructing an empirical cover to design powerful general learning algorithms. These algorithms can be successful in certain situations (that is, for certain function classes and probability distributions) in which approximate-SEM algorithms fail. As we shall see in the next chapter, this difference cannot occur in the learning problem studied here, since approximate-SEM algorithms lead to learning algorithms for every learnable function class.

19

The Sample Complexity of Learning Real Function Classes

19.1 Introduction

In Chapter 16, we encountered the notion of an *approximate-SEM* algorithm for a function class F, which takes as input a sample z and a positive real number ϵ and returns a function $\mathcal{A}(z,\epsilon) \in F$ such that $\text{êr}_z\left(\mathcal{A}(z,\epsilon)\right) < \inf_{f \in F} \text{êr}_z(f) + \epsilon$. We proved that if a function class is totally bounded with respect to the L_∞ metric, then it is learnable by an algorithm derived, as in Theorem 16.5, from any approximate-SEM algorithm. In this chapter we use the uniform convergence results of Chapter 17 and the covering number bounds of Chapter 18 to extend this result to other function classes by showing that, provided F has finite fat-shattering dimension, then any approximate-SEM algorithm can be used to construct a learning algorithm for F. We also give lower bounds on the sample complexity of any learning algorithm, in terms of the fat-shattering dimension of the function class. These results show that a function class is learnable if and only if it has finite fat-shattering dimension.

19.2 Classes with Finite Fat-Shattering Dimension

The main result

The main result of this chapter, which makes use of the uniform convergence result obtained in Chapter 17 and the covering number bounds of Chapter 18, is as follows.

Theorem 19.1 *Suppose that F is a class of functions mapping from a domain X into the real interval $[0,1]$, and suppose also that F has finite fat-shattering dimension. Let $\mathcal{A}$ be any approximate-SEM algorithm for*

F and define, for $z \in Z^m$, $L(z) = \mathcal{A}(z, \epsilon_0/6)$, where $\epsilon_0 = 16/\sqrt{m}$. Then L is a learning algorithm for F, and its sample complexity satisfies

$$m_L(\epsilon, \delta) \leq m_0(\epsilon, \delta) = \frac{256}{\epsilon^2} \left(18 \, \mathrm{fat}_F\left(\epsilon/256\right) \ln^2 \left(\frac{128}{\epsilon}\right) + \ln \left(\frac{16}{\delta}\right) \right)$$

for all $\epsilon, \delta > 0$.

We say that the learning algorithm L described in Theorem 19.1 is *based on the approximate-SEM algorithm* $\mathcal{A}$.

Proof By Theorem 17.1,

$$P^m \left\{ \exists f \in F, \, |\mathrm{er}_P(f) - \hat{\mathrm{er}}_z(f)| \geq \epsilon/2 \right\} \leq 4 \mathcal{N}_1 \left(\epsilon/32, F, 2m\right) e^{-\epsilon^2 m/128}.$$

We claim that this quantity is at most $\delta/2$, provided $m \geq m_0(\epsilon, \delta)$. Let $d = \mathrm{fat}_F(\epsilon/256)$. If $d = 0$, it is clear that $\mathcal{N}_1(\epsilon/32, F, 2m) \leq 1$, and the claim follows, so assume that $d \geq 1$. Theorem 18.2 then shows that

$$4 \mathcal{N}_1 \left(\epsilon/32, F, 2m\right) e^{-\epsilon^2 m/128} < 8 \left(\frac{128}{\epsilon}\right)^{3d \log_2(512em/(d\epsilon))} e^{-\epsilon^2 m/128}.$$

For this to be at most $\delta/2$, we need

$$\frac{\epsilon^2 m}{128} \geq \ln \left(\frac{16}{\delta}\right) + 3d \ln \left(\frac{128}{\epsilon}\right) \log_2 \left(\frac{512em}{d\epsilon}\right),$$

which is equivalent to

$$\frac{\epsilon^2 m}{128} \geq \ln \left(\frac{16}{\delta}\right) + 3d \ln \left(\frac{128}{\epsilon}\right) \log_2 \left(\frac{512e}{d\epsilon}\right) + 3d \ln \left(\frac{128}{\epsilon}\right) \log_2 m.$$

We now use Inequality (1.2) of Appendix 1, $\ln m \leq \alpha m - \ln \alpha - 1$, choosing α appropriately, to verify the claim. (The details of the calculation are omitted.)

Suppose then that $m \geq m_0(\epsilon, \delta)$, and that $z \in Z^m$. Then, with probability at least $1 - \delta/2$, a P^m-random $z \in Z^m$ is such that

$$|\mathrm{er}_P(f) - \hat{\mathrm{er}}_z(f)| < \frac{\epsilon}{2}, \quad \text{for all } f \in F. \tag{19.1}$$

Furthermore, since $\epsilon_0 = \sqrt{256/m}$, and $m \geq m_0(\epsilon, \delta) \geq 256/\epsilon^2$, we have $\epsilon_0 \leq \epsilon$, so it follows that

$$\hat{\mathrm{er}}_z \left(L(z)\right) = \hat{\mathrm{er}}_z \left(\mathcal{A}(z, \epsilon_0/6)\right) < \inf_{f \in F} \hat{\mathrm{er}}_z(f) + \frac{\epsilon_0}{6} \leq \inf_{f \in F} \hat{\mathrm{er}}_z(f) + \frac{\epsilon}{6}. \tag{19.2}$$

Suppose that $f^* \in F$ satisfies

$$\mathrm{er}_P(f^*) < \mathrm{opt}_P(F) + \frac{\epsilon}{6}. \tag{19.3}$$

Hoeffding's inequality (Inequality (1.16) in Appendix 1) implies that, with probability at least $1 - \delta/2$,

$$\hat{\mathrm{er}}_z(f^*) \leq \mathrm{er}_P(f^*) + \frac{\epsilon}{6}, \qquad (19.4)$$

provided $m \geq (18/\epsilon^2)\ln(2/\delta)$. Thus, for $m \geq m_0(\epsilon, \delta)$, with probability at least $1 - \delta$ we have

$$
\begin{aligned}
\mathrm{er}_P(L(z)) \quad &< \quad \hat{\mathrm{er}}_z(L(z)) + \frac{\epsilon}{2} \qquad \text{(by 19.1)} \\
&< \quad \inf_{f \in F} \hat{\mathrm{er}}_z(f) + \frac{4\epsilon}{6} \qquad \text{(by 19.2)} \\
&\leq \quad \hat{\mathrm{er}}_z(f^*) + \frac{4\epsilon}{6} \\
&\leq \quad \mathrm{er}_P(f^*) + \frac{5\epsilon}{6} \qquad \text{(by 19.4)} \\
&< \quad \mathrm{opt}_P(F) + \epsilon, \qquad \text{(by 19.3)}
\end{aligned}
$$

and it follows that L is a learning algorithm whose sample complexity is bounded above by $m_0(\epsilon, \delta)$. □

19.3 Classes with Finite Pseudo-Dimension

Bounding sample complexity with pseudo-dimension

If a function class has finite pseudo-dimension, then it also has finite fat-shattering dimension. Hence, by the results of the previous section, it is clear that F is learnable by an algorithm derived as above from an approximate-SEM algorithm. We can, however, use Theorem 18.4 to obtain an upper bound on the sample complexity of such algorithms in terms of the pseudo-dimension.

Theorem 19.2 *Suppose that F is a class of functions mapping from a domain X into the interval $[0,1]$ of real numbers, and that F has finite pseudo-dimension. Let A be any approximate-SEM algorithm for F and let L be as described in the statement of Theorem 19.1 (that is, the learning algorithm based on A). Then L is a learning algorithm for F and its sample complexity is bounded as follows:*

$$m_L(\epsilon, \delta) \leq m_0(\epsilon, \delta) = \frac{128}{\epsilon^2}\left(2\,\mathrm{Pdim}(F)\,\ln\left(\frac{34}{\epsilon}\right) + \ln\left(\frac{16}{\delta}\right)\right),$$

for all $0 < \epsilon, \delta < 1$.

Proof By Theorem 17.1 and Theorem 18.4, if $d = \text{Pdim}(F)$ and $m \geq d$,

$$P^m \{\exists f \in F, \ |\text{er}_P(h) - \hat{\text{er}}_z(h)| \geq \epsilon/2\}$$

$$< \ 8 \left(\frac{64e}{\epsilon} \ln \left(\frac{256e}{\epsilon} \right) \right)^d \exp \left(-\frac{\epsilon^2 m}{128} \right).$$

This is easily checked to be at most $\delta/2$ when $m \geq m_0(\epsilon, \delta)$. The rest of the proof proceeds as in the proof of Theorem 19.1. $\qquad\square$

For a function class of finite pseudo-dimension, the sample complexity bound of Theorem 19.2 is better than that implied by Theorem 19.1 for small values of ϵ. However, Theorem 19.1 is more widely applicable, since not all classes with finite fat-shattering dimension have finite pseudo-dimension.

19.4 Results for Neural Networks

Combining Theorems 19.1 and 19.2 with upper bounds on the fat-shattering dimension or pseudo-dimension of a neural network function class immediately gives sample complexity bounds for learning algorithms for that class. The following two corollaries describe two such bounds. Similar results can be obtained for other classes of networks considered in Chapters 6, 8 and 14.

The first corollary concerns feed-forward networks with a bounded number of computation units, each with a piecewise-polynomial activation function. Theorem 8.8 gives a bound on the VC-dimension of this function class, and Theorem 14.1 extends this to a bound on the pseudo-dimension, which implies the following result.

Corollary 19.3 *Suppose that a feed-forward network N has W weights and k computation units arranged in L layers. Suppose that each computation unit has a fixed piecewise-polynomial activation function with p pieces and degree no more than l. Let F be the class of functions computed by N. Then any approximate-SEM algorithm for F can be used to define a learning algorithm for F, and for fixed p and l, the sample complexity of this learning algorithm is*

$$O \left(\frac{1}{\epsilon^2} \left((WL \ln W + WL^2) \ln \left(\frac{1}{\epsilon} \right) + \ln \left(\frac{1}{\delta} \right) \right) \right).$$

The second corollary concerns two-layer networks with bounded parameters, but an arbitrary number of first-layer units. Theorem 14.19

gives a bound on the fat-shattering dimension of the class of functions computed by such a network. Rather than combine this with Theorem 19.1, we use the covering number bounds of Corollary 14.16 directly, giving an improvement of log factors.

Corollary 19.4 *Consider the class of two-layer networks defined in Corollary 14.16, with inputs in $[-A, A]^n$, where each computation unit has a bound V on the sum of the magnitudes of the associated parameters, and an activation function that is bounded and satisfies a Lipschitz constraint. Let F be the class of functions computed by this network. Any approximate-SEM algorithm can be used to define a learning algorithm L for F that has sample complexity satisfying*

$$m_L(\epsilon, \delta) = O\left(\frac{1}{\epsilon^2}\left(\frac{V^6 A^2}{\epsilon^4}\ln n + \ln\left(\frac{1}{\delta}\right)\right)\right).$$

19.5 Lower Bounds

The following theorem gives a lower bound on the sample complexity of any learning algorithm, in terms of the fat-shattering dimension of the function class. Together with Theorem 19.1, this shows that finiteness of the fat-shattering dimension of a function class is a necessary and sufficient condition for the existence of a learning algorithm for the class.

Theorem 19.5 *Suppose that F is a class of functions mapping from X to $[0, 1]$. Then for $B \geq 2$, $0 < \epsilon < 1$ and $0 < \delta < 1/100$, any learning algorithm L for F has sample complexity satisfying*

$$m_L(\epsilon, \delta, B) \geq \frac{\text{fat}_F(\epsilon/\alpha) - 1}{16\alpha},$$

for any $0 < \alpha < 1/4$.

By suitable choice of α, this theorem implies that the sample complexity of a learning algorithm for any function class F is $\Omega(1/\epsilon)$ and $\Omega(\text{fat}_F(4\epsilon))$.

There is a considerable gap between this result, which shows that the sample complexity of any learning algorithm for a class F satisfies

$$m(\epsilon, \delta, B) = \Omega\left(\frac{1}{\epsilon} + \text{fat}_F(4\epsilon)\right), \tag{19.5}$$

and Theorem 19.1, which describes a learning algorithm with sample complexity (for fixed B and δ)

$$m(\epsilon, \delta, B) = O\left(\frac{1}{\epsilon^2}\left(\mathrm{fat}_F\left(\epsilon/256\right)\ln^2\left(\frac{1}{\epsilon}\right)\right)\right).$$

For instance, suppose that F is a class with $\lim_{\epsilon \to 0} \mathrm{fat}_F(\epsilon) = \mathrm{Pdim}(F) < \infty$. Then the upper bound shows that the sample complexity grows as $1/\epsilon^2$ (ignoring log factors), whereas the lower bound shows that it grows at least as $1/\epsilon$. This gap is inevitable; we shall see in the next chapter that the sample complexity of a convex class F with finite pseudo-dimension grows as $1/\epsilon$, ignoring log factors, but for a non-convex class sample complexity grows as $1/\epsilon^2$. There are also examples that illustrate that the second term in (19.5) cannot be improved in general. In particular, in Chapter 26, we describe a learning algorithm for the class of two-layer networks with an arbitrary number of first-layer units and constraints on the size of the parameters. This algorithm is an approximate sample error minimization algorithm that returns a function from a certain restricted subset of the class. It has sample complexity $O(\mathrm{fat}_F(\epsilon))$, ignoring log factors.

Proof (of Theorem 19.5) The idea of the proof is to reduce the learning problem to a related learning problem in the restricted model for pattern classification. Consider the class H_d of all functions mapping from the finite set $\{x_1, \ldots, x_d\} \subseteq X$ to $\{0, 1\}$. Theorem 5.3 shows that any learning algorithm for H_d has sample complexity at least $(d-1)/(32\epsilon)$ for suitably small ϵ and δ. We shall show that, for any fixed α between 0 and $1/4$, any learning algorithm for the class F that learns to accuracy ϵ can be used to construct a learning algorithm for H_d that learns to accuracy $\alpha/2$, where $d = \mathrm{fat}_F(\epsilon/\alpha)$.

Fix $0 < \alpha < 1/4$ and $0 < \epsilon < 1$, and let $d = \mathrm{fat}_F(\epsilon/\alpha)$. We can assume that $d > 1$, because the theorem is trivial otherwise. Suppose $\{x_1, \ldots, x_d\}$ is ϵ/α-shattered by F, witnessed by $r_1, \ldots, r_d$. Without loss of generality, we suppose that $X = \{x_1, \ldots, x_d\}$. Suppose that L is a learning algorithm for F. Then we can construct a learning algorithm for H_d as follows. For each labelled example (x_i, y_i), the algorithm passes to L the labelled example $(x_i, \tilde{y}_i)$, where $\tilde{y}_i = 2$ if $y_i = 1$ and $\tilde{y}_i = -1$ if $y_i = 0$. Let P be the original distribution on $X \times \{0, 1\}$, and $\tilde{P}$ the resulting distribution on $X \times \{-1, 2\}$. Then given a function $f : X \to [0, 1]$ produced by L, the algorithm for H_d outputs the function

$h : X \rightarrow \{0, 1\}$, where $h(x_i) = 1$ if and only if $f(x_i) > r_i$. We claim that if $\mathrm{er}_{\tilde{P}}(f) - \mathrm{opt}_{\tilde{P}}(F) < \epsilon$ then $\mathrm{er}_P(h) < \alpha/2$.

To see this, notice that

$$
\begin{aligned}
\mathrm{opt}_{\tilde{P}}(F) &= \inf_{g \in F} \mathrm{er}_{\tilde{P}}(g) \\
&= \inf_{g \in F} \mathbf{E}(g(x) - \tilde{y})^2 \\
&\leq \mathbf{E} \min \left\{ (\hat{y} - \tilde{y})^2 : \hat{y} \in \{r(x) \pm \epsilon/\alpha\} \right\},
\end{aligned}
$$

where $r(x_i) = r_i$. The inequality follows from the fact that the distribution is concentrated on a shattered set. It follows that

$$
\begin{aligned}
&\mathrm{er}_{\tilde{P}}(f) - \mathrm{opt}_{\tilde{P}}(F) \\
&\geq \mathbf{E} \left[(f(x) - \tilde{y})^2 - \min \left\{ (\hat{y} - \tilde{y})^2 : \hat{y} \in \{r(x) \pm \epsilon/\alpha\} \right\} \right].
\end{aligned}
$$

Consider the quantity inside the square brackets. For $x = x_i$ with $y_i = 0$, $\tilde{y}_i = -1$ and this quantity is

$$
\begin{aligned}
&(f(x_i) + 1)^2 - \left(r_i - \frac{\epsilon}{\alpha} + 1 \right)^2 \\
&= \left(f(x_i) - r_i + \frac{\epsilon}{\alpha} \right)^2 + 2 \left(f(x_i) - r_i + \frac{\epsilon}{\alpha} \right) \left(r_i - \frac{\epsilon}{\alpha} + 1 \right) \\
&\geq 2 \left(f(x_i) - r_i + \frac{\epsilon}{\alpha} \right).
\end{aligned}
$$

Hence for $y = 0$, if

$$
(f(x) - \tilde{y})^2 - \widetilde{\min} \left\{ (\hat{y} - \tilde{y})^2 : \hat{y} \in \{r(x) \pm \epsilon/\alpha\} \right\} < \frac{2\epsilon}{\alpha},
$$

then $f(x) < r(x)$, and hence $h(x) = y$. A similar argument applies when $y = 1$. Thus,

$$
\begin{aligned}
&\mathrm{er}_P(h) \\
&\leq \tilde{P} \left\{ (f(x) - \tilde{y})^2 - \min \left\{ (\hat{y} - \tilde{y})^2 : \hat{y} \in \{r(x) \pm \epsilon/\alpha\} \right\} \geq \frac{2\epsilon}{\alpha} \right\} \\
&\leq \frac{\alpha}{2\epsilon} \mathbf{E} \left[(f(x) - \tilde{y})^2 - \min \left\{ (\hat{y} - \tilde{y})^2 : \hat{y} \in \{r(x) \pm \epsilon/\alpha\} \right\} \right] \\
&\leq \frac{\alpha}{2\epsilon} \left(\mathrm{er}_{\tilde{P}}(f) - \mathrm{opt}_{\tilde{P}}(F) \right),
\end{aligned}
$$

where the second last inequality is Markov's inequality (Inequality (1.10) in Appendix 1). This implies the result. $\qquad \square$

19.6 Remarks

It is possible to improve on the upper bound of Theorem 19.1 for specific classes with infinite pseudo-dimension, using a chaining technique. (We have seen an example of this technique in Section 4.6; it led to an improved sample complexity result for the classification problem.) However, the interesting cases of neural network classes with infinite pseudo-dimension are networks with constraints on the size of the parameters but no constraint on the number of parameters. In Chapter 20 we show that all convex classes like this exhibit faster rates of uniform convergence than one would expect from Theorem 19.1. In Chapter 26, we use this result to show that a learning algorithm for these networks has a sample complexity that matches the lower bound of Theorem 19.5.

It is easy to extend Theorems 19.1 and 19.2 to the case where the bound $B \geq 1$. Using the result from Section 17.2 in place of Theorem 17.1 gives the following sample complexity bounds, in terms of the fat-shattering dimension and pseudo-dimension respectively.

$$m_L(\epsilon, \delta, B) \leq \frac{256B^4}{\epsilon^2} \left(18 \, \text{fat}_F \left(\frac{\epsilon}{256B} \right) \ln^2 \left(\frac{128B}{\epsilon} \right) + \ln \left(\frac{16}{\delta} \right) \right),$$

$$m_L(\epsilon, \delta, B) \leq \frac{128B^4}{\epsilon^2} \left(2 \, \text{Pdim}(F) \, \ln \left(\frac{37B}{\epsilon} \right) + \ln \left(\frac{16}{\delta} \right) \right).$$

Restricted model

Just as in previous parts of the book, we can define a restricted version of the learning framework for real prediction, in which the labelled examples presented to the learning algorithm are of the form $(x, f(x))$ for some $f \in F$. However such a model can have some unnatural features that arise because the value $f(x)$ can encode an arbitrary amount of information about f. (In previous models, the label could provide only one bit.) The following example describes an extreme case of this phenomenon, in which a single labelled example $(x, f(x))$ serves to uniquely identify the function f. In this case, the fat-shattering dimension of F is not an appropriate measure of its complexity.

Example 19.6 *For a positive integer d, let $S_0, \ldots, S_{d-1}$ be disjoint subsets of X with $\bigcup_j S_j = X$. Define the class of $[0,1]$-valued functions*

$$F_d = \left\{ f_{b_0, \ldots, b_{d-1}} : b_i \in \{0, 1\}, i = 0, \ldots, d-1 \right\},$$

where

$$f_{b_0,\ldots,b_{d-1}}(x) = \frac{3}{4} \sum_{j=0}^{d-1} 1_{S_j}(x)b_j + \frac{1}{8} \sum_{k=0}^{d-1} b_k 2^{-k},$$

and 1_{S_j} is the indicator function for S_j. That is, the labels b_j determine the two most significant bits of the binary representation of the value of the function in S_j, and the d least significant bits of its value at any $x \in X$ encode the identity of the function. Clearly, for any $\gamma \leq 1/4$, $\text{fat}_{F_d}(\gamma) = d$. Hence, the union of these classes, $F = \bigcup_{d=1}^{\infty} F_d$ has $\text{fat}_F(\gamma) = \infty$ for $\gamma \leq 1/4$, but any f in F can be identified from a single example $(x, f(x))$.

There are less restricted models that avoid these pathological cases. For instance, if the labels are noisy versions of the function values (so that labelled examples are of the form $(x, f(x) + \eta)$, for some noise variable η) or if the labels are quantized versions of the function values, the amount of information passed to a learner in a label is restricted. Typically, the fat-shattering dimension is the appropriate measure of complexity in such cases, in the sense that a function class is learnable in the appropriate sense if and only if its fat-shattering dimension is finite. We shall consider one such model at the end of the next chapter: in that case the labels are noisy versions of the function values, and the noise is such that the conditional expectation function $\mathbf{E}(y|x)$ is in the class F.

Relative uniform convergence results

We shall see in the next chapter that the rate of uniform convergence of $\text{er}_P(f)$ to $\hat{\text{er}}_z(f)$ for non-convex classes cannot be faster than $1/\sqrt{m}$. However, as in Parts 1 and 2, it is possible to obtain a faster rate of uniform convergence of $\text{er}_P(f)$ to a value slightly larger than $\hat{\text{er}}_z(f)$. The following theorem is analogous to Theorems 5.7 and 13.7.

Theorem 19.7 *Suppose that F is a set of $[0, 1]$-valued functions defined on a set X and that P is a probability distribution on $Z = X \times [0, 1]$. For $\alpha, \epsilon > 0$ and m a positive integer, we have*

$$P^m \{\exists f \in F : \text{er}_P(f) > (1 + \alpha)\hat{\text{er}}_z(f) + \epsilon\}$$

$$\leq 4 \mathcal{N}_1\left(\frac{\epsilon}{4(2 + \alpha)}, F, 2m\right) \exp\left(\frac{-2m\alpha\epsilon}{(2 + \alpha)^2}\right).$$

The theorem is a consequence of the following result, since $\mathrm{er}_P(f) > (1 + \alpha)\hat{\mathrm{er}}_z(f) + \epsilon$ if and only if

$$\frac{\mathrm{er}_P(f) - \hat{\mathrm{er}}_z(f)}{\mathrm{er}_P(f) + \hat{\mathrm{er}}_z(f) + 2\epsilon/\alpha} > \frac{\alpha}{2 + \alpha}.$$

Theorem 19.8 *For F and P as in Theorem 19.7, $\nu > 0$ and $0 < \beta < 1$,*

$$P^m \left\{ \exists f \in F : \frac{|\mathrm{er}_P(f) - \hat{\mathrm{er}}_z(f)|}{\mathrm{er}_P(f) + \hat{\mathrm{er}}_z(f) + \nu} > \beta \right\}$$

$$\leq 4 \mathcal{N}_1 \left(\frac{\beta \nu}{8}, F, 2m \right) \exp \left(-\frac{m \nu \beta^2}{8} \right).$$

We omit the proof.

Model selection

It is possible to derive model selection results for learning real function classes that are analogous to those presented in Chapter 15 for the case of pattern classification. Consider an indexed family of function classes $\{F_t : t \in \mathbb{R}^+\}$ with increasing fat-shattering dimension. The estimation error bounds of this chapter, together with the techniques of Chapter 15 give error bounds for algorithms that choose a function from these classes to minimize a sum of the sample error for a function f and a complexity penalty for f.

19.7 Bibliographical Notes

Alon, Ben-David, Cesa-Bianchi and Haussler (1997) gave the first uniform convergence result in terms of the fat-shattering dimension. A learning result like Theorem 19.1 (but in terms of absolute loss, rather than quadratic loss) is given in (Bartlett, Long and Williamson, 1996) using the results of Alon *et al.*, together with a result like Lemma 17.6 relating covering numbers of a class to those of the loss function class.

For a description of the chaining technique, see, for example, (Pollard, 1984; Pollard, 1990). Long (1998b) uses this technique to analyse a class with infinite pseudo-dimension that improves on the results presented in this chapter. Birgé and Massart (1993) give examples of function classes and learning algorithms for these classes that have faster convergence of estimation error than sample error minimization algorithms.

Bartlett, Long and Williamson (1996) showed that the finiteness of the fat-shattering dimension of a class F characterizes the learnability of F when the labels are noisy versions of the value of a target function from the class F. Anthony and Bartlett (1995) showed that the same property characterizes learnability for a deterministic noise model, and when the labels are quantized versions of a target function's value. (See also (Bartlett, 1994).) Simon (1997) gave lower bounds in terms of a different scale-sensitive dimension.

The lower bound result, Theorem 19.5, is new. The example that illustrates the problem with obtaining lower bounds in the restricted model appeared in (Bartlett, Long and Williamson, 1996). Theorem 19.8 is due to Haussler; it is an improvement of a result due to Pollard (1984). A similar inequality, expressed in terms of d_∞ covering numbers, can also be derived from a stronger result that is similar to Inequality (5.11), but for real-valued functions (see (Bartlett and Lugosi, 1999)).

Model selection results for neural networks and related classes of real-valued functions have been presented by a number of authors, including Barron (1991; 1994), Krzyżak et al. (1996), and Lugosi and Zeger (1995).

20
Convex Classes

20.1 Introduction

We have seen in the previous chapter that finiteness of the fat-shattering dimension is necessary and sufficient for learning. Unfortunately, there is a considerable gap between our lower and upper bounds on sample complexity. Even for a function class with finite pseudo-dimension, the bounds show only that the sample complexity is $\Omega(1/\epsilon)$ and $O(1/\epsilon^2)$. In this chapter, we show that this gap is not just a consequence of our lack of skill in proving sample complexity bounds: there are function classes demonstrating that both rates are possible. More surprisingly, we show that the sample complexity or, equivalently, the estimation error rate is determined by the 'closure convexity' of the function class. (Closure convexity is a slightly weaker condition than convexity.) Specifically, for function classes with finite pseudo-dimension, if the class is closure convex, the sample complexity grows roughly as $1/\epsilon$; if it is not closure convex, the sample complexity grows roughly as $1/\epsilon^2$, and no other rates are possible (ignoring log factors).

To understand the intuition behind these results, consider a domain X of cardinality one. In this case, a function class is equivalent to a bounded subset of the real numbers, and the learning problem is equivalent to finding the best approximation from that subset to the expectation of a bounded random variable. It is a standard result of probability theory that the squared difference between the sample average and the expectation of such a random variable decreases as $1/m$. If the function class is a closed interval in $\mathbb{R}$, then clearly the excess error of the value returned by a sample error minimization algorithm (which returns the best approximation in the class to the sample average) also decreases as $1/m$, and so the sample complexity is $O(1/\epsilon)$. On the other hand, if the function class consists of two disjoint closed intervals and the expectation of the random variable falls between the intervals, a learning algorithm is forced to choose an estimate from one or other of the intervals. If the expectation is ϵ away from the centre of the gap between the two intervals, the additional squared error that arises from choosing the wrong interval is linear in ϵ. For a suitably chosen probability distribution, this learning problem is equivalent to the problem of estimating the expectation of a Bernoulli random variable, and the lower bound result of Lemma 5.1 shows that $\Omega(1/\epsilon^2)$ examples are necessary.

The results in this chapter generalize these observations. The single closed interval is an example of a convex function class, and the sample complexity of this class is of order $1/\epsilon$. (Recall that a function class F is convex if, for all f_1, f_2 in F and $0 < \alpha < 1$, the convex combination $\alpha f_1 + (1 - \alpha)f_2$ is also in F.) The union of two disjoint closed intervals is an example of a non-convex function class, and the sample complexity in this case is of order at least $1/\epsilon^2$.

20.2 Lower Bounds for Non-Convex Classes

For the sample complexity results in this chapter, we make use of the notion of 'closure convexity', a slightly weaker condition than convexity. To understand why a modification of convexity will be relevant, consider again a function class F defined on a domain X of cardinality one (so that F is equivalent to a subset of $\mathbb{R}$). If the class F is the union of the intervals $[0, 1/2)$ and $(1/2, 1]$, then it is not convex, but it is clear that the learning problem is equivalent to that involving the convex class $[0, 1]$, since F contains arbitrarily good approximations to the missing point. This example suggests that we do not need convexity in order to obtain fast estimation rates; rather, convexity of the closure of the class might suffice. The appropriate topology in which to define the closure depends on the probability distribution on the domain X, as the following definition demonstrates.

Definition 20.1 *For a probability distribution P_X on X, define the norm induced by P_X on the set of functions $f : X \to \mathbb{R}$ as*

$$\|f\| = \left(\int_X f^2(x)\, dP_X(x) \right)^{1/2}.$$

For a class F of real-valued functions defined on a set X and a probability distribution P_X on X, let $\bar{F}$ denote the closure of F with respect to this norm. *We say that such a class F is* closure convex *if, for all probability distributions P_X on X, $\bar{F}$ is convex.*

The following theorem is the main result of this section. It shows that the sample complexity of a class that is not closure convex is $\Omega(1/\epsilon^2)$.

Theorem 20.2 *For every class F that is not closure convex, there is a positive constant k and a bound B' such that for all $0 < \delta < 1$, all sufficiently small $\epsilon > 0$, all $B \geq B'$, and all learning algorithms L for F, the sample complexity satisfies*

$$m_L(\epsilon, \delta, B) \geq \frac{k \ln(1/\delta)}{\epsilon^2}.$$

The proof of the theorem involves two lemmas. In the first lemma, we think of the function class F as a subset of the Hilbert space of real-valued functions equipped with the scalar product

$$(f, g) = \int_X f(x)g(x)\, dP_X(x),$$

where P_X is the probability distribution on X. This lemma shows that we may assume that the closure of F is compact (that is, every open cover of $\bar{F}$ has a finite subcover). The lemma follows from Theorem 19.5, the fact (Theorem 18.8) that finiteness of the fat-shattering dimension implies total boundedness in $L_2(P)$, and the fact that every closed, totally bounded subset of a Hilbert space is compact.

Lemma 20.3 *If a class F of real-valued functions is learnable, then for any probability distribution P_X on X, $\bar{F}$ is compact.*

The next lemma shows that if F is not closure convex, then we can find an open ball in Hilbert space that does not intersect the class, and whose surface intersects $\bar{F}$ in at least two points. Figure 20.1 illustrates the functions defined in the lemma.

Lemma 20.4 *If $\bar{F}$ is compact and not convex, then there is a bounded interval $Y \subset \mathbb{R}$, a function $c : X \to Y$, and two functions $f_1, f_2 \in \bar{F}$, such that for all f in F, $\|c - f\| \geq \|c - f_1\| = \|c - f_2\|$.*

Proof Since $\bar{F}$ is not convex, there are functions $g, h \in \bar{F}$ and a constant $\alpha \in (0, 1)$ for which the function $f = \alpha g + (1 - \alpha)h$ is not in $\bar{F}$. (See Figure 20.1.) To show that the desired functions c, f_1, and f_2 exist, we consider the smallest ball around f that touches a point in $\bar{F}$. (This is

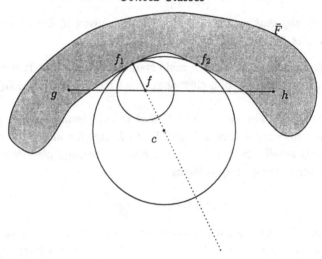

Fig. 20.1. A two-dimensional slice through Hilbert space, illustrating the function class F, the functions f_1, f_2, and c defined in Lemma 20.4, and the construction used in the proof of that lemma. (Notice that g and h need not lie in the same plane as f, f_1, and f_2.)

represented by the small circle in Figure 20.1.) Thus, the radius of this ball is $\delta = \min\{\|f' - f\| : f' \in \bar{F}\}$. (Notice that the minimum exists and is positive because $\bar{F}$ is compact.) If the set $\{f' \in \bar{F} : \|f' - f\| = \delta\}$ contains more than one function, the lemma is proved, with $c = f$. If the set contains only one function f_1, we consider the smallest ball that touches $\bar{F}$ at f_1 and some other point, and has its centre on the ray from f_1 that passes through f. That is, we set $c = (1 + \beta)f - \beta f_1$ with the smallest $\beta > 0$ such that some f' in $\bar{F}$ has $\|f' - f_1\| > 0$ and $\|f' - c\| = \|f_1 - c\|$. (The set of suitable points c is represented by the dotted line in Figure 20.1.) We show that such a β exists by showing that, for sufficiently large β, the ball includes either g or h.

Now,

$$
\begin{aligned}
&\|f_1 - c\|^2 - \|g - c\|^2 \\
&= \|f_1 - f\|^2 + \|f - c\|^2 + 2(f_1 - f, f - c) \\
&\quad - \left(\|g - f\|^2 + \|f - c\|^2 + 2(g - f, f - c)\right) \\
&= \|f_1 - f\|^2 - \|g - f\|^2 + 2(f_1 - g, f - c).
\end{aligned}
$$

A similar calculation with h replacing g shows that

$$
\alpha\left(\|f_1 - c\|^2 - \|g - c\|^2\right) + (1 - \alpha)\left(\|f_1 - c\|^2 - \|h - c\|^2\right)
$$

$$= \|f_1 - f\|^2 - \alpha\|g - f\|^2 - (1 - \alpha)\|h - f\|^2 + 2(f_1 - f, f - c)$$
$$= \|f_1 - f\|^2 - \alpha\|g - f\|^2 - (1 - \alpha)\|h - f\|^2 + 2\beta\|f_1 - f\|^2.$$

For sufficiently large β, this is greater than zero, so one of the terms on the left hand side is greater than zero. In that case, c is closer to either g or h than to f_1. □

These lemmas establish that for every non-convex class, we can find a ball in Hilbert space whose interior does not intersect the class, but whose surface touches the class in at least two distinct places. This is enough to show that, by positioning the conditional expectation function $\mathbf{E}(y|x)$ inside the ball approximately equidistant from these two functions, we can make the learning problem as difficult as the problem of estimating the probability of a Bernoulli random variable. That is the idea behind the proof of Theorem 20.2. We omit some details of the proof; they are tedious but straightforward to verify.

Proof (**of Theorem 20.2**) We show that the problem can be reduced to the Bernoulli random variable decision problem described in Lemma 5.1. Let $(\xi_1, \ldots, \xi_m)$ in $\{0,1\}^m$ be a sequence of m i.i.d. random variables with $\Pr(\xi_i = 1) = \alpha$ and $\alpha \in \{\alpha_-, \alpha_+\}$, where $\alpha_- = 1/2 - \gamma/2$ and $\alpha_+ = 1/2 + \gamma/2$. A learning algorithm for F can be used to construct a randomized decision rule (that is, a function A mapping from sequences in $\{0,1\}^m$ to random variables in $\{\alpha_-, \alpha_+\}$) for this problem. The idea is to pick two uniformly bounded functions f_1' and f_2' with certain properties. For an input sequence $(\xi_1, \ldots, \xi_m) \in \{0,1\}^m$, $A(\xi_1, \ldots, \xi_m)$ is computed by first choosing $x_1, \ldots, x_m \in X$ i.i.d. according to the probability distribution P_X. Then, for each i, if $\xi_i = 1$, A passes $(x_i, f_1'(x_i))$ to the learning algorithm, otherwise it passes $(x_i, f_2'(x_i))$. If the learning algorithm returns $f \in F$ with $\|f - f_1\| < \|f - f_2\|$, A returns $1/2 + \gamma/2$, otherwise it returns $1/2 - \gamma/2$.

The functions we construct are illustrated in Figure 20.2. The details are omitted, but it is possible to choose functions f_1' and f_2' so that the following conditions are satisfied.

(i) Define the functions f_1^* and f_2^* as the conditional expectation of the label passed to the learning algorithm when $\alpha = \alpha_+$ and when $\alpha = \alpha_-$ respectively,

$$f_1^* = \alpha_+ f_1' + (1 - \alpha_+) f_2',$$
$$f_2^* = \alpha_- f_1' + (1 - \alpha_-) f_2'.$$

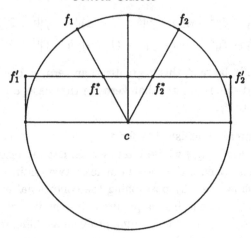

Fig. 20.2. A two-dimensional slice through Hilbert space, illustrating the functions used in the proof of Theorem 20.2.

(ii) We can write

$$f_1^* = pf_1 + (1-p)c,$$
$$f_2^* = pf_2 + (1-p)c,$$

for some constant $0 < p < 1$, and hence when $\alpha = \alpha_+$, f_1 is the function in $\bar{F}$ that gives the minimal error, $\|f_1 - f_1^*\|^2 = \inf_{f \in F} \|f - f_1^*\|^2$, and similarly when $\alpha = \alpha_-$, $\|f_2 - f_2^*\|^2 = \inf_{f \in F} \|f - f_2^*\|^2$.

(iii) For $\epsilon = c_1\gamma$ (where c_1 depends only on the class F), every $f \in F$ satisfies

$$\|f - f_1^*\|^2 < \|f_1 - f_1^*\|^2 + \epsilon \implies \|f - f_1\| < \|f - f_2\|,$$
$$\|f - f_2^*\|^2 < \|f_2 - f_2^*\|^2 + \epsilon \implies \|f - f_2\| < \|f - f_1\|.$$

So, if the learning algorithm returns a function $f \in F$ with $\mathrm{er}_P(f) < \mathrm{opt}_P(F) + \epsilon$, then the decision rule A returns the correct answer for the Bernoulli problem.

These conditions, together with the lower bound of Lemma 5.1, show that to find a function in F with $\mathrm{er}_P(f) < \mathrm{opt}_P(F) + \epsilon$, a learning algorithm requires $\Omega(\ln(1/\delta)/\epsilon^2)$ examples.

To see that the labels passed to the learning algorithm lie in a bounded interval in $\mathbb{R}$, first observe that the functions f_1, f_2 and c are uniformly bounded, and the bound depends only on the function class F. Furthermore, we can write f_1' and f_2' as convex combinations (where the coefficients depend on ϵ) of fixed linear combinations of the functions f_1, f_2, and c. □

As an example, consider the class F_k of two-layer networks, with a linear output unit and k first-layer computation units, each with the standard sigmoid activation function, $\sigma(\alpha) = 1/(1 + e^{-\alpha})$.

Theorem 20.5 *For any $k \in \mathbb{N}$, the class F_k is not convex, even if the input space is $X = \mathbb{R}$.*

As a result, if the parameters are restricted to any compact set, it is immediate that the class F_k is not closure convex. From Theorems 8.13 and 14.1, the pseudo-dimension of F_k is finite, so the sample complexity of this class grows as $\ln(1/\delta)/\epsilon^2$, ignoring log factors.

The proof of Theorem 20.5 uses the following result, which shows that the functions computed by the first-layer units are linearly independent. The proof uses ideas from complex analysis, and can be skipped without loss of continuity.

Lemma 20.6 *Let $\sigma : \mathbb{R} \to \mathbb{R}$ be the standard sigmoid function. Choose $k \in \mathbb{N}$ and $w_1, w_{1,0}, w_2, w_{2,0}, \ldots, w_k, w_{k,0} \in \mathbb{R}$, such that $w_j \neq 0$ and $(w_j, w_{j,0}) \neq \pm(w_{j'}, w_{j',0})$ for all j and all $j' \neq j$. Then the set*

$$\{x \mapsto \sigma(w_j x + w_{j,0}) : 1 \leq j \leq k\} \cup \{x \mapsto 1\}$$

of real functions defined on $\mathbb{R}$ is linearly independent.

Proof We use i to denote the square root of -1. Consider the complex function defined by $\sigma(z) = 1/(1 + e^{-z})$ for $z \in \mathbb{C}$. This function has poles at $\pm n\pi i$ for all odd n, and is analytic in the strip $\{z \in \mathbb{C} : |\Im(z)| < \pi\}$, (where $\Im(z)$ denotes the imaginary part of z). Hence, for a sequence of values of z contained in this strip and converging to πi, the product $(z - \pi i)\sigma(z)$ converges to a constant, the residue of the pole at πi. The proof uses this fact to "isolate" functions and show that the corresponding coefficient is zero.

Now, suppose that $\alpha_0 + \sum_{j=1}^{k} \alpha_j \sigma(w_j x + w_{j,0}) = 0$ for all $x \in \mathbb{R}$. Without loss of generality, assume that $0 < |w_1| \leq |w_2| \leq \cdots \leq |w_k|$. Then if we consider the analytic continuation of this function in the complex plane, it is identically zero on the strip $\{x \in \mathbb{C} : |\Im(w_k x)| < \pi\}$.

It follows that the limit as x approaches $(\pi i - w_{k,0})/w_k$ of

$$\left(x - \frac{(\pi i - w_{k,0})}{w_k}\right)\left(\alpha_0 + \sum_{j=1}^{k}\alpha_j\sigma(w_jx + w_{j,0})\right)$$

is 0. Now, $|w_j| \le |w_k|$ for all $j < k$, and if some $j < k$ has $|w_j| = |w_k|$ then $w_{j,0} \ne w_{k,0}$, so the limit of $w_jx + w_{j,0}$ is in the analytic region of σ. This implies

$$\lim_{x\to(\pi i - w_{k,0})/w_k}\left(x - \frac{(\pi i - w_{k,0})}{w_k}\right)\left(\alpha_0 + \sum_{j=1}^{k}\alpha_j\sigma(w_jx + w_{j,0})\right)$$

$$=\lim_{x\to(\pi i - w_{k,0})/w_k}\left(x - \frac{(\pi i - w_{k,0})}{w_k}\right)\alpha_k\sigma(w_kx + w_{k,0})$$

$$= 0,$$

and hence $\alpha_k = 0$. A similar argument shows that $\alpha_j = 0$ for $j = 1, \ldots, k-1$, and so the set is linearly independent. $\qquad\square$

Proof (of Theorem 20.5) Suppose that the class F_k of functions defined on $X = \mathbb{R}$ is convex. Then choose two functions $f_1, f_2 \in F_k$ defined by

$$f_1(x) = \sum_{j=1}^{k}v_j\sigma(w_jx + w_{j,0}),$$

$$f_2(x) = \sum_{j=k+1}^{2k}v_j\sigma(w_jx + w_{j,0}),$$

and suppose that $v_j \ne 0$, $w_j \ne 0$ and $(w_j, w_{j,0}) \ne \pm(w_{j'}, w_{j',0})$ for all j and all $j' \ne j$. Since F_k is convex, there must be parameters $\tilde{w}_1, \tilde{w}_{1,0}, \ldots, \tilde{w}_k, \tilde{w}_{k,0}$ and $\tilde{v}_1, \ldots, \tilde{v}_k$ such that

$$\sum_{j=1}^{k}\tilde{v}_j\sigma(\tilde{w}_jx + \tilde{w}_{j,0}) - \frac{1}{2}\sum_{j=1}^{2k}v_j\sigma(w_jx + w_{j,0})$$

is identically zero. An easy inductive argument using Lemma 20.6 shows that for all $j \in \{1, \ldots, k\}$ either $\tilde{w}_j = 0$ or there is a $j' \in \{1, \ldots, 2k\}$ such that $(\tilde{w}_j, \tilde{w}_{j,0}) = \pm(w_{j'}, w_{j',0})$. It follows that there are coefficients $v'_0, \ldots, v'_{2k}$, not all zero, for which

$$v'_0 + \sum_{j=1}^{2k}v'_j\sigma(w_jx + w_{j,0})$$

is identically zero, which contradicts Lemma 20.6. Thus F_k is not convex.

□

20.3 Upper Bounds for Convex Classes

The following theorem is a strong converse to Theorem 20.2. It shows that closure convexity leads to a smaller sample complexity.

Theorem 20.7 *Suppose F is a closure convex class of functions that map to the interval $[0, 1]$, A is an approximate-SEM algorithm for F, and $L(z) = A(z, 1/m)$ for $z \in Z^m$. Suppose that the distribution P on $X \times \mathbb{R}$ is such that $|f(x) - y| \leq B$ almost surely. Then*

$$\mathcal{P}^m \left\{ \mathrm{er}_P(L(z)) \geq \inf_{f \in F} \mathrm{er}_P(f) + \epsilon \right\}$$

$$\leq \ 6 \mathcal{N}_1 \left(\frac{\epsilon}{96B^3}, F, 2m \right) \exp \left(-\frac{\epsilon m}{5216B^4} \right).$$

Hence, if F has finite fat-shattering dimension, then L is a learning algorithm with

$$m_L(\epsilon, \delta) = O \left(\frac{B^4}{\epsilon} \left(d \ln^2 \left(\frac{B}{\epsilon} \right) + \ln \left(\frac{1}{\delta} \right) \right) \right),$$

where $d = \mathrm{fat}_F \left(\epsilon/(768B^3) \right)$. Furthermore, if $d = \mathrm{Pdim}(F)$ is finite, L is a learning algorithm, and

$$m_L(\epsilon, \delta) = O \left(\frac{B^4}{\epsilon} \left(d \ln \left(\frac{B}{\epsilon} \right) + \ln \left(\frac{1}{\delta} \right) \right) \right).$$

The classes of functions defined in Section 14.4 (see, for example, Theorems 14.14 and 14.17) are examples of closure convex function classes. In fact, each of these classes can be represented as the convex combination of an arbitrary number of functions from a certain class. For example, a two-layer network with a bound V on the sum of the magnitudes of the output weights can be thought of as a convex combination of an arbitrary number of first-layer unit functions (scaled by the bound V). Clearly, this class is convex, since a convex combination of two such functions is also in the class.

The remainder of this section gives an outline of the proof of Theorem 20.7. The following lemma is the key uniform convergence result. It uses information on the variances of the random variables it considers to give a faster convergence rate than earlier results.

Lemma 20.8 *Fix constants $K_1 > 0$ and $K_2 \geq 1$. Consider a class G of real functions defined on a set Z, and suppose that for every $g \in G$ and every $z \in Z$, $|g(z)| \leq K_1$. Let P be a probability distribution on Z for which $\mathbf{E}g(z) \geq 0$ and $\mathbf{E}(g(z))^2 \leq K_2\mathbf{E}g(z)$ for all g in G. Then for $\epsilon > 0$, $0 < \alpha \leq 1/2$ and $m \geq \max\{4(K_1 + K_2)/(\alpha^2\epsilon), K_1^2/(\alpha^2\epsilon)\}$,*

$$
P^m\left\{\exists g \in G, \frac{\mathbf{E}g - \hat{\mathbf{E}}_zg}{\mathbf{E}g + \epsilon} \geq \alpha\right\}
$$

$$
\leq\ 2\mathcal{N}_1\left(\frac{\alpha\epsilon}{8}, G, 2m\right)\exp\left(-\frac{3\alpha^2\epsilon m}{8K_1 + 324K_2}\right) +
$$

$$
4\mathcal{N}_1\left(\frac{\alpha\epsilon}{8K_1}, G, 2m\right)\exp\left(-\frac{\alpha^2\epsilon m}{4K_1^2}\right),
$$

where $\hat{\mathbf{E}}_zg = \frac{1}{m}\sum_{i=1}^m g(z_i)$ for $z = (z_1, \ldots, z_m)$.

The proof of this lemma is similar to that of Theorem 19.8, except that Bernstein's inequality is used in the place of Hoeffding's inequality (see (1.21) in Appendix 1) to give tighter bounds when the random variables have small variance. To prove Theorem 20.7, we apply this lemma to the class G of excess quadratic loss, $G = \{\ell_f - \ell_{f_a} : f \in F\}$, where f_a is the best approximation in $\bar{F}$ to the conditional expectation $\mathbf{E}(y|x)$, and $\ell_f(x, y) = (y - f(x))^2$ is the quadratic loss function. (We need to allow $f_a \in \bar{F}$ in case the infimum of the quadratic loss is not achieved in F.) The following lemma shows that the class G satisfies the variance condition of Lemma 20.8 if F is closure convex.

Lemma 20.9 *Suppose that a class F of functions mapping from X to $[0, 1]$ is closure convex. If f is in F and P is such that $|y - f(x)| \leq B$ almost surely, then for $f_a \in \bar{F}$ satisfying $\mathbf{E}(y - f_a(x))^2 = \inf_{f \in F} \mathbf{E}(y - f(x))^2$, we have*

$$
\mathbf{E}\left[(y - f(x))^2 - (y - f_a(x))^2\right]^2
$$
$$
\leq\ 4B^2\mathbf{E}(f(x) - f_a(x))^2
$$
$$
\leq\ 4B^2\mathbf{E}\left[(y - f(x))^2 - (y - f_a(x))^2\right].
$$

Proof It is easy to show that

$$
\mathbf{E}\left[(y - f(x))^2 - (y - f_a(x))^2\right]^2
$$
$$
=\ \mathbf{E}\left[(y - f_a(x) + y - f(x))^2(f_a(x) - f(x))^2\right]
$$
$$
\leq\ 4B^2\mathbf{E}(f_a(x) - f(x))^2,
$$

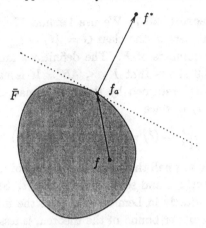

Fig. 20.3. A two-dimensional slice through Hilbert space, illustrating why the inner product between the vectors $f^* - f_a$ and $f_a - f$ is always nonnegative for a convex class $\bar{F}$. See Lemma 20.9.

which is the first inequality. To see the second inequality, notice that

$$
\begin{aligned}
\mathbf{E}\left[(y - f(x))^2 - (y - f_a(x))^2\right] \\
= \mathbf{E}\left[(f_a(x) - f(x))^2 + 2(y - f_a(x))(f_a(x) - f(x))\right] \\
= \|f_a - f\|^2 + 2(f^* - f_a, f_a - f),
\end{aligned}
$$

where $f^*(x) = \mathbf{E}(y|x)$ and, as always, the inner product is defined by $(f, g) = \int f(x)g(x)\,dP(x)$, Hence, we need to show that the inner product $(f^* - f_a, f_a - f)$ is nonnegative. It is clear from Figure 20.3 why this should be true. By definition of f_a, for all $g \in \bar{F}$, $\|f^* - f_a\|^2 \le \|f^* - g\|^2$. In particular, since $\bar{F}$ is convex, we can take $g = \alpha f + (1 - \alpha)f_a$ for $\alpha \in [0, 1]$ to obtain

$$
\|f^* - f_a\|^2 \le \|f^* - f_a + \alpha(f_a - f)\|^2,
$$

from which it follows that

$$
2\alpha(f^* - f_a, f_a - f) \ge -\alpha^2 \|f_a - f\|^2,
$$

and hence

$$
(f^* - f_a, f_a - f) \ge -\frac{\alpha}{2}\|f_a - f\|^2.
$$

But for this to hold for all $\alpha > 0$, $(f^* - f_a, f_a - f)$ must be nonnegative. The second inequality follows. $\qquad\square$

Proof (**of Theorem 20.7**) We use Lemma 17.6 to give bounds on the covering numbers of the class $G = \{\ell_f - \ell_{f_a} : f \in F\}$, in terms of the covering numbers of F. The definitions imply that $K_1 \leq B^2$, and Lemma 20.9 shows that $K_2 \leq 4B^2$. It is easy to see that the function $f = L(z)$ returned by the approximate-SEM algorithm has $\hat{\mathbf{E}}_z(\ell_f - \ell_{f_a}) \leq 1/m$, since

$$\inf_{f \in F} \hat{\mathbf{E}}_z(\ell_f - \ell_{f_a}) \leq \hat{\mathbf{E}}_z(\ell_{f_a} - \ell_{f_a}) = 0.$$

Now, either m is so small that the upper bound of the theorem is larger than one, or $1/m < \epsilon$ and so $\hat{\mathbf{E}}_z(\ell_f - \ell_{f_a}) < \epsilon$. Setting $\alpha = 1/2$ and scaling ϵ appropriately in Lemma 20.8 gives the first inequality of the theorem. (If the upper bound of the theorem is less than one, the condition on m in Lemma 20.8 is satisfied.) The pseudo-dimension and fat-shattering dimension results follow immediately from the covering number bounds of Theorems 18.4 and 18.2.   □

20.4 Remarks

Uniqueness of parameterization

For any parameterized function class, it is natural to ask whether the parameterization is unique; that is, whether for every distinct pair of parameter settings, the corresponding functions are distinct. (This question is important in the design of gradient-based optimization schemes, since non-uniqueness can lead to numerical difficulties.) Lemma 20.6 was used to show that the class of functions computed by two-layer sigmoid networks with a fixed number of first-layer units,

$$F_k = \left\{ x \mapsto \sum_{i=1}^{k} v_i \sigma(w_i \cdot x + w_{i,0}) + v_0 : v_i, w_{i,j} \in \mathbb{R} \right\},$$

is not convex. In fact, it also tells us something about the uniqueness of the parameterization of this function class. Clearly, the parameterization is not unique: if the output weight v_i of first-layer unit i is zero, we can arbitrarily change the values of the input weights $w_i, w_{i,0}$ associated with first-layer unit i, without changing the function computed. Similarly, if we swap the labels of the input weights and output weights associated with two first-layer units, the function computed is unchanged. Also, by exploiting the fact that $\sigma(\alpha) = 1 - \sigma(-\alpha)$, we can negate the input weights and output weight of a first-layer unit and add one to the output bias v_0, and the function computed is unchanged. However,

Lemma 20.6 can be used in an easy inductive proof to show that, apart from these obvious invariances, the parameterization is unique. More precisely, these invariances define equivalence classes over the set of network states, and any two states that are in distinct equivalence classes correspond to different functions.

Restricted model

Section 19.6 discussed the restricted version of the real prediction problem. In that section, we observed that unnatural phenomena can occur unless the amount of information passed to the learning algorithm is limited, for example by observation noise in the labels. The following theorem shows that, for any function class F, if the noise has zero mean, so that the conditional expectation $\mathbf{E}(y|x)$ is in F, the rate of uniform convergence is the same as the fast rate achieved by convex classes (see Theorem 20.7).

Theorem 20.10 *Suppose that F is a class of functions that map to the interval $[0,1]$, $\mathcal{A}$ is an approximate-SEM algorithm for F, $L(z) = \mathcal{A}(z, 1/m)$ for $z \in Z^m$, and the distribution P on $X \times \mathbb{R}$ is such that $|f(x) - y| \leq B$ almost surely and $\mathbf{E}(y|x)$ is in F. Then*

$$P^m \left\{ \text{er}_P(L(z)) \geq \inf_{f \in F} \text{er}_P(f) + \epsilon \right\}$$

$$\leq 6 \mathcal{N}_1 \left(\frac{\epsilon}{96B^3}, F, 2m \right) \exp \left(-\frac{\epsilon m}{5216B^4} \right).$$

Clearly, the sample complexity bounds in Theorem 20.7 that are expressed in terms of pseudo-dimension and fat-shattering function are also valid in this case.

The proof is essentially identical to the proof of Theorem 20.7, except that the last step of the proof of Lemma 20.9, where we used convexity to show that $(f^* - f_a, f_a - f) \geq 0$, is immediate in this case, since $f_a = f^*$.

Subsets of a closure convex set

The proof of Theorem 20.7 implies the following slightly stronger result. This shows that we can achieve the same fast rate of convergence of empirical averages to expected values in the class $G = \{\ell_f - \ell_{f_a} : f \in F\}$, even when the class F is not closure convex, as long as F is contained in a closure convex class F', and the best approximation f_a is chosen from $\bar{F}'$.

Lemma 20.11 *Suppose that F' is a closure convex class of functions that map from X to the interval $[0,1]$, and that $F \subseteq F'$. Let P be a probability distribution on $X \times \mathbb{R}$ for which almost surely $|f(x) - y| \le B$ for all $f \in F'$. Then for $\epsilon > 0$, $0 < \alpha \le 1/2$ and $m \ge \max\{5B^2/(\alpha^2\epsilon), B^4/(\alpha^2\epsilon)\}$,*

$$P^m \left\{ \exists f \in F, \frac{\mathbf{E}g_f - \hat{\mathbf{E}}_z g_f}{\mathbf{E}g_f + \epsilon} \ge \alpha \right\}$$

$$\le 2\mathcal{N}_1\left(\frac{\alpha\epsilon}{16B}, F, 2m\right) \exp\left(-\frac{3\alpha^2\epsilon m}{1304B^2}\right) +$$

$$4\mathcal{N}_1\left(\frac{\alpha\epsilon}{16B^3}, F, 2m\right) \exp\left(-\frac{\alpha^2\epsilon m}{4B^4}\right),$$

where $g_f = \ell_f - \ell_{f_a}$, and $f_a \in \bar{F}'$ satisfies $\mathbf{E}(y - f_a(x)) = \inf_{f \in F'} \mathbf{E}(y - f(x))$.

20.5 Bibliographical Notes

Theorem 20.2 is due to Lee, Bartlett and Williamson (1998) (see also Lee's PhD thesis (1996)). For further information on the definitions and results from topology used in the proof of that theorem (including a proof of the fact that every closed, totally bounded subset of a Hilbert space is compact), see, for example, (Kolmogorov and Fomin, 1975, Chapter 3).

The linear independence argument (Lemma 20.6) used to prove that two-layer sigmoid networks are not convex is due to Albertini, Sontag and Maillot (1993). They were interested in the uniqueness of parameterization of sigmoid networks. There are many related results that apply to a broad family of activation functions of the first-layer units (see (Sussmann, 1992; Fefferman, 1994)).

Theorem 20.7 is also due to Lee et al. (1996) (Lee, 1996). Theorem 20.10 is also in (Lee et al., 1996). This theorem generalizes several earlier results. In particular, it was already known that the faster convergence rate can be achieved in two situations: when the labels are generated by a function in the class and the class has finite pseudo-dimension (see (Haussler, 1992; Pollard, 1995)), and when the conditional expectation is in the class and the class has finite L_∞ covering numbers (see (Barron, 1994; McCaffrey and Gallant, 1994)). In fact, the proof of Lemma 20.8 extends ideas from these proofs, which also used Bernstein's inequality to take advantage of the small variance of the estimates.

21

Other Learning Problems

21.1 Loss Functions in General

In Chapter 16, we made the observation that in the context of learning real function classes, it is inappropriate simply to define the error of a function f as the probability that $f(x) \neq y$ for a randomly drawn (x, y). Instead, we defined the error of f to be the expected value of $(f(x) - y)^2$. The quantity $(f(x) - y)^2$ may be thought of as the 'loss' of f on (x, y). It might have occurred to the reader that there would be other approaches, based on different methods of measuring such a loss. One straightforward variant comes, for instance, when we instead define the error of f to be the expected value of $|f(x) - y|$. In order to discuss the use of different 'loss functions' in some more generality, we shall assume that our function class F maps from a set X into the interval $[0, 1]$, and that the label y is chosen from some set $Y \subseteq \mathbb{R}$. (Usually, as before, Y will be the interval $[0, 1]$.) A *bounded loss function* is a function $\ell : [0, 1] \times Y \to \mathbb{R}^+$, for which there is a $B > 0$ such that $\ell(y_1, y_2) \leq B$ for all $y_1 \in [0, 1]$ and $y_2 \in Y$. In what follows, we shall assume that ℓ maps to the interval $[0, 1]$. Two examples of loss functions are the *quadratic loss* given by $\ell(y, y') = (y - y')^2$, and the *absolute loss* given by $\ell(y, y') = |y - y'|$.

Given a particular loss function ℓ, we define, for $f \in F$, the function $\ell_f : X \times Y \to [0, 1]$ by

$$\ell_f(x, y) = \ell(f(x), y),$$

and we let $\ell_F = \{\ell_f : f \in F\}$ be the corresponding *loss class*. The ℓ-error of $f \in F$ with respect to a distribution P on $Z = X \times Y$ is the expected value of ℓ_f with respect to P,

$$\mathrm{er}_P^\ell(f) = \mathbf{E}\,\ell_f = \mathbf{E}\,\ell(f(x), y),$$

284

and, for $z \in Z^m$, the ℓ-sample error $\hat{\mathrm{er}}_z^\ell(f)$ is

$$\hat{\mathrm{er}}_z^\ell(f) = \frac{1}{m} \sum_{i=1}^m \ell_f(x_i, y_i) = \frac{1}{m} \sum_{i=1}^m \ell(f(x_i), y_i).$$

21.2 Convergence for General Loss Functions

As in Chapter 17, we can bound the rate at which sample errors converge to errors in terms of covering numbers. As is clear from its proof, the symmetrization result of Lemma 17.2 still holds when we replace the error $\mathrm{er}_P(f)$ by $\mathrm{er}_P^\ell(f)$ and the sample error $\hat{\mathrm{er}}_z(f)$ by $\hat{\mathrm{er}}_z^\ell(f)$. Lemma 17.3 and Lemma 17.4 relate the covering numbers of the loss class ℓ_F to those of F itself. The proof of Theorem 17.1 contains the following result, which holds for any loss function.

Theorem 21.1 *Suppose that F is a class of functions mapping into the interval $[0, 1]$, and that $\ell : [0, 1] \times Y \to [0, 1]$ is a loss function. Let P be any probability distribution on $Z = X \times Y$, $0 < \epsilon < 1$, and m any positive integer. Then*

$$P^m \left\{ |\mathrm{er}_P^\ell(h) - \hat{\mathrm{er}}_z^\ell(h)| \geq \epsilon \text{ for some } h \in F \right\}$$

$$\leq 4 \mathcal{N}_1 \left(\frac{\epsilon}{8}, \ell_F, 2m \right) \exp \left(-\frac{\epsilon^2 m}{32} \right).$$

To move from this general 'uniform convergence' result to more useful results, we might want to bound the rate of convergence in terms of the pseudo-dimension or fat-shattering dimension of the class F. One approach would be to use the results of previous chapters to bound the covering numbers of the loss class in terms of its pseudo-dimension or fat-shattering dimension, and then to relate these dimensions to those of F itself. Another approach is to obtain a direct relationship between the covering numbers of ℓ_F and the covering numbers of F and then apply the results of earlier chapters. This is the approach that was taken in Chapter 17 for the quadratic loss function. Lemma 17.6 shows that this approach is suitable for any bounded loss function satisfying a Lipschitz condition. The triangle inequality implies the appropriate Lipschitz condition for the absolute loss, which leads to the following result.

Corollary 21.2 *Let ℓ denote the absolute loss function. Then, for all positive integers k and for all positive numbers ϵ,*

$$\mathcal{N}_1\left(\epsilon, \ell_F, k\right) \le \mathcal{N}_1\left(\epsilon, F, k\right).$$

Having related the covering numbers of ℓ_F to those of F, the rate of convergence of sample errors to errors may be bounded in terms of the dimensions of F. One can, in a manner similar to Chapter 19, devise learning algorithms derived from approximate sample error minimization algorithms (where the sample error is that corresponding to the loss function). The details are omitted in this discussion.

21.3 Learning in Multiple-Output Networks

A general approach

The types of problems considered so far—and the loss functions used— deal with the case in which the set of functions under consideration maps into some subset of the real numbers. But the context of loss functions is more general than this and, in particular, will allow us to analyse learnability for function classes that map into a subset of $\mathbb{R}^s$ where $s > 1$. This encompasses, for instance, the sets of functions computed by neural networks with s output units.

Suppose that F maps from a set X into $\mathbb{R}^s$. How should we define a suitable loss function on F? If we were to use the bounded loss function ℓ for a class mapping into $\mathbb{R}$, then it would seem appropriate to use the loss function $\ell^s : \mathbb{R}^s \times \mathbb{R}^s \to [0, 1]$, defined as follows:

$$\ell^s(y, y') = \frac{1}{s} \sum_{i=1}^{s} \ell(y_i, y_i').$$

For instance, if the class F is the set of functions computed by an s-output neural network, and ℓ is the quadratic loss function, then ℓ^s measures the loss as the average quadratic loss over the outputs,

$$\ell^s(y, y') = \frac{1}{s} \sum_{i=1}^{s} (y_i - y_i')^2.$$

For a given i between 1 and s and $f \in F$, let f_i denote the *projection* of f on the ith co-ordinate, defined by

$$f_i(x) = (f(x))_i,$$

the ith entry of $f(x) \in \mathbb{R}^s$, and let $F_i = \{f_i : f \in F\}$. For $f \in F$, we define $\ell_{f_i} : \mathbb{R}^s \times \mathbb{R}^s \to [0,1]$ by

$$\ell_{f_i}(x,y) = \ell(f_i(x), y_i)$$

and we let $\ell_{F_i} = \{\ell_{f_i} : f \in F\}$. Then we have the following useful relationship between the covering numbers for the loss class ℓ_F^s and the covering numbers for the loss classes ℓ_{F_i}.

Theorem 21.3 *With the above notations,*

$$\mathcal{N}_1\left(\epsilon, \ell_F^s, k\right) \leq \mathcal{N}_1\left(\epsilon, \ell_{F_1}, k\right) \mathcal{N}_1\left(\epsilon, \ell_{F_2}, k\right) \cdots \mathcal{N}_1\left(\epsilon, \ell_{F_s}, k\right)$$

$$= \prod_{i=1}^{s} \mathcal{N}_1\left(\epsilon, \ell_{F_i}, k\right),$$

for all positive integers k and all $\epsilon > 0$.

Proof Let $z \in Z^k$ be given, and suppose that for each i between 1 and s, C_i is an ϵ-cover for $\ell_{F_i|_z}$. Suppose that $f \in F$ and that, for $1 \leq j \leq s$, $v_j \in C_j$ is such that $d_1(\ell_{f_j}(z), v_j) < \epsilon$. (Such a v_j exists since C_j is an ϵ-cover for $\ell_{F_i|_z}$.) Then

$$d_1\left(\ell_f^s(z), \frac{1}{s}\sum_{j=1}^{s} v_j\right) = \frac{1}{k}\sum_{i=1}^{k}\left|\ell_f^s(z_i) - \left(\frac{1}{s}\sum_{j=1}^{s} v_j\right)_i\right|$$

$$= \frac{1}{k}\sum_{i=1}^{k}\left|\frac{1}{s}\sum_{j=1}^{s}\ell_{f_j}(z_i) - \frac{1}{s}\sum_{j=1}^{s}(v_j)_i\right|$$

$$= \frac{1}{ks}\sum_{j=1}^{s}\left(\sum_{i=1}^{k}|\ell_{f_j}(z_i) - (v_j)_i|\right)$$

$$= \frac{1}{s}\sum_{j=1}^{s}d_1\left(\ell_{f_j}(z), v_j\right)$$

$$< \epsilon.$$

It follows that

$$C = \left\{\frac{1}{s}\sum_{j=1}^{s} v_j : v_j \in C_j,\ 1 \leq j \leq s\right\}$$

is an ϵ-cover for ℓ_F^s. Observing that $|C| \leq |C_1||C_2|\cdots|C_s|$, the result follows. $\square$

Relating the covering numbers of the loss spaces ℓ_{F_i} to those of F_i, we obtain the following corollary.

Corollary 21.4 *If ℓ is the quadratic loss function then*

$$\mathcal{N}_1\left(\epsilon, \ell_F^s, k\right) \leq \mathcal{N}_1\left(\frac{\epsilon}{2}, F_1, k\right) \mathcal{N}_1\left(\frac{\epsilon}{2}, F_2, k\right) \cdots \mathcal{N}_1\left(\frac{\epsilon}{2}, F_s, k\right)$$

$$= \prod_{i=1}^{s} \mathcal{N}_1\left(\frac{\epsilon}{2}, F_i, k\right),$$

for all positive integers k and all $\epsilon > 0$. If ℓ is the absolute loss function, then

$$\mathcal{N}_1\left(\epsilon, \ell_F^s, k\right) \leq \prod_{i=1}^{s} \mathcal{N}_1\left(\epsilon, F_i, k\right)$$

for all ϵ and k.

Application to specific neural networks

We can define the sample complexity of a learning algorithm for a class of vector-valued functions in the obvious way, with the loss function ℓ^s replacing the quadratic loss ℓ in Definition 16.1. We can define an approximate-SEM algorithm for such a class by extending Definition 16.4 in the same way. Then combining Theorem 21.1, Corollary 21.4, and the bounds on covering numbers for neural networks given in Chapter 18, and using the same arguments as in the proof of Theorem 19.1 gives upper bounds on the sample complexity of learning algorithms for neural networks with s outputs. These bounds are no more than s times the corresponding upper bounds for a network with one output. For instance, the following results give bounds for networks with few parameters and networks with small parameters. These bounds are a factor of s larger than the corresponding bounds described in Corollaries 19.3 and 19.4.

Theorem 21.5 *Suppose that a feed-forward network N has W weights and k computation units arranged in L layers, where s of these computation units are output units. Suppose that each computation unit has a fixed piecewise-polynomial activation function with p pieces and degree no more than l. Let F be the class of functions computed by N. Then any approximate-SEM algorithm for F can be used to define a learning algorithm for F, and for fixed p and l, the sample complexity of this* *algorithm is*

$$O\left(\frac{1}{\epsilon^2}\left(s\left(WL\ln W + WL^2\right)\ln\left(\frac{1}{\epsilon}\right) + \ln\left(\frac{1}{\delta}\right)\right)\right).$$

Theorem 21.6 *Consider the class of two-layer networks defined in Corollary 14.16, but with s output units. These networks have inputs in $[-A, A]^n$, and each computation unit has a bound V on the sum of the magnitudes of the associated parameters, and an activation function that is bounded and satisfies a Lipschitz constraint. Let F be the class of vector-valued functions computed by this network. Any approximate-SEM algorithm can be used to define a learning algorithm L for F that has sample complexity satisfying*

$$m_L(\epsilon, \delta) = O\left(\frac{1}{\epsilon^2}\left(\frac{sV^6A^2}{\epsilon^4}\ln n + \ln\left(\frac{1}{\delta}\right)\right)\right).$$

21.4 Interpolation Models

Learning and approximate interpolation

In this section, we take a fresh approach to the question of how to extend the basic learning model of Part I for binary classification to models of learning applicable to real-valued function classes. Specifically, we extend in two different ways the restricted model of learning for $\{0, 1\}$-classes. Recall that in this restricted model of learning, we have a class of functions H mapping from X to $\{0, 1\}$, a fixed (but unknown) probability distribution μ on the set X of all possible examples, and some *target function* $t \in H$. The error of $h \in H$ is then the μ-probability that $h(x) \neq t(x)$, and the aim is to guarantee that with high probability (at least $1 - \delta$, in the usual notation), the error is small (at most ϵ). This could be extended to classes of real-valued functions using absolute or quadratic loss functions in the obvious manner, but a different approach can be taken, as follows. Suppose F is a class of functions mapping from X to the interval $[0, 1]$, that t is any function from X to $[0, 1]$ (not necessarily in the class F), and that μ is a probability distribution on X. Let us suppose that we have a learning algorithm that, given a sample $x = (x_1, x_2, \ldots, x_m)$, produces a function $f \in F$ that *approximately interpolates* the target function t on the sample, in the sense that $|f(x_i) - t(x_i)| < \eta$ for $i = 1, 2, \ldots, m$, where η is a small positive number (perhaps prescribed in advance). What performance might we reasonably demand of such an output hypothesis? It is clear that since the values of f match

those of t very closely on each example in the sample, the sample error
with respect to either the absolute or quadratic loss function is small and
therefore we might expect that our algorithm produces hypotheses that,
with high probability, have small absolute or quadratic loss. However,
we might be able to ask for more. To see why, let us concentrate on the
absolute loss. The fact that $|f(x_i) - t(x_i)| < \eta$ for $i = 1, 2, \ldots, m$ means
that the absolute loss on the sample is the average of m numbers, each of
which is less than η, and hence is itself less than η. However, one could
not, conversely, deduce from the fact that the sample error is small that
all the differences $|f(x_i) - t(x_i)|$ were very small: indeed, if all we knew
was that the sample error was at most η, then the only general bound
we could place on each of these differences would be $m\eta$. In this sense,
therefore, the condition that $|f(x_i) - t(x_i)| < \eta$ for each i is *stronger*
than the condition that the sample error is less than η. Consequently, we
might be able to demand more of such functions f. We shall ask, roughly
speaking, that, with high probability the output hypothesis f is such
that the values $f(x)$ and $t(x)$ are close almost everywhere (rather than
simply close 'on average', which would be what the usual approach—a
bound on the error with respect to absolute loss—would entail). We
shall take two distinct approaches to what we mean by 'close almost
everywhere'. First, we shall ask that f approximates to t as well as
it does on the sample, almost everywhere, in the sense that, for all x,
except for those from a set of probability at most ϵ, $|f(x) - t(x)| < \eta$.
This is analogous to the restricted model of learning a binary-valued
class: there, from the fact that h equals t on a sample, we demand that
(with high probability) h equals t almost everywhere on X. To obtain
the present model, we simply replace 'equals' by 'is within η of'.

Definition 21.7 *Suppose that F is a class of functions mapping from
a set X to the interval $[0,1]$. Then F strongly generalizes from approx-
imate interpolation if for any $\epsilon, \delta, \eta \in (0,1)$, there is $m_0(\epsilon, \delta, \eta)$ such
that for $m \geq m_0(\epsilon, \delta, \eta)$, for any probability distribution μ in X and
any function $t : X \to [0,1]$, the following holds: with probability at least
$1 - \delta$, if $x = (x_1, x_2, \ldots, x_m) \in X^m$, then for any $f \in F$ satisfying
$|f(x_i) - t(x_i)| < \eta$ for $i = 1, 2, \ldots, m$, we have*

$$\mu \{x : |f(x) - t(x)| < \eta\} > 1 - \epsilon.$$

We now turn to our second way of thinking about what 'close almost
everywhere' should mean. It might at first appear that strong generalization from interpolation is a rather demanding condition: simply from

the fact that $|f(x_i) - t(x_i)| < \eta$ for each x_i in the sample, we want that (for most samples x), $f(x)$ is at least as accurate an estimate of $t(x)$ on almost all of the examples X. That is, we expect the same high level of approximation almost everywhere. Clearly—and as might have been anticipated from the use of the word 'strongly' in Definition 21.7—we can weaken the definition by requiring a less accurate level of approximation. Specifically, instead of requiring $|f(x) - t(x)| < \eta$ for almost all x, we might instead relax the condition a little and ask that $|f(x) - t(x)| < \eta + \gamma$ for almost all x, where γ is a small, positive, number. In this new model, therefore, with high probability, from approximate interpolation to accuracy η on a sample, we expect to deduce approximation within the slightly larger 'margin' of $\eta + \gamma$ on almost all of X (that is, on all but a subset of X of probability less than ϵ). We arrive at the following definition.

Definition 21.8 *Suppose that F is a class of functions mapping from a set X to the interval $[0,1]$. Then F generalizes from approximate interpolation if for any $\epsilon, \delta, \eta, \gamma \in (0,1)$, there is $m_0(\epsilon, \delta, \eta, \gamma)$ such that for $m \geq m_0(\epsilon, \delta, \eta, \gamma)$, for any probability distribution μ in X and any function $t : X \to [0,1]$, the following holds: with probability at least $1 - \delta$, if $x = (x_1, x_2, \ldots, x_m) \in X^m$, then for any $f \in F$ satisfying $|f(x_i) - t(x_i)| < \eta$ for $i = 1, 2, \ldots, m$, we have*

$$\mu\{x : |f(x) - t(x)| < \eta + \gamma\} > 1 - \epsilon.$$

Characterizing strong generalization from interpolation

The problem of strong generalization from approximate interpolation may be considered within the loss functions framework. To see this, let us fix $\eta \in (0,1)$ and take ℓ^η to be the loss function given by

$$\ell^\eta(y, y') = \begin{cases} 0 & \text{if } |y - y'| < \eta, \\ 1 & \text{otherwise.} \end{cases}$$

Then, *for fixed η*, strong generalization from interpolation follows from convergence of sample errors to errors for the loss function ℓ^η. We know from previous results that we have such convergence if the fat-shattering dimension of the loss class is finite. In this case, the loss class ℓ_F^η is $\{0, 1\}$-valued, so its fat-shattering dimension is precisely its VC-dimension, which depends on η. We therefore find the following scale-sensitive dimension relevant.

Definition 21.9 *For a class of functions mapping from a set X into $[0,1]$, and for $\eta \in (0,1)$, let the* band dimension *be*

$$\text{band}(F,\eta) = \text{VCdim}(\ell_F^\eta).$$

The following characterization of strong generalization from approximate interpolation can be obtained. The proof is omitted (but note that the upper bound on sample complexity follows immediately from Theorem 4.8).

Theorem 21.10 *Let F be a set of functions from X to $[0,1]$. Then F strongly generalizes from approximate interpolation if and only if $\text{band}(F,\eta)$ is finite for all $\eta \in (0,1)$. When this condition holds, a suitable $m_0(\epsilon,\delta,\eta)$ is*

$$\frac{4}{\epsilon}\left(\text{band}(F,\eta)\ln\left(\frac{12}{\epsilon}\right) + \ln\left(\frac{2}{\delta}\right)\right).$$

Furthermore, we must have

$$m_0(\epsilon,\delta,\eta) \geq \max\left(\frac{1-\epsilon}{\epsilon}\ln\left(\frac{1}{\delta}\right), \frac{1}{24\epsilon}(\text{band}(F,\eta) - 2)\right)$$

when $\delta \leq 1/6$ and $\text{band}(F,\eta) \geq 4$.

This theorem provides a characterization of strong generalization form approximate interpolation in terms of the the scale-sensitive band dimension, and furthermore it shows that the sample size m_0 is quantified fairly precisely by this dimension. However, the band dimension is not one of the standard dimensions we have encountered thus far. The following result relates it to the more familiar pseudo-dimension. The (non-trivial, technical) proof is omitted.

Theorem 21.11 *Suppose that F is a class of functions mapping into $[0,1]$. Then F has finite band dimension if and only if it has finite pseudo-dimension. Furthermore, for all $\eta \in (0,1)$,*

$$\frac{\text{Pdim}(F)}{10\ln(2/\eta)} \leq \text{band}(F,\gamma) \leq 15\,\text{Pdim}(F).$$

We therefore have the following, more appealing, characterization of strong generalization from approximate interpolation.

Theorem 21.12
Suppose that F is a set of functions from a set X to $[0,1]$. Then F

*strongly generalizes from approximate interpolation if and only if F has
finite pseudo-dimension. Furthermore, if F has finite pseudo-dimension*
Pdim(F) *then a sufficient sample length function for generalization from
approximate interpolation is*

$$m_0(\epsilon,\delta,\eta) = \frac{4}{\epsilon}\left(15\,\mathrm{Pdim}(F)\ln\left(\frac{12}{\epsilon}\right)+\ln\left(\frac{2}{\delta}\right)\right),$$

and any suitable sample length function must satisfy

$$m_0(\epsilon,\delta,\eta) \geq \frac{1}{24\epsilon}\left(\frac{\mathrm{Pdim}(F)}{2\ln(2/\eta)}-1+6\ln\left(\frac{1}{\delta}\right)\right)$$

for all $\eta > 0$, $\epsilon \in (0,1/2)$ and $\delta \in (0,1)$.

Thus, although it looks like a very difficult definition to satisfy, strong
generalization from approximate interpolation holds for all classes of
finite pseudo-dimension. The fact that finite pseudo-dimension is *necessary* is in contrast to the learnability results of previous chapters, where
it is enough to have finite fat-shattering dimension.

Characterizing generalization from interpolation

Since finite pseudo-dimension is a sufficient condition for strong generalization from approximate interpolation, it is also a sufficient condition for (the weaker) generalization from approximate interpolation. It
should be noted that in analysing generalization from interpolation, we
cannot express the problem within the loss functions framework, since
the 'sample-based' condition $|f(x_i) - t(x_i)| < \eta$ is a statement about
the sample error for the loss function ℓ^η (explicitly, the sample error
with respect to ℓ^η is zero), whereas the required approximation condi-
tion, $\mu\{x : |f(x) - t(x)| < \eta + \gamma\}$ is a statement about the *different* loss
function $\ell^{\eta+\gamma}$. It is, however, possible to obtain the following 'convergence result'.

Theorem 21.13 *Suppose that F is a class of functions mapping from a
domain X to the real interval [0, 1] and that F has finite fat-shattering
dimension. Let t be any function from X to $\mathbb{R}$ and let $\gamma,\eta,\epsilon \in (0,1)$.
Let μ be any probability distribution on X and m any positive integer.
Define P_{bad} to be the probability of $x \in X^m$ for which there exists $f \in F$
with*

$$\mu\{x \in X : |f(x) - t(x)| \geq \eta + \gamma\} > \epsilon$$

and

$$|f(x_i) - t(x_i)| < \eta, (1 \leq i \leq m).$$

Then

$$P_{\text{bad}} < 2 \mathcal{N}_\infty \left(\frac{\gamma}{2}, F, 2m \right) 2^{-\epsilon m/2}.$$

We then have the following characterization of generalization from approximate interpolation. The sufficiency follows from Theorem 21.13; the proof of necessity is omitted.

Theorem 21.14 *Suppose that F is a class of functions mapping into $[0,1]$. Then F generalizes from approximate interpolation if and only if F has finite fat-shattering dimension. Furthermore, there is a constant c such that if F has finite fat-shattering dimension, then a sufficient sample length for generalization from approximate interpolation is*

$$m_0(\epsilon, \delta, \gamma, \eta) = \frac{c}{\epsilon} \left(\ln \left(\frac{1}{\delta} \right) + \text{fat}_F \left(\frac{\gamma}{8} \right) \ln^2 \left(\frac{\text{fat}_F (\gamma/8)}{\gamma \epsilon} \right) \right).$$

It should be noted that for generalization from interpolation, it suffices to have finite fat-shattering dimension, whereas the stronger condition of finite pseudo-dimension must hold for strong generalization. The two models therefore turn out to be quite different.

A result on large margin classification

It is useful to compare some earlier results with those just given. In particular, it is possible to use our results on generalization from approximate interpolation to derive a result useful for a restricted form of the classification learning model of Part 2. Recall that in this framework, we consider a real function class F that is used for classification. For a probability distribution P on $X \times \{0,1\}$, a positive number γ, and $f \in F$, we define

$$\text{er}_P^\gamma(f) = P\left\{ (x,y) : \text{margin}(f(x), y) < \gamma \right\}.$$

In Chapter 10, we proved the following convergence result: with the usual notation,

$$P^m \left\{ \text{some } f \text{ in } F \text{ has } \text{er}_P(f) \geq \hat{\text{er}}_z^\gamma(f) + \epsilon \right\}$$
$$\leq 2 \mathcal{N}_\infty \left(\frac{\gamma}{2}, F, 2m \right) \exp \left(-\frac{\epsilon^2 m}{8} \right).$$

The following result is similar to this, but is more specialized in two ways: first, it concerns only distributions P that correspond to a target function $t : X \to \{0,1\}$ together with a probability distribution μ on X (rather than some arbitrary distribution on $X \times \{0,1\}$); secondly, it bounds the probability that $\mathrm{er}_P(f) \geq \epsilon$ *and* $\hat{\mathrm{er}}_z^\gamma(f) = 0$, rather than providing a bound on the probability that these two quantities differ by a certain amount (where the latter can be non-zero).

Theorem 21.15 *Suppose that F is a set of functions mapping from a set X to $[0,1]$, that $t : X \to \{0,1\}$, and that μ is a probability distribution on X. Let $\gamma \in (0,1/2]$ and $\epsilon \in (0,1)$. For $f \in F$, define $\mathrm{er}_\mu(f,t)$ to be $\mu\{x : \mathrm{sgn}(f(x) - 1/2) \neq t(x)\}$, the error incurred in using the function f for binary classification. Let P_{bad} be the probability of $x \in X^m$ for which some $f \in F$ has $\mathrm{margin}(f(x_i), t(x_i)) > \gamma$ for $i = 1,\dots,m$, but $\mathrm{er}_\mu(f,t) \geq \epsilon$. Then $P_{\mathrm{bad}} \leq 2\mathcal{N}_\infty\left(\gamma/2, F, 2m\right) 2^{-\epsilon m/2}$.*

Proof To prove this, we use the result of Theorem 21.13, which states that for $\alpha, \gamma \in (0,1)$, if $Q \subseteq X^m$ is the set of x for which there exists $f \in F$ with

$$\mu\{x \in X : |f(x) - t(x)| \geq \alpha + \gamma\} > \epsilon$$

and

$$|f(x_i) - t(x_i)| < \alpha, (1 \leq i \leq m),$$

then $\mu^m(Q) < 2\mathcal{N}_\infty\left(\gamma/2, F, 2m\right) 2^{-\epsilon m/2}$. For a fixed γ, we take $\alpha = 1/2 - \gamma$. Then $\alpha + \gamma = 1/2$ and $|f(x) - t(x)| < \alpha + \gamma$ if and only if $\mathrm{sgn}(f(x) - 1/2) = t(x)$. Therefore,

$$\mu\{x \in X : |f(x) - t(x)| \geq \alpha + \gamma\} = \mathrm{er}_\mu(f,t).$$

Furthermore, $|f(x_i) - t(x_i)| < \alpha = 1/2 - \gamma$ is equivalent to

$$\mathrm{margin}(f(x_i), t(x_i)) > \gamma,$$

so it follows that Q is the set of x for which there is $f \in F$ with $\mathrm{er}_\mu(f,t) \geq \epsilon$ and such that $\mathrm{margin}(f(x_i), t(x_i)) > \gamma$ for $i = 1, 2, \dots, m$. The result follows immediately from this. $\square$

21.5 Remarks

Theorem 21.1 gives an upper bound on estimation error that decreases no faster than $1/\sqrt{m}$, with any suitable loss function. In Chapter 20, we proved faster convergence rates for convex function classes with quadratic loss. Unfortunately, this result relied on properties of Hilbert spaces that do not extend to arbitrary loss functions. The following example shows that simple convex classes can exhibit this slow convergence rate with the absolute loss function.

Example 21.16 *Consider the problem of learning the (convex) class of all $[0, 1]$-valued functions defined on a single point x, with respect to the absolute loss. This problem is equivalent to estimating a random $y \in [0, 1]$ by choosing a number $\hat{y} \in [0, 1]$ that approximately minimizes the expected absolute difference $\mathbf{E}|\hat{y} - y|$. Let the probability distribution of y satisfy $\Pr(y = 0) = \alpha$ and $\Pr(y = 1) = 1 - \alpha$, where α is chosen uniformly at random from the set $\{1/2 \pm \epsilon\}$. It is easy to see that unless $\hat{y}$ is to the same side of $1/2$ as α, then $\mathbf{E}|\hat{y} - y|$ is at least ϵ bigger than its optimal value. But Lemma 5.1 shows that this requires $\Omega((1/\epsilon^2)\ln(1/\delta))$ examples.*

21.6 Bibliographical Notes

The powerful loss function framework described in Section 21.1 is presented, for example, in (Vapnik, 1989). Haussler (1992) gives a lucid decision-theoretic description of this approach.

The results on interpolation and approximate interpolation are from (Anthony and Shawe-Taylor, 1994; Anthony and Bartlett, 1995; Anthony, Bartlett, Ishai and Shawe-Taylor, 1996). The connection between approximate interpolation and real classification learning was observed in (Shawe-Taylor et al., 1998).

We conjecture that Theorem 21.5, the sample complexity bound for multiple output networks, can be improved, since the proof of that theorem ignores the fact that the functions computed by different network outputs share common computation units. Certainly the result cannot be improved significantly for the case of a single network output. However it seems likely that the dependence on s given in that theorem is too strong. This conjecture is motivated by an analogous result when the network output units are linear threshold units and the loss function is the discrete loss (for which $\ell(y_1, y_2)$ takes the value 0 when $y_1 = y_2$, and 1 otherwise); see (Natarajan, 1989; Shawe-Taylor and Anthony, 1991; Anthony and Shawe-Taylor, 1993b).

Part four
Algorithmics

22
Efficient Learning

22.1 Introduction

In this part of the book, we turn our attention to aspects of the *time complexity*, or *computational complexity* of learning. Until now we have discussed only the sample complexity of learning, and we have been using the phrase 'learning algorithm' without any reference to algorithmics. But issues of running time are crucial. If a learning algorithm is to be of practical value, it must, first, be possible to implement the learning algorithm on a computer; that is, it must be *computable* and therefore, in a real sense, an *algorithm*, not merely a function. Furthermore, it should be possible to produce a good output hypothesis 'quickly'.

One subtlety that we have not so far explicitly dealt with is that a practical learning algorithm does not really output a hypothesis; rather, it outputs a *representation* of a hypothesis. In the context of neural networks, such a representation consists of a state of the network; that is, an assignment of weights and thresholds. In studying the computational complexity of a learning algorithm, one therefore might take into account the 'complexity' of the representation output by the learning algorithm. However, this will not be necessary in the approach taken here. For convenience, we shall continue to use notation suggesting that the output of a learning algorithm is a function from a class of hypotheses, but the reader should be aware that, formally, the output is a representation of such a function.

22.2 Graded Function Classes

Clearly, we have to be more precise about what we mean by a learning algorithm working 'quickly'. Suppose we have a learning algorithm for a general class of neural networks, such as, say, the class of perceptrons. If the algorithm is to be useful, then the time taken to learn using

299

the algorithm should scale fairly modestly with the size of the network, which in this case can be measured by the number of inputs. Otherwise the algorithm may work quickly enough on the smallest networks but impossibly slowly on the larger networks and would, arguably, be useful only for 'toy problems'.

To formalize this notion of 'scaling' with respect to the number of inputs, we use the idea of a *graded* function class. First, we assume that X_n is a subset of $\mathbb{R}^n$: usually, X_n will equal $\mathbb{R}^n$ or $\{0,1\}^n$. (In the above example, X_n would be the set of all possible inputs x to the n-input network in the class.) Furthermore, F_n will denote a set of real functions defined on X_n. (In the above example, this would be the set of functions computable by the network with n inputs.) In many cases, F_n will map just into $\{0,1\}$, in which case we call it a *binary* function class. (We shall often use the notation H_n for such classes.) Given a function class F_n for each positive integer n, we say that the union $F = \bigcup F_n$ is a *graded* function class. Using the graded function class framework will enable us to introduce some generality in our description of learning algorithms and, furthermore, it will allow us to address issues of scaling for learning algorithms.

Suppose that we have a family of neural networks $\{N_n\}$, one for each positive integer n, where N_n is a network on n inputs. Here, the appropriate graded function class is $F = \bigcup F_n$ where F_n is the set of functions computable by network N_n. We may want to consider what might be termed a 'general' learning algorithm for the class. This is an algorithm that works in essentially the same manner on each of the networks N_n. For example, as we shall demonstrate shortly, there is a learning algorithm for the perceptron that operates by solving a linear program. The only essential difference between its actions on, say, the perceptron with 17 inputs and the one with 25 inputs lies in the size of the linear program; the *method* is fundamentally the same.

To formalize these notions, we need to define what we mean by a learning algorithm for a graded function class. It is easy to modify the definitions of a learning algorithm for a binary function class in the model of Part 1, and of a learning algorithm for a real function class in the model of Part 3. (We shall not discuss the classification learning model of Part 2.) For a graded binary function class $H = \bigcup H_n$, we let $Z_n = X_n \times \{0,1\}$. Then a learning algorithm for H is a mapping

$$L : \bigcup_{n=1}^{\infty} \bigcup_{m=1}^{\infty} Z_n^m \to \bigcup_{n=1}^{\infty} H_n$$

such that if $z \in Z_n^m$, then $L(z) \in H_n$, and for each n, L is a learning algorithm for H_n, in the sense of Definition 2.1.

The only difference between this definition and the basic notion of a learning algorithm for an ungraded class is that we have now encapsulated some sense of the 'generality' of the algorithm in its action over all the H_n. We define a learning algorithm for a graded real function class $F = \bigcup F_n$ in the same way. It is now possible to study how the 'complexity' of a learning algorithm scales with n, and this is one of the topics of the next section.

22.3 Efficient Learning

We now assume that learning algorithms are algorithms in the proper sense (that is, that they are computable functions). We shall implicitly use the 'bit cost' model of computation, in which it is assumed that operations are performed on a fixed number of bits in one unit of time, and that a single bit can be read or written in one unit of time. Thus, even though we shall consider real-valued inputs and outputs, it is assumed that those values are represented using a finite number of bits. We would like the computation time of learning algorithms to grow only slowly as the difficulty of the problem is increased. For instance, we shall require that the computation time is polynomial in the input size. By this we mean that as the number of input bits increases, the computation time is no more than some fixed polynomial function of that number. For convenience, we shall assume that the number of bits used to represent each real number in the input is fixed, and consider how the computation time grows with the number of real number inputs.

Suppose that L is a learning algorithm for a graded real function class $F = \bigcup F_n$. (The same comments apply in the special case that F is a graded binary function class.) An input to L is a training sample, which consists of m labelled real vectors of length n (that is, m elements of $\mathbb{R}^n$). It would be possible to use the total number of binary digits in the input as the measure of input size, but there is some advantage in keeping track of m and n separately and assuming that each real number is represented with a constant number of bits. We shall use the notation $R_L(m, n)$ to denote the worst-case running time of L on a training sample of m labelled examples, each of 'size' n. Thus, $R_L(m, n)$ is the maximum number of computation steps required for L to produce an output hypothesis in F_n given a sample in Z_n^m. (Notice that this notation hides the dependence of running time on the precision of the real number inputs.) Clearly, n is not the only parameter with which the running time of the learning procedure as a whole should be allowed to vary, since decreasing either the confidence parameter δ or the accuracy parameter ϵ makes the learning task more difficult. The total time taken to produce an output hypothesis of accuracy ϵ, with confidence given by δ, should vary in some appropriate way as $1/\delta$ and $1/\epsilon$ increase, but we should not want a decrease in either ϵ or δ to result in too dramatic an increase in the time taken for the learning task. We could simply ask that the running time increases polynomially with $1/\delta$ and $1/\epsilon$, but it is reasonable for us to be more stringent about the dependence on $1/\delta$ for the following reason. If the length of training sample input to an efficient learning algorithm is doubled, we might expect the probability that the output hypothesis is 'bad' to be approximately squared. Motivated by this, we shall ask that the running time of a learning algorithm L be polynomial in m, and that the sample complexity $m_L(n, \delta, \epsilon)$ depend polynomially on $\ln(1/\delta)$. In the case of the accuracy parameter, we shall ask that the running time of L be polynomial in m, and that its sample complexity depend polynomially on $1/\epsilon$. If both these conditions hold, then the running time required to produce a 'good' output hypothesis is polynomial in n, $\ln(1/\delta)$ and $1/\epsilon$.

Combining these three notions of efficiency together, we can now formally define what we mean by an *efficient learning algorithm* for a graded function class.

Definition 22.1 *Let* $F = \bigcup F_n$ *be a graded class of functions and suppose that* L *is a learning algorithm for* F. *We say that* L *is* efficient *if:*

(i) *the worst-case running time* $R_L(m, n)$ *of* L *on samples* $z \in Z_n^m$ *is polynomial in* m *and* n, *and*

(ii) *the sample complexity* $m_L(n, \epsilon, \delta)$ *of* L *on* F_n *is polynomial in* $n, 1/\epsilon$ *and* $\ln(1/\delta)$.

22.4 General Classes of Efficient Learning Algorithms

In earlier chapters, much emphasis was placed on SEM (sample error minimization) and approximate-SEM algorithms. One can define a SEM algorithm for a graded binary class H in the obvious manner, as an algorithm that given any sample $z \in Z_n^m$, returns a function $h \in H_n$ that has minimal sample error $\hat{er}_z(h)$ on z. An approximate-SEM algorithm for a graded real function class $F = \bigcup F_n$ takes as input $z \in Z_n^m$ and $\epsilon \in (0,1)$ and returns $f \in F_n$ such that $\hat{\text{er}}_z(f) < \inf_{g \in F_n} \hat{\text{er}}_z(g) + \epsilon$. As we noted earlier, it will not be possible in general to have a SEM algorithm for a real function class, as the infimum may not be a minimum. It is quite possible to consider approximate-SEM algorithms for binary function classes, but given an approximate-SEM algorithm $\mathcal{A}$ for such a class, we can readily construct a SEM algorithm. To see this, suppose we are given a sample $z \in Z_n^m$ of length m, and that we take ϵ in the input to the approximate-SEM algorithm to be $1/m$. Then, the algorithm returns $h \in H_n$ such that

$$\hat{\text{er}}_z(h) < \inf_{g \in H_n} \hat{\text{er}}_z(g) + \frac{1}{m}.$$

But, since $\hat{\text{er}}_z(h)$ is $1/m$ times the number of z_i on which h is 'wrong', this means that

$$\hat{\text{er}}_z(h) = \inf_{g \in H_n} \hat{\text{er}}_z(g).$$

In other words, given a sample z, the algorithm L given by $L(z) = \mathcal{A}(z, 1/m)$, for z of length m, is a SEM algorithm. Thus the notion of an approximate-SEM algorithm is crucial only for real function classes.

The following results show that the rate of growth with n of the 'expressive power'—which, for a binary class, is the VC-dimension and, for a real class is the fat-shattering dimension—determines the sample complexity of learning algorithms. These theorems are immediate consequences of the corresponding results for each subclass, H_n (Theorems 4.2 and 5.2) or F_n (Theorems 19.1 and 19.5).

Theorem 22.2 *Let $H = \bigcup H_n$ be a graded binary function class.*

(i) *If $\text{VCdim}(H_n)$ is polynomial in n, then any SEM algorithm for H is a learning algorithm with sample complexity $m_L(n, \epsilon, \delta)$ polynomial in $n, 1/\epsilon$ and $\ln(1/\delta)$.*

(ii) *If there is an efficient learning algorithm for H, then $\text{VCdim}(H_n)$ is polynomial in n.*

Theorem 22.3 *Let $F = \bigcup F_n$ be a graded real function class.*

(i) *If the fat-shattering dimension $\text{fat}_{F_n}(\alpha)$ is polynomial in n and $1/\alpha$, and L is the learning algorithm based on any approximate-SEM algorithm $\mathcal{A}$ (as in Theorem 19.1), then L has sample complexity $m_L(n, \epsilon, \delta)$ polynomial in n, $1/\epsilon$ and $\ln(1/\delta)$.*

(ii) *If there is an efficient learning algorithm for F, then $\mathrm{fat}_{F_n}(\alpha)$ is polynomial in n and $1/\alpha$.*

We now turn our attention to the running time of SEM algorithms and approximate-SEM algorithms. Having seen that, in many circumstances, such algorithms yield learning algorithms, we now investigate the *efficiency* of these derived learning algorithms. Theorem 22.5 below shows that the following definition of efficiency of SEM and approximate-SEM algorithms is sufficient.

Definition 22.4 *An* efficient approximate-SEM algorithm *for the graded real function class $F = \bigcup F_n$ is an algorithm that takes as input $z \in Z_n^m$ and $\epsilon \in (0,1)$ and, in time polynomial in m, n and $1/\epsilon$, produces an output hypothesis $f \in F_n$ such that*

$$\hat{\mathrm{er}}_z(f) < \inf_{g \in F_n} \hat{\mathrm{er}}_z(g) + \epsilon.$$

An efficient SEM algorithm *for the graded binary function class $H = \bigcup H_n$ is an algorithm that takes as input $z \in Z_n^m$ and, in time polynomial in m and n, returns $h \in H_n$ such that*

$$\hat{\mathrm{er}}_z(h) = \min_{g \in H_n} \hat{\mathrm{er}}_z(g).$$

Theorem 22.5 *(i) Suppose that $H = \bigcup H_n$ is a graded binary function class and that $\mathrm{VCdim}(H_n)$ is polynomial in n. Then, any efficient SEM algorithm for H is an efficient learning algorithm for H.*

(ii) Suppose that $F = \bigcup F_n$ is a graded real function class and that $\mathrm{fat}_{F_n}(\alpha)$ is polynomial in n and $1/\alpha$. Then any learning algorithm for F based on an efficient approximate-SEM algorithm is efficient.

Proof We prove the second part of the theorem, the proof of the first part being similar (and more straightforward). Suppose $\mathcal{A}$ is an efficient approximate-SEM algorithm for the graded real class $F = \bigcup F_n$ and that $\mathrm{fat}_{F_n}(\alpha)$ is polynomial in n and $1/\alpha$. Let L be the learning algorithm based on $\mathcal{A}$ (as described in Theorem 19.1). Theorem 22.3 shows that the sample complexity $m_L(n, \epsilon, \delta)$ is polynomial in $n, 1/\epsilon$ and $\ln(1/\delta)$. Given $z \in Z_n^m$, L computes $\mathcal{A}(z, \epsilon_0)$, where $\epsilon_0 = 16/\sqrt{m}$. Since $\mathcal{A}$ is efficient, the time taken to produce $\mathcal{A}(z, \epsilon_0)$ is polynomial in m, n and $1/\epsilon_0 = \sqrt{m}/16$; thus, $R_L(m, n)$ is polynomial in m and n. $\square$

22.5 Efficient Learning in the Restricted Model

We now briefly describe how the preceding approach can be modified to enable us to discuss efficient learnability of binary classes in the *restricted model* of learning. Suppose that we have, as usual, a graded binary function class $H = \bigcup H_n$, where H_n is defined on some subset X_n of $\mathbb{R}^n$. Recall that, in the restricted model of learning, rather than having labelled examples generated according to some distribution on one of the sets $Z_n = X_n \times \{0,1\}$, we instead have some *target function t*, belonging to H_n, together with a probability distribution μ on X_n. The *error* of $h \in H_n$ with respect to t and μ is then defined to be

$$\mathrm{er}_\mu(h,t) = \mu\left\{x \in X_n : h(x) \neq t(x)\right\}.$$

The training samples (rather than being arbitrary members of Z_n^m) are of the form

$$z = ((x_1, t(x_1)), (x_2, t(x_2)), \ldots, (x_m, t(x_m))),$$

which we call the training sample corresponding to x and t. A learning algorithm L for the graded class (in the restricted model) maps from such training samples to H, and satisfies the following conditions for $z \in Z_n^m$.

  (i) $L(z) \in H_n$, and
  (ii) L is a learning algorithm for H_n (in the restricted model).

As described earlier, the restricted model may be regarded as a straightforward special case of the standard model of learning of Part 1. In the restricted model, a learning algorithm is said to be *efficient* if its sample complexity $m_L(n, \epsilon, \delta)$ (the least sufficient value of $m_0(n, \epsilon, \delta)$ for learning) is polynomial in $n, 1/\epsilon$ and $\ln(1/\delta)$, and its worst-case running time $R_L(m, n)$ on training samples of length m for target functions in H_n, is polynomial in m and n.

Given that the training samples arise from functions in H, for any training sample z in the restricted model, there will always be a function in H with zero sample error on z; in other words, there will always be some function h *consistent* with z. *Efficient consistent-hypothesis-finders* are the natural counterpart in the restricted model to the SEM algorithms for general learning of binary classes.

Definition 22.6 *An algorithm L is an* efficient consistent-hypothesis-finder *for the graded binary class $H = \bigcup H_n$ if, given any training sample*

z of length m for a target function in H_n, L halts in time polynomial in m and n and returns $h = L(z) \in H_n$ such that $\hat{\mathrm{er}}_z(h) = 0$.

Theorem 22.7 *Suppose that $H = \bigcup H_n$ is a binary graded function class and that $\mathrm{VCdim}(H_n)$ is polynomial in n. Then any algorithm that is an efficient consistent-hypothesis-finder for H is an efficient learning algorithm for H.*

Proof Suppose L is an efficient consistent-hypothesis-finder for H. Then, by Theorem 4.8, L is a learning algorithm for H and its sample complexity on H_n is bounded by

$$\frac{4}{\epsilon}\left(\mathrm{VCdim}(H_n)\ln\left(\frac{12}{\epsilon}\right) + \ln\left(\frac{2}{\delta}\right)\right),$$

which is polynomial in n, $1/\epsilon$ and $\ln(1/\delta)$. Furthermore, from the definition, its worst-case running time $R_L(m,n)$ is polynomial. $\qquad\square$

22.6 Bibliographical Notes

Valiant (1984b; 1984a), in describing the model of learning that came to be known as the 'probably approximately correct' model (and which we have termed the restricted model), placed great emphasis on considerations of computational complexity. The efficiency of learning in the restricted model was further investigated by Blumer et al. (1989). (See also (Haussler et al., 1991).) The definitions we give of efficient learning algorithms, where the running time of the algorithm and its sample complexity are separated, are standard or based on standard definitions: other definitions are possible, but they are all, in a sense, equivalent; see (Haussler et al., 1991) for the case of the restricted model. For a detailed treatment of the bit cost model of computing, see (Aho and Ullman, 1992).

23

Learning as Optimization

23.1 Introduction

The previous chapter demonstrated that efficient SEM and approximate-SEM algorithms for graded classes $F = \bigcup F_n$ give rise to efficient learning algorithms, provided the expressive power of F_n grows polynomially with n (in, respectively, the binary classification and real prediction learning models). In this chapter we show that *randomized* SEM and approximate-SEM algorithms suffice, and that a converse result then holds: if efficient learning is possible then there must exist an efficient randomized approximate-SEM algorithm. (Hence, for the case of a binary function class, there must be an efficient randomized SEM algorithm.) This will establish that, in both models of learning, efficient learning is intimately related to the optimization problem of finding a hypothesis with small sample error.

23.2 Randomized Algorithms

For our purposes, a *randomized* algorithm has available to it a random number generator that produces a sequence of independent, uniformly distributed bits. We shall assume that examining one bit of this random sequence takes one unit of time. (It is sometimes convenient to assume that the algorithm has access to a sequence of independent uniformly distributed integers in the set $\{0, 1, \ldots, I\}$, for some $I \geq 1$; it is easy to construct such a sequence from a sequence of random bits.) The randomized algorithm $\mathcal{A}$ uses these random bits as part of its input, but it is useful to think of this input as somehow 'internal' to the algorithm, and to think of the algorithm as defining a mapping from an 'external' input to a probability distribution over outputs. The computation carried out by the algorithm is, of course, determined by its input, so that, in particular, it depends on the particular sequence produced by the random number generator, as well as on the 'external' input. When we speak of the 'probability' that A has a given outcome on an (external) input x, we mean the probability that the stream of random numbers gives rise to that outcome when the external input to the algorithm is x.

The following definition is really two definitions in one. It describes both what is meant by an efficient randomized learning algorithm for a graded binary class in the model of Part 1, and for a graded real function class in the model of Part 3. In order to simplify the notation, we shall let $Z_n = X_n \times \{0,1\}$ if $H = \bigcup H_n$ is a graded binary function class, and $Z_n = X_n \times [0,1]$ if $F = \bigcup F_n$ is a graded class of real functions. Generally, it will be clear from the context which of these is intended. A training sample of length m is then an element of Z_n^m for some positive integer n. Notice that the meaning of the input space Z_n and the measure of error are different in the two cases.

Definition 23.1 *With the above notation, a* randomized learning algorithm *for the graded class $F = \bigcup F_n$ is a mapping*

$$L : \{0,1\}^* \times \bigcup_{n=1}^{\infty} \bigcup_{m=1}^{\infty} Z_n^m \to \bigcup_{n=1}^{\infty} F_n$$

such that if $z \in Z_n^m$, then $L(b,z) \in F_n$, and:

- *given any $\epsilon \in (0,1)$,*
- *given any $\delta \in (0,1)$,*
- *for any positive integer n,*

there is an integer $m_0(n,\epsilon,\delta)$ such that if $m \geq m_0(n,\epsilon,\delta)$ then

- *for any probability distribution P on Z_n,*

if z is a training sample of length m, drawn randomly according to the product probability distribution P^m, and b is a sequence of independent, uniformly chosen bits, then with probability at least $1 - \delta$, the hypothesis $L(z)$ output by L satisfies

$$\mathrm{er}_P(L(b,z)) < \mathrm{opt}_P(F_n) + \epsilon.$$

That is, for $m \geq m_0(n,\epsilon,\delta)$,

$$\mathbf{E}P^m\{\mathrm{er}_P(L(b,z)) < \mathrm{opt}_P(F_n) + \epsilon\} \geq 1 - \delta.$$

We say that $F = \bigcup F_n$ is learnable *if there is a learning algorithm for F.*

We shall be interested in randomized SEM and approximate-SEM algorithms.

Definition 23.2 *(i) A randomized algorithm $\mathcal{A}$ is an* efficient randomized SEM *algorithm for the graded binary function class $H = \bigcup H_n$ if given any $z \in Z_n^m$, $\mathcal{A}$ halts in time polynomial in n and m and outputs $h \in H_n$ which, with probability at least $1/2$, satisfies*

$$\hat{\mathrm{er}}_z(h) = \min_{g \in H_n} \hat{\mathrm{er}}_z(g).$$

(ii) A randomized algorithm $\mathcal{A}$ is an efficient randomized approximate-SEM *algorithm for the graded function class $F = \bigcup F_n$ if the following holds: given any $z \in Z_n^m$, and any $\epsilon \in (0,1)$, $\mathcal{A}$ halts in time polynomial in n, m and $1/\epsilon$ and outputs $f \in F_n$ which, with probability at least $1/2$, satisfies*

$$\hat{\mathrm{er}}_z(f) < \inf_{g \in F_n} \hat{\mathrm{er}}_z(g) + \epsilon.$$

Suppose we run a randomized approximate-SEM algorithm k times on a fixed input (z, ϵ), keeping the output hypothesis $f^{(k)}$ with minimal sample error among all the k hypotheses returned. In other words, we take the *best of k iterations* of the algorithm. Then the probability that $f^{(k)}$ has error that is *not* within ϵ of the optimal is at most $(1/2)^k$, since the algorithm will have 'failed' k times to find a good hypothesis. This is the basis of the following result, which shows that, as far as its applications to learning are concerned, an efficient randomized approximate-SEM algorithm is as useful as its deterministic counterpart.

Theorem 23.3 *(i) Suppose that $H = \bigcup H_n$ is a graded binary function class and that $\mathrm{VCdim}(H_n)$ is polynomial in n. If there is an efficient randomized SEM algorithm $\mathcal{A}$ for H, then there is an efficient learning algorithm for H that uses $\mathcal{A}$ as a subroutine.*

(ii) Suppose that $F = \bigcup F_n$ is a graded real function class with $\mathrm{fat}_{F_n}(\alpha)$ polynomial in n and $1/\alpha$. If there is an efficient randomized approximate SEM algorithm $\mathcal{A}$ for H, then there is an efficient learning algorithm for F that uses $\mathcal{A}$ as a subroutine.

Proof We first prove (i). The key idea is that we take the best of k iterations of $\mathcal{A}$ for a suitable k, absorbing the randomness in the action of $\mathcal{A}$ into the 'δ' of learning. Suppose then that $\mathcal{A}$ is a randomized SEM algorithm. Theorem 4.3 shows that, for any probability distribution P on Z_n, we have

$$|\mathrm{er}_P(h) - \hat{\mathrm{er}}_z(h)| < \epsilon \qquad \text{for all } h \in H_n \qquad (23.1)$$

with probability at least $1 - 4\,\Pi_H(2m)\exp\left(-\epsilon^2 m/8\right)$. If (23.1) holds and $h \in H_n$ has

$$\hat{\mathrm{er}}_z(h) = \min_{g \in H_n} \hat{\mathrm{er}}_z(g),$$

then, as in the proof of Theorem 4.2, we have $\mathrm{er}_P(h) < \mathrm{opt}_P(H_n) + 2\epsilon$. Now, given a random sample $z \in Z_n^m$, we take z as the input to the randomized SEM algorithm $\mathcal{A}$, and run $\mathcal{A}$ a total of k times on this input, taking $h^{(k)}$ to be the best of these k iterations. Because $\mathcal{A}$ is a randomized SEM algorithm, the probability that $h^{(k)}$ satisfies

$$\hat{\mathrm{er}}_z(h^{(k)}) = \min_{g \in H_n} \hat{\mathrm{er}}_z(g)$$

is at least $1 - 1/2^k$. Hence,

$$\mathbf{E}P^m \left\{ \mathrm{er}_P(h^{(k)}) \geq \mathrm{opt}_P(H_n) + 2\epsilon \right\}$$

$$\leq \quad \mathbf{E}P^m \left\{ \mathrm{er}_P(h^{(k)}) \geq \mathrm{opt}_P(H_n) + 2\epsilon \,\bigg|\, \hat{\mathrm{er}}_z(h^{(k)}) = \min_{g \in H_n} \hat{\mathrm{er}}_z(g) \right\}$$

$$+ 1/2^k$$

$$\leq \quad 4\,\Pi_H(2m)\exp\left(-\epsilon^2 m/8\right) + 1/2^k.$$

If we choose k such that $1/2^k \leq \delta/2$, we have

$$\mathbf{E}P^m \left\{ \mathrm{er}_P(h^{(k)}) \geq \mathrm{opt}_P(H_n) + \sqrt{\frac{32}{m}\ln\left(8\,\Pi_H(2m)/\delta\right)} \right\} \leq \delta.$$

Define

$$m_0(n, \epsilon, \delta) = \frac{64}{\epsilon^2}\left(\mathrm{VCdim}(H_n)\ln(128/\epsilon^2) + \ln(8/\delta)\right),$$

and choose $k = m/32 + 1$. Then for $m \geq m_0(n, \epsilon, \delta)$, we have $1/2^k \leq \delta/2$, and so

$$\mathbf{E}P^m \left\{ \mathrm{er}_P(h^{(k)}) \geq \mathrm{opt}_P(H_n) + \epsilon \right\} \leq \delta.$$

Thus, the algorithm L that iterates the randomized SEM algorithm $k = m/32 + 1$ times and takes the best of k iterations is a learning algorithm. Its sample complexity is no more than m_0. Since $\mathrm{VCdim}(H_n)$ is polynomial in n, $m_0(n, \epsilon, \delta)$ is polynomial in $n, 1/\epsilon$ and $\ln(1/\delta)$. Furthermore, its worst-case running time on a sample in Z_n^m is at most k

times the worst-case running time of $\mathcal{A}$. Since k is linear in m, and since the running time of $\mathcal{A}$ is polynomial in m and n, the running time of L is polynomial in m and n.

The proof of (ii) is similar, and makes use of Theorem 19.1. □

23.3 Learning as Randomized Optimization

We have seen that efficient approximate-SEM and SEM algorithms (both deterministic and randomized) can in many cases be used to construct efficient learning algorithms. The next result proves, as a converse, that if there is an efficient learning algorithm for a graded class then *necessarily* there is an efficient randomized SEM or approximate-SEM algorithm (depending on whether the class is real or binary).

Theorem 23.4 *(i) If there is an efficient learning algorithm for the graded binary class $H = \bigcup H_n$, then there is an efficient randomized SEM algorithm.*

(ii) If there is an efficient learning algorithm for the graded real function class $F = \bigcup F_n$ then there is an efficient randomized approximate-SEM algorithm.

Proof (i) is implied by (ii) and the observation that the existence of an efficient approximate-SEM algorithm for a binary class implies the existence of an efficient SEM algorithm for the class. Hence, we need only prove (ii). Suppose that L is an efficient learning algorithm for the real class $F = \bigcup F_n$. We construct the following randomized algorithm $\mathcal{A}$, which we shall prove is an efficient randomized approximate-SEM algorithm. Given as input to $\mathcal{A}$ the sample $z \in Z_n^m$ and the number $\epsilon \in (0,1)$, we use the randomization allowed in $\mathcal{A}$ to form a sample of length $m^* = m_L(n, \epsilon, 1/2)$, in which each labelled example is drawn according to the distribution P that is uniform on the labelled examples in z and zero elsewhere on $X_n \times [0,1]$. (This probability is defined with multiplicity; that is, for instance, if there are two labelled examples in z each equal to z, we assign the labelled example z probability $2/m$ rather than $1/m$.) Let z^* denote the resulting sample. Feeding z^* into the learning algorithm, we receive as output $f^* = L(z^*)$ and we take this to be the output of the algorithm $\mathcal{A}$; that is, $\mathcal{A}(z, \epsilon) = f^* = L(z^*)$. With probability at least $1/2$ (since we took '$\delta = 1/2$' when determining the length m^* of z^*),

$$\mathrm{er}_P(f^*) < \mathrm{opt}_P(F) + \epsilon.$$

But for any f, by the definition of P, $\mathrm{er}_P(f) = \hat{\mathrm{er}}_z(f)$. So with probability at least $1/2$,

$$\begin{aligned} \hat{\mathrm{er}}_z(f^*) = \mathrm{er}_P(f^*) \quad &< \quad \mathrm{opt}_P(F) + \epsilon \\ &= \quad \inf_{g \in F_n} \mathrm{er}_P(g) + \epsilon \\ &= \quad \inf_{g \in F_n} \hat{\mathrm{er}}_z(g) + \epsilon. \end{aligned}$$

This means that $\mathcal{A}$ is a randomized approximate-SEM algorithm. Because L is efficient, $m^* = m_L(n, \epsilon, 1/2)$ is polynomial in n and $1/\epsilon$. Since the sample z^* has length m^*, and since L is efficient, the time taken by L to produce f^* is polynomial in m^*, n and $1/\epsilon$, and hence $\mathcal{A}$ has running time polynomial in n, m and $1/\epsilon$, as required. $\square$

23.4 A Characterization of Efficient Learning

We may summarize the results of this and the previous chapter in the following theorem.

Theorem 23.5 *Suppose that $F = \bigcup F_n$ is a graded function class. Then F is efficiently learnable if and only if $\mathrm{fat}_{F_n}(\alpha)$ is polynomial in n and $1/\alpha$ and there is an efficient randomized approximate-SEM algorithm for F.*

A special case of this result applies to binary classes.

Theorem 23.6 *Suppose that $H = \bigcup H_n$ is a graded binary function class. Then H is efficiently learnable if and only if $\mathrm{VCdim}(H_n)$ is polynomial in n and there is an efficient randomized SEM algorithm for H.*

23.5 The Hardness of Learning

We concentrate now on graded binary function classes. In order to discuss further the computational complexity of learning, we shall assume that the reader has a rudimentary understanding of the basic concepts of computational complexity theory—in particular, the notion of an 'NP-hard' problem. (Loosely speaking, a problem is NP-hard if it is at least as hard as one of a number of standard problems that are thought *not* to be solvable by a polynomial-time algorithm.) We have seen that H can be efficiently learned only if there is an efficient randomized SEM algorithm for H. In order to prove that it is unlikely that such an algorithm exists, it is enough to show that a certain decision problem associated with H is NP-hard. To this end, we define the following decision problems. The first asks if there is a function h in H achieving a certain fit to the sample—that is, disagreeing on at most a specified number of entries of the sample. The second asks if there is a function in H consistent with the sample.

H-FIT
Instance: $z \in (\mathbb{R}^n \times \{0,1\})^m$ and an integer k between 1 and m.
Question: Is there $h \in H_n$ such that $\text{êr}_z(h) \leq k/m$?

H-CONSISTENCY
Instance: $z \in (\mathbb{R}^n \times \{0,1\})^m$.
Question: Is there $h \in H_n$ such that $\text{êr}_z(h) = 0$?

Clearly H-CONSISTENCY is a sub-problem of H-FIT, obtained by setting $k = 0$. Thus, any algorithm for H-FIT can be used also to solve H-CONSISTENCY.

To obtain hardness results for learning, we need some more standard notions from computational complexity theory. We say that a randomized algorithm $\mathcal{A}$ solves a decision problem Π if the algorithm always halts and produces an output—either 'yes' or 'no'—such that if the answer to Π on the given instance is 'no', the output of $\mathcal{A}$ is 'no', and if the answer to Π on the given instance is 'yes' then, with probability at least $1/2$, the output of $\mathcal{A}$ is 'yes'. A randomized algorithm is said to be *polynomial-time* if its worst-case running time (over all instances) is polynomial in the size of its input. (In both of the decision problems defined above, the size of the input is m.) The class of decision problems Π that can be solved by a polynomial-time randomized algorithm is denoted by RP.

Theorem 23.7 *Let $H = \bigcup H_n$ be a graded binary function class. If there is an efficient learning algorithm for H then there is a polynomial-time randomized algorithm for H-FIT; in other words, H-FIT is in RP.*

Proof If H is efficiently learnable then, by Theorem 23.4, there exists an efficient randomized SEM algorithm $\mathcal{A}$ for H. Using $\mathcal{A}$, we construct a polynomial-time randomized algorithm $\mathcal{B}$ for H-FIT as follows. Suppose that $z \in (\mathbb{R} \times \{0,1\})^m$ and k together constitute an instance of H-FIT,

314 *Learning as Optimization*

and hence an input to $\mathcal{B}$. The first step of the algorithm $\mathcal{B}$ is to compute $h = \mathcal{A}(z)$, the output of $\mathcal{A}$ on z. This function belongs to H_n and, with probability at least $1/2$, $\hat{\mathrm{er}}_z(h)$ is minimal among all functions in H_n. The next step in $\mathcal{B}$ is to check whether $\hat{\mathrm{er}}_z(h) \leq k/m$. If so, then the output of $\mathcal{B}$ is 'yes' and, if not, the output is 'no'. It is clear that $\mathcal{B}$ is a randomized algorithm for H-FIT. Furthermore, since $\mathcal{A}$ runs in time polynomial in m and n, and since the time taken for $\mathcal{B}$ to calculate $\hat{\mathrm{er}}_z(h)$ is linear in the size of z, $\mathcal{B}$ is a polynomial-time algorithm. $\qquad\square$

Of course, this result also shows that if H is efficiently learnable then there is a polynomial-time randomized algorithm for H-CONSISTENCY. If we believe that RP $\neq$ NP—and this is widely held to be the case—then the following two immediate results will enable us to prove that in some cases efficient learning is impossible, as we shall see in the next two chapters.

Theorem 23.8 *Suppose* RP $\neq$ NP *and that H is a graded class of binary functions. If H-FIT is NP-hard then there is no efficient learning algorithm for H.*

Corollary 23.9 *Suppose* RP $\neq$ NP *and that H is a graded class of binary functions. If H-CONSISTENCY is NP-hard then there is no efficient learning algorithm for H.*

23.6 Remarks

For a class F of real-valued functions, it is easy to show that the following 'multiple choice' decision problem can be efficiently solved if and only if the class is efficiently learnable.

APPROX-F-FIT
Instance: $z \in (\mathbf{R}^n \times \{0,1\})^m$, and $\alpha, \epsilon \in [0,1]$.
Question: Choose one of
(a) $\inf_{f \in F} \hat{\mathrm{er}}_z(f) > \alpha$,
(b) $\inf_{f \in F} \hat{\mathrm{er}}_z(f) \leq \alpha + \epsilon$.

We require that a randomized algorithm produces a correct response with probability at least $1/2$ in time polynomial in $1/\epsilon$ and the input size. Notice that, in contrast with H-FIT (the corresponding problem for binary classes), sometimes both responses to the decision problem are correct. This arises because in this case we only need to solve an *approximate* SEM problem. We do not consider the APPROX-F-FIT problem further; in what follows, it is convenient to deal with the approximate-SEM problem directly.

The restricted model

Just as efficient learning of binary classes is linked to the existence of an efficient SEM algorithm, it can be shown that in the *restricted* model of learning binary classes, efficient learning is related to the existence of an efficient consistent-hypothesis-finder, as the following result shows. Here, the notion of an efficient *randomized* consistent-hypothesis-finder is the obvious one, obtained from the definition of a (deterministic) consistent-hypothesis-finder in the same way that the definition of an efficient randomized SEM algorithm is obtained from that of an efficient SEM algorithm. Also, the definition of a randomized learning algorithm is the obvious generalization of the definition in Section 2.4. The result can be proved in a way analogous to the proofs of Theorems 23.3 and 23.4.

Theorem 23.10 *Suppose that $H = \bigcup H_n$ is a graded binary function class. Then H is efficiently learnable in the restricted model if and only if $\mathrm{VCdim}(H_n)$ is polynomial in n and there is an efficient randomized consistent-hypothesis-finder for H.*

In particular, therefore, if the H-CONSISTENCY problem is NP-hard, and RP $\neq$ NP, then H is not efficiently learnable *even in the restricted model*, an observation that strengthens Corollary 23.9.

23.7 Bibliographical Notes

The importance of consistent-hypothesis-finders in the restricted model of learning was demonstrated by Blumer et al. (1989) and Pitt and Valiant (1988). The link between the consistency problem and efficient learning in the restricted model was also discussed in (Natarajan, 1989). The classic book on complexity theory is (Garey and Johnson, 1979); there have been many more recent books, including that of Cormen, Leiserson and Rivest (1990).

24

The Boolean Perceptron

24.1 Introduction

In this chapter, we consider the computational complexity of learning the class of functions computed by the boolean perceptron (the simple perceptron with binary inputs). Section 24.2 shows that learning with this class is difficult, and so we consider two relaxations of this learning problem: learning the subclass of simple perceptrons that have fixed fan-in (that is, those in which the number of non-zero weights is constrained), and learning in the restricted model. In both cases, there are efficient learning algorithms.

24.2 Learning is Hard for the Simple Perceptron

Let BP_n denote the set of boolean functions from $\{0,1\}^n$ to $\{0,1\}$ computed by the boolean perceptron, and let $BP = \bigcup BP_n$ be the corresponding graded function class. The BP-FIT problem is as follows.

BP-FIT
Instance: $z \in (\{0,1\}^n \times \{0,1\})^m$ and an integer k between 1 and m.
Question: Is there $h \in BP_n$ such that $\acute{e}r_z(h) \leq k/m$?

In this section, we show that this problem is NP-hard by establishing that it is at least as hard as a well-known NP-hard problem in graph theory.

A *graph* $G = (V, E)$ consists of a set V of vertices and a set E of unordered pairs of vertices. Thus, if the vertices are labelled with the numbers $1, 2, \ldots, n$, then a typical edge is a 2-set $\{i, j\}$. For convenience, we denote this simply by ij (which, it should be realized, means the same as ji). A *vertex cover* of the graph is a set U of vertices such that for each edge ij of the graph, at least one of the vertices i, j belongs to U. The following decision problem is known to be NP-hard.

VERTEX COVER
Instance: A graph $G = (V, E)$ and an integer $k \leq |V|$.
Question: Is there a vertex cover $U \subseteq V$ such that $|U| \leq k$?

Note that if the graph has r edges and the vertex set V has cardinality n, then the size of an instance of this problem is $O(rn)$.

Our proof that BP-FIT is NP-hard is a standard reduction argument: we show that, given an instance of the VERTEX COVER problem, we can construct (in polynomial time) an instance of BP-FIT (of a size polynomially related to that of the instance of the vertex covering problem) in such a way that the answer to BP-FIT on this constructed instance is the same as the answer to VERTEX COVER on the original instance. This establishes that, if there was a polynomial-time algorithm for BP-FIT, then we could solve VERTEX COVER in polynomial time by transforming any instance of this problem to one of BP-FIT and applying the algorithm for BP-FIT. The details of this transformation are given below.

A typical instance of VERTEX COVER is a graph $G = (V, E)$ together with an integer $k \leq |V|$. We shall assume, for simplicity, that $V = \{1, 2, \ldots, n\}$ and we shall denote the number of edges, $|E|$, by r. Notice that the size of an instance of VERTEX COVER is $\Omega(r + n)$. We construct $z = z(G) \in (\{0,1\}^{2n} \times \{0,1\})^{2r+n}$ as follows. For any two distinct integers i, j between 1 and $2n$, let $e_{i,j}$ denote the binary vector of length $2n$ with ones in positions i and j and zeroes elsewhere. The sample $z(G)$ consists of the labelled examples $(e_{i,n+i}, 1)$ for $i = 1, 2, \ldots, n$ and, for each edge $ij \in E$, the labelled examples $(e_{i,j}, 0)$ and $(e_{n+i,n+j}, 0)$. Note that the 'size' of z is $(2r + n)(2n + 1)$, which is polynomial in the size of the original instance of VERTEX COVER, and that $z(G)$ can be computed in polynomial time.

For example, if a graph G has vertex set $V = \{1, 2, 3, 4\}$ and edge set $E = \{12, 23, 14, 13\}$, then the sample $z(G)$ consists of the following 12 labelled examples:

$$(10001000, 1), (01000100, 1), (00100010, 1), (00010001, 1),$$
$$(11000000, 0), (00001100, 0), (01100000, 0), (00000110, 0),$$
$$(10100000, 0), (00001010, 0), (10010000, 0), (00001001, 0).$$

Lemma 24.1 *Given any graph $G = (V, E)$ with n vertices, and any integer $k \leq n$, let $z = z(G)$ be as defined above. Then, there is $h \in BP_{2n}$*

such that $\hat{er}_z(h) \leq k/(2n)$ *if and only if there is a vertex cover of G of cardinality at most k.*

Proof Suppose first that there is such an h and that this is represented by the state $\omega = (w_1, w_2, \ldots, w_{2n}, \theta)$ of the boolean perceptron on $2n$ inputs. (Thus $w = (w_1, w_2, \ldots, w_{2n}) \in \mathbb{R}^{2n}$ is a weight vector and θ a threshold.) We construct a subset U of V as follows. If $h(e_{i,n+i}) = 0$, then we include i in U; if, for $i \neq j$, $h(e_{i,j}) = 1$ or $h(e_{n+i,n+j}) = 1$ then we include *either one* of i, j in U. Because h is 'wrong' on at most k of the examples in z, the set U consists of at most k vertices. We claim that U is a vertex cover. To show this, we need to verify that given any edge $ij \in E$, at least one of i, j belongs to U. It is clear from the manner in which U is constructed that this is true if either $h(e_{i,n+i}) = 0$ or $h(e_{j,n+j}) = 0$, so suppose that neither of these holds; in other words, suppose that $h(e_{i,n+i}) = 1 = h(e_{j,n+j})$. Then we may deduce that

$$w_i + w_{n+i} \geq \theta, \ w_j + w_{n+j} \geq \theta,$$

and so

$$w_i + w_j + w_{n+i} + w_{n+j} \geq 2\theta;$$

that is,

$$(w_i + w_j) + (w_{n+i} + w_{n+j}) \geq 2\theta.$$

From this, we see that either $w_i + w_j \geq \theta$ or $w_{n+i} + w_{n+j} \geq \theta$ (or both); thus, $h(e_{i,j}) = 1$ or $h(e_{n+i,n+j}) = 1$, or both. Because of the way in which U is constructed, it follows that at least one of the vertices i, j belongs to U. Since ij was an arbitrary edge of the graph, this shows that U is indeed a vertex cover.

We now show, conversely, that if there is a vertex cover of G consisting of at most k vertices, then there is a function in BP_{2n} with sample error at most $k/(2n)$ on $z(G)$. Suppose U is a vertex cover and $|U| \leq k$. Define a state $\omega = (w_1, w_2, \ldots, w_{2n}, \theta)$ of the boolean perceptron as follows: let $\theta = 1$ and, for $i = 1, 2, \ldots, n$,

$$w_i = w_{n+i} = \begin{cases} -1 & \text{if } i \in U \\ 1 & \text{if } i \notin U. \end{cases}$$

We claim that $\hat{er}_z(h) \leq k/(2n)$. Observe that if $ij \in E$, then, since U is a vertex cover, at least one of i, j belongs to U and hence the inner products $w^T e_{i,j}$ and $w^T e_{n+i,n+j}$ are both either 0 or -2, less than θ, so $h(e_{i,j}) = h(e_{n+i,n+j}) = 0$. The function h is therefore correct on all the examples in $z(G)$ arising from the edges of G. We now consider the other types of labelled example in $z(G)$: those of the form $(e_{i,n+i}, 1)$. Now, $w^T e_{i,n+i}$ is -2 if $i \in U$ and is 2 otherwise, so $h(e_{i,n+i}) = 0$ if $i \in U$ and $h(e_{i,n+i}) = 1$ otherwise. It follows that h is 'wrong' only on the examples $e_{i,n+i}$ for $i \in U$ and hence

$$ \hat{\mathrm{er}}_z(h) = \frac{|U|}{2n} \leq \frac{k}{2n}, $$

as claimed.   □

This result shows that the answer to BP-FIT on the instance $(z(G), k)$ is the same as the answer to VERTEX COVER on instance (G, k). Given that $z(G)$ can be computed from G in time polynomial in the size of G, we therefore establish the following hardness result.

Theorem 24.2 BP-FIT *is NP-hard.*

Corollary 24.3 *If* RP $\neq$ NP *then there is no efficient learning algorithm for* $BP = \bigcup BP_n$.

24.3 Learning is Easy for Fixed Fan-In Perceptrons

Since Theorem 24.2 shows that learning the simple perceptron is difficult, it is natural to seek easier versions of this learning problem, so that we can determine what features of the problem make it difficult. In this section, we consider simple perceptrons in which the number of non-zero weights is constrained.

We say that a simple perceptron with weights $w \in \mathbb{R}^n$ and threshold $\theta \in \mathbb{R}$ has *fan-in* k if the number of non-zero components of w is no more than k. An easy VC-dimension argument shows that such functions can compute no more than

$$ (em/(k+1))^{k+1} \binom{n}{k} = O(m^{k+1} n^k) $$

dichotomies of $m \geq k$ points in $\mathbb{R}^n$. For fixed k, this is polynomial in m and n, so an obvious candidate for an efficient learning algorithm is an algorithm that enumerates all dichotomies that fixed fan-in perceptrons can compute, and returns the one with minimal sample error. It turns out that, for fixed k, there is such an efficient learning algorithm.

Figure 24.1 shows pseudocode for the procedure Splitting which, given a training set S of size m, returns a set of dichotomies of S.

argument: Training set, $S = \{x_1, \ldots, x_m\} \subset \mathbb{R}^n$
returns: Set of weights and thresholds, $W = \{(w, \theta)\}$

```
function Splitting(S)
    W := ∅
    P := ∅
    for all t₁ < ··· < tₖ from {1,...,n}
        for all l from {1,...,k+1}
            for all r₁ < ··· < rₗ from {1,...,m}
                for all α₁,···,αₗ from {±1}
                    if there is a solution (w,θ) to the system
                       of linear equations
                       xᵣᵢ · w + θ = αᵢ          i = 1,...,l
                       satisfying
                       {i : wᵢ ≠ 0} = {t₁,t₂,...,tₖ}
                    then
                       S' := {x ∈ S : w · x − θ < 0}
                       S'' := {x ∈ S : w · x − θ ≥ 0}
                       if {S',S''} ∉ P
                       then
                              W := W ∪ {(w,θ)}
                              P := P ∪ {S',S''}
                       endif
                    endif
                endfor
            endfor
        endfor
    endfor
    return W
end
```

Fig. 24.1. Pseudocode for the Splitting procedure.

Theorem 24.4 *The procedure* Splitting *returns all dichotomies of its argument* $S \subset \mathbb{R}^n$ *that can be computed by some simple perceptron with fan-in no more than* k. *For* $|S| = m$, *it takes time* $O(n^{2k} 2^k m^{2k+3})$.

Proof We first show that the procedure returns all dichotomies. Notice that any dichotomy computed by a perceptron with fewer than k non-zero weights can be computed by one with exactly k non-zero weights. Since Splitting enumerates all possible k-subsets of the n weights, we need only show that, for any dichotomy $\{S', S''\}$ of m points in $S \subset \mathbb{R}^k$ that can be computed by a simple perceptron (that is, a perceptron with k inputs), there is a subset of the m points $\{x_{r_1}, \ldots, x_{r_l}\}$ of size no more than $k+1$, and a sequence $(\alpha_1, \ldots, \alpha_l) \in \{\pm 1\}^l$, so that for every solution (w, θ) to the equations

$$x_{r_i} \cdot w + \theta = \alpha_i \qquad i = 1, \ldots, l$$

the simple perceptron with weights w and threshold θ computes the dichotomy. To see this, consider a dichotomy $\{S', S''\}$ computed by a simple perceptron. By suitably shifting and scaling θ and w, we can obtain a pair (w, θ) for which

$$w \cdot x_i + \theta \begin{cases} \geq 1 & \text{if } x_i \in S', \\ \leq -1 & \text{if } x_i \in S''. \end{cases}$$

These m inequalities define a closed nonempty polyhedron in the space $\mathbb{R}^{k+1}$ of parameters (w, θ). It is well known that every closed nonempty polyhedron in $\mathbb{R}^{k+1}$ contains the nonempty intersection of some number $s \leq k + 1$ of the hyperplanes that make up its surfaces. Hence, we can choose some set of $s \leq k + 1$ equations of the form

$$w \cdot x_i + \theta = \alpha_i$$

(for $\alpha_i \in \{\pm 1\}$), and for all solutions (w, θ), the simple perceptron with those parameters computes the dichotomy $\{S', S''\}$ of S. Hence, Splitting enumerates all possible dichotomies.

We now prove the bound on the computation time of the algorithm. Clearly, the innermost loop (searching for a solution to the system of linear equations) is executed

$$\binom{n}{k} \sum_{l=1}^{k+1} \binom{m}{l} 2^l \leq n^k 2^{k+1} m^{k+1}$$

times. Each iteration involves the solution of no more than $k + 1$ linear equations in no more than $k + 1$ variables, and so takes time $O(k^3)$ (using, for instance, Gaussian elimination). Since P contains distinct dichotomies of S, it has size $O(m^{k+1} n^k)$, and so checking whether $\{S', S''\}$ is in P takes time $O(|P|m) = O(m^{k+2} n^k)$. So the total time is

$$O(n^k 2^{k+1} m^{k+1}(k^3 + m^{k+2} n^k)) = O(n^{2k} 2^k m^{2k+3}).$$

$\square$

Corollary 24.5 *For fixed k, define the graded class $H^k = \bigcup_n H_n^k$, where H_n^k is the class of simple perceptrons defined on $\mathbb{R}^n$ with fan-in no more than k. The class H^k is efficiently learnable.*

24.4 Perceptron Learning in the Restricted Model

We now turn our attention to the learnability of the boolean perceptron in the restricted model of learning. As we shall see, there is an efficient learning algorithm in the restricted model, in contrast to the results of Section 24.2. By Theorem 22.7, since VCdim(BP_n) = $n + 1$, which is certainly polynomial in n, any efficient consistent-hypothesis-finder for BP_n will constitute an efficient learning algorithm. We discuss here two distinct consistent-hypothesis-finders for BP_n; one based on linear programming and one based on the perceptron learning algorithm (as described in Chapter 1).

Using linear programming

Suppose that $z = ((x_1, y_1), \ldots, (x_m, y_m))$ is a training sample for some function in BP_n. For a weight vector $w \in \mathbb{R}^n$, threshold $\theta \in \mathbb{R}$ and real number γ, define the column vector

$$\tilde{w} = \begin{pmatrix} w \\ \theta \\ \gamma \end{pmatrix},$$

and the row vectors

$$v_i = \left((2y_i - 1)x_i^T, 1 - 2y_i, -1 \right),$$

for $i = 1, \ldots, m$. Then $v_i \tilde{w} \geq 0$ is equivalent to

$$x_i^T w - \theta \geq \gamma \quad \text{if} \quad y_i = 1, \text{ and} \tag{24.1}$$
$$x_i^T w - \theta \leq -\gamma \quad \text{if} \quad y_i = 0. \tag{24.2}$$

Hence, a solution $\tilde{w}$ to the linear program

$$\text{maximize } \gamma \text{ subject to } \begin{pmatrix} v_1 \\ v_2 \\ \vdots \\ v_m \end{pmatrix} \tilde{w} \geq 0$$

that has $\gamma > 0$ corresponds to a consistent hypothesis. Clearly, the feasible region is nonempty, since $\tilde{w} = 0$ satisfies the constraints. (Notice that, if there is a solution with $\gamma > 0$, the feasible region is unbounded. This is easy to remedy, by adding the condition $\sum_{i=1}^{n} |w_i| + |\theta| \leq 1$, which can be represented with the addition of $n + 1$ slack variables and another $2n + 3$ linear constraints.)

It is known that there are algorithms for linear programming that are efficient. For instance, interior point methods such as Karmarkar's algorithm have polynomial running time. We have therefore established the following result.

Theorem 24.6 *The consistent-hypothesis-finder described above, using any efficient algorithm for linear programming (such as Karmarkar's algorithm), constitutes an efficient consistent-hypothesis-finder (and hence is an efficient learning algorithm in the restricted model) for the boolean perceptron.*

Using the perceptron learning algorithm

The well-known *perceptron learning algorithm* (discussed in Chapter 1) was originally motivated by biological considerations and is 'incremental', in the sense that small changes are made to the weight vector in response to each labelled example in turn. For any *learning constant* $\eta > 0$, the perceptron learning algorithm L_η acts sequentially as follows. Suppose that $z \in Z_n^m$ is a training sample. The algorithm L_η maintains a *current state*, $\omega = (w, \theta)$, where $w \in \mathbb{R}^n$ and $\theta \in \mathbb{R}$, which initially has the all-0 vector as weight vector, and threshold 0. The state is updated sequentially as the algorithm cycles through each of the labelled examples in the training sample. When the algorithm considers a labelled example (x, y), where $x \in \mathbb{R}^n$ and $y \in \{0, 1\}$, it calculates the label $h(x) = \text{sgn}(w \cdot x - \theta)$ assigned to x by the perceptron in state ω (where, as before, $w \cdot x = w^T x$, the inner product of w and x) and it updates the state to the new state, $\omega' = (w', \theta')$ given by

$$
\begin{aligned}
w' &= w + \eta \left(y - h(x) \right) x, \\
\theta' &= \theta - \eta \left(y - h(x) \right).
\end{aligned}
$$

Notice that the state ω is only updated on a labelled example if the perceptron in state ω misclassifies the example. It is convenient to think of the algorithm L_η as maintaining the hypothesis h, which is updated each time it misclassifies an example. The algorithm operates on a training sample by repeatedly cycling through the m examples, and when it has completed a cycle through the training data without updating its hypothesis, it returns that hypothesis. The following result, the *Perceptron Convergence Theorem* shows that if the training sample is consistent with some simple perceptron, then this algorithm converges after a finite number of iterations. Since the theorem allows examples in $\mathbb{R}^n$, it implies the corresponding result for examples in $\{0,1\}^n$ that are consistent with some $t \in BP_n$.

Theorem 24.7 *Define $Z_n = \mathbb{R}^n \times \{0,1\}$, and fix a training sample $z = ((x_1,y_1),\ldots,(x_m,y_m)) \in Z_n^m$. Suppose that there is a weight vector w^* and threshold θ^* satisfying $\|w^*\|^2 + \theta^{*2} = 1$ for which $y_i = \mathrm{sgn}\,(w^* \cdot x_i - \theta^*)$ for $i = 1,\ldots,m$. Define*

$$\gamma = \min\{|w^* \cdot x_i - \theta^*| : i = 1,\ldots,m\},$$

and suppose $\gamma > 0$. Then for all $\eta > 0$, the hypothesis maintained by the perceptron algorithm L_η converges after no more than $(R^2 + 1)/\gamma^2$ updates, where $R = \max_i \|x_i\|$, and the limiting hypothesis is consistent with the training data z.

Proof Let (w_i, θ_i) be the state maintained by L_η immediately before the ith update. Suppose that the ith update occurs on example (x_j, y_j). This example must have been misclassified by the perceptron with state (w_i, θ_i), so $\mathrm{sgn}(w_i \cdot x_j - \theta_i) = 1 - y_j$, and hence

$$\begin{aligned}
w_{i+1} &= w_i + \eta\,(y_j - \mathrm{sgn}(w_i \cdot x_j - \theta_i))\,x_j \\
&= w_i + (2y_j - 1)\eta x_j.
\end{aligned}$$

Similarly, $\theta_{i+1} = \theta_i - (2y_j - 1)\eta$.

Now, to measure the progress of the algorithm, we consider the evolution of the squared norm, $\|w_i\|^2 + \theta_i^2$, and observe that it grows with each mistake. In particular,

$$\begin{aligned}
w^* \cdot w_{i+1} + \theta^* \theta_{i+1} &= w^* \cdot w_i + \theta^* \theta_i + (2y_j - 1)\eta(w^* \cdot x_j - \theta^*) \\
&\geq w^* \cdot w_i + \theta^* \theta_i + \eta\gamma,
\end{aligned}$$

and so $w^* \cdot w_{i+1} + \theta^* \theta_{i+1} \geq i\eta\gamma$. Since $\|w^*\|^2 + \theta^{*2} = 1$, this implies—by the Cauchy-Schwarz inequality (Inequality (1.7) in Appendix 1)—that $\|w_{i+1}\|^2 + \theta_i^2 \geq (i\eta\gamma)^2$.

On the other hand, this squared norm cannot be too large, since

$$\begin{aligned}
&\|w_{i+1}\|^2 + \theta_{i+1}^2 \\
&= \|w_i\|^2 + \theta_i^2 + \eta^2\,(\|x_j\|^2 + 1) + 2(2y_j - 1)\eta\,(w_i \cdot x_j - \theta_i) \\
&\leq \|w_i\|^2 + \theta_i^2 + \eta^2\,(\|x_j\|^2 + 1)
\end{aligned}$$

and so $\|w_{i+1}\|^2 + \theta_i^2 \leq i\eta^2(R^2 + 1)$. Combining these inequalities shows that

$$(i\eta\gamma)^2 \leq \|w_{i+1}\|^2 + \theta_i^2 \leq i\eta^2(R^2 + 1),$$

and so $i \leq (R^2 + 1)/\gamma^2$ as required.   □

Since the perceptron algorithm makes an update at least once in every cycle through the training data, and each iteration involves $O(n)$ computation steps, this theorem implies that L_η has time complexity $O((R^2 + 1)mn/\gamma^2)$.

A natural question is whether this consistent-hypothesis-finder is efficient. Clearly, if the margin γ is sufficiently large (for instance, if $1/\gamma$ is no larger than some polynomial in n), then the algorithm would be efficient. However, for samples of size polynomial in n, the margin γ can be exponentially small in n. We shall show that, in fact, the algorithm is not efficient by proving that for a sample of size polynomial in n, the number of complete cycles required can be exponential in n.

In order to show that this procedure is inefficient, we consider the boolean function f_{2n} of $2n$ variables that has formula

$$f_{2n} = u_{2n} \wedge (u_{2n-1} \vee (u_{2n-2} \wedge (u_{2n-3} \vee (\ldots (u_2 \wedge u_1))\ldots))).$$

Here, we use the standard notation for describing boolean functions in terms of the literals $u_1, u_2, \ldots,$ the OR connective $\vee$ and the AND connective $\wedge$. We shall use the following two lemmas.

Lemma 24.8 *Let the set $S_n \subseteq \{0,1\}^{2n}$ of cardinality $2n + 1$ be defined for each positive integer n as follows. $S_1 = \{01, 10, 11\}$, and, for $n \geq 1$,*

$$S_{n+1} = \{x01 : x \in S_n\} \cup \{11\ldots10, 00\ldots011\}.$$

Then the only function $h \in BP_{2n}$ consistent with f_{2n} on S_n is f_{2n} itself.

Proof We prove by induction that the only $h \in BP_{2n}$ consistent with f_{2n} on S_n is f_{2n} itself and that, if f_{2n} is represented by the state (w, θ) of the perceptron, then each weight w_i is positive. This is easily seen to be true for $n = 1$. For, suppose that $h \in BP_2$ is such that h agrees with f_2 on S_1. If h is represented by weight vector (w_1, w_2) and threshold θ then, since $h(10) = f_2(10) = 0$ and $h(01) = f_2(01) = 0$, we have $w_1 < \theta$ and $w_2 < \theta$. But we also know that $h(11) = f_2(11) = 1$, so $w_1 + w_2 > \theta$. It follows that $w_1, w_2 > 0$ and hence $\theta > 0$. Therefore $h(00) = 0 = f_2(00)$. Since $h(x) = f_2(x)$ for all four elements of $\{0,1\}^2$, h equals f_2, as required. Let us now make the inductive hypothesis that $n \geq 1$ and that if $h \in BP_{2n}$ agrees with f_{2n} on S_n, then $h = f_{2n}$ (in other words,

S_n specifies f_{2n}) and, furthermore, that any weight vector representing f_{2n} has all its weights positive. Now suppose that $h \in BP_{2n+2}$ agrees with f_{2n+2} on S_{n+1}. Suppose also that h is represented by weight vector $(w_1, w_2, \ldots, w_{2n}, w_{2n+1}, w_{2n+2})$ and threshold θ. The examples $x01$, for $x \in S_n$, are in S_{n+1} and so h agrees with f_{2n+2} on all such examples. But, since $f_{2n+2}(y01) = f_{2n}(y)$ for all y, and since S_n specifies f_{2n}, the function g defined by $g(y) = h(y01)$ must equal f_{2n}. Therefore, for all $y \in \{0, 1\}^{2n}$,

$$h(y01) = f_{2n}(y) = f_{2n+2}(y01).$$

Now, for $y \in \{0, 1\}^{2n}$,

$$f_{2n}(y) = g(y) = h(y01) = \mathrm{sgn}\left(\sum_{i=1}^{2n} w_i y_i + w_{2n+2} - \theta\right),$$

and so f_{2n} is represented by weight vector $(w_1, w_2, \ldots, w_{2n})$ and threshold $\theta - w_{2n+2}$. Given the inductive hypothesis, we deduce that

$$w_1, w_2, \ldots, w_{2n} > 0.$$

This, coupled with the fact that $h(11\ldots 10) = f_{2n+2}(11\ldots 10) = 0$, implies that for all $y \in \{0, 1\}^{2n}$,

$$h(y10) = 0 = f_{2n+2}(y10),$$

because for any $y \in \{0, 1\}^{2n}$, we have

$$(y10) \cdot w \le (11 \cdots 10) \cdot w < \theta.$$

Similarly, since $h(00 \ldots 011) = f_{2n+2}(00 \ldots 011) = 1$,

$$h(y11) = 1 = f_{2n+2}(y11)$$

for all $y \in \{0, 1\}^{2n}$. Let z be any element of $\{0, 1\}^{2n}$ such that $f_{2n}(z) = 0$. From the fact (established above) that $h(y01) = f_{2n}(y)$ for all y, we have $h(z01) = f_{2n}(z) = 0$; furthermore, $h(z11) = 1$, as just shown. Since changing x_{n+1} from 0 to 1 changes $h(zx_{n+1}1)$ from 0 to 1, $w_{2n+1} > 0$ and hence, since $h(11 \ldots 10) = 0$, we have that for all $y \in \{0, 1\}^{2n}$,

$$h(y00) = 0 = f_{2n+2}(y00).$$

We have now shown that $h(x) = f_{2n+2}(x)$ for all $x \in \{0, 1\}^{2n+2}$, and hence $h = f_{2n+2}$, and we have also established that $w_i > 0$ for $i = 1, 2, \ldots, 2n + 1$. Since $h(11 \ldots 10) = 0$ and $h(00 \ldots 011) = 1$, we have

$$w_{2n+2} + w_{2n+1} \ge \theta > \sum_{i=1}^{2n} w_i + w_{2n+1}$$

and hence

$$w_{2n+2} > \sum_{i=1}^{2n} w_i > 0,$$

completing the proof.   □

Lemma 24.9 *Let n be any positive integer and suppose f_{2n} is represented by the state $\omega = (w, \theta)$ of the boolean perceptron, where $w \in \mathbb{R}^{2n}$ and $\theta \in \mathbb{R}$. Then $w_{2n} \geq \left(\sqrt{3}\right)^{n-1} \min(w_1, w_2)$.*

Proof We prove the result by induction on n. It is clearly true when $n = 1$. For $n = 2$, since $f_4((0011)) = 1$ and $f_4((1110)) = 0$, we have $w_4 + w_3 > \theta$ and $w_3 + w_2 + w_1 < \theta$. Combining these inequalities gives

$$w_4 > w_2 + w_1 \geq 2 \min(w_1, w_2).$$

Suppose the result is true for $n = s$ and consider $n = s + 1$. Now, if f_{2s+2} is represented by (w, θ) then f_{2s} is represented by weight vector $(w_1, \ldots, w_{2s})$ and threshold $\theta - w_{2s+1}$. To see this, observe that

$$\sum_{i=1}^{2s} w_i x_i \geq \theta - w_{2s+1} \iff \sum_{i=1}^{2s} w_i x_i + w_{2s+1} \geq \theta$$

$$\iff f_{2s+2}(x_1, x_2, \ldots, x_{2s}, 0, 1) = 1,$$

and this last condition holds precisely when $f_{2s}(x_1, \ldots, x_n) = 1$. So, by the induction hypothesis, for each $k \leq s$, $w_{2k} \geq \sqrt{3}^{k-1} \min(w_1, w_2)$. Now, for each $j \leq s$, there are x, y such that $f_{2s+2}(x) = 0$, $f_{2s+2}(y) = 1$ and such that x, y differ only in entries $2j$ and $2j+1$, with $(x)_{2j+1} = 0 = (y)_{2j}$, and $(x)_{2j} = 1 = (y)_{2j+1}$. Hence $w \cdot x < \theta \leq w \cdot y$, so that $w_{2j+1} > w_{2j}$. Also, since $f_{2s+2}((110101\ldots101)) = 1$ and $f_{2s+2}((111\ldots10)) = 0$, we have

$$w_1 + w_2 + w_3 + \cdots + w_{2s+1} < \theta \leq w_1 + w_2 + w_4 + \cdots + w_{2s+2},$$

so that

$$w_{2s+2} > w_3 + w_5 + \cdots + w_{2s-1} + w_{2s+1} > w_2 + w_4 + \cdots + w_{2s},$$

this last inequality since $w_{2j+1} > w_{2j}$. Consider the case $s = 2$: here, using the fact that $w_4 > 2 \min(w_1, w_2)$, we obtain

$$w_6 > \min(w_1, w_2)(1 + 2) = \sqrt{3}^{3-1} \min(w_1, w_2),$$

as required. For general $s > 2$, by the inductive hypothesis,

$$
\begin{aligned}
w_{2s+2} &> \min(w_1, w_2)(1 + \sqrt{3} + \sqrt{3}^2 + \ldots + \sqrt{3}^{s-1}) \\
&= \min(w_1, w_2)(\sqrt{3}^s - 1)/(\sqrt{3} - 1),
\end{aligned}
$$

and the result follows from the fact that

$$
(\sqrt{3}^s - 1)/(\sqrt{3} - 1) > \sqrt{3}^s,
$$

for $s \geq 3$. $\qquad\qquad\qquad\qquad\qquad\qquad\qquad\qquad\qquad\qquad$ $\square$

Combining these two results, we obtain the following result, which shows that the consistent-hypothesis-finder is inefficient.

Theorem 24.10 *For any fixed $\eta > 0$, the consistent-hypothesis-finder arising from the perceptron learning algorithm L_η is not efficient.*

Proof Suppose we take the target t to be f_{2n} and we take as the input to the consistent-hypothesis-finder a sample $z^{(n)}$ consisting of the members of S_n, labelled by their classifications according to f_{2n}. Suppose the initial state of the perceptron is $((00, \ldots, 0), 0)$. Let u be the number of updates made before a function h, consistent with the sample, is produced. By Lemma 24.8, this consistent function h must be f_{2n} itself. Therefore, if it is represented by the state (w, θ), $w_1, w_2 > 0$ and, by Lemma 24.9, $w_{2n} \geq (\sqrt{3})^{n-1} \min(w_1, w_2)$. After u updates, the maximum entry in the new weight vector w' is at most $u\eta$ and the minimum non-zero entry is certainly at least η. Hence the ratio of maximum entry to minimum non-zero entry is at most u. But, since in the final output weight vector this ratio is at least $w_{2n}/\min(w_1, w_2) > (\sqrt{3})^{n-1}$, it follows that $u \geq (\sqrt{3})^{n-1}$, which is exponential in n, and hence in the size of the sample z. $\qquad\qquad\qquad\qquad\qquad\qquad$ $\square$

This result also holds if $\eta = \eta(n)$ is any function of n, and also if the initial state of the perceptron is chosen differently.

24.5 Remarks

The perceptron convergence theorem (Theorem 24.7) tells us something about the computational cost of learning simple perceptrons in a restricted version of the real classification problem defined in Chapter 9. (In this restricted model, we assume that there is some target function in the class of simple perceptrons that classifies all examples correctly, with some positive margin γ.) We can define efficient learning in this model in the obvious way. Since a simple perceptron is a thresholded linear function, the graded class BP is equivalent to the family of thresholded versions of functions in $F = \bigcup_n F_n$, where the linear functions in F_n satisfy

$$f(x) = w \cdot x - \theta$$

for some $w \in \mathbb{R}^n$ and $\theta \in \mathbb{R}$ and any $x \in \{0, 1\}^n$, and

$$\|w\|^2 + \theta^2 = 1. \tag{24.3}$$

The perceptron convergence theorem implies that there is a polynomial-time classification learning algorithm for F (in this restricted sense).

Instead of restricting the functions in F_n with (24.3) so that the Euclidean norm of the augmented weight vector is bounded by 1, we could insist that the 1-norm is bounded by 1, that is,

$$\sum_{i=1}^{n} |w_i| + |\theta| = 1.$$

In this case, the linear programming approach shows that there is a polynomial-time classification learning algorithm for F in this restricted sense.

24.6 Bibliographical Notes

The problem of finding a half-space that best matches an arbitrary dichotomy of a set of points in $\{0, 1\}^n$ is listed in (Garey and Johnson, 1979) as an NP-complete problem; see (Johnson and Preparata, 1978) and (Höffgen, Simon and Horn, 1995). (However, modified versions of the perceptron algorithm perform reasonably well in practice; see, for example, (Gallant, 1990).)

The procedure Splitting for enumerating dichotomies computed by perceptrons with bounded fan-in was presented in (Lee et al., 1996). It is similar to an algorithm earlier proposed by Faragó and Lugosi (1993). For details on Gaussian elimination, see (Watkins, 1991). The simple general approach of constructing learning algorithms that enumerate all dichotomies of the training examples was discussed by Blumer et al. (1989).

The linear programming approach to finding a consistent perceptron is well-known. Polynomial-time algorithms for linear programming are described in (Karmarkar, 1984). In fact, the time grows polynomially in the number of bits required to represent the solution. Thus, the boolean perceptron is efficiently learnable in the restricted model only if the weights and threshold of some perceptron consistent with the data can be represented in only polynomially many bits. Fortunately, any boolean perceptron can be represented by another with integer weights in which the ratio of the largest to the smallest weight is no more than $2^{O(n \ln n)}$. (See (Muroga, 1965; Muroga, 1971).)

Pitt and Valiant (1988) showed that, if the weights of a boolean perceptron are restricted to the set $\{0, 1\}$, then even in the restricted case, learning is hard.

Rosenblatt (1958) gives a proof of the perceptron convergence theorem; see also (Block, 1962; Nilsson, 1965).

The fact that the perceptron algorithm can be inefficient is shown in (Anthony and Shawe-Taylor, 1993c; Anthony and Shawe-Taylor, 1993a) (see also (Anthony et al., 1995)). Baum (1990a) has shown that the algorithm is efficient in the restricted model when the training data is uniformly distributed on the unit sphere in $\mathbb{R}^n$. Bylander (1994; 1997) shows that modifications of the algorithm can be efficient for certain distributions, even in the presence of certain types of random classification noise.

25

Hardness Results for Feed-Forward Networks

25.1 Introduction

In this chapter we show that the consistency problem can be hard for some very simple feed-forward neural networks. In Section 25.2, we show that, for certain graded spaces of feed-forward linear threshold networks with binary inputs, the consistency problem is NP-hard. This shows that for each such family of networks, unless RP = NP, there can be no efficient learning algorithm in the restricted learning model and hence, in particular, no efficient learning algorithm in the standard model of Part 1. These networks are somewhat unusual in that the output unit is constrained to compute a conjunction. In Section 25.3, we extend the hardness result to networks with an arbitrary linear threshold output unit, but with real inputs. In Section 25.4, we describe similar results for graded classes of feed-forward sigmoid networks with linear output units, showing that approximately minimizing sample error is NP-hard for these classes. Unless RP = NP, this shows that there can be no efficient learning algorithm in the restricted learning model of Part 3.

25.2 Linear Threshold Networks with Binary Inputs

For each positive integer n, we define a neural network on n inputs as follows. The network has n binary inputs and $k+1$ linear threshold units ($k \geq 1$). It has two layers of computation units, the first consisting of k linear threshold units, each connected to all of the inputs. The output unit is also a linear threshold unit, with a connection of fixed weight 1 from each of the other k threshold units. The output unit has fixed threshold k. The effect of this arrangement is that the output unit computes the conjunction of the first-layer linear threshold units. We

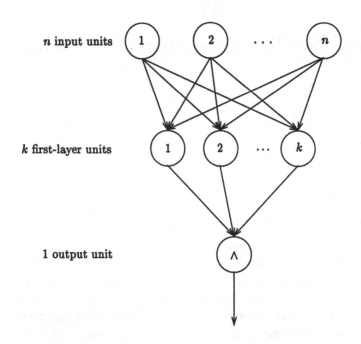

n input units

k first-layer units

1 output unit

Fig. 25.1. The feed-forward two-layer linear threshold network that computes the function class $N_{\wedge,n}^{k}$.

shall refer to this network (and the set of functions it computes) as $N_{\wedge,n}^{k}$. The network is illustrated in Figure 25.1.

The consistency problem for the graded space $N_{\wedge}^{k} = \bigcup_{n} N_{\wedge,n}^{k}$ is as follows.

$N_{\wedge}^{k}$-CONSISTENCY
Instance: $z \in (\{0,1\}^{n} \times \{0,1\})^{m}$.
Question: Is there $h \in N_{\wedge,n}^{k}$ such that $\text{êr}_{z}(h) = 0$?

We shall prove that $N_{\wedge}^{k}$-CONSISTENCY is NP-hard (provided $k \geq 3$), by relating the problem to a well-known NP-hard problem in graph theory.

Let G be a graph with vertex set V and edge set E. For a positive integer k, a *k-colouring* of G is a function $\chi : V \rightarrow \{1, 2, \ldots, k\}$ with the property that, whenever $ij \in E$, then $\chi(i) \neq \chi(j)$. The following decision problem for k-colourings is known to be NP-hard for each $k \geq 3$.

k-COLOURING
Instance: A graph G.
Question: Does G have a k-colouring?

Note that the integer k is not part of the instance. The assertion that k-COLOURING is NP-hard for $k \geq 3$ therefore means that, for each *fixed* $k \geq 3$, it is NP-hard to determine whether a given graph has a k-colouring. Thus, for example, it is NP-hard to determine whether a given graph is 3-colourable.

Let G be a graph with vertex set $V = \{1, 2, \ldots, n\}$ and edge set E, with $r = |E|$. We construct a training sample

$$z = z(G) \in (\{0, 1\}^n \times \{0, 1\})^{n+r+1}$$

as follows. Denoting by e_i the vector in $\{0, 1\}^n$ with a 1 in position i and 0 elsewhere, the sample z consists of the following labelled examples:

- $(e_i, 0)$, for $i = 1, 2, \ldots, n$;
- $(e_i + e_j, 1)$ for each edge $ij \in E$;
- $(\mathbf{0}, 1)$, where $\mathbf{0}$ is the all-0 vector.

For example, suppose that G is the graph on vertex set $\{1, 2, 3, 4, 5\}$, with edge set $\{12, 14, 15, 23, 34, 45\}$. Then the corresponding training sample $z(G)$ consists of the 12 labelled examples

$$(10000, 0), (01000, 0), (00100, 0), (00010, 0), (00001, 0),$$

$$(11000, 1), (10010, 1), (10001, 1), (01100, 1), (00110, 1), (00011, 1),$$

$$(00000, 1).$$

The following result establishes the link between the consistency problem for the neural network and the graph colouring problem.

Theorem 25.1 *There is a function in $N_{\wedge, n}^k$ that is consistent with $z(G)$ if and only if the graph G is k-colourable.*

Proof A state ω of $N_{\wedge, n}^k$ is described completely by the thresholds on each of the first-layer units and by the weights on the connections between each of these and each of the input units. We shall denote by w_l and θ_l the weight vector and threshold of the lth unit in the first layer, for $l = 1, 2, \ldots, k$, so that $w_{l,i}$ is the weight on the connection from input unit i to first-layer unit l.

Consider a function $h \in N_{\wedge, n}^k$, and let $h_1, h_2, \ldots, h_k : \mathbb{R}^n \to \{0, 1\}$ be the k functions computed by the units in the first layer. By the construction of the network, h is the conjunction $h = h_1 \wedge h_2 \wedge \cdots \wedge h_k$ of these functions. Suppose that h is consistent with the training sample. This means that there are weight vectors $w_1, w_2, \ldots, w_k$ and thresholds

$\theta_1, \theta_2, \ldots, \theta_k$ such that, for all l between 1 and k, $h_l(x) = 1$ if and only if the inner product $w_l^T x$ is at least θ_l. Note that, since 0 is labelled as a positive example, we have $\theta_l \leq 0$ for each l between 1 and k. For each vertex i in G, $h(e_i) = 0$, and so there is at least one function h_m $(1 \leq m \leq k)$ for which $h_m(e_i) = 0$. Thus we may define $\chi : V \to \{1, 2, \ldots, k\}$ by

$$\chi(i) = \min\{m : h_m(e_i) = 0\}.$$

It remains to prove that χ is a colouring of G. Suppose that $\chi(i) = \chi(j) = m$, so that $h_m(e_i) = h_m(e_j) = 0$. Then,

$$w_m^T e_i < \theta_m, \qquad w_m^T e_j < \theta_m$$

and so, recalling that $\theta_m \leq 0$, we have

$$w_m^T(e_i + e_j) = w_m^T e_i + w_m^T e_j < \theta_m + \theta_m \leq \theta_m.$$

It follows that $h_m(e_i + e_j) = 0$ and, hence, $h(e_i + e_j) = 0$. Now if ij were an edge of G, then we should have $h(e_i + e_j) = 1$, because we assumed that h is consistent with the training sample. Thus ij is not an edge of G, and χ is a colouring, as claimed.

Conversely, suppose we are given a colouring $\chi : V \to \{1, 2, \ldots, k\}$. For l between 1 and k, define the weight vector w_l as follows:

$$w_{l,i} = \begin{cases} -1, & \text{if } \chi(i) = l, \\ 1, & \text{otherwise,} \end{cases}$$

and take the threshold θ_l to be $-1/2$. Let $h_1, h_2, \ldots, h_k$ be the corresponding linear threshold functions, and h their conjunction (which is computable by $N_{\wedge,n}^k$). We claim that h is consistent with $z(G)$. Since $0 \geq \theta_l = -1/2$ it follows that $h_l(0) = 1$ for each l, and so $h(0) = 1$. In order to evaluate $h(e_i)$, note that if $\chi(i) = m$ then

$$w_m^T e_i = w_{m,i} = -1 < -\frac{1}{2},$$

so $h_m(e_i) = 0$ and $h(e_i) = 0$, as required. Finally, for any l between 1 and k, and for any edge ij, we know that at least one of $\chi(i)$ and $\chi(j)$ is not l. Therefore, for any l,

$$w_l^T(e_i + e_j) = w_{l,i} + w_{l,j},$$

where either both of the terms on the right-hand side are 1, or one is 1 and the other is -1. In either case, the inner product exceeds the threshold $-1/2$, and $h_l(e_i + e_j) = 1$ for each l. Thus $h(e_i + e_j) = 1$. $\square$

Given the NP-hardness of k-COLOURING, and the fact that $z(G)$ can be computed in polynomial time, this reduction establishes the hardness of the consistency problem.

Corollary 25.2 *Let $k \geq 3$ be any fixed integer. Then $N_\wedge^k$-CONSISTENCY is NP-hard.*

Having established that the consistency problem is NP-hard for each of the classes of networks, we now have the following hardness result for learning.

Corollary 25.3 *Let k be any fixed integer, $k \geq 3$. Suppose that $N_{\wedge,n}^k$ is the network described above and let H_n be the set of functions computable by $N_{\wedge,n}^k$. Then, unless RP = NP, there is no efficient learning algorithm for the graded class $H = \bigcup H_n$.*

25.3 Linear Threshold Networks with Real Inputs

The result of the previous section is limited, since it shows that learning is difficult for a rather unusual network class, that of two-layer linear threshold networks in which the output unit is constrained to compute a conjunction. In this section, we extend the result to linear threshold networks with an arbitrary linear threshold output unit.

For each $k \geq 3$ and $n \geq 1$, define the class N_n^k of two-layer linear threshold networks as follows. A network in N_n^k has n real inputs, k linear threshold units in the first layer, and one linear threshold output unit. The following result extends Corollary 25.3 from the class $N_\wedge^k$ to the class $N^k = \bigcup_n N_n^k$.

Theorem 25.4 *Let k be any fixed integer that is at least 3. Suppose that N_n^k is the network described above and let H_n be the set of functions computable by N_n^k. Then, unless RP = NP, there is no efficient learning algorithm for the graded class $H = \bigcup H_n$.*

Proof We use the reduction of Theorem 25.1, and augment the inputs with two extra (real) components, which we use to force the output unit to compute a conjunction.

Specifically, given a graph G with $n \geq 3$ vertices, we show that there is a training sample $\tilde{z}(G)$ that is consistent with a function in N_n^k if and only if G is k-colourable. Furthermore, $\tilde{z}(G)$ can be computed in

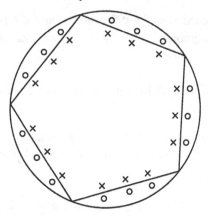

Fig. 25.2. The sets S_{in} and S_{out} used in the proof of Theorem 25.4, for the case $k = 5$. The points in S_{in} are marked as crosses; those in S_{out} are marked as circles.

polynomial time. The sample $\tilde{z} = \tilde{z}(G)$ consists of the following labelled examples:

- $((0, 0, e_i), 0)$, for $i = 1, 2, \ldots, n$;
- $((0, 0, e_i + e_j), 1)$ for each edge $ij \in E$;
- $(\mathbf{0}, 1)$, where $\mathbf{0}$ is the all-0 vector;
- $((s, 0), 1)$, for $s \in S_{\text{in}} \subset \mathbb{R}^2$; and
- $((s, 0), 0)$, for $s \in S_{\text{out}} \subset \mathbb{R}^2$,

where S_{in} and S_{out} will be defined shortly. Here, the first three types of labelled examples are those used in the reduction described in the proof of Theorem 25.1, augmented with two real inputs set to zero. The sets S_{in} and S_{out} both have cardinality $3k$. Each point in S_{in} is paired with a point in S_{out}, and this pair straddles some edge of a regular k-sided polygon in $\mathbb{R}^2$ that has vertices on the unit circle centred at the origin, as shown in Figure 25.2. (We call this pair of points a 'straddling pair'.) The midpoint of each pair lies on some edge of the polygon, and the line passing through the pair is perpendicular to that edge. The set of $3k$ midpoints (one for each pair) and the k vertices of the polygon are equally spaced around the polygon. Let α denote the distance between a point in $S_{\text{in}} \cup S_{\text{out}}$ and its associated edge. Clearly, since the points in $\{(s, 0) : s \in S_{\text{in}}\}$ are labelled 1 and those in $\{(s, 0) : s \in S_{\text{out}}\}$ are labelled 0, for every straddling pair described above, any consistent function in N_n^k has some hidden unit whose decision boundary separates the pair. It is easy to show using elementary trigonometry that there is a constant c such that, if $\alpha < c/k$, no line in $\mathbb{R}^2$ can pass between more than three of these pairs, and no line can pass between three unless they all straddle the same edge of the polygon. Since k lines must separate $3k$ straddling pairs, and the origin must be classified as 1, any function in N_n^k that is consistent with $\tilde{z}$ can be represented as a conjunction of k linear threshold functions. Clearly, the extra input components do not affect the reduction from the proof of Theorem 25.1. Thus, there is a function in N_n^k consistent with $\tilde{z}(G)$ if and only if the graph G is k-colourable. One can show fairly directly that this is also true if the components of vectors in S_{in} and S_{out} must be ratios of integers, provided the integers are allowed to be as large as ck^2, for some constant c (the proof is omitted). Hence, for each k, the number of bits in $\tilde{z}(G)$ is linear in the size of the graph G. $\qquad\square$

It is clear from the proof that the same result is true if the output unit is chosen from any class of boolean functions that contains conjunction.

25.4 Sigmoid Networks

Fix a positive constant K and let $\sigma : \mathbb{R} \to [0,1]$ be a monotone function satisfying the Lipschitz constraint

$$|\sigma(\alpha_1) - \sigma(\alpha_2)| \le |\alpha_1 - \alpha_2|$$

for all $\alpha_1, \alpha_2 \in \mathbb{R}$. Then define $N_{\sigma,n}^2$ as the class of two-layer sigmoid network with n real inputs, two units in the first layer, each with the activation function σ, and a single linear output unit, with weights bounded by K and no threshold. That is, $N_{\sigma,n}^2$ computes the class

$$
\begin{aligned}
F = \quad &\{x \mapsto w_1\sigma\left(v_1 \cdot x + v_{1,0}\right) + w_2\sigma\left(v_2 \cdot x + v_{2,0}\right) : \\
&|w_1|, |w_2| \le K,\ v_1, v_2 \in \mathbb{R}^n,\ v_{1,0}, v_{2,0} \in \mathbb{R}\} \, .
\end{aligned}
$$

Consider the following approximate-SEM problem for the graded space $N_\sigma^2 = \bigcup_n N_{\sigma,n}^2$.

N_σ^2-APPROX-SEM
Instance: $z = ((x_1, y_1), \ldots, (x_m, y_m)) \in (\mathbb{R}^n \times \{0,1\})^m$.
Problem: Find $f \in N_{\sigma,n}^2$ such that

$$\hat{\text{er}}_z(f) = \frac{1}{m}\sum_{i=1}^{m}(f(x_i) - y_i)^2 < \inf_{g \in F} \hat{\text{er}}_z(f) + \frac{1}{100m}.$$

The following theorem implies that the class N_σ^2 is not efficiently learnable in the restricted model of Part 3, unless RP = NP. We omit the proof.

Theorem 25.5 *The problem N_σ^2-APPROX-SEM is NP-hard.*

A similar result applies to larger networks. Let $\sigma : \mathbb{R} \to [0,1]$ be a monotone function, and define $N_{\sigma,n}^k$ as the class of two-layer sigmoid network with n real inputs, k units in the first layer, each with the activation function σ, and a single linear output unit, with positive weights summing to one, and no threshold. That is, $N_{\sigma,n}^k$ computes the class

$$F = \left\{ x \mapsto \sum_{i=1}^{k} w_i \sigma \left(v_i \cdot x + v_{i,0} \right) : \right.$$

$$\left. v_i \in \mathbb{R}^n, \ v_{i,0} \in \mathbb{R}, \ w_i \geq 0, \ \sum_{i=1}^{k} w_i = 1 \right\}.$$

Consider the following approximate-SEM problem for the graded space $N_\sigma^p = \bigcup_n N_{\sigma,n}^{p(n)}$, where p is some polynomial.

N_σ^p-APPROX-SEM
Instance: $z = ((x_1, y_1), \ldots, (x_m, y_m)) \in (\mathbb{R}^n \times \{0,1\})^m$.
Question: Find $f \in N_{\sigma,n}^{p(n)}$ such that

$$\hat{\mathrm{er}}_z(f) = \frac{1}{m} \sum_{i=1}^{m} (f(x_i) - y_i)^2 < \inf_{g \in F} \hat{\mathrm{er}}_z(f) + \frac{1}{16p(n)^5 m}.$$

The following theorem shows that, unless RP = NP, N_σ^p is not efficiently learnable in the restricted model of Part 3. We omit the proof.

Theorem 25.6 *There is a polynomial p such that N_σ^p-APPROX-SEM is NP-hard.*

25.5 Remarks

Two hidden unit linear threshold networks

Corollary 25.2 shows that N^k-CONSISTENCY is NP-hard for $k \geq 3$. In fact, this problem is also NP-hard for $k = 2$, but the graph-colouring reduction does not establish this (since 2-colouring is easy). Instead, we show that N^2-CONSISTENCY is at least as hard as the SET-SPLITTING decision problem, defined as follows:

SET-SPLITTING

Instance: A set $S = \{x_1, x_2, \ldots, x_n\}$ and a collection $\mathcal{A} = \{A_1, A_2, \ldots, A_l\}$ of subsets of S.

Question: Are there subsets S_1, S_2 of S such that $S = S_1 \cup S_2$ and such that, for each i between 1 and l, A_i does *not* lie entirely within S_1 or S_2?

In fact, the set-splitting problem is a generalization of 2-colouring. The pair $(S, \mathcal{A})$ is a hypergraph—a graph in which edges are sets of vertices of arbitrary size—and the set-splitting problem is equivalent to finding a 2-colouring of this hypergraph so that no edge in $\mathcal{A}$ has all vertices of the same colour.

For a given instance of SET-SPLITTING, let us define a training sample $z(\mathcal{A}) \in (\{0, 1\}^n \times \{0, 1\})^{n+l}$ as follows. The negative examples in $z(\mathcal{A})$ are $v_1, v_2, \ldots, v_n$, where, for i between 1 and n, v_i has a 1 in position i and 0 in every other position. The positive examples in $z(\mathcal{A})$ are $a_1, a_2, \ldots, a_l$ where, for i between 1 and l, a_i has a 1 in position j if $x_j \in A_i$ and a 0 in position j if $x_j \notin A_i$. It can be shown that the answer to the SET-SPLITTING problem in instance $\mathcal{A}$ is 'yes' *if and only if* the answer to N^2-CONSISTENCY on instance sample $z(\mathcal{A})$ is 'yes'. From this, the NP-hardness of N^2-CONSISTENCY follows.

25.6 Bibliographical Notes

The reduction used to prove Theorem 25.1 and the corresponding result for networks with two units in the first layer (described in Section 25.5) are due to Blum and Rivest (1992) (see also (Anthony and Biggs, 1992)). The proof is based on a proof due to Pitt and Valiant (1988) that learning k-term DNF is hard in the restricted model. Blum and Rivest also gave an extension to networks with two hidden units and an arbitrary linear threshold unit at the output. The extension of Theorem 25.4, using real inputs, is from (Bartlett and Ben-David, 1999).

Earlier, Judd (1990) proved NP-hardness results for an approximate-SEM problem for certain linear threshold networks. DasGupta, Siegelmann and Sontag (1995) proved NP-hardness of binary classification learning with two layer networks of units in which the first-layer units' activation function is a certain piecewise-linear function.

It has long been known that gradient descent algorithms for sigmoid networks can fail because of local minima (see, for example, (Sontag and Sussmann, 1989)). In fact, Auer, Herbster and Warmuth (1996) have shown that the number of local minima can be exponentially large in the number of network parameters. See also (Sontag, 1995), which gives upper bounds on the number of such local minima.

The results of Section 25.4, and the proofs of Theorems 25.5 and 25.6 are due to Jones (1997). Vu (1998) presents stronger results for sigmoid networks with an additional condition on the rate at which the activation function σ approaches its asymptotic values. In that case, he shows that approximate sample error minimization over N_σ^k is hard for all $k \geq 3$, provided the approximation error is smaller than some threshold that depends only on k and n, and not on the sample size m. Vu also gives hardness results for approximate sample error minimization over two-layer networks with linear threshold hidden units and a linear output unit. Related results are given in (Bartlett and Ben-David, 1999). Bartlett and Ben-David (1999) also show that approximate sample error minimization over certain classes of linear threshold network is hard. (The approximate sample error minimization problem is defined for binary-valued function classes in the obvious way, although it is not sufficient for the pattern classification problem studied in Part 1.)

The results of this chapter do not rule out the possibility that we can efficiently choose a function with error near-minimal over a certain neural network class, provided that the function is not restricted to the same class. For instance, if we use the class of linear threshold networks with two units in the first hidden layer as our touchstone class (see Section 2.5), it may be possible to efficiently choose a function that has error not much worse than that of the best network in the touchstone class. Baum (1990b) has shown that this is possible with a fixed input dimension, and with arbitrary input dimension provided the distribution is spherically symmetric. Another approach is to allow the training algorithm to also determine the size of the network; a number of algorithms of this kind have been proposed (see, for example, (Frean, 1990; Brent, 1991)), and we shall see two such algorithms in the next chapter.

Another way to make the learning problem easier is to give the learning algorithm more power. For instance, if we allow the algorithm to ask an expert for the labels associated with points in the input space of its choosing, this can significantly simplify the learning problem. There are a number of positive results for neural networks in models that allow *membership queries* (see (Angluin, 1988; Angluin, 1992; Kearns and Vazirani, 1995)) of this kind. For instance, Hancock, Golea and Marchand (1994) have proved such a result for two-layer linear threshold networks in which each input unit is connected to no more than one first-layer unit, and Baum (1990c; 1991) has proved a result of this kind for linear threshold networks with up to four hidden units.

26

Constructive Learning Algorithms for Two-Layer Networks

26.1 Introduction

In this chapter, we consider learning algorithms for classes F of real-valued functions that can be expressed as convex combinations of functions from some class G of basis functions. The key example of such a class is that of feed-forward networks with a linear output unit in which the sum of the magnitudes of the output weights is bounded by some constant B. In this case, the basis function class G is the set of functions that can be computed by any non-output unit in the network, and their negations, scaled by B. We investigate two algorithms. Section 26.2 describes Construct, an algorithm for the real prediction problem, and Section 26.3 describes Adaboost, an algorithm for the restricted version of the real classification problem. Both algorithms use a learning algorithm for the basis function class to iteratively add basis functions to a convex combination, leaving previous basis functions fixed.

26.2 Real Estimation with Convex Combinations of Basis Functions

Theorem 14.10 (Section 14.4) shows that any convex combination of bounded basis functions can be accurately approximated (with respect to the distance $d_{L_2(P)}$, for instance) using a small convex combination. This shows that the approximate-SEM problem for the class $co(G)$ can be solved by considering only small convex combinations of functions from G. In fact, the problem can be simplified even further. The following theorem shows that we can construct a small convex combination in an iterative way, by greedily minimizing error as each basis function is added.

342

Theorem 26.1 *Let V be a vector space with an inner product, and let* $\|f\| = \sqrt{(f, f)}$ *be the induced norm on V. Suppose that $G \subset V$ and that, for some $B > 0$, $\|g\| \leq B$ for all $g \in G$. Fix $f \in V$, $k \in \mathbb{N}$, and $c \geq B^2$, and define $\hat{f}_0 = 0$. Then for $i = 1, \ldots, k$, choose $g_i \in G$ such that*

$$\|f - \hat{f}_i\|^2 \leq \inf_{g \in G} \|f - ((1 - \alpha_i)\hat{f}_{i-1} + \alpha_i g)\|^2 + \epsilon_i,$$

where $\alpha_i = 2/(i + 1)$, $\epsilon_i \leq 4(c - B^2)/(i + 1)^2$, and we define

$$\hat{f}_i = (1 - \alpha_i)\hat{f}_{i-1} + \alpha_i g_i.$$

Then

$$\|f - \hat{f}_k\|^2 < \inf_{\hat{f} \in \mathrm{co}(G)} \|f - \hat{f}\|^2 + \frac{4c}{k}.$$

Proof Let $d_f = \inf_{\hat{f} \in \mathrm{co}(G)} \|\hat{f} - f\|$. Given $\delta > 0$, let f_δ be a point in the convex hull of G with $\|f_\delta - f\| \leq d_f + \delta$. Thus $f_\delta = \sum_{j=1}^{N} \gamma_j g_j$ with $g_j \in G$, $\gamma_j \geq 0$ and $\sum_{j=1}^{N} \gamma_j = 1$ for some sufficiently large N. Then for all $1 \leq i \leq k$ and $\alpha_i \in [0, 1]$,

$$
\begin{aligned}
&\|(1 - \alpha_i)\hat{f}_{i-1} + \alpha_i g - f\|^2 \\
&= \|(1 - \alpha_i)\hat{f}_{i-1} + \alpha_i g - f_\delta + f_\delta - f\|^2 \\
&= \|(1 - \alpha_i)\hat{f}_{i-1} + \alpha_i g - f_\delta\|^2 + \|f_\delta - f\|^2 \\
&\quad + 2((1 - \alpha_i)\hat{f}_{i-1} + \alpha_i g - f_\delta, f_\delta - f).
\end{aligned}
$$

Thus,

$$
\begin{aligned}
&\|(1 - \alpha_i)\hat{f}_{i-1} + \alpha_i g - f\|^2 - \|f_\delta - f\|^2 \\
&= \|(1 - \alpha_i)\hat{f}_{i-1} + \alpha_i g - f_\delta\|^2 + 2((1 - \alpha_i)\hat{f}_{i-1} + \alpha_i g - f_\delta, f_\delta - f) \\
&= \|(1 - \alpha_i)(\hat{f}_{i-1} - f_\delta) + \alpha_i(g - f_\delta)\|^2 \\
&\quad + 2((1 - \alpha_i)\hat{f}_{i-1} + \alpha_i g - f_\delta, f_\delta - f) \\
&= (1 - \alpha_i)^2\|\hat{f}_{i-1} - f_\delta\|^2 + \alpha_i^2\|g - f_\delta\|^2 \\
&\quad + 2(1 - \alpha_i)\alpha_i(\hat{f}_{i-1} - f_\delta, g - f_\delta) \\
&\quad + 2((1 - \alpha_i)\hat{f}_{i-1} + \alpha_i g - f_\delta, f_\delta - f).
\end{aligned}
$$

Let g be independently drawn from the set $\{g_1, \ldots, g_N\}$ with $\Pr(g = g_j) = \gamma_j$. Recall that $f_\delta = \sum_{j=1}^{N} \gamma_j g_j$. Hence, the average value of

$\|(1 - \alpha_i)\hat{f}_{i-1} + \alpha_i g - f\|^2 - \|f_\delta - f\|^2$ is

$$\sum_{j=1}^{N} \gamma_j \left((1 - \alpha_i)^2 \|\hat{f}_{i-1} - f_\delta\|^2 + \alpha_i^2 \|g_j - f_\delta\|^2 \right.$$

$$+ 2(1 - \alpha_i)\alpha_i(\hat{f}_{i-1} - f_\delta, g_j - f_\delta)$$

$$\left. + 2((1 - \alpha_i)\hat{f}_{i-1} + \alpha_i g_j - f_\delta, f_\delta - f) \right)$$

$$= (1 - \alpha_i)^2 \|\hat{f}_{i-1} - f_\delta\|^2 + \alpha_i^2 \sum_{j=1}^{N} \gamma_j \|g_j - f_\delta\|^2$$

$$+ 2((1 - \alpha_i)\hat{f}_{i-1} + \alpha_i f_\delta - f_\delta, f_\delta - f)$$

$$= (1 - \alpha_i)^2 \|\hat{f}_{i-1} - f_\delta\|^2$$

$$+ \alpha_i^2 \left(\sum_{j=1}^{N} \gamma_j \left(\|g_j\|^2 - 2(g_j, f_\delta) + \|f_\delta\|^2 \right) \right)$$

$$+ 2(1 - \alpha_i)(\hat{f}_{i-1} - f_\delta, f_\delta - f)$$

$$= (1 - \alpha_i)^2 \|\hat{f}_{i-1} - f_\delta\|^2 + \alpha_i^2 \left(\sum_{j=1}^{N} \gamma_j \|g_j\|^2 - \|f_\delta\|^2 \right)$$

$$+ 2(1 - \alpha_i)(\hat{f}_{i-1} - f_\delta, f_\delta - f)$$

$$\leq (1 - \alpha_i)^2 \|\hat{f}_{i-1} - f_\delta\|^2 + \alpha_i^2 B^2 + 2(1 - \alpha_i)(\hat{f}_{i-1} - f_\delta, f_\delta - f)$$

Since the average is bounded in this way, there must be some g $\{g_1, \ldots, g_N\}$ such that

$$\|(1 - \alpha_i)\hat{f}_{i-1} + \alpha_i g - f\|^2 - \|f_\delta - f\|^2$$

$$\leq (1 - \alpha_i)^2 \|\hat{f}_{i-1} - f_\delta\|^2 + \alpha_i^2 B^2 + 2(1 - \alpha_i)(\hat{f}_{i-1} - f_\delta, f_\delta - f)$$

$$= (1 - \alpha_i)\left((1 - \alpha_i)\|\hat{f}_{i-1} - f_\delta\|^2 + 2(\hat{f}_{i-1} - f_\delta, f_\delta - f) \right) + \alpha_i^2 B$$

$$\leq (1 - \alpha_i)\left(\|\hat{f}_{i-1} - f_\delta\|^2 + 2(\hat{f}_{i-1} - f_\delta, f_\delta - f) \right) + \alpha_i^2 B^2, \quad (26$$

where the last inequality holds since $\alpha_i \geq 0$. Noting that

$$\|\hat{f}_{i-1} - f\|^2 = \|\hat{f}_{i-1} - f_\delta\|^2 + \|f_\delta - f\|^2 + 2(\hat{f}_{i-1} - f_\delta, f_\delta - f),$$

we get

$$\|\hat{f}_{i-1} - f\|^2 - \|f_\delta - f\|^2 = \|\hat{f}_{i-1} - f_\delta\|^2 + 2(\hat{f}_{i-1} - f_\delta, f_\delta - f).$$

Substituting into Inequality (26.1) and taking the limit as δ goes to 0, we get

$$\inf_{g \in G} \|(1-\alpha_i)\hat{f}_{i-1} + \alpha_i g - f\|^2 - d_f^2 \leq (1-\alpha_i)\left(\|\hat{f}_{i-1} - f\|^2 - d_f^2\right) + \alpha_i^2 B^2.$$

$$(26.2)$$

Setting $i = 1$, $\alpha_1 = 1$ and $\hat{f}_0 = 0$, we see that

$$\inf_{g \in G} \|g - f\|^2 - d_f^2 \leq B^2.$$

Hence the theorem is true for $k = 1$. Assume, as an inductive hypothesis, that

$$\|\hat{f}_{i-1} - f\|^2 - d_f^2 < \frac{4c}{(i-1)}.$$

Then (26.2) implies that

$$\inf_{g \in G} \|(1-\alpha_i)\hat{f}_{i-1} + \alpha_i g - f\|^2 - d_f^2 + \epsilon_i < \frac{(1-\alpha_i)4c}{(i-1)} + \alpha_i^2 B^2 + \frac{4(c-B^2)}{(i+1)^2}.$$

Setting $\alpha_i = 2/(i+1)$ gives

$$\inf_{g \in G} \|(1-\alpha_i)\hat{f}_{i-1} + \alpha_i g - f\|^2 - d_f^2 + \epsilon_i$$

$$< \frac{4c}{i-1}\left(1 - \frac{2}{i+1}\right) + \frac{4B^2}{(i+1)^2} + \frac{4(c-B^2)}{(i+1)^2}$$

$$= \frac{4c}{(i+1)} + \frac{4c}{(i+1)^2}$$

$$= \frac{4c(i^2+2i)}{(i^2+2i+1)i}$$

$$< \frac{4c}{i}.$$

The theorem follows. $\square$

As always, we are concerned with a vector space of functions, and we interpret the squared norm $\|f - \hat{f}_k\|^2$ as the error of $\hat{f}_k$ in approximating a target function f. Theorem 26.1 improves Theorem 14.10 in two ways. First, it shows how to iteratively construct an approximating function $\hat{f}_k$, whereas Theorem 14.10 proved only the existence of such a function. Second, it is concerned with approximating any function f, not just a function in the convex hull of G. It gives the same rate as Theorem 14.10. That is, the error of a convex combination of k functions from G in approximating any function f decreases to the error of an arbitrary convex combination at the same rate as it would if f were itself a convex combination.

The algorithm Construct

At step i of the construction described by Theorem 26.1, the basis function g_i is chosen to approximately minimize

$$\|f - ((1 - \alpha_i)\hat{f}_{i-1} + \alpha_i g)\|^2.$$

Notice that we can express this as approximately minimizing $\alpha_i^2\|\tilde{f}_i - g\|^2$, where

$$\tilde{f}_i = \frac{1}{\alpha_i}f - \frac{1 - \alpha_i}{\alpha_i}\hat{f}_{i-1}.$$

This observation suggests a constructive algorithm that uses an approximate-SEM algorithm for a class G to approximately minimize sample error over the class $\mathrm{co}(G)$. To apply Theorem 26.1, we define the inner product of functions f_1 and f_2 to be

$$(f_1, f_2) = \frac{1}{m}\sum_{i=1}^{m} f_1(x_i)f_2(x_i).$$

For $z = ((x_1, y_1), \dots, (x_m, y_m))$, we define f^* as the empirical conditional expectation of y given some x_i,

$$f^*(x_i) = \hat{\mathbb{E}}_z[y|x_i] = \frac{\sum\{y_j : x_j = x_i\}}{|\{j : x_j = x_i\}|}.$$

Then we have

$$
\begin{aligned}
\hat{\mathrm{er}}_z(f) &= \frac{1}{m}\sum_{i=1}^{m}(y_i - f(x_i))^2 \\
&= \|f - f^*\|^2 + \frac{2}{m}\sum_{i=1}^{m}(y_i - f^*(x_i))\,(f(x_i) - f^*(x_i)) \\
&\quad + \frac{1}{m}\sum_{i=1}^{m}(y_i - f^*(x_i))^2 \\
&= \|f - f^*\|^2 + \frac{1}{m}\sum_{i=1}^{m}(y_i - f^*(x_i))^2.
\end{aligned}
$$

Since the choice of f cannot affect the second term, choosing f to minimize the first term corresponds to minimizing $\hat{\mathrm{er}}_z(f)$.

Figure 26.1 shows pseudocode for the algorithm $\mathrm{Construct}_L$, which makes use of an approximate-SEM algorithm L for the basis function class G.

Corollary 26.2 *Suppose that $G = \bigcup_n G_n$ is a graded class of real-valued functions that map to some bounded interval, and L is an efficient*

```
arguments: Training set, S = {(x₁,y₁),...,(xₘ,yₘ)} ⊂ (X × ℝ)ᵐ
           Number of iterations, k
           Bound, B, on range of functions in G
returns:   Convex combination of functions from G, f̂ₖ = Σᵏᵢ₌₁ γₖgₖ
```

function Construct$_L$ (S, k, B)
  $\hat{f}_0 := 0$
  for $i := 1$ to k
    $\alpha_i := 2/(i+1)$
    for $j := 1$ to m
      $\tilde{y}_j = (1/\alpha_i) \left(y_j - (1-\alpha_i)\hat{f}_{i-1}(x_j) \right)$
    end for
    $\tilde{S} = \{(x_1, \tilde{y}_1), \ldots, (x_m, \tilde{y}_m)\}$
    $g_i := L(\tilde{S}, B^2)$
    $\hat{f}_i := (1-\alpha_i)\hat{f}_{i-1} + \alpha_i g_i$
  endfor
  return $\hat{f}_k$
end

Fig. 26.1. Pseudocode for the Construct$_L$ algorithm. (L is an approximate-SEM algorithm for $G \subset [-B, B]^X$.)

approximate-SEM algorithm for G, with running time $O(p(m, n, 1/\epsilon))$ for some polynomial p. Then the algorithm Construct$_L$ can be used as the basis of an efficient approximate-SEM algorithm for $co(G) = \bigcup_n co(G_n)$, and this algorithm has running time $O(p(m, n, 1/\epsilon^2)/\epsilon)$.

Proof Suppose that functions in G map to $[-B, B]$. Given a training set S and desired error ϵ, if we set $k = \lceil 8B^2/\epsilon \rceil$ and call the algorithm Construct$_L(S, k, B)$, then Theorem 26.1 implies that the function $f \in co(G)$ returned by the algorithm satisfies

$$\hat{\text{er}}_z(f) < \inf_{\hat{f} \in co(G)} \hat{\text{er}}_z(\hat{f}) + \frac{8B^2}{k} \leq \inf_{\hat{f} \in co(G)} \hat{\text{er}}_z(\hat{f}) + \epsilon,$$

so this is an approximate-SEM algorithm for $co(G)$. It is easy to check that the running time of the algorithm is $O(p(m, n, 1/\epsilon^2)/\epsilon)$.   □

Sample complexity

We have seen that, if there is a learning algorithm L for a class G of bounded real-valued functions, then Construct$_L$ can be used to give a learning algorithm for the convex hull $co(G)$ of the class. If we appeal to the error bounds for convex classes given in Theorem 20.7, together with the covering number bounds for convex combinations of functions that follow from Theorems 14.11 and 12.8, we obtain the following sample complexity bound for this learning algorithm.

Theorem 26.3 *There is a constant c such that for any class G of $[-B, B]$-valued functions with finite fat-shattering dimension, if there is an approximate-SEM algorithm for G then it can be used to construct a learning algorithm L for co(G) that has sample complexity*

$$m_L(\epsilon, \delta) = O\left(\frac{B^4}{\epsilon}\left(\frac{B^6}{\epsilon^2}\text{fat}_G\left(c\epsilon/B^3\right)\ln^2\left(\frac{B}{\epsilon}\right) + \ln\left(\frac{1}{\delta}\right)\right)\right).$$

In some cases, it is possible to obtain a better sample complexity bound by using the approximation result of Theorem 26.1 more directly.

Theorem 26.4 *Let G be a class of $[-B, B]$-valued functions, and define the set $\text{co}_k(G)$ of convex combinations of k functions from G,*

$$\text{co}_k(G) = \left\{\sum_{i=1}^{k}\alpha_i g_i : g_i \in G, \alpha_i \geq 0, \sum_{i=1}^{k}\alpha_i = 1\right\}.$$

If there is a learning algorithm L for G, then the algorithm Construct$_L$ can be used as the basis of a learning algorithm for co(G). There is a constant c such that the sample complexity m of this learning algorithm satisfies

$$m \leq \frac{cB^4}{\epsilon}\ln\left(\frac{\mathcal{N}_1\left(\epsilon/(64B^3), \text{co}_k(G), 2m\right)}{\delta}\right),$$

where $k = \lceil 16B^2/\epsilon \rceil$.

Proof Fix a probability distribution P and suppose that $f_a \in \overline{\text{co}(G)}$ satisfies $\mathbf{E}(y - f_a(x)) = \inf_{f \in F'}\mathbf{E}(y - f(x))$. Lemma 20.11 shows that

$$P^m\left\{\exists f \in \text{co}_k(G), \frac{\mathbf{E}g_f - \hat{\mathbf{E}}_z g_f}{\mathbf{E}g_f + \epsilon/2} \geq \frac{1}{2}\right\}$$

$$\leq 2\mathcal{N}_1\left(\frac{\epsilon}{64B}, \text{co}_k(G), 2m\right)\exp\left(-\frac{3\epsilon m}{10432B^2}\right)$$

$$+ 4\mathcal{N}_1\left(\frac{\epsilon}{64B^3}, \text{co}_k(G), 2m\right)\exp\left(-\frac{\epsilon m}{32B^4}\right), \quad (26.3)$$

where $g_f = \ell_f - \ell_{f_a}$. The inequality inside the probability statement is true for some $f \in \mathrm{co}_k(G)$ precisely when

$$\mathbf{E}((y - f(x))^2 - (y - f_a(x))^2) \geq 2\hat{\mathbf{E}}_z((y - f(x))^2 - (y - f_a(x))^2) + \epsilon/2.$$

Now, the algorithm ensures that

$$\hat{\mathbf{E}}_z(y - \hat{f}_k(x))^2 \leq \hat{\mathbf{E}}_z(y - f_a(x))^2 + \frac{4B^2}{k},$$

so the probability that some $f \in \mathrm{co}_k(G)$ has

$$\mathbf{E}((y - f(x))^2 - (y - f_a(x))^2) \geq \frac{8B^2}{k} + \frac{\epsilon}{2}$$

is no more than the quantity on the right hand side of Inequality (26.3). Choosing $k = \lceil 16B^2/\epsilon \rceil$ and rearranging gives the result. $\square$

Neural networks

Theorem 26.4 has an immediate corollary for two-layer neural networks. Let G be the class of scaled and possibly negated linear threshold functions defined on $\mathbb{R}^n$, $G = BH \cup -BH$, with

$$H = \left\{ x \mapsto \mathrm{sgn}(w^T x + w_0) : w \in \mathbb{R}^n,\, w_0 \in \mathbb{R} \right\},$$

and $BH = \{Bh : h \in H\}$. Then $F = \mathrm{co}(G)$ is the class of two-layer networks with linear threshold units in the first layer and a linear output unit with the constraint that the magnitudes of the output weights sum to B.

Theorem 26.5 *There is a learning algorithm L for the class F of two-layer networks defined above, and L has sample complexity*

$$m_L(\epsilon, \delta) = O\left(\frac{B^4}{\epsilon} \left(\frac{nB^2}{\epsilon} \ln\left(\frac{B}{\epsilon} \right) + \ln\left(\frac{1}{\delta} \right) \right) \right).$$

Proof The algorithm Splitting described in Figure 24.1 enumerates all restrictions to the training sample of linear threshold functions with fan-in bounded by k. Clearly, this can be used as the basis of a SEM algorithm for this class. If $k = n$, it leads to a SEM algorithm for the class H of linear threshold functions (although the algorithm takes time exponential in n in that case). By separately enumerating the restriction to the sample of all functions in BH and $-BH$ and returning the function with minimum sample error, we can use Splitting as the basis of a SEM algorithm, and hence learning algorithm L for G. Then the algorithm $\texttt{Construct}_L$ is an approximate-SEM algorithm for the class F.

To prove the sample complexity bound, first notice that Theorems 3.4 and 3.7 imply $\Pi_H(m) < (em/n)^n$ for $m \geq n$. Hence we have

$$
\begin{aligned}
\mathcal{N}_1\left(\epsilon, \mathrm{co}_k(G), m\right) &\leq \binom{2\Pi_H(m)}{k} \\
&\qquad \times \max\left\{\mathcal{N}_1\left(\epsilon, \mathrm{co}(S), m\right) : S \subseteq G, |S| = k\right\} \\
&\leq \left(\frac{em}{n}\right)^{2nk} e(k+1)\left(\frac{2eB}{\epsilon}\right)^k \\
&= \left(\frac{2eB}{\epsilon}\left(\frac{em}{n}\right)^{2n}\right)^k e(k+1),
\end{aligned}
$$

where the second inequality follows from Theorem 18.4. Substituting into Theorem 26.4 and applying Inequality (1.2) from Appendix 1 gives the result. □

It is interesting that the algorithm in Theorem 26.5, which minimizes sample error over some restricted subset of the class, has a better sample complexity bound than that implied by Theorem 26.3 for a simple SEM algorithm. In contrast, we saw in Section 5.4 that in the pattern classification problem, sample error minimization gives optimal sample complexity.

The learning algorithm L that features in Theorem 26.5 is the algorithm $\texttt{Construct}$, based on a learning algorithm for linear threshold functions. Unfortunately, results in Chapter 24 show that the problem of learning linear threshold functions is computationally difficult. If, instead of this class, we consider the class H^k of linear threshold functions with fan-in bounded by k (see Section 24.3), then the algorithm $\texttt{Splitting}$ can be used as the basis of an efficient learning algorithm for this class. $\texttt{Construct}$, based on this algorithm, then leads to an efficient learning algorithm for the class of two-layer networks containing linear threshold units with bounded fan-in in the first layer and a linear output unit with bounded weights.

Theorem 26.6 *Let H_n^k be the set of bounded fan-in linear threshold functions,*

$$
H_n^k = \left\{x \mapsto \mathrm{sgn}(w^T x + w_0) : w \in \mathbb{R}^n, |\{i : w_i \neq 0\}| \leq k, w_0 \in \mathbb{R}\right\},
$$

and let $F_n^k = \mathrm{co}(BH_n^k \cup -BH_n^k)$. *Then the algorithm* Construct, *based on the algorithm* Splitting, *is an efficient learning algorithm for the graded class* $F^k = \bigcup_n F_n^k$.

Clearly, the sample complexity bound of Theorem 26.5 is also valid in this case, since F_n^k is a subset of the class F considered in that theorem.

26.3 Classification Learning using Boosting

This section describes a learning algorithm for a convex combination of binary-valued functions from some set H. We show that, provided the algorithm has access to a learning algorithm for H, it is successful in the restricted model of classification learning with real functions. In this model, we assume that for some $\gamma > 0$ the distribution P on $X \times \{0, 1\}$ is such that for some function $f \in F$ we have $\mathrm{margin}(f(x), y) \geq \gamma$ with probability 1. (Recall that $\mathrm{margin}(f(x), y)$ is $f(x) - 1/2$ if $y = 1$ and $1/2 - f(x)$ otherwise.) If $F = \mathrm{co}(H)$, the following lemma shows that this condition implies that some $h \in H$ is a weak predictor of the label y, in the sense that $h(x)$ disagrees with y slightly less frequently than a random guess.

Lemma 26.7 *Suppose that the sample* $z = ((x_1, y_1), \ldots, (x_m, y_m))$ *and the function* $f \in \mathrm{co}(H)$ *are such that* $\mathrm{margin}(f(x_i), y_i) \geq \gamma$ *for* $i = 1, \ldots, m$. *Then for all distributions* D *on* $\{(x_1, y_1), \ldots, (x_m, y_m)\}$, *some* $h \in H$ *has*

$$\mathrm{er}_D(h) \leq \frac{1}{2} - \gamma.$$

Proof We use the probabilistic method. Suppose that $f = \sum_{i=1}^N \alpha_i h_i$ with $h_i \in H$, $\alpha_i \geq 0$ and $\sum_{i=1}^N \alpha_i = 1$. Choose $h \in \{h_1, \ldots, h_N\}$ randomly with $\Pr(h = h_i) = \alpha_i$. Then

$$
\begin{aligned}
\mathbf{E}\,\mathrm{er}_D(h) &= \sum_{i=1}^N \alpha_i \sum_{j=1}^m D(x_j, y_j) 1_{h_i(x_j) \neq y_j} \\
&= \sum_{j=1}^m D(x_j, y_j) \sum_{i=1}^N \alpha_i 1_{h_i(x_j) \neq y_j}.
\end{aligned}
$$

Consider the inner sum, and suppose first that $y_j = 0$. Clearly, the indicator function $1_{h_i(x_j) \neq y_j} = h_i(x_j)$ in that case, so the inner sum is $f(x_j)$. Since $\mathrm{margin}(f(x_j), y_j) \geq \gamma$, we have $f(x_j) \leq 1/2 - \gamma$. Similarly, if $y_j = 1$, the inner sum is $1 - f(x_j) \leq 1/2 - \gamma$. Hence, $\mathrm{Eer}_D(h) \leq 1/2 - \gamma$, and the result follows. □

This lemma shows that in the restricted model of classification learning for a class $F = \mathrm{co}(H)$, some function in the basis class H can provide useful predictions. A converse result is also true: if, for any distribution on a training set there is a function in H that has error slightly better than random guessing, then some $f \in \mathrm{co}(H)$ has large margins. The proof of this is constructive. We show that we can use a SEM algorithm for H to construct a large margin SEM algorithm for $\mathrm{co}(H)$. Actually, we need something slightly stronger than a SEM algorithm for H: we need an algorithm that can minimize *weighted* sample error. By this, we mean that for any distribution D on a training sample $\{(x_1, y_1), \ldots, (x_m, y_m)\}$, the algorithm returns $h \in H$ minimizing $\mathrm{er}_D(h)$. The algorithm Adaboost, illustrated in Figure 26.2, iteratively combines basis functions returned by a weighted SEM algorithm L. The idea behind Adaboost is to start with a uniform weighting over the training sample, and progressively adjust the weights to emphasize the examples that have been frequently misclassified by the basis functions. The basis functions returned by the algorithm L are combined, with convex coefficients that depend on their respective weighted errors. The following theorem shows that Adaboost is a large margin SEM algorithm.

Recall that the sample error of a function f with respect to γ on a sample z is

$$\hat{\mathrm{er}}_z^\gamma(f) = \frac{1}{m} \left| \{ i : \mathrm{margin}(f(x_i), y_i) < \gamma \} \right|,$$

where the margin is the amount by which $f(x_i)$ is to the correct side of the threshold value of $1/2$.

Theorem 26.8 *If L is a weighted sample error minimization algorithm for H, then Adaboost returns a function f that satisfies*

$$\hat{\mathrm{er}}_z^\gamma(f) \leq \prod_{t=1}^{T} 2\sqrt{\epsilon_t^{1-2\gamma}(1 - \epsilon_t)^{1+2\gamma}}.$$

In particular, if $\epsilon_t \leq 1/2 - 4\gamma$, then

$$\hat{\mathrm{er}}_z^\gamma(f) < (1 - \gamma^2)^{T/2},$$

and this is less than ϵ for $T \geq (2/\gamma^2) \ln(1/\epsilon)$.

argument: Training sample, $z = ((x_1, y_1), \ldots, (x_m, y_m)) \in (X \times \{0, 1\})^m$
            Number of iterations, T
returns: Convex combination of functions from H, $f = \sum_{i=1}^{T} \gamma_i h_i$.
function Adaboost(z, T)
    for all i from $i = 1, \ldots, m$
        $D_1(i) := 1/m$
    endfor
    for all t from $\{1, \ldots, T\}$
        $h_t := L(z, D_t)$

$$\epsilon_t := \sum_{i=1}^{m} D_t(i) 1_{h_t(x_i) \neq y_i}$$

$$\alpha_t := \frac{1}{2} \ln \left(\frac{1 - \epsilon_t}{\epsilon_t} \right)$$

$$Z_t := 2\sqrt{\epsilon_t(1 - \epsilon_t)}$$

    for all i from $i = 1, \ldots, m$

$$D_{t+1}(i) := \begin{cases} D_t(i)e^{-\alpha_t}/Z_t & \text{if } y_i = h_t(x_i) \\ D_t(i)e^{\alpha_t}/Z_t & \text{otherwise,} \end{cases}$$

        endfor
    endfor
    return $f = \dfrac{\sum_{t=1}^{T} \alpha_t h_t}{\sum_{i=1}^{T} \alpha_t}$.
end

Fig. 26.2. Pseudocode for the Adaboost algorithm. (L is a weighted sample error minimization algorithm.)

Proof Although the algorithm Adaboost specifies the choice of the coefficients α_t, for now we leave them unspecified, and at each step choose Z_t as an overall normalization factor so that D_{t+1} is always a distribution. Later, we shall show that the choice of α_t (and Z_t) specified in the algorithm is optimal.

It is convenient to scale the variables $y_1, \ldots, y_m$ and the basis functions $h_1, \ldots, h_m$ so that they take values in $\{-1, 1\}$. Define $\tilde{y}_i = 2y_i - 1$, $\tilde{h}_t = 2h_t - 1$, and $\tilde{f} = 2f - 1$. Then it is clear that margin$(f(x_i), y_i) < \gamma$ if and only if $\tilde{y}_i \tilde{f}(x_i) < 2\gamma$, which is equivalent to

$$\tilde{y}_i \sum_{t=1}^{T} \alpha_t \tilde{h}_t(x_i) < 2\gamma \sum_{t=1}^{T} \alpha_t,$$

and this implies

$$\exp\left(-\tilde{y}_i \sum_{t=1}^{T} \alpha_t \tilde{h}_t(x_i) + 2\gamma \sum_{t=1}^{T} \alpha_t\right) \geq 1.$$

It follows that

$$\hat{er}_z^\gamma(f) \leq \frac{1}{m} \sum_{i=1}^{m} \exp\left(-\tilde{y}_i \sum_{t=1}^{T} \alpha_t \tilde{h}_t(x_i) + 2\gamma \sum_{t=1}^{T} \alpha_t\right)$$

$$= \frac{1}{m} \exp\left(2\gamma \sum_{t=1}^{T} \alpha_t\right) \sum_{i=1}^{m} \exp\left(-\tilde{y}_i \sum_{t=1}^{T} \alpha_t \tilde{h}_t(x_i)\right).$$

Now,

$$D_{t+1}(i) = \frac{D_t(i) \exp\left(-\tilde{y}_i \tilde{h}_t(x_i) \alpha_t\right)}{Z_t},$$

and so

$$\exp\left(-\tilde{y}_i \sum_{t=1}^{T} \alpha_t \tilde{h}_t(x_i)\right) = \prod_{t=1}^{T} \exp\left(-\tilde{y}_i \tilde{h}_t(x_i) \alpha_t\right)$$

$$= \prod_{t=1}^{T} \frac{D_{t+1}(i)}{D_t(i)} Z_t$$

$$= \frac{D_{T+1}(i)}{D_1(i)} \prod_{t=1}^{T} Z_t.$$

It follows that

$$\hat{er}_z^\gamma(f) \leq \frac{1}{m} \exp\left(2\gamma \sum_{t=1}^{T} \alpha_t\right) \sum_{i=1}^{m} m D_{T+1}(i) \prod_{t=1}^{T} Z_t$$

$$= \exp\left(2\gamma \sum_{t=1}^{T} \alpha_t\right) \prod_{t=1}^{T} Z_t. \qquad (26.4)$$

To minimize this, we choose α_t to minimize, at each step, the normalization factor Z_t. We have

$$Z_t = \sum_{i=1}^{m} D_t(i) \exp\left(-\tilde{y}_i \tilde{h}_t(x_i) \alpha_t\right)$$

$$= \sum_{i:y_i=h_t(x_i)} D_t(i) e^{-\alpha_t} + \sum_{i:y_i \neq h_t(x_i)} D_t(i) e^{\alpha_t}$$

$$= (1 - \epsilon_t) e^{-\alpha_t} + \epsilon_t e^{\alpha_t}.$$

Differentiating with respect to α_t, setting to zero, and solving shows that $\alpha_t = (1/2)\ln((1 - \epsilon_t)/\epsilon_t)$ gives the minimum value $Z_t = 2\sqrt{(1 - \epsilon_t)\epsilon_t}$, and these values of α_t and Z_t are used in the Adaboost algorithm. Substituting into (26.4) gives the first inequality of the theorem. □

Theorem 23.4 shows that if there is an efficient learning algorithm for a binary class, then there is an efficient randomized SEM algorithm. It is clear that the proof of this theorem can be extended to show that in that case there is also an efficient randomized *weighted* sample error minimization algorithm. This, together with Theorem 26.8, shows that if a class H of binary-valued functions is learnable, then co(H) is learnable in the restricted real classification model. It is clear that Adaboost calls the learning algorithm L for H only $T = O((1/\gamma^2)\ln(1/\epsilon))$ times, so if L is an efficient learning algorithm for H, the Adaboost algorithm based on L is an efficient learning algorithm for co(H) in the restricted real classification model.

26.4 Bibliographical Notes

The iterative approximation result described in Theorem 26.1 is an improvement, due to Lee et al. (1996), of a result of Barron (1993). A weaker result (with a slower rate) was independently obtained by Koiran (1994). Darken, Donahue, Gurvits and Sontag (1997) extend the approximation result to non-Hilbert spaces. The algorithm Construct and the sample complexity bound Theorem 26.5 are also from (Lee et al., 1996) (see also (Lee et al., 1995b)). A similar result follows from more recent work of Auer, Kwek, Maass and Warmuth (1996), who consider learning two-layer networks in an online model.

Boosting algorithms were first proposed by Schapire (1990) to illustrate the equivalence of weak binary classification learning (producing a hypothesis with error slightly better than random guessing) and probably approximately correct learning (learning a binary class in the restricted model, using some richer class of hypotheses). There were a number of improvements of this result (see, for example, (Freund, 1995)). Subsequently, experimental machine learning researchers observed that this approach can give improvements in pattern classification problems (see, for instance, (Drucker, Cortes, Jackel, LeCun and Vapnik, 1994)). The algorithm Adaboost was introduced by Freund and Schapire (1997), and its experimental properties studied in (Freund and Schapire, 1996). A number of researchers noticed that this algorithm gave reductions in error when more basis functions were introduced, even after the sample error of the convex combination had been reduced to zero (Drucker and Cortes, 1996; Quinlan, 1996; Breiman, 1998). Theorem 26.8 suggests that in these cases Adaboost is increasing the margins of training examples, and the results of Part 2 show why the estimation error decreases. Theorem 26.8 is due to Schapire et al. (1998), extending in a straightforward way a similar result from (Freund and Schapire, 1997) for binary sample error.

The derivation of the optimal values of α_t and Z_t in the proof of Theorem 26.8 can be extended to show that the Adaboost algorithm chooses the basis functions h_t and their coefficients α_t to minimize in a greedy way the sample average of an exponential function of the margin of the linear combination $\sum_{t=1}^{T} \alpha_t h_t$ (see (Breiman, 1999; Frean and Downs, 1998)). Friedman, Hastie and Tibshirani (1998) interpret Adaboost as an approximate stagewise maximum likelihood algorithm, by viewing the exponential function as an approximate likelihood cost function. Mason, Bartlett and Baxter (1999) and Mason, Baxter, Bartlett and Frean (1999) have shown that minimizing the sample average of other functions of the margin (that do not penalize mistakes so fiercely) can give significant advantages. Grove and Schuurmans (1998) give experimental evidence suggesting that maximizing the minimum margin does not give optimal estimation error.

Appendix 1
Useful Results

This appendix is a collection of various inequalities and technical results that are useful in a number of places throughout the book.

A1.1 Inequalities

Estimates for natural logarithms

Elementary calculus shows that

$$1 + x \le e^x \qquad \text{for all } x \in \mathbb{R}. \qquad (1.1)$$

Setting $x = ab - 1$ and rearranging shows that

$$\ln a \le ab + \ln \frac{1}{b} - 1 \qquad \text{for all } a, b > 0, \qquad (1.2)$$

with equality only if $ab = 1$.

Another useful inequality is the following. For positive numbers a, b with $b < 1$ and $ab \ge 1$,

$$\ln^2 a \le 6ab + 3\ln^2(1/b). \qquad (1.3)$$

To prove this, we make use of two facts: first, for $x \ge 1$, $\ln^2 x \le 4x$ and, secondly, for $a, b > 0$,

$$\ln a \le \frac{ab}{\ln(1/b)} + \ln\left(\frac{\ln(1/b)}{b}\right).$$

The first of these can be shown easily, and the second follows from

$$\ln\left(\frac{ab}{\ln(1/b)}\right) \le \frac{ab}{\ln(1/b)}.$$

357

So, since $ab \geq 1$, we have $\ln^2(ab) \leq 4ab$, and

$$
\begin{aligned}
\ln^2 a \;\; &\leq\;\; 4ab - \ln^2 b - 2\ln a \ln b \\
&=\;\; 4ab - \ln^2 b + 2\ln(1/b)\left(\frac{ab}{\ln(1/b)} + \ln\left(\frac{\ln(1/b)}{b}\right)\right) \\
&\leq\;\; 4ab - \ln^2 b + 2ab + 2\ln(1/b)\left(\ln\left(\frac{1}{b}\right) + \ln\ln\left(\frac{1}{b}\right)\right) \\
&\leq\;\; 4ab - \ln^2 b + 2ab + 4\ln^2\left(\frac{1}{b}\right) \\
&=\;\; 6ab + 3\ln^2(1/b).
\end{aligned}
$$

Euler's inequality

Elementary calculus shows that $(1 + 1/x)^x < e$ and $(1 - 1/x)^x < e^{-1}$ for all $x > 0$. This implies that, for all $x > 0$ and $a \in \mathbb{R}$, if $a \neq 0$,

$$
\left(1 + \frac{a}{x}\right)^x < e^a. \tag{1.4}
$$

Stirling's approximation

For any $n \in \mathbb{N}$,

$$
n^n e^{-n}\sqrt{2\pi n}\, e^{1/(12n+1)} < n! < n^n e^{-n}\sqrt{2\pi n}\, e^{1/(12n)}. \tag{1.5}
$$

For a proof, see (Feller, 1968), for example.

Binomial theorem

It is easy to prove by induction that, for all $a \in \mathbb{R}$ and $d \in \mathbb{N}$,

$$
(1 + a)^d = \sum_{i=0}^{d} \binom{d}{i} a^i. \tag{1.6}
$$

Jensen's inequality

For a vector space X, a convex function $f : X \to \mathbb{R}$ is one for which

$$
f(\alpha a + (1 - \alpha)b) \leq \alpha f(a) + (1 - \alpha)f(b),
$$

for all $a, b \in X$ and $0 < \alpha < 1$. If f is a convex function, and x is a random variable in X, then

$$
\mathbf{E}\left(f(x)\right) \geq f\left(\mathbf{E}(x)\right).
$$

For a proof, see, for example, (Kolmogorov and Fomin, 1975).

Cauchy-Schwarz inequality

For any elements a, b of an inner product space,

$$(a, b) \leq \|a\|\|b\|, \tag{1.7}$$

where $\|a\|^2 = (a, a)$. To see why this is true, notice that the inequality is trivially true if $b = 0$, and if $b \neq 0$ we can write

$$\|a\|^2 - \frac{(a, b)^2}{\|b\|^2} = \left\|a - \frac{(a, b)b}{\|b\|^2}\right\|^2 \geq 0.$$

Hölder inequalities

For $a, b \in \mathbb{R}^k$, the standard inner product (a, b) may be bounded as follows:

$$
\begin{aligned}
(a, b) = \sum_{i=1}^{k} a_i b_i &\leq \sum_{i=1}^{k} |a_i||b_i| \\
&\leq \left(\sum_{i=1}^{k} |a_i|\right) \max_i |b_i| \\
&= \|a\|_1 \|b\|_\infty.
\end{aligned} \tag{1.8}
$$

This inequality and the Cauchy-Schwarz inequality are both special cases of *Hölder's inequality*. This states that if p, q are such that $1/p + 1/q = 1$ (which is interpreted in the obvious way if one of these numbers is infinite), then for $a, b \in \mathbb{R}^k$,

$$
\begin{aligned}
(a, b) = \sum_{i=1}^{k} a_i b_i &\leq \left(\sum_{i=1}^{k} a_i^p\right)^{1/p} \left(\sum_{i=1}^{k} b_i^q\right)^{1/q} \\
&= \|a\|_p \|b\|_q.
\end{aligned} \tag{1.9}
$$

(See, for example, (Kolmogorov and Fomin, 1975).) The p-norm and the q-norm are said to be *dual*.

A1.2 Tails of Distributions

Markov's inequality

If a random variable x is almost surely nonnegative, then

$$\Pr(x \geq a) \leq \frac{\mathbf{E}(x)}{a} \tag{1.10}$$

for all $a > 0$. To see this, notice that $\mathbf{E}(x) \geq \mathbf{E}(x|x \geq a)\Pr(x \geq a) \geq a\Pr(x \geq a)$.

Chebyshev inequality

For a random variable x with mean μ and variance σ^2,

$$\Pr(|x - \mu| \geq a) \leq \frac{\sigma^2}{a^2} \tag{1.11}$$

for all $a > 0$. This follows immediately from Markov's inequality applied to the random variable $(x - \mu)^2$.

Chernoff bounds

Suppose $m \in \mathbb{N}$ and $x_1, \ldots, x_m$ are independent $\{0,1\}$-valued random variables with $\Pr(x_i = 1) = p_i$, where $0 \leq p_i \leq 1$ for $i = 1, \ldots, m$. Let

$$\mu = \frac{1}{m}\sum_{i=1}^{m} p_i.$$

Then for $\epsilon \geq 0$, we have

$$\Pr\left(\frac{1}{m}\sum_{i=1}^{m} x_i \geq (1+\epsilon)\mu\right) \leq \exp\left(-\epsilon^2\mu m/3\right), \tag{1.12}$$

$$\Pr\left(\frac{1}{m}\sum_{i=1}^{m} x_i \leq (1-\epsilon)\mu\right) \leq \exp\left(-\epsilon^2\mu m/2\right). \tag{1.13}$$

Proofs of these bounds may be found in the original paper of Chernoff (1952), and in (Hagerup and Rub, 1990).

The special cases of the Chernoff bounds in which all the probabilities p_i are equal is frequently useful. Suppose that each p_i equals p. Then $\mu = p$ and the probability on the left-hand-side of Inequality (1.12) is the probability that the number of x_i equal to 1 is at least $m(1+\epsilon)\mu = m(1+\epsilon)p$. The probability of obtaining at least k 'successes' in an experiment repeated m independent times, in which the probability of 'success' is p, is denoted $\text{GE}(p, m, k)$, and the probability of at most k successes is similarly denoted $\text{LE}(p, m, k)$. By the Chernoff bounds, we immediately have

$$\text{GE}\,(p, m, (1 + \epsilon)mp) = \sum_{i=\lceil(1+\epsilon)mp\rceil}^{m} \binom{m}{i} p^i (1-p)^{m-i} \leq \exp\left(-\epsilon^2 pm/3\right),$$

$$\text{LE}\,(p, m, (1 - \epsilon)mp) = \sum_{i=0}^{\lfloor(1-\epsilon)mp\rfloor} \binom{m}{i} p^i (1-p)^{m-i} \leq \exp\left(-\epsilon^2 pm/2\right).$$

Generally, it follows that

$$\text{GE}\,(p, m, k) \;\leq\; \exp\left(-(k - pm)^2/3pm\right) \qquad (1.14)$$

for $k > pm$ and

$$\text{LE}\,(p, m, k) \;\leq\; \exp\left(-(pm - k)^2/2pm\right) \qquad (1.15)$$

for $k < pm$. See also (Angluin and Valiant, 1979).

Hoeffding's inequality

Let X be a set, D a probability distribution on X, and $f_1, \ldots, f_m$ real-valued functions defined on X, with $f_i : X \to [a_i, b_i]$ for $i = 1, \ldots, m$, where a_i and b_i are real numbers satisfying $a_i < b_i$. Then we have the following inequality (due to Hoeffding (1963)).

$$\Pr\left(\left|\left(\frac{1}{m}\sum_{i=1}^{m} f_i(x_i)\right) - \left(\frac{1}{m}\sum_{i=1}^{m} \int f_i(x)D(x)\right)\right| \geq \epsilon\right)$$
$$\leq 2\exp\left(\frac{-2\epsilon^2 m^2}{\sum_{i=1}^{m}(b_i - a_i)^2}\right), \qquad (1.16)$$

where the probability is over the random sequence $(x_1, \ldots, x_m)$ chosen according to D^m.

Inequality (1.16) follows immediately from the two 'one-sided' bounds

$$\Pr\left(\left(\frac{1}{m}\sum_{i=1}^{m} f_i(x_i)\right) - \left(\frac{1}{m}\sum_{i=1}^{m} \int f_i(x)D(x)\right) \geq \epsilon\right)$$
$$\leq \exp\left(\frac{-2\epsilon^2 m^2}{\sum_{i=1}^{m}(b_i - a_i)^2}\right), \qquad (1.17)$$

$$\Pr\left(\left(\frac{1}{m}\sum_{i=1}^{m}f_i(x_i)\right)-\left(\frac{1}{m}\sum_{i=1}^{m}\int f_i(x)D(x)\right)\le-\epsilon\right)$$

$$\le\exp\left(\frac{-2\epsilon^2 m^2}{\sum_{i=1}^{m}(b_i-a_i)^2}\right).\qquad(1.18)$$

To prove Inequality (1.17), we follow the proof in (Devroye et al., 1996; Lugosi, 1998). (Inequality (1.18) is proved similarly.) Let $y_1, y_2, \dots, y_m$ be independent random variables, each with mean 0, such that $y_i \in [c_i, d_i]$. We first note that for any $s > 0$,

$$\begin{aligned}\Pr\left(\sum_{i=1}^{m}y_i\ge\alpha\right) &= \Pr\left(\exp\left(s\sum_{i=1}^{m}y_i\right)\ge e^{s\alpha}\right)\\ &\le \frac{\mathbf{E}\left(\exp\left(s\sum_{i=1}^{m}y_i\right)\right)}{e^{s\alpha}}\\ &= e^{-s\alpha}\prod_{i=1}^{m}\mathbf{E}(e^{sy_i}),\qquad(1.19)\end{aligned}$$

where we have used Markov's inequality and the independence of the random variables e^{sy_i}. Now choose any i between 1 and m and let us denote y_i, c_i, d_i simply by y, c, d. By the convexity of the function $x \mapsto e^{sx}$ for $s > 0$, we have

$$e^{sy}\le\frac{y-c}{d-c}e^{sd}+\frac{d-y}{d-c}e^{sc},$$

and so (taking expectations and using the fact that $\mathbf{E}y = 0$),

$$\mathbf{E}e^{sy}\le\frac{-c}{d-c}e^{sd}+\frac{d}{d-c}e^{sc}=\left(1-p+pe^{s(d-c)}\right)e^{-ps(d-c)}=e^{g(u)},$$

where $p = -c/(d-c), u = s(d-c)$ and $g(u) = -pu + \ln(1-p+pe^u)$. It is easy to verify that $g(0) = g'(0) = 0$ and $g''(u) \le 1/4$ for $u > 0$. By Taylor's theorem, for some $\xi \in [0, u]$,

$$g(u)=\frac{u^2}{2}g''(\xi)\le\frac{u^2}{8}=\frac{s^2(d-c)^2}{8}.$$

Thus $\mathbf{E}(e^{sy}) \le e^{g(u)} \le e^{s^2(d-c)^2/8}$, and substituting into (1.19) gives

$$\Pr\left(\sum_{i=1}^{m}y_i\ge\alpha\right)\le e^{-s\alpha}\prod_{i=1}^{m}e^{s^2(d_i-c_i)^2/8}.\qquad(1.20)$$

To apply this result, let f_i, x_i be as above and define, for each i,

$$y_i=\frac{1}{m}\left(f_i(x_i)-\mathbf{E}(f_i)\right)=\frac{1}{m}\sum_{i=1}^{m}f_i(x_i)-\left(\frac{1}{m}\sum_{i=1}^{m}\int f_i(x)D(x)\right).$$

A1.2 Tails of distributions 363

Then $\mathbf{E}y_i = 0$ and, taking $d_i = (b_i - \mathbf{E}f_i)/m$ and $c_i = (a_i - \mathbf{E}f_i)/m$, we obtain from (1.20) that

$$
\Pr\left(\left(\frac{1}{m}\sum_{i=1}^{m}f_i(x_i)\right) - \left(\frac{1}{m}\sum_{i=1}^{m}\int f_i(x)D(x)\right) \geq \epsilon\right)
$$

$$
= \Pr\left(\sum_{i=1}^{m}y_i \geq \epsilon\right)
$$

$$
\leq \exp\left(-s\epsilon + \sum_{i=1}^{m}\frac{s^2(d_i - c_i)^2}{8}\right)
$$

$$
= \exp\left(-s\epsilon + \frac{s^2\sum_{i=1}^{m}(b_i - a_i)^2}{8m^2}\right),
$$

for any $s > 0$. Choosing $s = 4m^2\epsilon/\left(\sum_{i=1}^{m}(b_i - a_i)^2\right)$ yields (1.17).

Bernstein's inequality

Bernstein's inequality is more useful than Hoeffding's inequality when functions $f_1,\ldots,f_m$ and i.i.d. random variables $x_1,\ldots,x_m$ are such that the variances $\mathrm{var}(f_i) = \mathbf{E}\left(f_i(x) - \mathbf{E}f_i(x)\right)^2$ are small. It states that if $|f_i(x) - \mathbf{E}f_i(x)| \leq M$ for all i with probability 1 and $\sigma^2 = \frac{1}{m}\sum_{i=1}^{m}\mathrm{var}(f_i(x_i))$, then

$$
\Pr\left(\frac{1}{m}\sum_{i=1}^{m}f_i(x_i) - \frac{1}{m}\sum_{i=1}^{m}\mathbf{E}f_i(x) > \epsilon\right) \leq \exp\left(-\frac{\epsilon^2 m}{2\sigma^2 + 2M\epsilon/3}\right).
$$

$$(1.21)$$

See (Bernstein, 1946).

Slud's inequality

Let B be a binomial (m,p) random variable with $p \leq 1/2$, and suppose that $mp \leq k \leq m(1-p)$. Then

$$
\Pr(B \geq k) \geq \Pr\left(Z \geq \frac{k - mp}{\sqrt{mp(1-p)}}\right),
$$

$$(1.22)$$

where Z is a normal $(0,1)$ random variable. (See (Slud, 1977; Devroye et al., 1996).)

Normal tail bounds

If Z is a normal $(0,1)$ random variable and $x > 0$, then

$$\Pr(Z \geq x) \geq \frac{1}{2}\left(1 - \sqrt{1 - e^{-x^2}}\right). \tag{1.23}$$

(See (Patel and Read, 1982, p64), (Tate, 1953).)

A1.3 Sard's Theorem

We say that a set $S \subseteq \mathbb{R}^n$ has (outer) measure zero if for all $\epsilon > 0$ there is a sequence $B_1, B_2, \ldots$ of balls in $\mathbb{R}^n$ with

$$A \subseteq \bigcup_{i=1}^{\infty} B_i$$

and

$$\sum_{i=1}^{\infty} \text{vol}(B_i) < \epsilon,$$

where $\text{vol}(B_i)$ is the volume (Lebesgue measure) of the ball B_i.

For a C^1 function $f : \mathbb{R}^n \to \mathbb{R}^m$, we say that $x \in \mathbb{R}^n$ is a *critical point* of f if $\text{rank} f'(x) < m$. (Recall that for a function $f : \mathbb{R}^n \to \mathbb{R}^m$, if $f(x) = (f_1(x), \ldots, f_m(x))$, then the *Jacobian* of f at $x \in \mathbb{R}^n$, denoted $f'(x)$, is the $n \times m$ matrix with entry i,j equal to $D_i f_j(x)$, the partial derivative of $f_j(x)$ with respect to the ith component of $x = (x_1, \ldots, x_n)$.) We say that $y \in \mathbb{R}^m$ is a *critical value* of f if some $x \in \mathbb{R}^n$ satisfying $f(x) = y$ is a critical point of f.

Theorem 1.1 (Sard's Theorem) *For $n, m \geq 1$, if $f : \mathbb{R}^n \to \mathbb{R}^m$ is C^k and $k \geq \max(1, n - m + 1)$, then the set of critical values of f has measure zero.*

For a proof, see (Sternberg, 1964, Chapter II).

Bibliography

Aho, A. V. and Ullman, J. D. (1992). *Foundations of computer science,* Principles of computer science, Computer Science Press. [306]

Akaike, H. (1974). A new look at the statistical model identification, *IEEE Transactions on Automatic Control* AC-19: 716-723. [227]

Albertini, F., Sontag, E. D. and Maillot, V. (1993). Uniqueness of weights for neural networks, *in* R. J. Mammone (ed.), *Artificial Neural Networks for Speech and Vision,* Chapman & Hall, London, pp. 115-125. [282]

Aldous, D. and Vazirani, U. (1990). A Markovian extension of Valiant's learning model, *Proceedings of the 31st Symposium on the Foundations of Computer Science,* IEEE Computer Society Press, Los Alamitos, CA, pp. 392-396. [28]

Alexander, K. S. (1984). Probability inequalities for empirical processes and a law of the iterated logarithm, *Annals of Probability* 12: 1041-1067. [58]

Alon, N. (1983). On the density of sets of vectors, *Discrete Mathematics* 46: 199-202. [41]

Alon, N., Ben-David, S., Cesa-Bianchi, N. and Haussler, D. (1993). Scale-sensitive dimensions, uniform convergence, and learnability, *Proceedings of the 34rd Annual Symposium on Foundations of Computer Science,* IEEE Computer Society Press, Los Alamitos, CA, pp. 292-301. [183, 256]

Alon, N., Ben-David, S., Cesa-Bianchi, N. and Haussler, D. (1997). Scale-sensitive dimensions, uniform convergence, and learnability, *Journal of the ACM* 44(4): 616-631. [267]

Anderson, J. A. and Rosenfeld, E. (eds) (1988). *Neurocomputing: Foundations of Research,* MIT Press. [9]

Angluin, D. (1988). Queries and concept learning, *Machine Learning* 2(4): 319-342. [28, 340]

Angluin, D. (1992). Computational learning theory: survey and selected bibliography, *Proceedings of the 24th Annual ACM Symposium on Theory of Computing,* ACM Press, New York, NY, pp. 351-369. [28, 340]

Angluin, D. and Laird, P. (1988). Learning from noisy examples, *Machine Learning* 2(4): 343-370. [27]

Angluin, D. and Valiant, L. G. (1979). Fast probabilistic algorithms for Hamiltonian circuits and matchings, *Journal of Computer and System Sciences* 18(2): 155-193. [361]

Anthony, M. (1995). Classification by polynomial surfaces, *Discrete Applied*

Mathematics **61**: 91–103. [163]

Anthony, M. and Bartlett, P. L. (1995). Function learning from interpolation, *Computational Learning Theory: Eurocolt '95*, Springer-Verlag, pp. 211–221. [139, 183, 192, 268, 296]

Anthony, M., Bartlett, P. L., Ishai, Y. and Shawe-Taylor, J. (1996). Valid generalisation from approximate interpolation, *Combinatorics, Probability, and Computing* **5**: 191–214. [296]

Anthony, M. and Biggs, N. (1992). *Computational Learning Theory*, Cambridge Tracts in Theoretical Computer Science (30), Cambridge University Press. [9, 339]

Anthony, M., Biggs, N. and Shawe-Taylor, J. (1990). The learnability of formal concepts, *Proceedings of the 3rd Annual Workshop on Computational Learning Theory*, Morgan Kaufmann, San Mateo, CA, pp. 246–257. [58]

Anthony, M., Brightwell, G. and Shawe-Taylor, J. (1995). On specifying Boolean functions by labelled examples, *Discrete Applied Mathematics* **61**: 1–25. [28, 330]

Anthony, M. and Holden, S. B. (1993). On the power of polynomial discriminators and radial basis function networks, *Proceedings of the 6th Annual Workshop on Computational Learning Theory*, ACM Press, New York, NY, pp. 158–164. [163]

Anthony, M. and Holden, S. B. (1994). Quantifying generalisation in linearly-weighted neural networks, *Complex Systems* **8**: 91–114. [163]

Anthony, M. and Shawe-Taylor, J. (1993a). Bounds on the complexity of testing and loading neurons, *ICANN'93: Proceedings of the International Conference on Artificial Neural Networks, 1993*, Springer-Verlag. [330]

Anthony, M. and Shawe-Taylor, J. (1993b). A result of Vapnik with applications, *Discrete Applied Mathematics* **47**(3): 207–217. See also erratum (1994) **52**: 211. [73, 296]

Anthony, M. and Shawe-Taylor, J. (1993c). Using the perceptron algorithm to find consistent hypotheses, *Combinatorics, Probability and Computing* **4**(2): 385–387. [330]

Anthony, M. and Shawe-Taylor, J. (1994). Valid generalisation of functions from close approximations on a sample, *Computational Learning Theory: Eurocolt '93*, Vol. 53 of *The Institute of Mathematics and its Applications Conference Series*, Oxford University Press, Oxford, pp. 94–108. [296]

Assouad, P. (1983). Densité et dimension, *Ann. Inst. Fourier* pp. 233–282. [41]

Auer, P., Herbster, M. and Warmuth, M. K. (1996). Exponentially many local minima for single neurons, *in* D. S. Touretzky, M. C. Mozer and M. E. Hasselmo (eds), *Advances in Neural Information Processing Systems 8*, MIT Press, pp. 316–322. [339]

Auer, P., Kwek, S., Maass, W. and Warmuth, M. K. (1996). Learning of depth two neural networks with constant fan-in at the hidden nodes, *Proceedings of the 9th Annual Conference on Computational Learning Theory*, ACM Press, New York, NY, pp. 333–343. [355]

Babai, L. and Frankl, P. (1992). *Linear Algebra Methods in Combinatorics, with Applications to Geometry and Computer Science*, The University of Chicago, Department of Computer Science. [183]

Barron, A. R. (1991). Complexity regularization with application to artificial neural networks, *in* G. Roussas (ed.), *Nonparametric Functional Estimation and Related Topics*, Kluwer Academic, pp. 561–576. [227, 268]

Barron, A. R. (1992). Neural net approximation, *Proceedings of the 7th Yale Workshop on Adaptive and Learning Systems*. [216]

Barron, A. R. (1993). Universal approximation bounds for superpositions of a sigmoidal function, *IEEE Transactions on Information Theory* **39**: 930–945. [216, 355]

Barron, A. R. (1994). Approximation and estimation bounds for artificial neural networks, *Machine Learning* **14**(1): 115–133. [9, 216, 227, 240, 268, 282]

Bartlett, P. L. (1992). Learning with a slowly changing distribution, *Proceedings of the 5th Annual Workshop on Computational Learning Theory*, ACM Press, New York, NY, pp. 243–252. [28]

Bartlett, P. L. (1993a). Lower bounds on the Vapnik-Chervonenkis dimension of multi-layer threshold networks, *Proceedings of the 6th Annual Workshop on Computational Learning Theory*, ACM Press, New York, NY, pp. 144–150. [85]

Bartlett, P. L. (1993b). Vapnik-Chervonenkis dimension bounds for two- and three-layer networks, *Neural Computation* **5**(3): 371–373. [85]

Bartlett, P. L. (1994). Learning quantized real-valued functions, *Proceedings of Computing: the Australian Theory Seminar*, University of Technology Sydney, pp. 24–35. [268]

Bartlett, P. L. (1998). The sample complexity of pattern classification with neural networks: the size of the weights is more important than the size of the network, *IEEE Transactions on Information Theory* **44**(2): 525–536. [138, 139, 150, 183, 192, 217, 227]

Bartlett, P. L. and Ben-David, S. (1999). Hardness results for neural network approximation problems, *in* P. Fischer and H. Simon (eds), *Proceedings of the 4th European Conference on Computational Learning Theory*, Springer. [339, 340]

Bartlett, P. L., Ben-David, S. and Kulkarni, S. R. (1996). Learning changing concepts by exploiting the structure of change, *Proceedings of the 9th Annual Conference on Computational Learning Theory*, ACM Press, New York, NY, pp. 131–139. [28]

Bartlett, P. L., Fischer, P. and Höffgen, K.-U. (1994). Exploiting random walks for learning, *Proceedings of the 7th Annual ACM Workshop on Computational Learning Theory*, ACM Press, New York, NY, pp. 318–327. [28]

Bartlett, P. L., Kulkarni, S. R. and Posner, S. E. (1997). Covering numbers for real-valued function classes, *IEEE Transactions on Information Theory* **43**(5): 1721–1724. [183, 256]

Bartlett, P. L. and Long, P. M. (1995). More theorems about scale-sensitive dimensions and learning, *Proceedings of the 8th Annual Conference on Computational Learning Theory*, ACM Press, New York, NY, pp. 392–401. [183, 256]

Bartlett, P. L. and Long, P. M. (1998). Prediction, learning, uniform convergence, and scale-sensitive dimensions, *Journal of Computer and System Sciences* **56**: 174–190. [183]

Bartlett, P. L., Long, P. M. and Williamson, R. C. (1996). Fat-shattering and the learnability of real-valued functions, *Journal of Computer and*

System Sciences **52**(3): 434–452. [246, 267, 268]

Bartlett, P. L. and Lugosi, G. (1999). An inequality for uniform deviations of sample averages from their means, *Statistics and Probability Letters* **44**: 55–62. [268]

Bartlett, P. L., Maiorov, V. and Meir, R. (1998). Almost linear VC-dimension bounds for piecewise polynomial networks, *Neural Computation* **10**: 2159–2173. [129]

Bartlett, P. L. and Shawe-Taylor, J. (1999). Generalization performance of support vector machines and other pattern classifiers, *in* B. Schölkopf, C. J. C. Burges and A. J. Smola (eds), *Advances in Kernel Methods: Support Vector Learning*, MIT Press, pp. 43–54. [217]

Bartlett, P. L. and Williamson, R. C. (1996). The Vapnik-Chervonenkis dimension and pseudodimension of two-layer neural networks with discrete inputs, *Neural Computation* **8**: 653–656. [129]

Barve, R. D. and Long, P. M. (1997). On the complexity of learning from drifting distributions, *Information and Computation* **138**(2): 101–123. [28]

Baum, E. B. (1988). On the capabilities of multilayer perceptrons, *Journal of Complexity* **4**: 193–215. [85]

Baum, E. B. (1990a). The perceptron algorithm is fast for nonmalicious distributions, *Neural Computation* **2**: 248–260. [330]

Baum, E. B. (1990b). A polynomial time algorithm that learns two hidden net units, *Neural Computation* **2**: 510–522. [340]

Baum, E. B. (1990c). Polynomial time algorithms for learning neural nets, *Proceedings of the 3rd Annual Workshop on Computational Learning Theory*, Morgan Kaufmann, San Mateo, CA, pp. 258–272. [341]

Baum, E. B. (1991). Neural net algorithms that learn in polynomial time from examples and queries, *IEEE Transactions on Neural Networks* **2**: 5–19. [341]

Baum, E. B. and Haussler, D. (1989). What size net gives valid generalization?, *Neural Computation* **1**(1): 151–160. [85]

Baxter, J. (1998). A model of inductive bias learning, *Technical report*, Department of Systems Engineering, Australian National University. [72]

Ben-David, S., Cesa-Bianchi, N., Haussler, D. and Long, P. M. (1995). Characterizations of learnability for classes of $\{0, \ldots, n\}$-valued functions, *Journal of Computer and System Sciences* **50**(1): 74–86. [183]

Ben-David, S. and Lindenbaum, M. (1993). Localization vs. identification of semi-algebraic sets, *Proceedings of the 6th Annual Workshop on Computational Learning Theory*, ACM Press, New York, NY, pp. 327–336. [107]

Ben-David, S. and Lindenbaum, M. (1997). Learning distributions by their density levels: A paradigm for learning without a teacher, *Journal of Computer and System Sciences* **55**(1): 171–182. [72]

Benedek, G. M. and Itai, A. (1988). Nonuniform learnability, *Proceedings of ICALP*, pp. 82–92. [28]

Benedek, G. M. and Itai, A. (1991). Learnability with respect to fixed distributions, *Theoretical Computer Science* **86**(2): 377–389. [28]

Benedetti, R. and Risler, J.-J. (1990). *Real algebraic and semi-algebraic sets*, Hermann. [129]

Bernstein, S. N. (1946). *The Theory of Probabilities*, Gastehizdat Publishing House. [363]

Billingsley, P. (1986). *Probability and Measure*, Wiley, New York, NY. [27]

Birgé, L. and Massart, P. (1993). Rates of convergence for minimum contrast estimators, *Probability Theory and Related Fields* **97**: 113–150. [267]

Bishop, C. M. (1995). *Neural Networks for Pattern Recognition*, Oxford University Press, Oxford. [9]

Block, H. D. (1962). The perceptron: a model for brain functioning, *Reviews of Modern Physics* **34**: 123–135. [330]

Blum, A. and Chalasani, P. (1992). Learning switching concepts, *Proceedings of the 5th Annual Workshop on Computational Learning Theory*, ACM Press, New York, NY, pp. 231–242. [28]

Blum, A. and Rivest, R. L. (1992). Training a 3-node neural network is NP-complete, *Neural Networks* **5**(1): 117–127. [339]

Blumer, A., Ehrenfeucht, A., Haussler, D. and Warmuth, M. K. (1989). Learnability and the Vapnik-Chervonenkis dimension, *Journal of the ACM* **36**(4): 929–965. [27, 58, 306, 315, 329]

Bollobás, B. (1986). *Combinatorics: Set systems, hypergraphs, families of vectors, and combinatorial probability*, Cambridge University Press, Cambridge. [41]

Boser, B. E., Guyon, I. M. and Vapnik, V. N. (1992). A training algorithm for optimal margin classifiers, *Proceedings of the 5th Annual Workshop on Computational Learning Theory*, ACM Press, New York, NY, pp. 144–152. [139, 217]

Breiman, L. (1998). Arcing classifiers, *Annals of Statistics* **26**(3): 801–849. [356]

Breiman, L. (1999). Prediction games and arcing algorithms, *Neural Computation* **11**(7): 1493–1517. [356]

Brent, R. P. (1991). Fast training algorithms for multilayer neural nets, *IEEE Transactions on Neural Networks* **2**(3): 346–354. [340]

Buescher, K. L. and Kumar, P. R. (1991). Simultaneous learning of concepts and simultaneous estimation of probabilities, *Proceedings of the 4th Annual Workshop on Computational Learning Theory*, Morgan Kaufmann, San Mateo, CA, pp. 33–42. [257]

Buescher, K. L. and Kumar, P. R. (1992). Learning stochastic functions by smooth simultaneous estimation, *Proceedings of the 5th Annual Workshop on Computational Learning Theory*, ACM Press, New York, NY, pp. 272–279. [257]

Bylander, T. (1994). Learning linear threshold functions in the presence of classification noise, *Proceedings of the 7th Annual ACM Workshop on Computational Learning Theory*, ACM Press, New York, NY, pp. 340–347. [330]

Bylander, T. (1997). Learning probabilistically consistent linear threshold functions, *Proceedings of the 10th Annual Conference on Computational Learning Theory*, ACM Press, New York, NY, pp. 62–71. [330]

Carl, B. (1982). On a characterization of operators from l_q into a Banach space of type p with some applications to eigenvalue problems, *Journal of Functional Analysis* **48**: 394–407. [216]

Cesa-Bianchi, N., Fischer, P., Shamir, E. and Simon, H. U. (1997). Randomized hypotheses and minimum disagreement hypotheses for learning with noise, *Computational Learning Theory: Eurocolt '97*, Springer-Verlag, pp. 119–133. [27]

Cesa-Bianchi, N. and Haussler, D. (1998). A graph-theoretic generalization of

the Sauer-Shelah lemma, *Discrete Applied Mathematics* **86**(1): 27–35.
[183]

Chari, S., Rohatgi, P. and Srinivasan, A. (1994). Improved algorithms via
approximations of probability distributions, *Proceedings of the
Twenty-Sixth Annual ACM Symposium on the Theory of Computing*,
pp. 584–592. [41]

Chernoff, H. (1952). A measure of asymptotic efficiency for tests of a
hypothesis based on the sum of observations, *Annals of Mathematical
Statistics* **23**: 493–509. [360]

Cormen, T., Leiserson, C. and Rivest, R. L. (1990). *Introduction to
Algorithms*, MIT Press. [315]

Cortes, C. and Vapnik, V. N. (1995). Support-vector networks, *Machine
Learning* **20**(3): 273–297. [217]

Cover, T. M. (1965). Geometrical and statistical properties of systems of
linear inequalities with applications in pattern recognition, *IEEE
Transactions on Electronic Computers* **EC-14**: 326–334. [41]

Cover, T. M. (1968). Capacity problems for linear machines, *in* L. Kanal
(ed.), *Pattern Recognition*, Thompson, pp. 283–289. [85]

Cover, T. M. and Thomas, J. (1991). *Elements of Information Theory*, Wiley.
[85]

Cybenko, G. (1989). Approximation by superpositions of a sigmoidal
function, *Mathematics of Control, Signals and Systems* **2**(4): 303–314.
(Correction in vol. 5, p455, 1992). [10]

Darken, C., Donahue, M., Gurvits, L. and Sontag, E. D. (1997). Rates of
convex approximation in non-Hilbert spaces, *Constructive
Approximation* **13**: 187–220. [355]

DasGupta, B., Siegelmann, H. T. and Sontag, E. D. (1995). On the
complexity of training neural networks with continuous activation
functions, *IEEE Transactions on Neural Networks* **6**(6): 1490–1504. [339]

DasGupta, B. and Sontag, E. D. (1996). Sample complexity for learning
recurrent perceptron mappings, *IEEE Transactions on Information
Theory* **42**: 1479–1487. [130]

Devroye, L. (1982). Any discrimination rule can have an arbitrarily bad
probability of error for finite sample size, *IEEE Transactions on Pattern
Analysis and Machine Intelligence* **4**: 154–157. [27]

Devroye, L., Györfi, L. and Lugosi, G. (1996). *A probabilistic theory of pattern
recognition*, Applications of Mathematics: Stochastic Modelling and
Applied Probability (31), Springer. [27, 106, 362, 363]

Devroye, L. and Lugosi, G. (1995). Lower bounds in pattern recognition and
learning, *Pattern Recognition* **28**(7): 1011–1018. [27, 72]

Drucker, H. and Cortes, C. (1996). Boosting decision trees, *Advances in
Neural Information Processing Systems*, Vol. 8, pp. 479–485. [356]

Drucker, H., Cortes, C., Jackel, L. D., LeCun, Y. and Vapnik, V. N. (1994).
Boosting and other machine learning algorithms, *Proceedings of the 11th
International Conference on Machine Learning*, Morgan Kaufmann,
pp. 53–61. [355]

Duda, R. O. and Hart, P. E. (1973). *Pattern Classification and Scene
Analysis*, Wiley. [27, 138]

Dudley, R. M. (1978). Central limit theorems for empirical measures, *Annals
of Probability* **6**(6): 899–929. [41, 58, 256]

Dudley, R. M. (1987). Universal Donsker classes and metric entropy, *Annals of Probability* **15**(4): 1306–1326. [163, 216]

Ehrenfeucht, A., Haussler, D., Kearns, M. J. and Valiant, L. G. (1989). A general lower bound on the number of examples needed for learning, *Information and Computation* **82**: 247–261. [72]

Erlich, Y., Chazan, D., Petrack, S. and Levy, A. (1997). Lower bound on VC-dimension by local shattering, *Neural Computation* **9**(4): 771–776. [85]

Faragó, A. and Lugosi, G. (1993). Strong universal consistency of neural network classifiers, *IEEE Transactions on Information Theory* **39**(4): 1146–1151. [227, 329]

Fefferman, C. (1994). Reconstructing a neural network from its output, *Rev. Mat. Iberoamericana* **10**: 507–555. [282]

Feller, W. (1968). *An Introduction to Probability Theory and its Applications*, Vol. 1, John Wiley and Sons. [358]

Feller, W. (1971). *An Introduction to Probability and its Applications*, Vol. 2, John Wiley and Sons. [27]

Frankl, P. (1983). On the trace of finite sets, *Journal of Combinatorial Theory, Series A* **34**: 41–45. [41]

Frean, M. (1990). The upstart algorithm: a method for constructing and training feedforward neural networks, *Neural Computation* **2**: 198–209. [340]

Frean, M. and Downs, T. (1998). A simple cost function for boosting, *Technical report*, Department of Computer Science and Electrical and Computer Engineering, University of Queensland. [356]

Freund, Y. (1995). Boosting a weak learning algorithm by majority, *Information and Computation* **121**(2): 256–285. [355]

Freund, Y. and Mansour, Y. (1997). Learning under persistent drift, *Computational Learning Theory: Eurocolt '97*, Springer-Verlag, pp. 109–118. [28]

Freund, Y. and Schapire, R. E. (1996). Experiments with a new boosting algorithm, *Proceedings of the 13th International Conference on Machine Learning*, Morgan Kaufmann, pp. 148–156. [355]

Freund, Y. and Schapire, R. E. (1997). A decision-theoretic generalization of on-line learning and an application to boosting, *Journal of Computer and System Sciences* **55**(1): 119–139. [355, 356]

Friedman, J., Hastie, T. and Tibshirani, R. (1998). Additive logistic regression : A statistical view of boosting, *Technical report*, Stanford University. [356]

Gallant, S. (1990). Perceptron-based learning algorithms, *IEEE Transactions on Neural Networks* **1**(2): 179–191. [329]

Garey, M. R. and Johnson, D. S. (1979). *Computers and intractability: A guide to the theory of NP-completeness*, W. H. Freeman and Company. [315, 329]

Goldberg, P. W. and Jerrum, M. R. (1995). Bounding the Vapnik-Chervonenkis dimension of concept classes parametrized by real numbers, *Machine Learning* **18**(2/3): 131–148. [107, 129]

Goldman, S. A. and Kearns, M. J. (1991). On the complexity of teaching, *Proceedings of the 4th Annual Workshop on Computational Learning Theory*, Morgan Kaufmann, San Mateo, CA, pp. 303–314. [28]

Grenander, U. (1981). *Abstract Inference*, Wiley. [227]

Grove, A. J. and Schuurmans, D. (1998). Boosting in the limit: Maximizing the margin of learned ensembles, *Proceedings of the Fifteenth National Conference on Artificial Intelligence*, pp. 692–699. [356]

Guo, Y., Bartlett, P. L., Shawe-Taylor, J. and Williamson, R. C. (1999). Covering numbers for support vector machines, *Proc. 12th Annual Workshop on Computational Learning Theory*, pp. 267–277. [217]

Gurvits, L. (1997a). Linear algebraic proofs of VC-dimension based inequalities, *Computational Learning Theory: Eurocolt '97*, Springer-Verlag, pp. 238–250. [183]

Gurvits, L. (1997b). A note on a scale-sensitive dimension of linear bounded functionals in Banach spaces, *Technical report*, NEC Research Institute. [217]

Gurvits, L. and Koiran, P. (1997). Approximation and learning of convex superpositions, *Journal of Computer and System Sciences* 55(1): 161–170. [216]

Hagerup, T. and Rub, C. (1990). A guided tour of Chernov bounds, *Information Processing Letters* 33: 305–308. [360]

Hancock, T. R., Golea, M. and Marchand, M. (1994). Learning nonoverlapping perceptron networks from examples and membership queries, *Machine Learning* 16(3): 161–184. [340]

Haussler, D. (1992). Decision theoretic generalizations of the PAC model for neural net and other learning applications, *Information and Computation* 100(1): 78–150. [27, 58, 163, 216, 240, 246, 256, 282, 296]

Haussler, D. (1995). Sphere packing numbers for subsets of the Boolean *n*-cube with bounded Vapnik-Chervonenkis dimension, *Journal of Combinatorial Theory, Series A* 69(2): 217–232. [58, 256]

Haussler, D., Kearns, M. J., Littlestone, N. and Warmuth, M. K. (1991). Equivalence of models for polynomial learnability, *Information and Computation* 95(2): 129–161. [27, 306]

Haussler, D., Littlestone, N. and Warmuth, M. K. (1994). Predicting {0, 1} functions on randomly drawn points, *Information and Computation* 115(2): 284–293. [27]

Haussler, D. and Long, P. M. (1995). A generalization of Sauer's lemma, *Journal of Combinatorial Theory, Series A* 71(2): 219–240. [183]

Haussler, D. and Welzl, E. (1987). Epsilon-nets and simplex range queries, *Discrete Computational Geometry* 2: 127–151. [41]

Haykin, S. (1994). *Neural Networks: a Comprehensive Foundation*, Macmillan, New York, NY. [9]

Hebb, D. (1949). *The Organization of Behavior*, Wiley, New York. [9]

Helmbold, D. P. and Long, P. M. (1994). Tracking drifting concepts by minimizing disagreements, *Machine Learning* 14(1): 27–45. [28]

Hertz, J., Krogh, A. and Palmer, R. G. (1991). *Introduction to the Theory of Neural Computation*, Addison-Wesley, Redwood City, California. [9, 227]

Hoeffding, W. (1963). Probability inequalities for sums of bounded random variables, *Journal of the American Statistical Association* 58(301): 13–30. [361]

Höffgen, K.-U., Simon, H. U. and Horn, K. S. V. (1995). Robust trainability of single neurons, *Journal of Computer and System Sciences* 50(1): 114–125. [329]

Hornik, K., Stinchcombe, M. and White, H. (1990). Universal approximation of an unknown mapping and its derivatives using multilayer feedforward networks, *Neural Networks* 3: 551–560. [10]

Horváth, M. and Lugosi, G. (1998). A data-dependent skeleton estimate and a scale-sensitive dimension for classification, *Discrete Applied Mathematics* **86**(1): 37–61. [192]

Jackson, J. and Tomkins, A. (1992). A computational model of teaching, *Proceedings of the 5th Annual Workshop on Computational Learning Theory*, ACM Press, New York, NY, pp. 319–326. [28]

Jacobs, R. A., Jordan, M. I., Nowlan, S. J. and Hinton, G. E. (1991). Adaptive mixtures of local experts, *Neural Computation* **3**: 79–87. [130]

Ji, C. and Psaltis, D. (1991). The VC-dimension vs. the statistical capacity for two layer networks with binary weights, *Proceedings of the 4th Annual Workshop on Computational Learning Theory*, Morgan Kaufmann, San Mateo, CA, pp. 250–256. [85]

Johnson, D. S. and Preparata, F. P. (1978). The densest hemisphere problem, *Theoretical Computer Science* **6**: 93–107. [329]

Jones, L. K. (1992). A simple lemma on greedy approximation in Hilbert space and convergence rates for projection pursuit regression and neural network training, *Annals of Statistics* **20**(1): 608–613. [216]

Jones, L. K. (1997). The computational intractability of training sigmoidal neural networks, *IEEE Transactions on Information Theory* **43**(1): 167–173. [340]

Judd, J. S. (1990). *Neural Network Design and the Complexity of Learning*, MIT Press. [339]

Karmarkar, N. (1984). A new polynomial-time algorithm for linear programming, *Combinatorica* **4**(4): 373–395. [329]

Karpinski, M. and Macintyre, A. J. (1997). Polynomial bounds for VC dimension of sigmoidal and general Pfaffian neural networks, *Journal of Computer and System Sciences* **54**: 169–176. [107, 130]

Kearns, M. J. and Li, M. (1993). Learning in the presence of malicious errors, *SIAM Journal of Computing* **22**: 807–837. [27]

Kearns, M. J., Mansour, Y., Ng, A. Y. and Ron, D. (1997). An experimental and theoretical comparison of model selection methods, *Machine Learning* **27**: 7–50. [227]

Kearns, M. J. and Schapire, R. E. (1994). Efficient distribution-free learning of probabilistic concepts, *Journal of Computer and System Sciences* **48**(3): 464–497. [139, 163]

Kearns, M. J., Schapire, R. E. and Sellie, L. M. (1994). Toward efficient agnostic learning, *Machine Learning* **17**(2/3): 115–142. [27]

Kearns, M. J. and Vazirani, U. (1995). *Introduction to Computational Learning Theory*, MIT Press, Cambridge, MA. [9, 340]

Khovanskii, A. G. (1991). *Fewnomials*, Vol. 88 of *Translations of Mathematical Monographs*, American Mathematical Society. [129]

Koiran, P. (1994). Efficient learning of continuous neural networks, *Proceedings of the 7th Annual ACM Workshop on Computational Learning Theory*, ACM Press, New York, NY, pp. 348–355. [139, 355]

Koiran, P. and Sontag, E. D. (1997). Neural networks with quadratic VC dimension, *Journal of Computer and System Sciences* **54**(1): 190–198. [85, 129]

Koiran, P. and Sontag, E. D. (1998). Vapnik-Chervonenkis dimension of recurrent neural networks, *Discrete Applied Math* **86**: 63–79. [130]

Kolmogorov, A. N. and Fomin, S. V. (1975). *Introductory Real Analysis*, Dover. [282, 359]

Kolmogorov, A. N. and Tihomirov, V. M. (1961). ε-entropy and ε-capacity of sets in function spaces, *American Mathematics Society Translations (2)* **17**: 277–364. [150, 183]

Kowalczyk, A. (1997). Dense shattering and teaching dimensions for differentiable families, *Proceedings of the 10th Annual Conference on Computational Learning Theory*, ACM Press, New York, NY, pp. 143–151. [41]

Krzyżak, A., Linder, T. and Lugosi, G. (1996). Nonparametric estimation and classification using radial basis function nets and empirical risk minimization, *IEEE Transactions on Neural Networks* **7**(2): 475–487. [106, 130, 227, 268]

Kuh, A., Petsche, T. and Rivest, R. L. (1991). Learning time-varying concepts, *Advances in Neural Information Processing Systems 3*, Morgan Kaufmann, pp. 183–189. [28]

Lee, W. S. (1996). *Agnostic learning and single hidden layer neural networks*, PhD thesis, Department of Systems Engineering, Research School of Information Sciences and Engineering, Australian National University, Canberra, Australia. [282]

Lee, W. S., Bartlett, P. L. and Williamson, R. C. (1995a). Lower bounds on the VC-dimension of smoothly parameterized function classes, *Neural Computation* **7**(5): 1040–1053. (Correction in *Neural Computation*, vol. 9(4), pp. 765–769, 1997). [85]

Lee, W. S., Bartlett, P. L. and Williamson, R. C. (1995b). On efficient agnostic learning of linear combinations of basis functions, *Proceedings of the 8th Annual Conference on Computational Learning Theory*, ACM Press, New York, NY, pp. 369–376. [139, 355]

Lee, W. S., Bartlett, P. L. and Williamson, R. C. (1996). Efficient agnostic learning of neural networks with bounded fan-in, *IEEE Transactions on Information Theory* **42**(6): 2118–2132. [139, 216, 282, 329, 355]

Lee, W. S., Bartlett, P. L. and Williamson, R. C. (1998). The importance of convexity in learning with squared loss, *IEEE Transactions on Information Theory* **44**(5): 1974–1980. [282]

Leshno, M., Lin, V., Pinkus, A. and Schocken, S. (1993). Multilayer feedforward networks with a nonpolynomial activation function can approximate any function, *Neural Networks* **6**: 861–867. [10]

Li, M. and Vitányi, P. M. B. (1991). Learning simple concepts under simple distributions, *SIAM Journal of Computing* **20**: 911–935. [28]

Li, M. and Vitányi, P. M. B. (1993). *An Introduction to Kolmogorov Complexity and Its Applications*, Text and Monographs in Computer Science, Springer-Verlag. [28]

Linial, N., Mansour, Y. and Rivest, R. L. (1991). Results on learnability and the Vapnik-Chervonenkis dimension, *Information and Computation* **90**(1): 33–49. [227]

Long, P. M. (1998a). The complexity of learning according to two models of a drifting environment, *Proceedings of the 11th Annual Conference on Computational Learning Theory*, ACM Press, pp. 116–125. [58]

Long, P. M. (1998b). On the sample complexity of learning functions with bounded variation, *Proceedings of the 11th Annual Conference on Computational Learning Theory*, ACM Press, pp. 126–133. [267]

Lorentz, G. G. (1986). *Approximation of Functions*, Chelsea. [163]

Lugosi, G. (1995). Improved upper bounds for probabilities of uniform deviations, *Statistics and Probability Letters* **25**: 71–77. [58, 227]

Lugosi, G. (1998). On concentration-of-measure inequalities. (Seminar notes, Pompeu Fabra University, Barcelona). [362]

Lugosi, G. and Zeger, K. (1995). Nonparametric estimation via empirical risk minimization, *IEEE Transactions on Information Theory* **41**(3): 677–687. [268]

Lugosi, G. and Zeger, K. (1996). Concept learning using complexity regularization, *IEEE Transactions on Information Theory* **42**(1): 48–54. [227]

Maass, W. (1994). Neural nets with superlinear VC-dimension, *Neural Computation* **6**(5): 877–884. [85]

Maass, W. (1995). Agnostic PAC-learning of functions on analog neural networks, *Neural Computation* **7**(5): 1054–1078. [27]

Macintyre, A. J. and Sontag, E. D. (1993). Finiteness results for sigmoidal "neural" networks, *Proceedings of the Twenty-Fifth Annual ACM Symposium on the Theory of Computing*, pp. 325–334. [106, 130]

Makhoul, J., El-Jaroudi, A. and Schwartz, R. (1991). Partitioning capabilities of two-layer neural networks, *IEEE Transactions on Signal Processing* **39**(6): 1435–1440. [41]

Makovoz, Y. (1996). Random approximants and neural networks, *Journal of Approximation Theory* **85**: 98–109. [216]

Mason, L., Bartlett, P. L. and Baxter, J. (1999). Direct optimization of margins improves generalization in combined classifiers, *Advances in Neural Information Processing Systems*, Vol. 11, pp. 288–294. [217, 356]

Mason, L., Baxter, J., Bartlett, P. L. and Frean, M. (1999). Functional gradient techniques for combining hypotheses, *Technical report*, Research School of Information Sciences and Engineering, Australian National University. [356]

Matousek, J. (1995). Tight upper bounds for the discrepancy of half-spaces, *Discrete Computational Geometry* **13**: 593–601. [41]

McCaffrey, D. F. and Gallant, A. R. (1994). Convergence rates for single hidden layer feedforward networks, *Neural Networks* **7**(1): 147–158. [216, 240, 282]

Mhaskar, H. (1993). Approximation properties of a multilayered feedforward artificial neural network, *Advances in Computational Mathematics* **1**: 61–80. [10]

Milnor, J. (1964). On the Betti numbers of real varieties, *Proceedings of the AMS* **15**: 275–280. [107]

Minsky, M. and Papert, S. (1969). *Perceptrons*, MIT Press, Cambridge, MA. [9]

Muroga, S. (1965). Lower bounds of the number of threshold functions and a maximum weight, *IEEE Transactions on Electronic Computers* **14**: 136–148. [58, 330]

Muroga, S. (ed.) (1971). *Threshold logic and its applications*, Wiley. [58, 330]

Natarajan, B. K. (1989). On learning sets and functions, *Machine Learning* **4**(1): 67–97. [296, 315]

Natarajan, B. K. (1991a). *Machine Learning: A Theoretical Approach*, Morgan Kaufmann, San Mateo, CA. [9]

Natarajan, B. K. (1991b). Probably approximate learning of sets and functions, *SIAM Journal of Computing* **20**(2): 328–351. [183]

Natarajan, B. K. (1993). Occam's razor for functions, *Proceedings of the 6th*

Annual Workshop on Computational Learning Theory, ACM Press, New York, NY, pp. 370–376. [246]

Nilsson, N. J. (1965). *Learning Machines: foundations of trainable pattern-classifying systems*, McGraw-Hill. [85, 330]

Patel, J. K. and Read, C. B. (1982). *Handbook of the normal distribution*, Marcel Dekker. [364]

Pisier, G. (1981). Remarques sur un résultat non publié de B. Maurey, *Séminaire d'Analyse Fonctionelle 1980–1981*, Ecole Polytechnique, Centre de Mathématiques, Palaiseau, pp. V.1–V.12. [216]

Pitt, L. and Valiant, L. G. (1988). Computational limitations on learning from examples, *Journal of the ACM* **35**: 965–984. [315, 330, 339]

Pollard, D. (1984). *Convergence of Stochastic Processes*, Springer-Verlag. [58, 150, 163, 192, 246, 256, 267, 268]

Pollard, D. (1990). *Empirical Processes: Theory and Applications*, Vol. 2, Institute of Mathematical Statistics. [58, 163, 267]

Pollard, D. (1995). Uniform ratio limit theorems for empirical processes, *Scandinavian Journal of Statistics* **22**: 271–278. [282]

Powell, M. J. D. (1987). Radial basis functions for multivariable interpolation: A review, *Algorithms for Approximation*, Clarendon Press, Oxford, pp. 143–167. [130]

Quinlan, J. R. (1996). Bagging, boosting, and C4.5, *Proceedings of the Thirteenth National Conference on Artificial Intelligence*, pp. 725–730. [356]

Ripley, B. D. (1996). *Pattern Recognition and Neural Networks*, Cambridge University Press. [9]

Rissanen, J. (1978). Modeling by shortest data description, *Automatica* **14**: 465–471. [227]

Rissanen, J. (1986). Stochastic complexity and modeling, *Annals of Statistics* **14**(3): 1080–1100. [227]

Rissanen, J. (1989). *Stochastic Complexity in Statistical Inquiry*, Vol. 15 of *Series in Computer Science*, World Scientific. [227]

Rosenblatt, F. (1958). The perceptron: A probabilistic model for information storage and organization in the brain, *Psychological Review* **65**: 386–407. (Reprinted in *Neurocomputing* (MIT Press, 1988)). [9, 330]

Rumelhart, D. E., Hinton, G. E. and Williams, R. J. (1986a). Learning internal representations by error propagation, *Parallel Distributed Processing – Explorations in the Microstructure of Cognition*, MIT Press, chapter 8, pp. 318–362. [9]

Rumelhart, D. E., Hinton, G. E. and Williams, R. J. (1986b). Learning representations by back-propagating errors, *Nature* **323**: 533–536. [9]

Sakurai, A. (1993). Tighter bounds of the VC-dimension of three-layer networks, *Proceedings of the 1993 World Congress on Neural Networks*, Vol. 3, Erlbaum, Hillsdale, NJ, pp. 540–543. [85]

Sakurai, A. (1999). Tight bounds for the VC-dimension of piecewise polynomial networks, *in* M. S. Kearns, S. A. Solla and D. A. Cohn (eds), *Advances in NIPS 11*, MIT Press, Cambridge, MA. [129]

Sauer, N. (1972). On the density of families of sets, *Journal of Combinatorial Theory, Series A* **13**: 145–147. [41]

Schapire, R. E. (1990). The strength of weak learnability, *Machine Learning* **5**(2): 197–227. [355]

Schapire, R. E., Freund, Y., Bartlett, P. L. and Lee, W. S. (1998). Boosting the margin: a new explanation for the effectiveness of voting methods, *Annals of Statistics* **26**(5): 1651–1686. [217, 356]

Schläfli, L. (1950). *Gesammelte Mathematische Abhandlungen I*, Birkhäuser, Basel. [41]

Schölkopf, B., Burges, C. J. C. and Smola, A. J. (1999). *Advances in Kernel Methods: Support Vector Learning*, MIT Press. [217]

Schuurmans, D. (1995). Characterizing rational versus exponential learning curves, *Computational Learning Theory: Eurocolt '95*, Springer-Verlag, pp. 272–286. [73]

Shawe-Taylor, J. and Anthony, M. (1991). Sample sizes for multiple-output threshold networks, *Network* **2**: 107–117. [296]

Shawe-Taylor, J., Bartlett, P. L., Williamson, R. C. and Anthony, M. (1996). A framework for structural risk minimization, *Proceedings of the 9th Annual Conference on Computational Learning Theory*, ACM Press, New York, NY, pp. 68–76. [139, 217, 227]

Shawe-Taylor, J., Bartlett, P. L., Williamson, R. C. and Anthony, M. (1998). Structural risk minimisation over data-dependent hierarchies, *IEEE Transactions on Information Theory* **44**(5): 1926–1940. [217, 227, 296]

Shelah, S. (1972). A combinatorial problem: Stability and order for models and theories in infinity languages, *Pacific Journal of Mathematics* **41**: 247–261. [41]

Shinohara, A. and Miyano, S. (1991). Teachability in computational learning, *New Generation Computing* **8**: 337–347. [28]

Simon, H. U. (1996). General bounds on the number of examples needed for learning probabilistic concepts, *Journal of Computer and System Sciences* **52**(2): 239–254. [72, 192]

Simon, H. U. (1997). Bounds on the number of examples needed for learning functions, *SIAM Journal of Computing* **26**(3): 751–763. [164, 268]

Sloan, R. H. (1995). Four types of noise in data for PAC learning, *Information Processing Letters* **54**: 157–162. [27]

Slud, E. (1977). Distribution inequalities for the binomial law, *Annals of Probability* **5**: 404–412. [363]

Smola, A. J., Bartlett, P. L., Schölkopf, B. and Schuurmans, D. (1999). *Advances in Large Margin Classifiers*, MIT Press. (To appear). [217]

Sontag, E. D. (1992). Feedforward nets for interpolation and classification, *Journal of Computer and System Sciences* **45**: 20–48. [41, 85, 106]

Sontag, E. D. (1995). Critical points for least-squares problems involving certain analytic functions, with applications to sigmoidal nets, *Advances in Computational Mathematics* **5**: 245–268. [340]

Sontag, E. D. (1997). Shattering all sets of k points in "general position" requires $(k-1)/2$ parameters, *Neural Computation* **9**(2): 337–348. [41]

Sontag, E. D. and Sussmann, H. J. (1989). Backpropagation can give rise to spurious local minima even for networks without hidden layers, *Complex Systems* **3**(1): 91–106. [139, 339]

Steele, J. M. (1978). Existence of submatrices with all possible columns, *Journal of Combinatorial Theory, Series A* **24**: 84–88. [41]

Sternberg, S. (1964). *Lectures on Differential Geometry*, Prentice Hall. [364]

Stone, C. (1977). Consistent nonparameteric regression, *Annals of Statistics* **8**: 1348–1360. [27]

Sussmann, H. J. (1992). Uniqueness of the weights for minimal feedforward nets with a given input-output map, *Neural Networks* **5**: 589–593. [282]

Talagrand, M. (1994). Sharper bounds for Gaussian and empirical processes, *Annals of Probability* **22**: 28–76. [58]

Tate, R. F. (1953). On a double inequality of the normal distribution, *Annals of Mathematical Statistics* **24**: 132–134. [364]

Tikhomirov, V. M. (1969). Diameters of sets in function spaces and the theory of best approximations, *Russian Mathematical Surveys* **15**(3): 75–111. [163]

Valiant, L. G. (1984a). Deductive learning, *Philosophical Transactions of the Royal Society of London, Series A* **312**: 441–446. [306]

Valiant, L. G. (1984b). A theory of the learnable, *Communications of the ACM* **27**(11): 1134–1142. [27, 306]

van der Vaart, A. W. and Wellner, J. A. (1996). *Weak Convergence and Empirical Processes*, Springer. [216]

Vapnik, V. and Chervonenkis, A. (1974). *Theory of Pattern Recognition*, Nauka, Moscow. (in Russian). [72]

Vapnik, V. N. (1982). *Estimation of Dependences Based on Empirical Data*, Springer-Verlag, New York. [9, 58, 73, 139, 217, 227, 240]

Vapnik, V. N. (1989). Inductive principles of the search for empirical dependences (methods based on weak convergence of probability measures), *Proceedings of the 2nd Annual Workshop on Computational Learning Theory*, Morgan Kaufmann, San Mateo, CA, pp. 3–21. [296]

Vapnik, V. N. (1995). *The Nature of Statistical Learning Theory*, Springer-Verlag, New York. [9, 217]

Vapnik, V. N. and Chervonenkis, A. Y. (1971). On the uniform convergence of relative frequencies of events to their probabilities, *Theory of Probability and its Applications* **16**(2): 264–280. [27, 41, 58, 150, 192, 246]

Vidyasagar, M. (1997). *A Theory of Learning and Generalization, with Applications to Neural Networks and Control Systems*, Springer, New York. [9, 216, 246]

Vu, V. H. (1998). On the infeasibility of training neural networks with small squared errors, *in* M. I. Jordan, M. J. Kearns and S. A. Solla (eds), *Advances in Neural Information Processing Systems 10*, MIT Press, pp. 371–377. [340]

Wahba, G. (1990). *Spline models for observational data*, CBMS-NSF Regional Conference Series in Applied Mathematics, SIAM, Philadelphia. [217]

Wallace, C. S. and Boulton, D. M. (1968). An information measure for classification, *The Computer Journal* **11**(2): 185–194. [227]

Warren, H. E. (1968). Lower bounds for approximation by nonlinear manifolds, *Transactions of the AMS* **133**: 167–178. [107]

Watkins, D. S. (1991). *Fundamentals of Matrix Computations*, Wiley. [329]

Wenocur, R. S. and Dudley, R. M. (1981). Some special Vapnik-Chervonenkis classes, *Discrete Mathematics* **33**: 313–318. [41]

White, H. (1990). Connectionist nonparametric regression: Multilayer feedforward networks can learn arbitrary mappings, *Neural Networks* **3**: 535–549. [216]

Williamson, R. C., Smola, A. J. and Schölkopf, B. (1999). Entropy numbers, operators and support vector kernels, *Advances in Kernel Methods: Support Vector Learning*, MIT Press, chapter 9, pp. 127–144. [217]

Zuev, Y. A. (1989). Asymptotics of the logarithm of the number of threshold functions of the algebra of logic, *Soviet Mathematics Doklady* **39**: 512–513. [58]

Author index

Subject index